AT BERKELEY IN THE SIXTIES

IN THE SIXTIES

*The Education of an Activist,
1961–1965*

Jo Freeman

INDIANA
University Press

Bloomington & Indianapolis

Publication of this book is made possible in part with the assistance of a Challenge Grant from the National Endowment for the Humanities, a federal agency that supports research, education, and public programming in the humanities.

This book is a publication of

Indiana University Press
601 North Morton Street
Bloomington, Ind. 47404-3797 USA

http://iupress.indiana.edu

Telephone orders   800-842-6796
Fax orders   812-855-7931
Orders by e-mail   iuporder@indiana.edu

The paper used in this publication meets the minimum requirements of American National Standard for Information Sciences—Permanence of Paper for Printed Library Materials, ANSI Z39.48-1984.

Manufactured in the United States of America

Library of Congress Cataloging-in-Publication Data

Freeman, Jo.
At Berkeley in the sixties : the education of an activist, 1961–1965 / Jo Freeman.
p.   cm.
Includes bibliographical references and index.
ISBN 0-253-34283-X (alk. paper) — ISBN 0-253-21622-2 (pbk. : alk. paper)
1. University of California, Berkeley—History. 2. College students—California—Berkeley—Political activity—History. 3. Student movements—California—Berkeley—History. 4. Freeman, Jo. I. Title.
LD760.F73 2004
378.794'67—dc21

2003006318

1 2 3 4 5   09 08 07 06 05 04

To my mother
Helen Mitchell Freeman (1909–1973)
who got more than she expected
when she sent her kid to Cal

Contents

List of Illustrations

A Note on Nomenclature

I N THIS BOOK I've chosen to use the words typical of the time of which I write, even though some of them are no longer considered proper. "Negro" was the polite term for persons of African descent. "Chairman" was the designation for the head of a department, committee, or organization. Students were referred to as "boys" and "girls" regardless of age. "Gender" was not part of our vocabulary, though "sex" was. At Berkeley, adults were addressed directly by their educational or occupational titles—Dr., Dean, Chancellor—or referred to indirectly by only their last names, so I have done the same. Read these terms with the understanding that they are used to capture the flavor of the era.

Acronyms and Abbreviations

American Association of University Professors (AAUP)
American Civil Liberties Union (ACLU)
Associated Students of the University of California (ASUC)
Bay Area Students' Committee against HUAC (BASCAHUAC)
Burns Committee (California Senate Fact-Finding Subcommittee on Un-
   American Activities)
California College Republicans (CCR)
California Conservatives for Political Action (CCPA)
California Democratic Council (CDC)
California Federation of Young Democrats (CFYD)
Cal Students for Goldwater (CSG)
Committee on Academic Freedom (CAF)
Communist Party (CP or CPUSA)
Congress of Racial Equality (CORE)
Congressional District (C.D.)
Council of Federated Organizations (COFO)
Democratic Socialist Club (DSC)
Emergency Executive Committee (EEC)
Executive Committee (Ex Com)
Fellowship of Reconciliation (FOR)
Free Speech Movement (FSM)
Free Student Union (FSU)
Fuck Defense Fund (FDF)
Graduate Coordinating Committee (GCC)
House Un-American Activities Committee (HUAC)
International Longshoremen's and Warehousemen's Union (ILWU)
Independent Socialist Club (ISC)
May 2nd Movement (M2M)
Mississippi Freedom Democratic Party (MFDP)
Mississippi Sovereignty Commission (MSC)
National Association for the Advancement of Colored People (NAACP)

Progressive Labor Movement (PLM)
Progressive Labor Party (PL)
Reserve Officer Training Corps (ROTC)
Socialist Workers Party (SWP)
Southern Christian Leadership Conference (SCLC)
Stiles Hall (YMCA)
Student Nonviolent Coordinating Committee (SNCC)
Student Peace Union (SPU)
Students for a Democratic Society (SDS)
Study Committee on Campus Political Activity (SCCPA)
Summer Community Organization for Political Education (SCOPE)
Toward an Active Student Community (TASC)
University Civil Liberties Committee (UCLC)
University Society of Individualists (USI)
University Young Democrats (UYD)
University Young Republicans (UYR)
Vietnam Day Committee (VDC)
Young Democrats (YD)
Young People's Socialist League (YPSL)
Young Republicans (YR)
Young Socialist Alliance (YSA)

Preface and Acknowledgments

In 1994 I started a feminist memoir of the sixties to show through personal experience how feminist consciousness emerged in that contentious decade. I had participated in three major sixties movements—the Berkeley Free Speech Movement (FSM), the southern Civil Rights Movement, and the early Women's Liberation Movement—and observed or been on the periphery of several others. Those of us who started women's liberation were not born feminists, and the times in which we grew up were, if anything, anti-feminist. I wanted to use my own experience to talk about where we came from and why.

Much of that experience resided in file folders. In 1963, when my mother asked me what I wanted for my eighteenth birthday, I asked her to buy a file cabinet—a four-drawer legal-sized file cabinet—and give me a place to keep it. During my first two years at Cal I had collected many of the leaflets and pamphlets passed out by the political groups at Bancroft and Telegraph or put out at student meetings held in the local YMCA. I did not then know what I would do with all of these, but they fascinated me. My archival instinct needed a place to store its treasures.

I became a collector of political literature. Most of it was lefty/liberal literature because that's what the Berkeley groups passed out. But some right-wing literature came my way and some that was neither. I also collected other stuff—news clippings about current events, Democratic Party ephemera, my own correspondence describing what I saw and experienced. Whenever I went home, I spent hours carefully filing it all away. During the 1964 Free Speech Movement, I systematically collected one or more of everything produced by or about the FSM that crossed my path; enough to fill one entire drawer. By the time I graduated, the file cabinet was almost full. I had no idea what I would do with all of this. I had some vague idea of going to graduate school one day and maybe using it for a dissertation.

After my mother died in 1973, that file cabinet along with all the other stuff in her house went into storage. In 1985, I moved it to my xvi | *Preface and Acknowledgments*

home in Brooklyn, New York. To lessen the weight, I threw many things away, including (to my great regret) about half the contents of the file cabinet. What's left forms the core of this book.

My mother was also a collector of paper, and among her papers I found most of the letters I wrote her. I salvaged those and read them for this book. While it's sometimes painful to realize how narrow was the view from which I saw the world at that age, they were very useful in reconstructing the student perspective. Some of my letters contain detailed descriptions of major events on campus and in the nearby community and what we thought was behind those events. Term papers written about off-campus political actions were also helpful in reminding me of what the newspapers missed, or never knew. Occasionally I quote these verbatim, but usually I rely on them as source material.

By the time I started this book, I was more of a scholar than an activist and needed to know what happened from multiple points of view. I began reading oral histories done of administrators at UC Berkeley, interviews of key participants done by others years ago, old newspapers, legal documents, and early publications and books on California history. Personal experience is rarely unique. The more I looked at the context — the historical precedents, the political actors, the way in which institutions and values molded our perceptions — the more the book expanded beyond its original purpose. At some point the history took over the book. After writing 150 pages before reaching the 1964 Free Speech Movement, I realized that it was volume one, not part one.

What I soon called the Berkeley book would have to stand on its own; there wasn't enough feminist consciousness in the early sixties for that to be the theme. Since Berkeley was in the vanguard, and the FSM was the first student uprising to make international headlines, it became a case study of student protest. Initially I intended to cover only the years from 1961 to 1965 because those were the years I was a student at Berkeley. They were crucial years in the decade of the sixties. One could see on one campus the evolution of student thought from liberalism to radicalism, and student activism from polite protests to building occupation.

All history has antecedents; to understand those four years, I had to go back in time. This led me to people I had known slightly or not at all who had put into motion the wheels of history on which I rode. Some whose names I knew as a student I met for the first time in the 1990s as I expanded the book to include their experiences. The book remained a memoir, but one which described not only my own journey but that of other students who worked for social change and were changed by the experience of doing so. This journey begins in the mid-1950s, when a few dissenters appear in the midst of "the silent generation" and ask the university to change a few rules. It ends in a very different place than any of us thought it would end.

My research was greatly facilitated by two invitations. Early in 1997, Reginald Zelnik, chairman of the History Department at Berkeley, invited me to give a paper at a panel commemorating the life of Mario Savio that he and Robby Cohen were organizing for the April meeting of the Organization of American Historians (OAH). A new faculty member at Berkeley during the 1964 Free Speech Movement, Zelnik became a friend of Mario Savio. It was Mario's untimely death on November 6, 1996, which prompted this panel. This invitation gave me an opportunity to research the origins of Mario's commitment to civil rights and social justice as well as a trip to the Bay Area, where I spent a useful week talking to people and going through archives and personal papers. An edited version of the paper I wrote is in the volume Zelnik edited with Robert Cohen.

In 1999, Clark Kerr, president of the University of California from September 1958 to January 1967, asked me to review a draft of volume two of his memoirs, which covered his presidential years. Since it was a work in progress I have not quoted or cited any pages but used it for background to understand his outlook. From it I gained a perspective on the politics of the era. Kerr's research assistant, Marian Gade, became an invaluable colleague. On trips to Berkeley in May of 2000 and 2001, she allowed me to copy extensive material from her files. She also e-mailed other items on request, shared her thoughts, and told me about publications and people I might find useful. She relayed questions and answers between myself and President Kerr and sent me excerpts of Kerr's memoir as it progressed. Marian introduced me to John Douglass, who writes about university history. He provided crucial statistics and information on the university that I had not been able to find elsewhere. Kerr's secretary, Maureen Kawaoka, also sent me copies of Kerr's speeches and other materials from his files.

Two Berkeley student organizations in which I was involved figure prominently in these pages: SLATE and the FSM. Both had reunions in 1984, though I only made it to the FSM reunion. I went to the 30th-anniversary reunion of the FSM in 1994 and SLATE's second reunion in 2000. By the time of the second SLATE reunion, I was in the final stages of the book and used the occasion to interview people I hadn't seen in years. Both the FSM and SLATE kept some records of vets, which made it possible to track people down. I especially sought those who had not left interviews in the hands of prior archivists and researchers. Barbara Toby Stack, who maintains the FSM vets list, helped me find a few and also alerted me to newspaper stories and interviews I might have missed. E-mail made correspondence easy and led to some very interesting exchanges. The anecdotes in this book are richer, and there are a few less errors, because some of my colleagues and antagonists from Berkeley were willing to share their thoughts with me. I had particularly enlightening exchanges with Michael Rossman, Brad Cleaveland, Syd Stapleton, Brian Shannon, and Brian Turner. There are a few vets I could not find; if any of you read this book, please get in touch.

Several of my predecessors generously shared with me their own collection of papers and memories. Particularly valuable were the personal papers of Ken Cloke and Mike Miller, Berkeley activists at the end of the 1950s and beginning of the 1960s. I reviewed Ken's papers at the Southern California Library for Social Studies and Research in Los Angeles, California, and read a microfilm copy of his 1980 UCLA dissertation on Berkeley political groups from 1957 to 1965. He kindly sent me additional documents, including materials given to him by Mike Miller on the early days of SLATE. Mike invited me to go through his files in 1997; Marie Plezewski helped me copy from them extensively. That same trip I visited Beverly Axelrod, where I copied material from her files on the 1964 civil rights trials in San Francisco for which she was the lead attorney. I found more material in the Meicklejohn Civil Liberties Institute in Berkeley (now the Ann Fagan Ginger Collection at Bancroft Library).

Some of the events I describe in this book were researched by others, and I am grateful to those who shared their work with me. Max Heirich wrote his insightful and thoroughly researched dissertation for UC's Sociology Department on the Free Speech Movement, for which he interviewed many participants and observers in 1965. Early in 1997, Max sent me copies of the interviews he had done with me and with Mario Savio so I could better write my OAH paper. Later that year, a Brooklyn friend, Michael Shapiro, visited his alma mater, where Max taught. At my request he went to see Max, and by the time he left he had copied about half of the remaining interviews for me. During my 1997 trip to California, I contacted Mark Kitchell, who let me copy the transcripts of interviews he had done in preparation for his marvelous documentary film, *Berkeley in the Sixties*. I later found at Howard University's Moorland-Springarn Research Center some interviews with key figures in the 1964 Bay Area Civil Rights Movement, which filled in some details on the politics behind the demonstrations and what happened afterward. At Columbia University's Oral History Office I read oral history interviews done with sixties protestors, including some of Berkeley students (and one nonstudent).

It's fortunate I kept my clippings files, because they would have been hard to reproduce. When I tried to fill holes in my own collection, I found it impossible to get microfilm copies of the student newspaper the *Daily Cal,* or some local newspapers, through Interlibrary Loan. New York Public Library only had the *San Francisco Chronicle* and the *Los Angeles Times,* though they were useful. On my trips to Berkeley I spent as much time as I could copying stories from papers I could not get in New York. Since I lived through many of these events, I was well aware that the quality of coverage varied widely and that journalists never understood the student groups. But the stories in the papers were a rough outline of what happened when and alerted me to things I had not known, especially about how we were perceived by the rest of the world. I read news stories cautiously, constantly making judgments about what was credible and what was not.

Bancroft Library at Berkeley is the permanent repository of the campus papers, official and unofficial, including the Free Speech Movement archives. I found a few useful things there which supplemented my own files. Of much greater value was the help of Bill Roberts, the university archivist. He dug through old folders in collections I had never heard of to find background information and revealing memos written by administrators. Quite a few of these people also left oral histories, most done by the Regional Oral History Office. Three were on the Web and I got many more through interlibrary loan. Lisa Rubens sent me a couple I couldn't get through other means. Much of my understanding of how what we did as students looked to the administration, as well as what they did in response and why, comes from these oral histories. In addition, Ray Colvig, Berkeley's Public Information Officer from July of 1964 until he retired many years later, sent me useful material from his files.

Although I started by looking at campus life as a student, eventually I realized I needed to know what the Regents thought and did. They were the ultimate authority of the university and were much more concerned with campus events than most of us knew at the time. In January of 2000, I requested minutes for their meetings (open and closed), executive and general sessions, and Boards and Committees. After my request was approved by the Office of the President, Ann Shaw was given the job of responding to my requests. She did a thorough job of reviewing the minutes to identify those that might interest me as well as answering specific requests by date or topic as my research developed. James Holst, General Counsel of the Regents, reviewed minutes for the closed sessions. While some of these minutes were very sparse, others disclosed actions or clarified discussions of which I was otherwise unaware. I supplemented them with information from other sources, including oral histories and newspaper accounts. I cited few minutes other than those I quoted, but by looking at the dates in the references section of this book, one can easily tell which ones I relied on for regental thought and action for any particular meeting.

Less useful were the thousands of pages I *finally* received from the FBI. I made several FOIA requests in 1993. Subsequently, I sent an article based on the FBI files that was published in the *Daily Cal* at the time of the 20th-anniversary reunion of the FSM and asked for the same materials. Since most of this material had already been processed, I thought the FBI could just make a copy for me, for which I would pay. In 1996, after three years of writing futile letters, someone from the FBI phoned to tell me that I could get what I wanted from a "prior requestor." She gave me an address for Seth Rosenfeld, a reporter for the *San Francisco Examiner.* I eventually found out that he had the files that the FBI sent to the *Daily Cal* in 1984 and much more (including Clark Kerr's personal files). He had taken the FBI to court when it refused to give him all he asked for and eventually got "clean" copies of documents for which I only had the blacked-out versions. Contacting Rosenfeld was another exercise in futility; he didn't answer any of my letters, e-mails, or phone calls. I read the district and appellate court decisions, which had useful extracts from declarations and depositions. I later read the court files in California but found none of the declarations on which the court decisions rested. The FBI continued to send me form letters, asking me if I still wanted the files I had requested after so much time had passed.

Finally, in 1999, I wrote my New York senator, Daniel Patrick Moynihan, and asked for his help. Over the next year, boxes and boxes of badly copied pages arrived at my door (at ten cents a page). I read them all. Most were "public source documents" (e.g., newspaper clippings) which would have been quite useful at the beginning of my research, but by the time they arrived they told me little I didn't know. The rest told me more about the FBI and what it did with taxpayer money than they did about participants in the political activities of which I wrote. I describe the FBI's investigations into the Berkeley students in a chapter near the end of the book. I still have a few outstanding requests the FBI has yet to fill.

On June 9, 2002, Rosenfeld finally published the results of his years of litigation in the *San Francisco Chronicle* as a special eight-page section called "The Campus Files" <http://www.sfgate.com/campus>. I read it eagerly but found very little that I didn't already know and only one "clean" document of great interest. We have a somewhat different interpretation of the politics behind the politics of those days. I wrote Rosenfeld once more; once more he didn't reply. I also asked the FBI for the "clean" copies of documents the court ordered it to give to Rosenfeld, but I never got them. Apparently a court order doesn't apply to subsequent requestors, only those who go to court.

Long before I got the FBI files I had learned that it was not the only government agency which had a very strong interest in what students did at Berkeley. The California Senate Fact-Finding Subcommittee on Un-American Activities had been watching us for years. Indeed, it kept extensive files on faculty, students, and staff at all the UC campuses. It tried to influence who was hired and occasionally tried to fire people it did not like—including UC's President Clark Kerr. While the materials it collected over thirty years have not been opened to researchers, its biennial official reports told me much once I learned how to read them. In addition, the Mississippi Sovereignty Commission (MSC) had its own spy on the Berkeley campus; one result of student participation in the 1964 Mississippi Freedom Summer. Staff at the Mississippi Department of Archives and History helped me obtain copies of what this informant sent to the MSC as well as the few photographs of the FSM that were in the MSC files.

In addition to the people mentioned above, I am also indebted to many others for help with everything from locating and obtaining documents to giving me a place to sleep. They include Doug McAdam, Lillian Gwilliam, Mary Singleton, Marilyn Boxer, Carolyn and Tony Scarr, Sherry Warman, Theresa Ferrara, Janet Flammang, Allan Solomonow, Ofelia Alayeto, Susan Druding, Art Gatti, Gail and Chuck Roberts, Vanessa Tait, Mary C. McFadden, Nick Irons, Liz Cox, Sara Rowe-Sims, Nancy Henley, Jessica Moran, Beverly Goldberg, and Pat Lynden.

This manuscript benefited from the comments of those who read all or parts of it in draft. Carolyn Scarr read the first draft of the first hundred pages. Mal Burnstein vetted the chapter on the trial of the FSM defendants. Mike Miller, Robert Cohen, and Victoria Johnson read and critiqued the entire manuscript, recommending corrections and making useful suggestions. I thank them all, with the usual caveat that remaining errors are my own.

This book began as a memoir and evolved into a history. As a result it speaks with two voices, which are not always in harmony with each other. I began from the student perspective, wanting to give the reader some insight into how we saw things at the time. Reviewing the letters and term papers I wrote in my college years helped me to recapture that mindset. But as I delved more deeply into causes and consequences, aided by original sources and the writings of others, the middle-aged scholar began to take over. My years of training in finding and assessing evidence pushed me to understand events from multiple points of view and to give a more balanced presentation. The student and the scholar fought many battles inside my head on whether to portray events as we saw them at the time or as I see them now. Generally the student speaks louder when I relate experiences of which I had direct, personal knowledge and the scholar dominates those for which I relied on records written by others. Keep in mind when reading this book that the scholar doesn't always agree with the student.

One reason the scholar took over the book is because I discovered the fallibility of memory. Although I retain many memories of my four years at Berkeley, only some are clear. Most are rather hazy; full of impressions and feelings without the clarity of detail. Fortunately, the period I was there left many written records as well as the recorded memories of others. I didn't remember the past so much as I reconstructed it. And reconstruction in turn revived some memories that were deeply buried. Indeed, I now "remember" some events much more clearly than I did when I began this book.

Reading the memories of others, recorded closer to the time in interviews and oral histories, alerted me to how quickly memory degenerates. I found frequent factual flaws in interviews of participants less than a year after the events they described. Memory quickly reshaped itself to fit preconceived notions of what should have happened, even when it didn't happen and all evidence was to the contrary. I was constantly reminded of how easy it is to attribute bad motives to those we don't like and good motives to those we do. Indeed, some of the misconceptions students had at the time are still reported as facts even though research has long since shown them to be fiction. Judging from the oral histories I read of administrators, this was equally true for them, though most were a little less judgmental than we were.

By the time I finished the book, I had learned more than I ever knew as a resident about the politics of the state of California. I discovered that the Free Speech Movement was not a battle in the Civil Rights Movement, as we had thought at the time, but a skirmish in the Cold War. Indeed, by looking at the political context in which university administrators made their decisions, actions that at the time had seemed arbitrary, capricious, and stupid made sense. They were concerned with public perception; we prioritized principled action. They projected onto us the problems of the past; we identified them with the problems of the present. Neither understood the other, or wanted to.

Between the oral histories and the FSM vets list I was also able to find out what happened to many of us. The paths some of us followed are briefly covered in the last, and longest, chapter. While this book is not a collective biography, the pattern is clear. No one changed directions; "yippies" (or their forebears) did not become "yuppies" (or their equivalent). Our politics are a little more nuanced and we are a little more tolerant than we were as students, but no one has gone into reverse. Nonetheless, everyone was changed by our experience, and not always for the best. Overall, the university survived just fine, but the people who fought the ideological and sometimes physical battles of the early sixties were often damaged. Many soldiers of the sixties, like those in military conflicts, were injured. Yet I don't think any of us have regrets. We did what we had to do. By dismantling the restrictions and rules imposed by the Cold War, we broke the chains of the past and opened up the future.

AT BERKELEY IN THE SIXTIES

1 | *The Train to Berkeley*

THE TRAIN TRIP from Los Angeles to Berkeley took twelve hours. I later learned that the bus took only eight, but my mother wanted me to take the train; in those days, I generally did what she wanted. I had been admitted as a freshman to the University of California at Berkeley, one of the elite universities of the world but one which welcomed the children of ordinary people—at least those who were moderately bright residents of the state. Residents in the top eighth of state high school graduates were automatically admitted. It was September 1961. I had just turned 16.

Berkeley, like the train, was my mother's choice. Only a year earlier, I had started the eleventh grade in the brand-new Granada Hills High School, one of the many new schools that sprouted in the San Fernando Valley as its population boomed. I had enough high school credits to be in the twelfth grade, having spent two years at Birmingham High. But I was a couple of years ahead of my age-mates, and the general educational consensus was that fifteen was too young to graduate from high school, so I was supposed to take an extra year.

Sometime in the spring of 1961, someone changed their mind. I don't know who because no one told me. Obviously my mother, a junior high school history teacher who had known my high school principal when he taught at Birmingham, concurred. She knew that there were not enough academic courses in my new school to keep me occupied for two more years; I had told her that I would run out of math and science courses at the end of that year, and those were my best subjects. What else went into this decision I will never know; I was not consulted. In the middle of the spring semester I was transferred to the twelfth grade, which required changing a few courses so that all the required ones would show on my transcript, and in June I graduated with GH High's first class. My grade point average placed me at number 12 out of 410, but I didn't know the top 11. I knew the names of very few kids in my new twelfth grade courses; I didn't have a single friend in my graduating class.

I do know that none of them went to Berkeley. Most of my classmates didn't go to college at all. Those who did and who happened to
say where they were going went to Valley State (San Fernando Valley
State College, now known as California State University, Northridge),
conveniently located one block from my home. The more adventuresome
went to UCLA. While I didn't follow the lives of any seniors, my two
friends in the junior class, with whom I spent most of that year, went in
opposite directions. Sara went to Stanford, and Joan went to work. Sara
and I were the only two juniors who made the semifinals in the National
Merit Exam. We kept it secret from everyone except each other. In the
Valley, being smart was not something to brag about, especially if you
were a girl. Pretty and popular were the marks of success.

Most of my classmates led lives more like my cousin Linda than like
me. She grew up three miles away and never moved out of L.A. Eleven
months younger than I, she graduated three years later at the normal age,
but didn't go to college, at least not immediately. Linda wanted *stuff*
more than an education, so she worked as a receptionist while living at
home. After a while she began taking courses at Valley State and graduated many years later. The last time I saw her, at my mother's funeral
in 1973, she was still a receptionist. The following month I received
my Ph.D.

My mother was born in Hamilton, Alabama, in 1909 as Helen
Claire Mitchell, sixth child of Charles Erastus and Leota Ford Mitchell.
During my childhood, she was Helen M. Freeman. To her students, and
anyone younger than her, she was always Mrs. Freeman. In this book I
will call her Helen, though I certainly never called her that when she was
alive. She had a rebellious streak and an inquisitive mind, but graduating
from Alabama College for Women at the beginning of the Depression
didn't provide many outlets. Her first opportunity to explore the world
outside the South came with World War II. She joined the Women's
Army Corps and soon became a first lieutenant. During most of her service, she was stationed in Great Britain. Armed with a home economics
degree, she led a battery of cooks.

Helen returned to Alabama sometime before VE Day, pregnant with
me, and moved in with an older sister who lived near Birmingham. I was
born in a military hospital outside Atlanta shortly after VJ Day. She took
me back to Birmingham and six months later followed a younger sister
to Los Angeles, where she stayed the rest of her life. It is ironic that for
many of those years she taught at Birmingham Junior High, which was
on a converted army base in the middle of the San Fernando Valley that
was named for General P. Birmingham. If she had stayed in Alabama, I

might have grown up in Birmingham; instead I attended Birmingham Junior High and Birmingham Senior High in California, though I graduated from neither. Our classrooms were barracks, but the grounds were spacious and had a lot of facilities, such as a swimming pool, that were not present at the usual high school.

Helen got her M.A. from the University of Southern California on the GI Bill, taking me with her to class. I went to college before I went to kindergarten. She revered education. That's why she sent me to Berkeley, the largest and most prestigious campus of the University of California, despite my youth. She thought it would give me the best education she could afford.[1] The California public colleges traditionally admitted everyone who was eligible and did not charge tuition to residents. My only payment my first semester was a $60 "incidental" fee. It increased by $20 a semester every year until it was $120 a semester my senior year.[2]

Private colleges charged real tuition—several times what Berkeley charged nonresidents. When Helen found out there was time to apply to Stanford as well as Berkeley, she insisted that I apply to this prestigious private school, though she made it clear that I was going to Berkeley. "I can't afford Stanford," she said. It might not be too late to be admitted, but it was too late to get a scholarship. "If I can't go, why do you want me to apply?" I responded, not thrilled at filling out more forms and writing needless essays. "I just want to see if you can get in," was her definitive rejoinder. I didn't get in. The form rejection letter I received said there was only room for 825 men and 425 women in the entering class.[3] When later asked why I went to Berkeley, I would say it was the best school, for the least amount of money, the farthest away from home.

It was dark when the train arrived. I had never been on a train before and found the long chug through the central California valley boring. The train shook too much to read and the scenery—miles of produce growing in flat fields—was monotonous. I retrieved my trunk and dragged it to the front of the station where Helen had told me to find a taxi. I had never taken a taxi before either. At this point, almost everything was an adventure because I had never done it before.

At least I had a place to go, though I could only stay there for two weeks. My application was not too late for admission to Cal, but it was too late to get into the dorms. In August we drove to Berkeley to find a place for me to live, but everything was full. The dorms were full, the private boarding houses were full, the student co-operatives were full, even the private homes which rented rooms to students had no vacancies. The best we could find was a private rooming house near Cal, which rented to students attending Armstrong College, a local business school.

Since its classes began two weeks after Cal's, the rooming house had vacancies for the first two weeks of Cal classes. Helen paid for the two weeks. After that I was on my own.

For two weeks I coped with figuring out college classes and finding a place to live. I wasn't very successful. The leads at the housing office were from students sharing apartments who needed one more roommate, or rooms in private homes. Even if I had been up to the responsibilities of running a shared household, which I wasn't, no one wanted a 16-year-old roommate. The families renting out private rooms didn't want one either. It didn't help that with short straight hair and no make-up, I looked like I was 12. Just as my two weeks were up, someone told me about the Berkeley Inn, a geriatric hotel with mostly permanent residents only a few blocks south of campus. At $55 a month for the cheapest room, without a bath, it cost more than I wanted to spend, and there were no kitchen facilities, but it had a vacancy. The room even had a small desk, about twice the area occupied by my new Smith-Corona portable manual typewriter, along with a bed, a chair, and a floor lamp that were many years older than I was. I moved in and stayed until December, when space opened up in a girls' dorm. The dorm was farther from campus and I had to share my room, but at least the electrical circuits didn't blow and the lights go off every time the old folks turned on their electric heaters.

I had better luck with my classes, as well as a lot more advice. Ken Cloke, a Berkeley junior whose family lived across the street in Northridge, spent a couple of hours with me in August going over the course catalog. From him I learned there was an entire field called political science and it was something one could major in. He also told me that politics at Berkeley was much more fun than anything that went on in the San Fernando Valley.

Not much politics happened in the Valley, and what was there was electoral politics. In this I was trained practically from birth. Politics runs in families, and I inherited the political gene from my mother. Her father was a small-town lawyer and politician who served four years as alderman in her hometown of Hamilton and another four in the Alabama legislature. He represented Marion County in northwest Alabama between 1907 and 1911. For his time and place he was well educated, having gone to a state normal school and then obtained a law degree from the University of Alabama in 1893. In 1896, he married 17-year-old Leota Ford, daughter of the county probate judge and sister of another local lawyer. He died in 1942 at the age of 73. Helen left me with the impression that she didn't like her father very much, but she did follow him. Her secret ambition, which she never even attempted, was to be a lawyer. She let me know early in life that the law was what she wanted me to pursue. Of the twelve Mitchell children, none became lawyers and only two were interested in politics; the other was her next older sister. The political gene showed up in one other of the fourteen grandchildren; a cousin I never met was an aide to several Alabama senators.

Since Helen didn't tell me much about her childhood, I don't know what politics she practiced in Alabama before World War II. My earliest memory is of her denouncing Richard Nixon for red-baiting Helen Gahagan Douglas in the 1950 California senate campaign. In the 1952 presidential campaign she was a Stevenson volunteer. We spent many an evening at L.A. campaign headquarters and many a weekend walking precincts. At 7, I was their champion button-seller. While Helen handed out leaflets on the street, I walked up to total strangers and boldly asked them to buy "Stevenson for President" buttons. Few could resist a young child, so I outsold the adults, a point of great pride. When we canvassed door to door, Helen would take one side of the street and I would take the other. I offered to answer the questions of those who opened the door and said if I didn't know the answer I would go get my mother. Since she had trained me well and few voters asked complicated questions, I seldom had to do this. In the '56 campaign I had my own precincts, specifically the ones in our Van Nuys neighborhood of two-bedroom tract homes and created my own—temporary—political organization. I rode my bike with a basket full of campaign literature to each street and paid local kids a nickel each to lit-drop the block. I rode up and down to make sure they did what they were paid to do and then went on to the next block. If a voter had a question, the kids would signal me. It was much more efficient than doing it all by myself.

In 1960 we lived in Northridge. We didn't do much precinct work, but we did run the local Kennedy campaign headquarters on the weekends. I tried to organize a Kennedy campaign at Granada Hills High, but I mostly got into arguments with Nixon supporters. Not that Valley kids were very political, but those few that were all seemed to be rabid Republicans. Linda Montana, the immaculately dressed daughter of a local showman who had the locker across from mine at gym, thought Nixon was too liberal. She rooted for Goldwater. She also supported racial segregation, a position I found reprehensible. We argued all year during the five minutes of changing time before and after gym.

I was more of a dedicated Democrat than a Kennedy fanatic. Helen had taken me to the Democratic national convention that summer, conveniently held in Los Angeles, to picket for Adlai Stevenson, whom we both adored. But when Kennedy won the nomination she took me to the Coliseum to hear his acceptance speech, in which he made his ringing call for sacrifice from the American people and his proclamation of a New Frontier for the 1960s. While she referred to JFK as "that punk kid," a Kennedy bust and inaugural medallion graced her bookshelves until her death ten years to the day after his. She also did a lot of work for our local congressman, Jim Corman, even after reapportionment put her home outside his district. He gave her an engraved silver box as a thank-you, and when I later visited Washington on my own he treated me royally simply because I was Helen's daughter.

Being a dedicated Democrat didn't keep me from flirting with social-ism. Not that I knew much about it. In the conservative, conformist 1950s, socialism was one of those dirty words, slightly paler than communism, which one read about in the press. Helen had no interest in so-cialism.

As a nonconformist, the very fact that socialism was denigrated attracted me. Helen had taught me that if something was important enough to be feared, it was important enough to understand. The more I read, the better an idea socialism seemed. "From each according to their ability; to each according to their needs" didn't seem so monstrous. But beyond a few slogans, there wasn't much to read about socialism in the local library, so until I got to Berkeley it remained beyond my reach.

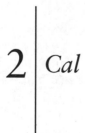

2 | Cal

NESTLED AT THE foot of the Berkeley hills, the flagship campus of the University of California slopes from east to west. There are many ravines and few plains. One is always walking up or down, entering the large buildings at different levels. On the Berkeley map it occupies a large rectangular area with a couple of rough edges. Hearst Avenue marks the northern and Bancroft Way runs along the southern boundary, with some buildings and most of the dorms located in the surrounding community. The campus does not give the appearance of having been planned but of expanding in response to need, like a medieval town. Indeed, the official southern entrance, known as Sather Gate, was a block inside the 1961 boundary of the campus. Buildings representing different styles and designs grew where there was space. Although some were surely built at the same time, none seemed to match and I cannot remember a single one I found aesthetically pleasing. In contrast, the landscaping was gorgeous. Trees abounded, grassy nooks were everywhere, and the variegated topography was skillfully used to create islands of seclusion in a very busy place. I thought Cal had some of the ugliest buildings on the most beautiful grounds I had ever seen.

Cal was big and seemed bigger. Over 25,000 students, two-thirds of them undergraduates, plus faculty and staff gave it the bustle of a city, not the languid pace of a small town. Four-fifths of the students came from California, especially Los Angeles. About 8 percent were foreign students, 4 percent came from New York, and the rest came from every other state.[1] The campus had discreet sections, each with its own geography and atmosphere. From the main library, which was almost dead center in the campus, the physical science and engineering buildings were north and east; the life sciences were to the west; the social science, humanities, and general education buildings were to the south. Buildings built for older disciplines (e.g., home economics and agriculture) were more to the north than those built for newer ones. Construction had begun on a social science high-rise, which would become Barrows Hall. T-buildings (for temporary), bungalows built during World War II, still lined University Drive, running the length of what had once been the geographic center. The law school was a self-contained unit at the far eastern edge; the main gym and tracks were to the west, two blocks down from the girls' gym, but the football stadium was east of campus, snug against the Berkeley hills. Disciplinary clustering made it possible to have back-to-back classes in different buildings and still go from one to the other in the ten minutes allotted between periods; it made it difficult to have back-to-back classes in different fields without practicing cross-country running. It also informally segregated everyone by field of study and even by discipline.

Even as I entered Berkeley in the fall of 1961, it was undergoing ma-

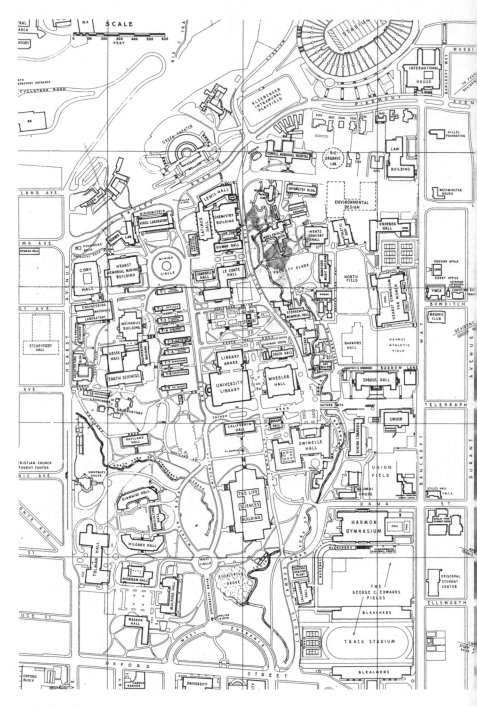

The Berkeley campus, 1963.

jor changes. On September 19, 1958, Clark Kerr was inaugurated as the twelfth president of the University of California. A graduate of Swarthmore College, Kerr had obtained his Ph.D. in economics from Cal in 1939 after getting an M.A. at Stanford in 1933. In 1945, he joined the faculty of the School of Business Administration and soon became the first director of the Institute of Industrial Relations, where he made his reputation as a mediator in labor disputes. Kerr brought a different management style to the office of university president. His predecessor, Robert Gordon Sproul, had reigned paternally from 1930 to 1958; until 1952 he was the chief *campus* officer as well as president of the entire university system. The system itself, like the state it served, was expanding rapidly with plans for several new campuses as part of an overall master plan passed by the legislature in 1960. Kerr had been the first chancellor of Berkeley under Sproul and chafed at the president's centralized control and interference in campus affairs. Kerr's strategy for the "multiversity," as he called it, was to decentralize, formalize, and bureaucratize relationships among the different university units; he would run the university and leave matters specific to each campus to its chancellor. Glenn Seaborg was Berkeley's chancellor from 1958 through 1960, when President Kennedy appointed him to head the Atomic Energy Commission. Berkeley's third chancellor was Edward W. Strong, a professor of philosophy who had run the Lawrence Radiation Laboratory during World War II and been vice chancellor for research under Seaborg.[2]

The campus had shifted geographically to the south and west since the first classes were held in South Hall in 1873. Telegraph Avenue had once run through Sather Gate, over Strawberry Creek, and right onto campus. After the main administration building was built in 1940, just south of the Sather Gate entrance, Telegraph turned west into Allston Way. The "Ad" building was renamed for Sproul when he retired, and he kept his office in its north wing. President Kerr's office was on the seventh floor of University Hall, across the street from the western entrance to the campus. Chancellor Strong kept quarters in Dwinelle Hall, not far from Sather Gate. In 1958, a block of stores across the street from Sproul Hall was demolished to make room for a large new student union and dining complex. Finished in 1960, the street between it and Sproul Hall became a large plaza ideal for student gatherings, except that none were permitted. In the middle of Sproul Plaza sat Ludwig's Fountain, informally named for the large dog that played in its waters.

The creation of Sproul Plaza moved the beginning of Telegraph Avenue to Bancroft Way. Lined by stores for many blocks, Telegraph Avenue was a major shopping street. North and south of it were blocks of low-rent housing heavily occupied by students. On most streets, large Victorian houses had been broken up into irregular apartments and/or rooms with ancient kitchens and bathrooms. Some streets had newer two- and three-story apartment buildings with higher rentals. A few blocks east of Telegraph Avenue, two enormous dorm complexes had opened only in 1960. Each had four high-rise buildings for 210 residents in two-bed rooms on eight floors surrounding a dining complex. Two were girls' dorms and two were for boys. Older low-rise dormitories and a few cooperative housing buildings were scattered off campus. Bancroft Way was lined with buildings owned by different religious institutions. The Episcopal student center, Wesley Foundation (Methodist), Westminster (Presbyterian), and Hillel (Jewish), all ministered to students of their faiths. The Newman Club (Catholic) was on the north side. West of Telegraph Avenue, on the corner of Dana Street, sat Stiles Hall, home of the YMCA. This was the student center for the political groups, a role it earned by making meeting space available for a small fee. The student groups which weren't allowed to meet on campus met here.

Because the buildings where the entry-level courses were taught were near Sather Gate and most dorms were south of campus, the intersection of Bancroft and Telegraph was the main entrance for hordes of new students. More advanced humanities and social science courses were also taught in these and nearby buildings mostly south of the main library. Between classes one could easily go to the library or to the student union complex, which had four eating areas catering to different tastes. From outside tables at The Terrace, one could watch the crowd pass by. This configuration created a bifurcated town square composed of Sproul Plaza on one side of Sather Gate and Dwinelle Plaza on the other. It was a town square populated heavily by undergraduates, especially those majoring in the social sciences and humanities. Students in the sciences, agriculture, law, engineering, and so forth stayed closer to their home buildings to the north and east. Geography fostered homogeneity despite disciplinary diversity. Our student newspaper, the *Daily Californian,* generally known as the *Daily Cal,* was the common denominator.

The sidewalk at Bancroft and Telegraph was laid with red brick. A large planter marked one side of what had once been a city street. The brick continued inside the campus proper for twenty-six feet. Where it stopped, four short obelisks protruded. Inlaid in the brick ten feet from the curb were two plaques, unnoticed by those who trod over them, demarcating the public sidewalk from the property of the Regents. To the casual glance, however, it appeared that the real campus border was at the posts where the red brick ended. By the time I graduated in 1965, the placing of the pillars and the bricks would have important political consequences because most people assumed that the land twenty-six feet into the campus belonged to the City of Berkeley.

It was in this area that the student political groups put up their tables, sold buttons and literature, and passed out leaflets announcing events. The university rules forbade them to do these things on campus. The ten feet of public sidewalk at Bancroft and Telegraph was too narrow for the many groups wanting to solicit students. Their presence would have created too much congestion if restricted to its width. Thus, it was a convenient fiction to assume that all the red bricks were on public property. Students coming on campus each day passed the political groups and could stop to browse but were not stopped by them. Nestled between the city and the campus was 1,000 square feet of political space which nourished the student marketplace of ideas.

3 | *Politics and the University*

THE UNIVERSITY ADMINISTRATION had long trod a fine line between the academic tradition of full and free inquiry and the pull of the public purse. Article IX, § 9 of the state constitution declared that the University of California was to be "entirely independent of all political or sectarian influence and kept free therefrom in the appointment of its Regents and in the administration of its affairs." This clause was put into the 1879 constitution to shield the university from the political turmoil that embroiled it in the 1870s, which led to a legislative investigation and resignation of the president in 1874. But an institution funded primarily by a political body—the state legislature—and largely populated by intelligent, educated citizens could never be free from politics. It would continue to be a political hot spot subject to repeated legislative threats and investigations.[1]

The drafters of Article IX, § 9 intended that the twenty-four members of the Board of Regents would set policy for the university without regard for the push and pull of political currents. Sixteen were appointed by the governor for 16-year terms, and eight were ex officio Regents by virtue of other offices they held. They reflected the important political, economic, and social interests within the state. In 1964, "members of the Board of Regents either headed or served on the boards of directors of 38 major corporations in the state and the nation."[2] While they did provide stability and also encouraged sizable donations from wealthy Californians, they did not render the university apolitical.

The legislature could not govern the university directly, but it did approve the budget, sometimes using this power to express its views on how the taxpayers' money was spent. Members of the legislature attacked the work of the university and the activities of its faculty and students as one way of raising their political profiles and scoring points with their constituencies. The reigning belief was that college students were still children in need of adult supervision, which would be provided by the campus administration in loco parentis (in lieu of the parents). Consequently, the administration was often held responsible for what its students did off, as well as on, campus.

During the 1930s, a small strata of student radicals formed political organizations at the university. Some were openly communist or socialist. Others, such as the Social Problems Club, were led by Communists, though anyone could join. These groups mobilized students for a variety of protests. In 1934, they supported the labor strikes that convulsed the Bay Area. In 1935, they led 4,000 Berkeley students in a nationwide strike against war, in which 175,000 participated. These actions "badly frightened" the Regents. Concerned that student radicals scared the public and provoked the legislature, President Sproul began a personal anticommunism campaign "to reassure the public its University was in safe hands." He adopted, with the approval of the Regents, a series of rules and policies to limit or prohibit use of the campus. Regulation 17 put control of all university facilities under the president. Regulation 5 allowed each campus administration to decide who was qualified to be on campus, in any capacity. These were used to keep Communists out. Sproul also initiated an intelligence network to gather information on student radicals. He assigned William Wadman, a young officer in the campus police, to keep track of radicals among the students and the faculty on the Berkeley campus. A music student from New Zealand who followed his father into police work, Wadman loved working at a university and soon established rapport with the students. He shared information with law enforcement officials all over the Bay Area. Some faculty, particularly political science professor and former UC president David Barrows, also provided information on students.[3]

Nonetheless, when students picketed and rallied, the newspapers editorialized, the public wrote letters, and the legislature looked for signs of subversion. Early in 1940, the state assembly created a committee to investigate subversive activities in the state relief administration. Chaired by Sam Yorty of Los Angeles, its creation was part of a struggle over power and patronage between assembly Democrats and the Democratic governor, Culbert Olson. Although campus radicalism was not on its agenda, it was on that of its successor, the joint Fact-Finding Subcommittee on Un-American Activities, created in 1941 and chaired by Assemblyman Jack Tenney (D-Los Angeles). Declaring that "tolerance [of Communists] is treason," Tenney ran his committee personally with minimal supervision from the legislature. He started a battle with the University of California that lasted for thirty years.[4]

This battle was not confined to the university's boundaries. Tenney also went after Stiles Hall for letting Cal's student political clubs hold meetings and hear speakers that weren't permitted on campus. In 1946, Tenney's committee subpoenaed Stiles's director—plus the director of the YWCA and several known Communists—to a hearing. It released their names to the newspapers before serving the subpoena. Among other things, Tenney attacked Stiles Hall for registering as "The University of California YMCA"; it changed its name to "University YMCA."[5]

In 1949, Tenney introduced thirteen bills to ferret out subversives, including a state constitutional amendment to "give the legislature power to insure the loyalty of officers and employees of the University." On recommendation of the university lobbyist, Vice President James H. Corley, President Sproul asked the Regents to preempt it with an oath of their own. The new university loyalty oath specifically disclaimed membership in the Communist Party or any other organization which advocated the overthrow of the government by force or violence. The faculty rebelled. Some objected to the very idea of an oath, others to the fact that this oath was strictly for university employees; others saw it as a threat to academic freedom or to tenure. Twenty percent refused to sign, even when the Regents emphasized that not signing would mean loss of their jobs. Some faculty contributed to a salary pool for those who were not reappointed. The controversy did not end until 1952—after thirty-one professors had been dismissed—when the California Supreme Court declared that a state loyalty oath passed in the interim preempted a special one for university personnel. The manner in which this matter was handled by the administration left bitter memories in the minds of many faculty members and tarnished Sproul's reputation. The special loyalty oath was one of many attempts by the university administration to avoid the wrath of red-hunting legislators through a strategy of anticipatory appeasement. Sometimes it worked, and sometimes it backfired.[6]

Tenney was forced out of his committee in 1949 after a committee staffer accused several legislators and prominent Democrats with being Communist "fellow travelers, dupes or dopes." He was replaced by Hugh Burns (D-Fresno), a committee member since its inception, who was expected to be a reasonable and moderate chairman. The Burns Committee kept a lower profile, no longer sponsoring anti-communist legislation or holding public hearings. But it did develop a network of informants to gather information on "subversives" and produce biennial reports. Its 1951 report "reflected a renewed and concentrated investigation of higher education." In his effort to shepherd the university budget, Vice President Corley developed a close working relationship with Burns, with whom he shared an antipathy to Communists.[7]

4 | SLATE

THE GREEK SYSTEM—fraternities and sororities—survived wartime retrenchment. Most of the student political groups did not. Since the Greeks shared living quarters and gave their members points for extra-curricular activities, they dominated the governing body of the Associated Students of the University of California (ASUC) and ran most student activities. Nonetheless, as the student body grew in size and new dormitories and co-op units provided alternative housing, fewer students pledged; in 1961, Greeks were less than 10 percent of undergraduates and 6 percent of all students.[1]

The last hurrah of the Greek houses came in 1956 when the fraternities turned a pre-finals water fight into a massive, destructive panty raid. Male invasions of female housing units were a campus fad in the early 1950s; over thirty colleges and universities saw their male students mount raiding parties of from several hundred to several thousand. While Berkeley students had rioted in previous years—notably in 1936, 1937, and 1948—these were largely prompted by excess football enthusiasm. On May 16, 1956, about 3,000 students invaded twenty-six women's living groups, looking for lingerie. They caused $12,000 in damage before finally dispersing. Those that could be identified were disciplined—two were expelled—and it gave the Greeks a bad name.[2]

One of those who was disciplined was Allan Solomonow, a freshman from Los Angeles who joined Alpha Epsilon Pi and became his class cheerleader. Allan was turned in by someone in a private women's residence (not a sorority) who recognized him while he was prowling its corridors. He was directed to report to Alex Sherriffs, a faculty member in the Psychology Department and an advisor to Chancellor Kerr. After admitting his entry into and removal of items from four residences, he was suspended for a year.

When Allan returned in the fall of 1957, the campus was a different place. Greek control of the student government was being challenged by GDIs, or God Damned Independents, as those students who did not pledge were called. Several had organized a campus political party, which they named TASC: Toward an Active Student Community. TASC was composed largely of students in the social sciences of varied, but mostly liberal to radical, persuasions. They felt that student government had become a "sandbox" where students played imaginary games that had little relation to the real world. They wanted it to address issues relevant to the current lives of students.

By 1957, the children of political activists from the 1930s were going to college. Although still seriously outnumbered by the "silent generation," as their cohorts were called, they carried the political gene and a set of common values, which moved them to make waves. Kindred spirits found each other at Stiles Hall, in co-op living groups, and in classes taught by such professors as Wolin, Schaar, and Jacobson in Political Science; Kornhauser, Coser, and Selznick in Sociology; and ten Broek in the Speech Department. They brought in their friends and roommates who were interested in politics but less likely to lead the charge into unknown territory. After Allan's roommate became involved in TASC, Allan became its parliamentarian.

One inspiration of these incipient activists was the southern Civil Rights Movement, which had been in the headlines throughout 1956. A federal court ordered Autherine Lucy admitted to the University of Alabama, but a white mob effectively kept her out. Negroes in Montgomery, Alabama, boycotted the city buses to protest segregated seating, and newspapers everywhere ran stories on their nonviolent protest. On November 13, 1956, the Supreme Court affirmed a federal court decision that this form of segregation was unconstitutional; on December 21st, the city announced it would comply. On February 19, 1957, ASUC graduate representative Ralph Shaffer asked the student government to deny recognition to any student organization which restricted membership on the basis of race, color, religion, or national origin. Although the Greek houses were not specifically named, they were his target because their national charters often restricted membership on the basis of race and religion (as well as sex). When the student government skirted a direct vote inimical to the Greeks, Ralph joined fellow students Fritjof Thygeson and Rick White to form TASC. They decided to run candidates in the spring ASUC elections on a common platform. In addition to speaking against racial discrimination in student housing, its candidates also spoke against apartheid in South Africa, loyalty oaths, compulsory military training (Reserve Officer Training Corps, or ROTC) for male undergraduates, and nuclear testing, as well as some strictly student concerns.[3]

Of all the candidates TASC supported, only Thygeson won a seat in the spring 1957 ASUC election. In the fall of 1957, senior Mike Miller, who had been elected to the ASUC government a year earlier, resigned and with the TASCers recruited a group to run on a common platform. They called themselves "the SLATE." While they lost, they were heartened to receive 40 percent of the vote in an election with twice the normal turnout. They decided to form a permanent student political party. In February of 1958, a convention of roughly 100 students founded SLATE to run candidates "committed to a common platform for student office in order to engage in issue-oriented political education both on and off campus." SLATE rented an office for $50 a month in a storefront across the street from the administration building and began publishing the *Cal*

Reporter, a four-page weekly. Since administration rules forbade its distribution on campus, the paper was available only on the city side of Sather Gate. The $23 cost to print 5,000 copies of each issue was largely met by holding off-campus beer parties at fifty cents per person.[4]

The idea of student political parties had been discussed at meetings of the National Student Association for years, and SLATE was not the first student party to form. One existed at the University of Chicago. On March 4, 1958, the ASUC executive committee voted to allow student parties; on March 19th, it changed its mind, ruling that candidates could not indicate a party affiliation on the ballot. The campus administration followed the lead of the student government and told SLATE it could not be a political party, only a "recognized student organization," until the issue of whether there should be campus political parties could be settled. According to Chancellor Seaborg, "Both Sherriffs and [Dean of Students Huford] Stone . . . took a dim view of Slate and *Cal Reporter.*" Sherriffs, who had been made vice-chancellor for student affairs by Kerr in one of his last acts as chief campus officer, wrote numerous memos to both of them warning that SLATE meant trouble. "The group deliberately misrepresents facts, opposes any kind of cooperation, fosters conflict, and seems to be systematically seeking means to embarrass the administration," he stated on October 1, 1958. The *Daily Cal* was also hostile. When it claimed that SLATE stood for nothing, the *Cal Reporter* responded that it meant "Student League Accused of Trying to Exist." Criticism heightened student interest in SLATE. By the end of the semester, SLATE had an office on campus with other student groups and its press was churning out leaflets from Allan's new apartment at 2514A Regent Street.[5]

For the next several years, SLATE membership averaged a few hundred students, of which thirty to forty came to meetings regularly. There were usually about a dozen active leaders. Roughly 850 students joined SLATE at one time or another. SLATEniks were a mixed group whose most common characteristic was an aversion to conformity. While men predominated, there were a lot more women in the SLATE leadership than that of the student government; women chaired SLATE for one semester each in 1959 and in 1962. Politically, members ranged from liberal to socialist. Though the curve was skewed to the left, I met a few liberal Republicans in SLATE. All had a commitment to civil liberties and civil rights. Many were active in off-campus political organizations, but not the same ones. What held them together was their distaste for the "sandbox" government of the ASUC, where students were not allowed to address real issues, and their belief that the campus should be a forum for real-world politics.[6]

Being a "recognized student organization" that wanted "to make meaningful politics legitimate on campus" brought continual conflict with Regulation 17. Some of the students who would join TASC had persuaded the administration to modify 17 in 1957 so that "off-campus student groups" could hold special meetings on campus to listen to suitable speakers approved by the administration, but this small gain had required a major effort. SLATE sought to increase the pressure for change through public action. In March of 1959, it asked permission to hold a rally at Wheeler Oak, which grew in Dwinelle Plaza near the bridge, to support a fair housing ordinance then on the Berkeley ballot and to protest the University Housing Office's listing of rental units for students that were only available to whites. Dean Stone said no because recognized student organizations were not allowed to "take positions on political and related controversies." SLATE then asked for permission to hold a rally on student participation in political activities, but this too was denied. SLATE held the rally anyway, defying the administration to take disciplinary action. It passed out leaflets demanding FREE SPEECH AT CAL. Wilson Carey McWilliams, Jr., whose father had gained some notoriety as a writer for and editor of the left-wing magazine *The Nation*, was the chief speaker.[7]

A dozen students were called into the dean's office for disciplinary hearings. Ernest Besig of the northern California chapter of the American Civil Liberties Union (ACLU) acted as their attorney and also wrote letters objecting to the denial of "a campus meeting by a recognized student group because it intended to state its position on an off-campus issue." California attorney general Stanley Mosk wrote an informal opinion that no laws would be violated by such activity. The *Daily Cal* editorialized: "The University administration seems so immersed in the concept of remaining free from partisan disputes that it attaches a mystical sanctity to the obviously inept regulations which attempt to enforce this policy."[8]

Instead of disciplining individual students, the administration robbed SLATE of its chief constituency, the graduate students. In the May 1959 elections, an exceptionally large turnout elected SLATE candidate David Armor as ASUC president by 33 votes, plus another four SLATE candidates to the senate, including two graduate students. Armor was the first non-Greek to become student body president since the war. The administration then announced that "a majority of graduate students wish to be separated from the undergraduate student government," and said that their elected representatives could not serve. This claim was based on a questionnaire returned by two-thirds of the graduate students who filed course lists during spring registration. They were asked to rank five alternatives that included continuing as members of the ASUC, withdrawing and having their student fees cut in half, and forming a separate organization. Although only 30 percent chose complete disassociation, when classes began in the fall of 1959, Chancellor Seaborg declared that graduate students were no longer represented in the student government. Graduate student fees, however, were increased to cover the costs of the new student union then being built. A Graduate Student Association was created, but without compulsory fees it soon became skeletal. SLATE continued to run candidates for ASUC office, but it won few seats.[9]

It also continued to irritate the administration. In May of 1959, Sherriffs and Stone sent memos to Seaborg urging him to keep the *Cal Reporter* off campus because it was "characterized very largely by a complete lack of responsibility to anyone." Two days later Kerr told Seaborg to let it be distributed on campus. However, the little paper had breathed its last for the year and would only gasp twice more, once in 1960 and again in 1963. This did not mean that SLATE no longer published its views. It regularly produced pamphlets, leaflets, and letters to the editor. At a retreat attended by the ASUC executive committee and several administrators in September 1959, SLATE representative Marvin Sternberg passed out song sheets with new words to old music lampooning several administrators in ways they found insulting. Sherriffs' memo said it was "a carefully worked out attack by slander, ridicule, and suggestion on representatives of the University." Nonetheless, SLATE was being heard.[10]

Partially prompted by SLATE's pushing the envelope of what were campus concerns, on October 22, 1959, President Kerr issued a series of regulations on student government, student organizations, and use of university facilities. Soon known as the Kerr Directives, they sought to consolidate, clarify, and in some cases liberalize the rules and policies that had evolved under Sproul. Essentially, they said that: (1) Student governments were creatures of the administration and could not take a position on any "off-campus issue" without its consent; (2) Recognized student organizations "must not be affiliated with any partisan political or religious group, or have as one of its principal purposes the taking of partisan positions identified with such a group." Those that did have such purposes could be "off-campus student organizations" and apply to use campus facilities for special events, but not for regular meetings; and (3) Use of university facilities was still carefully controlled, as were events sponsored by student organizations, but candidates for public office could speak on campus under some conditions. Much to Kerr's dismay, the new rules were denounced by students on four campuses, who saw them as limiting rather than liberating. The faculty weren't enamored with them either, though they didn't actively protest. Chancellor Seaborg asked the Academic Senate to create a committee to advise him on how best to apply the directives to the Berkeley campus. Its members were not the faculty civil libertarians, but after meeting for several months their only recommendations were ones to allow *more* political activity on campus and *greater* freedom to advocate positions and raise funds than permitted by the directives. Seaborg passed these on to Kerr, but no one acted on them.[11]

SLATE continued to *act* like a political party and even to *call* itself a political party, as did the *Daily Cal,* despite the fact that it could not officially *be* one. It was on the cutting edge of a new student activism emerging on campuses all over the country, like leaves of grass pushing their way through asphalt. In July of 1960, SLATE sponsored a conference at Mount Madonna Park near San Jose on how to be a student political party. It brought 140 members of liberal, religious, civil rights, and peace organizations from all over the country for a weekend of endless discussions.[12] Political parties had or would soon form on many campuses. Students organized PLATFORM at UCLA and DECLARE at UC Riverside. Tom Hayden spent several weeks with the SLATE leadership on his way to Los Angeles to cover the 1960 Democratic Convention for the *Michigan Daily.* When he returned to Ann Arbor he formed VOICE. POLIT was put together at the University of Chicago, TOCSIN at Harvard, the Progressive Student League at Oberlin, and the Political Action Club at Swarthmore.[13] In April of 1962, Oberlin hosted a conference for campus political parties. At this nascent New Left gathering there were representatives from the National Student Association, the budding Students for a Democratic Society (SDS), campus groups at Columbia University and in Utah, and several California colleges. Rich Fallenbaum, the SLATE member who reported on this meeting, was impressed with the desire for a "liberal and radical politics" and the "consciousness of the futility of local action in affecting national policy."[14]

Current events more than anything SLATE did thwarted administration efforts to build a wall at the campus edge. When SLATE tried to straddle that wall, insisting that what happened on the outside was relevant to what students studied on the inside, the administration built it

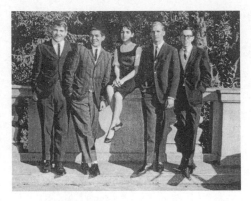

VOTE
TODAY

reps—at—large

    JERRY BERMAN

    RICH FALLENBAUM

    DAVE WALLS

lower division rep

    JEANNE VARON

men's rep

    MIKE MIKESELL

President Benjamin Ide Wheeler on
student government at Cal:

It must be, outright, a student affair
in its thinking and its doing. Otherwise
student self-government will be a farce.
It will be faculty government disguised
with a sweater.

The issue in this election is whether student
self-government should exist at Cal, or whether
the ASUC should be merely an arm of the
university administration. The present majority
of the Executive Committee has shown by its
actions that it does not believe in student
self-government.

SLATE believes that the student government
should have a voice in university affairs;
that it should have an effect on the living
and working conditions of students; that it
is the proper vehicle for expressing concerns
common to the majority of the student community
here.

SLATE does not believe that members of the
student community give up their rights and
responsibilities as citizens each time they
step onto the campus. Our participation in
an educational community, in fact, makes it
imperative that we participate more fully as
citizens in our society.

For a student government that represents
students with courage and independence,
vote SLATE. Support all five SLATE candidates.

✳ SLATE

Even though SLATE could not officially be a student political party, it ran a slate of
candidates committed to a common platform in every student government election.

higher, eventually forcing SLATE outside. It did not align itself with any
existing political party or organization—its members were too diverse
for this ever to happen—but it thought discussion of, and even action on,
off-campus issues belonged on campus. Removal of the graduate students
from the ASUC removed the possibility that SLATE could capture student government through elections. This encouraged SLATE to alter its

focus from the problems of student government to the problems of being a student in a rapidly changing world. Instead of being a campus political party, it became a campus gadfly.

5 | Exploring the Political Bazaar

BEFORE BERKELEY, THE only worlds I knew were the suffocating conformity of the San Fernando Valley—where Valley Girls set the standard long before the song was written—and Helen's Alabama family, which demanded conformity of a different kind. Berkeley was a whole new world; it made me realize that there was more to life than I had seen in my sixteen years. Eager to explore it and very shy, almost frightened, I became a turtle; I would stick my head out, look around for a while, and then pull it back in. My first morning in the business-school rooming house I stayed in bed until I heard no more noises in the house. My bladder was bursting, but I wouldn't get up and go to the bathroom because I was afraid to meet anyone. There was a kitchen but no dining room or common room, so in my two weeks of living there I only made one friend, and that friendship didn't survive my move to the Berkeley Inn.

Nonetheless, as I found my way into this variegated world my shyness slowly dissolved. Compared to the stifling sameness of the Valley, Cal was a kaleidoscope. There was so much to do. There were so many different people. There were so many different ideas. I tried a little bit of everything until I realized that my studies would suffer if I tried to do too much. I wasn't wedded to acing every course, but neither did I want to shame myself. After a few weeks I cut back. Ironically, the person I picked as my best friend for the semester, Karen Okamoto, was a serious student without my penchant for exploring the unknown. She kept re-minding me that my primary job was to study.

Every morning I crossed Bancroft at Telegraph and entered the po-litical fair between the pillars and the plaques. In front of each post were tables placed by different groups covered with brightly colored posters advertising their wares. I sampled from the Young Democrats (YD), SLATE, the Young Socialist Alliance (YSA), the Young People's Socialist League (YPSL), Fair Play for Cuba, the Student Peace Union (SPU), the Student Civil Liberties Union, BASCAHUAC (Bay Area Students' Com-mittee against HUAC), and probably more that I've long since forgotten. I took their leaflets and in between classes read them with curiosity and wonderment. There were so many different views that had never come to light in the parochial confines of the Valley. I read with particular inter-est the offerings of the socialist groups because years of hearing anti-communism campaigns had made me curious. But instead of plunging into one of them after reading their offerings, I went to several forums and asked questions. Once I satisfied my curiosity, the only political group I joined was not one for young socialists in any of its various fac-tional forms, but the University Young Democrats (UYD).

SLATE was the most active of the student political groups, and though I did not then join, I did put my name on its mailing list and went to some of its events. Its chairman my first semester was Ken Cloke, my Northridge neighbor, and its primary issue seemed to be nuclear testing. Until a moratorium was called in 1958, both the Soviet Union and the United States tested atomic devices above and below ground. There was a lot of discussion about the harmful effects of radioactive fallout from these blasts, but little hard evidence reached the public. The Atomic En-ergy Commission repeatedly assured us that U.S. tests were within safe limits, but with nothing to back this up, many just didn't believe the agency.[1]

In 1961, after France began nuclear testing, the USSR's Nikita Khrushchev threatened to resume its tests. Threats and counterthreats continued for months, until on August 31st the Soviet Union announced it would resume atmospheric testing of nuclear bombs. It detonated bombs throughout the fall; on October 30th, the largest-ever manmade explosion put cities all over the northern hemisphere under a "fallout alert." Since there was no Soviet outpost in the Bay Area—not even a trade mission in San Francisco—SLATE called for an all-night vigil on the steps of Sproul Hall on October 31st to protest *all* nuclear testing.

SLATE's efforts to sponsor anything tainted by politics often resulted in a ritual dance with the administration. The new dean of students, Katherine Towle, denied approval, writing that "action of a social or political nature by student organizations . . . is prohibited by University regulations." She suggested that "individual members of the campus community as individuals are, of course, free to assemble peaceably if they wish to do so." SLATE withdrew its sponsorship and called upon "individuals within the campus community to join in collective action as individuals." The vigil was held as planned.[2] Several hundred people spent all or part of the night holding candles under a banner reading "For Humanity's Sake, Stop All Nuclear Testing." I didn't last the night and was impressed by how many were still there when I returned for classes the next day.

President Kennedy had spoken against atmospheric testing when he campaigned the year before, but only three days after the Soviet super-blast he ordered its resumption. Now, it seemed, the dangers of fallout took a back seat to maintaining nuclear superiority. The United States was still dropping test bombs the following spring when Kennedy was the Charter Day speaker at Cal.[3] On March 22nd, he spoke to 88,000 people in Memorial Stadium at the largest event in university history. He was greeted with long picket lines at Bancroft and Telegraph and on a public street near the stadium. Not ready to picket my president, I nonetheless picked up leaflets and took photographs of the picket lines. Then I went inside to hear him speak, coming just close enough to take a blurry photo with my Brownie Bull's-Eye camera as the procession passed by.

YPSL was the youth group of the Socialist Party (SP). Founded at the turn of the century, the SP had had some illustrious leaders, including Eugene Debs and Norman Thomas. After the Soviet Union was founded, pro-Soviet members of the SP broke away to form the Communist Party (CPUSA) in 1919, and the two parties went their separate ways. Fractured by factional fights, witch hunts for Communists, and red scares, the SP only had a few thousand members nationwide by the early 1960s. YPSL, founded in the 1930s, only had a few hundred members. The UC chapter was composed mostly of graduate students who spent their time talking political theory in an arcane language I didn't understand. The YPSLs realized that the word "socialist" was anathema to most Americans, so they often worked through other groups, some of which they founded and some of which they simply joined en masse. One of these was the SPU, which worked for nuclear disarmament and denounced

Berkeley students picket President Kennedy at Bancroft and Telegraph before he addresses a Charter Day celebration on March 22, 1962. The issue of the day was opposition to nuclear testing, which both sides of the Cold War had resumed the year before. *Photograph by Jo Freeman.*

both the United States and the USSR as warmongers. In February of 1962, the SPU brought 5,000 students to Washington, D.C., for two days of lobbying and demonstrations.[4] Several people I later recognized as members of YPSL also worked through the UYDs. In the YDs they avoided socialist jargon and were very good workers. I never heard any resentment that they might be exercising too much influence. Of course, they were seriously outnumbered.

The YSA was organized in 1960 from youth clubs of the Socialist Workers Party (SWP). I quickly learned that members of both were called "Trotskyists." It took me longer to find out who Leon Trotsky was, since my high school history courses didn't say much about the Russian Revolution. The Trots had at various times been part of the SP until they formed their own SWP in 1938. Although they had a mere handful of active members locally, and a hundred or so nationwide, they were very active and impressed me with their energy and dedication. In 1963, the YSA table was usually manned by Syd Stapleton and Beth Gardner, a pleasant, cherubic couple quite unlike the stereotypes of socialists portrayed in the Valley papers. The SWP national newspaper, called *The Militant,* came out several times a year, and the local group sponsored regular forums. However, the forums weren't really for discussion of current issues, since the Trots already had a party line. Their primary purpose was recruitment of warm bodies to do work, and their primary focus was support of the Cuban revolution. Unlike many left-wing parties, the SWP ran its own candidates in major elections. They denounced the Democratic and Republican parties as two sides of the same capitalistic coin. Since I wasn't ready to give up on the Democratic Party, that line effectively ended any interest I might have in their version of socialism.[5]

BASCAHUAC, the Bay Area Students' Committee against the House Un-American Activities Committee, had the most sonorous name, though I never found out exactly what it did besides sell pamphlets calling for the abolition of HUAC. In 1938, Congress had formed a temporary committee to investigate subversive propaganda. The House Un-American Activities Committee (HUAC) became permanent in 1945. In the next fifteen years, it spent $5 million of the taxpayers' money to pay for 55 staff members, 5,000 subpoenas, and 50,000 published pages of hearings and reports. HUAC's strategy was to draw attention to Communist subversion through publicity. It held hearings around the country, subpoenaing numerous people to testify about their associations and those of people they knew. If they refused, they were jailed and blacklisted from their professions. Throughout my childhood HUAC had actively fueled anti-Communist hysteria and was associated in my mind with McCarthyism, even though Joe McCarthy was a U.S. senator, not a member of the House. McCarthyism, HUAC, and the Cold War dominated the childhood of all of us at Berkeley in the sixties. They generated an atmosphere of fear and repression which shaped our environment but also promoted resistance.

Tables came and went from Bancroft and Telegraph; some groups were shooting stars and some were regulars. Among the former was Students Associated Against Totalitarianism, a small group run by Charles Fox, a grad student in linguistics who wrote letters regularly to the

Daily Cal. The group disappeared when he left campus to set up shop on nearby Channing Way as a professional anti-Communist, dedicated to exposing Commiesymps (Communist sympathizers) in the Bay Area through a weekly sheet he called *Tocsin.* Among the latter was the campus chapter of the W. E. B. DuBois Clubs, one of several that appeared in the Bay Area in 1963. A national organization was officially founded in June of 1964. Its literature said it was a Marxist-oriented youth organization, but within the student political subculture it was known to be the youth group of the CP. Kayo Hallinan, one of its founders, said it was organized around "red diaper babies" (children of Communists) who didn't want to join the Party but were interested in issues. "We gave them a way to get into politics," he said.[6] W. E. B. DuBois was a distinguished black scholar, founder of the NAACP (National Association for the Advancement of Colored People), and editor of its magazine *The Crisis.* He joined the CP in 1961, two years before his death. Named in his honor, the DuBois Club was open to anyone who agreed with its principles; not all of its members were in the CP. Because of this shroud, the UC club could register with the Dean of Students as a recognized "off-campus" organization, hold rallies, and sponsor off-campus speakers other than open Communists (who were banned).

At the time I did not know that the political bazaar I found so fascinating was the direct descendent of the "Sather Gate Tradition." During the 1930s, when many national issues were being debated, students got around the prohibition against politics on campus by congregating inside Sather Gate—then the campus border—while speakers stood just outside the campus grounds and addressed them through bullhorns or loudspeakers from soapboxes, car roofs, and even from trucks parked at the curb. As plans were made to close the last block of Telegraph Avenue and deed it to the university, everyone from SLATE to Clark Kerr asked the campus administration what it was going to do. Vice-Chancellor Sherriffs wrote a long memo in the fall of 1958 on the importance of the Sather Gate Tradition as a safety valve for meetings "which might be embarrassing if held on the campus proper." He observed that when the City of Berkeley tried to curtail gatherings at the Gate during the McCarthy era, the uproar before the City Council was so tremendous that it backed off. He wanted "the valued tradition" to be moved to the northeast corner of Bancroft and Telegraph.[7]

SLATE objected to this new location because greater noise, heavy traffic, and limited sidewalk space would make effective communication

In the spring of 1958 SLATE founder Mike Miller addresses a student rally on the city side of Sather Gate, while two members of the Berkeley Police Red Squad observe.

difficult. It threatened to form a free speech committee. The ASUC asked that the Sather Gate Tradition be kept at Sather Gate. The *Daily Cal* urged that Regulation 17 be changed to allow for an "island of free speech at Sather Gate." President Kerr decided that the best solution was to deed back to the city a small amount of land at Bancroft and Telegraph. He asked the architects for the Student Union to put a little plaza into their design. The Regents agreed at their September 1959 meeting, but the return of land never happened; it fell between the cracks.[8] Sometime in the spring of 1960, student groups were told they could no longer put their tables up outside of Sather Gate; they had to go to Bancroft and Telegraph. There a little red-brick plaza awaited them, separated from the campus proper by pillars just like the ones that had previously sat at Sather Gate. No one paid attention to the plaques twenty-six feet away declaring that plaza to be the property of the Regents.

6 | The Young Democrats

The UYD was a member of the California Democratic Council (CDC) and the California Federation of Young Democrats (CFYD). Officially founded in late 1953, CDC was one product of the reform movement that swept the Democratic Party in the wake of the 1952 election. Although Adlai Stevenson lost to Eisenhower, his wry humor, elegant speeches, and image of intelligence and integrity reinvigorated the Democratic Party and "made it seem an open and exciting place for a generation of younger Americans who might otherwise never have thought of working for a political candidate."[1] During his campaign, thousands of political clubs were founded throughout the country, many of which continued to exist afterward in conflict with local party bodies. They brought into Democratic Party politics a new breed, the amateur Democrat—educated, middle class, professionally employed, motivated by issues rather than patronage. In areas dominated by traditional party machines, such as New York City, these amateur Democrats founded Independent Democratic Clubs and fought the regulars. However, California was run by Republicans, so Democratic leaders welcomed new blood. In California, reform meant a resurgence of the Democratic Party.[2]

Official political parties were weak in California as a result of legislation passed in the Progressive Era. Cross-filing was a legacy of Governor Hiram Johnson (1911–1916). After running for vice president with Theodore Roosevelt on the 1912 Progressive Party ticket, he engineered cross-filing through the legislature so he could run for the Senate in 1916 as the candidate of both the Progressive and Republican Parties. For the next forty years, cross-filing gave the Republicans an electoral advantage. In 1950, they held most elected offices even though almost 60 percent of the voters had registered Democratic since the days of FDR. Incumbents were listed at the top of the ballot for each race, so Republicans running in both party primaries were listed first on both ballots. CDC's purpose was to endorse candidates running in the Democratic primary to prevent Republicans who cross-filed from capturing the Democratic as well as the Republican nomination. Official parties were prohibited from endorsing any candidate in its primary; CDC wasn't an official party body. All of its endorsed candidates for statewide office won the Democratic primaries in 1954 and 1958, making it, with 70,000 members organized into 400 clubs, more influential than the official Democratic Party. After cross-filing was abolished in 1959, CDC continued to make pre-primary endorsements at conventions to which member clubs sent delegates. For the most part, CDC endorsed those on the liberal side of the party's ideological divide, describing itself as the "conscience of the party"; when it didn't, club members often sat on their hands.[3]

In the election of 1958, the Democratic Party did well throughout the country and very well in California. The Democrats took control of the state for the first time since 1888, including "both houses of the legislature, the congressional delegation, the Board of Equalization and five of the six state constitutional offices, [and] the governorship." Attorney General Edmund G. "Pat" Brown became governor. The Democratic sweep was aided by a vicious factional fight in the Republican Party. William F. Knowland, U.S. senator since 1945, wanted to be governor. He forced incumbent governor Goodwin Knight (who had replaced Earl Warren in 1953 when he was appointed chief justice of the Supreme Court) to run for the Senate so he (Knowland) could seek the state's highest office. Both lost badly.[4]

While CDC endorsed all but one of the Democratic incumbents in 1960, when Democrats captured and kept major offices, it was soon at odds with Democratic elected officials. The anti-power ethic, which had motivated many amateurs to join the clubs in the first place, was transferred from the state's Republican power structure to its Democratic incumbents. In the early 1960s, such classic liberals as Assembly Speaker Jesse Unruh was denounced as a "boss" and snidely called "Big Daddy" Unruh, a reference to his considerable girth as well as his power. In 1963, Democratic legislators tried to limit CDC's ability to "officially endorse" candidates. By 1966, antagonism was so great between elected Democrats and CDC that Governor Brown engineered the removal of CDC leader Si Casady. Casady opposed the Viet Nam War and didn't want CDC to endorse anyone who felt differently. His removal did not keep CDC from endorsing anti-war candidates in the Democratic primary over incumbents. At the 1966 CDC convention Governor Brown, and even State Controller Alan Cranston, CDC's first president, were booed.

That fall Brown lost his bid for a third term as governor to Ronald Reagan.[5]

Membership in the YDs was open to anyone between ages 16 to 36 who was a registered Democrat or who would be one if eligible to vote. Through the clubs, one joined the CFYD, the national Young Democratic Clubs of America, and CDC. Although the YDs contributed a lot of legwork in elections, its real value was as a training school for future political leaders. Separating the YDs from the big Ds created more offices to run for and conventions to go to and thus more experience in arguing one's positions in front of large groups and in running campaigns. I learned parliamentary procedure at YD meetings. When I finally joined SLATE, I was the only one who knew Robert's Rules of Order. At YD and CDC conventions I saw skilled chairmen handle with dispatch heated disputes in large meetings that practically crippled SLATE and other student groups whose members did not know Robert's Rules or, more often, did not want to know. I also learned that the important place to be at conventions was not the resolutions committee, where ideas were debated, but the organization committee, where one could watch the maneuvering over bylaws. It was organization that determined how power was distributed and thus what, if anything, happened to the resolutions.

To some extent, the YDs mirrored the senior party, and thus their faction fights gave insight into what was happening in the different states. However, the YDs, especially in California, were also the vanguard— certainly the coming leaders, so their policy positions, while having little immediate impact on the real world, did presage the future. In the early sixties, how to enforce minority civil rights was *the* issue. The field of battle was over housing discrimination, pitting the right to rent and buy where you chose against the right to rent and sell to whom you chose. The California YDs were firmly on the side of renters and buyers; some clubs joined CORE (Congress of Racial Equality) to picket builders who refused to sell homes to Negroes.

Next to fair housing, opposition to the death penalty generated the most heat. Coming up from the grassroots were new issues just entering the public realm, such as "Should abortion be legalized?" In between were issues on which there was a consensus but little action such as disarmament, reducing the voting age to 18, abolition of HUAC and loyalty oaths, state support of birth control, recognition of Red China, opposition to apartheid, and "compensatory measures" to achieve "full equality for all men."[6]

Sometimes liberalism and politics collided. At the May 1963 state convention, CFYD acting president Josiah Beeman of San Francisco was challenged for election to a full term as president by William B. Greene of Los Angeles. A state assembly employee who had been involved in the official Democratic Party but not the CFYD, Greene was rumored to be fronting for Big Daddy Unruh as part of an effort to divide or take over the CFYD. Political alliances created by the normal north/south conflict, with the north usually more liberal, were disrupted by the fact that Greene was a Negro with a record of civil rights activism as a field worker for CORE. An anonymous letter warning of a takeover of the CFYD by Negroes circulated and was denounced by both sides. Delegates from seventy-nine clubs representing 4,900 members assembled amid a swarm of charges and countercharges, in which the Beeman supporters were simultaneously accused of being racist and "ultra-liberal" (for supporting recognition of Red China, immediate cessation of nuclear testing, and abolition of HUAC). The UYD supported Beeman; he won by 2 percent of the vote.[7]

Much more than the adult clubs, the UYD was a heavily male domain. I can only remember one other woman ever speaking out at a meeting, though surely there were more. The unwritten rule was that offices were held by boys, except for secretary, which was reserved for a girl. I declined an opportunity to hold this office by claiming I couldn't take notes accurately. I ran for other offices but was never elected. Most of the boys were politically ambitious; their talk was full of the offices they wanted to run for and their strategies for obtaining them. For me, electoral politics was more of a civic religion; putting good people into public office was part of my obligation to make the world a better place. It's not that I never thought of running for anything; it just wasn't a priority, and no one ever told me it should be.

The unspoken assumption that men ran for office and women helped them do so was reinforced by the prevailing distribution of political jobs. The clubs and the campaigns were full of women. The elected offices were not. Between 1961 and 1965, the California assembly had one woman in it and the state senate had none. While Elizabeth Snyder had been chair of the Democratic Party State Central Committee in 1954–1956, she was the only woman to hold statewide office in the twenty years I lived in California, and it was a party office, not a public office. The second woman ever to be elected to the Los Angeles City Council won in 1953 at the tender age of 22. Rosalind Wyman held that office until 1965, when she lost her bid for reelection (and every other office she ran for thereafter). During her twelve years on the city council her age as much as her sex made her stand out—her name recognition in Los Angeles was 90 percent. However, both women took a lot of flak. Snyder was falsely accused of being an alcoholic and a professional gambler. Wyman later said that people resented her success and that women in particular thought she was too aggressive. Personal as well as political attacks never let up.[8]

Of all the ambitious young men I met in the UYD, only two impressed me as serious possibilities for public office. Jim Stanbery and Jerry Fishkin both came from L.A. and both majored in political science. Jim had high ideals, even though his language was studded with such words as "boodle" and "clout," used with a slight disdain. We sometimes talked on the phone as long as an hour while he paced at the end of his tether. I had met Jerry in 1960 when we both attended a special high school summer session for honors students. Jerry was a political pragmatist, headed for law school, and already calculating which Bay Area offices were likely to become vacant and when. Jim would get excited under pressure; Jerry always seemed in complete control no matter what happened. Both were basic liberals. Jim talked about what we ought to do, Jerry about how to get it done. I could see them both as members of Congress and would have happily helped elect either.

The one person I met in UYD who most shared my view of politics as an obligation of citizenship was Allan Solomonow. When I met him sometime in my first year, he had graduated from Berkeley, done graduate work in political science, and started at Hastings Law School. Allan was the consummate teacher. He took me under his wing and tutored me in Cal politics. Knowing Allan was like having a big brother. I could call him anytime with questions without feeling like I was either naïve or an imposition. He sometimes questioned my motives or my ideals, but never in a way that made me feel ignorant. He sometimes prodded me to do things he thought I should do, but accepted without censure my decisions about what I would do.

7 | *Student*

Berkeley was not a commuter school. I met very few students who lived with their parents in the Bay Area. Seventy percent of the undergraduates lived within a ten-minute walk of the campus.[1] The available dormitory space could house only a fraction of resident students, so most lived off campus, generally sharing space in apartments. In some ways living in apartments—being responsible for our own food, cleaning, and other needs; and paying our own bills while not having to earn all our income as well—made the transition from childhood to adulthood easier. But combined with course work, social life, and extracurricular activities, this responsibility added to the many things we had to learn.

Racial discrimination, where it existed, was challenged, but since racial minorities were less than 2 percent of the student body, and most of those were foreign students, such challenges had little real-world impact. Racial segregation was automatically assumed to be evil, but it was also seen as something *other* people did. Students protested against apartheid in South Africa and for admission of black students to white colleges in the south, against Jim Crow laws, and for passage of laws ensuring civil rights. Racism as something other than racial segregation or discrimination was not part of our vocabulary. Conceptually, it did not exist.

Segregation by sex was taken for granted, and not just in the separate dorms. As was typical of mixed-sex institutions, a place was made for women based on the assumption that women should not hold authority over men. During World War II, the absence of men had allowed women to take over most positions in student government and on the *Daily Cal*. By 1960, men had retaken their turf. The ASUC had two vice presidents. The first vice president was male; the second vice president was female. The first vice president was a voting member of the finance committee and succeeded the president in case of disability. The second vice president was the official ASUC hostess and chairman of the activities planning committee. The fact that the second vice president had to be female ensured that at least one woman sat on the ASUC executive committee; women were only occasionally elected to offices both sexes could fill. There were also two judicial committees, one for men and one for women. The chairman of the men's judicial committee was automatically the chairman of the joint student judicial committee; the women's chairman was joint vice-chairman. The belief that leadership was male was reflected in the September 29, 1964, story on the president's reception for new students. Wrote the *Daily Cal,* "Another attraction, but which is restricted to the new coeds, is the host committee. This 100 man group includes senior members of the football team and campus leaders. Also on hand will be 100 senior women, who will act as hostesses."

The girls' gym, built by and named for Phoebe Apperson Hearst, was two blocks from the boys' gym. Although Phoebe Hearst was a mentor to the university and a major contributor of scholarships and facilities for women, her gym was not as well equipped as the boys' facility. Most gym classes were sex segregated. The few that weren't (e.g., folk dancing, fencing) were held in the girls' gym. We were required to take four phys ed courses to graduate, and I naturally turned to the listings for girls without even wondering why they were separate. The one time I read the offerings for boys I spotted a karate course, something I'd always wanted to try, and inquired if I might be allowed to join since I was as big as the average boy and almost as strong. I was turned down because it was held in the boys' gym where there were no locker rooms for girls.

Even the football games fostered segregation. From sometime in the 1910s until the 1950s, college men had their own section on the 50-yard line and women on the 30- to 40-yard line. Alex Sherriffs later explained that when "the [male] rooting section became ugly and violent," the administration sought to integrate it in order to tame it. This "threatened the hell out of some of the males."[2]

The attitude of the university toward women was usually ahead of its time, at least for students. The College of California that opened in Oakland with eight young men in 1860 soon merged into the land-grant college set up after Congress passed the Morrill Act in 1862. When the new university admitted its first class in 1869 it was a boys' school, but the following year a few young women were added to the student body. The 1879 state constitution made this policy permanent by declaring that "no person shall be debarred admission to any of the collegiate departments of the University on account of sex." But it was twenty years before women were permitted on the faculty, and Phoebe Apperson Hearst didn't become the first female Regent until 1897. Sixty years later, all eligible women could become students, but they became professors only rarely. In 1958, when the university was desperately searching for bright young faculty, department heads were asked if "they would consider hiring women if no men were available." Only a few said yes.[3]

Unlike Stanford and many private schools, there were no ceilings on admissions of girls, but we were still only 40 percent of the undergraduates and 25 percent of the graduate students. Admission was based on grades in academic courses taken in high school. Even though girls got better grades than boys, there were still fewer of us at the university; this had always been true except during World War II.[4] The conventional wisdom was that good girls got married; only those who couldn't catch a man pursued a career. Girls' education might contribute to the general social good and certainly was good for their children but would not be put to any specific use.[5]

Undergraduate students didn't have a lot of contact with adults. Professors rarely saw students outside of class; even office hours were few. There was no socializing between professors and undergraduates and only a little with graduate students. Most basic classes were too large for professors to recognize their students if they met them in the halls. My first semester I took Poli Sci 1, Introduction to American Government, from John Schaar, a truly inspiring teacher. But I never met him, that semester or since. I sat with several hundred other students, avidly absorbing his thought-provoking lectures twice a week. Once a week we met in small sections run by graduate students to discuss the readings. On the other hand, both my Speech and Spanish[6] classes were small, with about thirty students each. My first-year Calculus course was taught via video; we could go to any of several small sections to see the professor lecture on a TV screen. Our homework was graded by a TA. Although many students resented the large lecture halls, I did not mind them. The quality was excellent; I could see no difference between a professor lecturing to twenty or two hundred. Even though one could buy the notes for basic courses, taken by professional note-takers, most of us went to class. I found many lectures inspiring and can remember some to this day. My high school teachers had taught me facts. My college professors taught me theories to help interpret facts. More important, they taught me that there were many ways to interpret facts.

Our professors' ability to open our minds to new ways of thinking coupled with the physical and social distance between us made professors into godlike authority figures. We believed in them perhaps more than we should have and looked to them for approval on those rare occasions for which that was possible. We also expected more than many were able to deliver and displayed no compassion when they didn't. In the large lectures we enlarged our minds, but it was in the smaller classes where we exercised them and made friends. There was something about the give-and-take of discussion over what Plato really meant that was so invigorating that arguments begun in class would continue outside. It was in the small classes that I found friends whom I kept for many years.

The best of these was Speech 1A, taught by Peter Dale Scott. The Speech Department had an eclectic collection of faculty, many of whom did not have Ph.D.s. It was the place for students who didn't know what to major in and faculty who didn't fit into traditional departments. I took Speech to avoid taking English, which had always been an unhappy experience. While I loved to read, I hated to write. Indeed, I had a paranoid fear of writing. I wrote term papers in high school when I had to, but I avoided courses with essay tests in favor of those with multiple choice, even when it meant taking a course of lesser quality. Cal required a year of composition, but it didn't have to be English. Speech was misnamed, as we neither read, studied, nor practiced rhetoric. The main difference between Speech and English was that we read nonfiction rather than fiction, including Plato, Aristotle, Freud, Mill, Dostoyevsky, Thoreau, and so forth.

I enrolled with fear and trepidation. Professor Scott was a relentless and rigorous teacher. We had to discuss the books three times a week and write a paper every ten days. Class discussion was the most fun I'd ever had in a class; writing was torture. I spent hours that seemed like days mentally chained to my portable manual typewriter waiting for inspiration to strike. I read and reread the great minds of the past, trying to figure out what I could say about what they said that would be half as interesting. I wrote a few words and tore up the pages. As a diversion from staring at blank sheets of white paper, I wrote the only poem I've ever written—an ode to sleep. Professor Scott was also a good editor. He wrote extensive comments, which, unlike my high school English teachers, actually showed me what I was doing wrong. When I did something right, he told me that, too. Slowly, as the weeks wore on, the writing became easier. By the time the semester ended I no longer feared writing. I still didn't think I was very good at it, and I certainly didn't like it, but it was no longer something I dreaded. This freed me to take a lot of courses I would not otherwise have taken as well as to choose a major that didn't rely on multiple-choice tests or mathematical calculations.[7]

All my professors were men. In my four years in one of the largest institutions of higher education in the world—and one with a progressive reputation—I not only never *had* a woman professor, I never even *saw* one. Worse yet, I didn't notice. Even today, the student life is probably the most egalitarian experience a woman will ever have. Going to school teaches you that individual merit is what counts, as measured in grades and athletic and other achievements. On the surface that appears to be true. Discrimination is more subtle, more covert, than in the outside world; so much so that unless your nose is rubbed in it, you don't see it. In the 1960s, less than 5 percent of the Berkeley faculty were women, and they were concentrated in "female" departments such as home economics.[8] I didn't see the absence of women professors, and if I was treated differently than male students, I didn't see that either. One reason I and so many other female students did not see the absence of women was that we were unconscious proponents of the "three sex" theory: there are men, women, and me. Thus, while we may have observed that women were scarce among the faculty and higher-level administrators, we assumed it was because they didn't want to be there, not that there were formal and informal rules which weeded them out.

I did have one female teaching assistant when I took Poli Sci 2, Comparative Government, in the spring of 1962. Laurel Weinstein had a very sharp mind. She ran a good class, almost as good as Speech 1A, and was the only TA who ever paid any special attention to me. After I wrote a 50-page term paper on one-party political systems, she spoke about it to the professor, Ernst Haas, and then took me to meet him. We had a pleasant short conversation which made me think seriously about majoring in political science. I never saw Laurel at UC after that semester but did run into her twenty years later when we were both students at New York University School of Law. She had left graduate school and gone into social work but hadn't found much there that was fulfilling, so she was switching to law. I had majored in political science and gone on to get a Ph.D. in it from the University of Chicago but couldn't find a full-time job, let alone a fulfilling one.

8 | Protest

STUDENT DISCONTENT THAT had been bubbling under the surface began to erupt in the spring of 1960. It began in the South. On February 1, 1960, four Negro students in Greensboro, North Carolina, sat down at a white lunch counter in the Woolworth five-and-dime and demanded to be served. After they were arrested, massive publicity spread the sit-in movement throughout the South, involving over 50,000 people and several thousand arrests. Throughout the spring, Bay Area students picketed Woolworth and Kress stores to support the southern students' desegregation efforts. Sometimes protest spread to other issues. On May 2nd, these students were inspired to turn a vigil against the death penalty into a sit-in on the road outside San Quentin Penitentiary while the State of California executed Caryl Chessman, the "red-light rapist" whose prison novels had made him famous.[1] All over the world people were protesting; in Turkey and Korea, students led the demonstrations.

These events prepared students to give a warm welcome to HUAC when it announced in April that it would soon hold hearings in the chambers of the Board of Supervisors at San Francisco's City Hall. HUAC had planned to come in 1959, but adverse publicity convinced it that the time was not yet ripe. Although it had put fear into the hearts of many for two decades, respectable people were now speaking out. On April 25, 1960, California congressman James Roosevelt denounced HUAC on the House floor because it had released to the press the names of California public schoolteachers that it had subpoenaed in June 1959. HUAC files of over ninety teachers were sent to local school boards. As a result, four were fired. Roosevelt said that

> more than 100 teachers have been in emotional turmoil for 10 months. Their teaching effectiveness has been impaired, and their sense of insecurity has communicated itself to their colleagues. . . . [Most were] on probationary status. . . . These may be quietly eased out of the teaching profession by the simple expedient of not renewing their contracts.[2]

HUAC sent out its subpoenas on April 26th. One went to Douglas Wachter, an 18-year-old Cal sophomore and SLATE member. Doug's friends in SLATE joined with other like-minded students to form the ad hoc group Students for Civil Liberties. It circulated a petition protesting HUAC. Within three days, 1,000 students and 300 faculty members had signed the petition and plans were made to picket the hearings. The *Daily Cal* printed excerpts from official HUAC records, urged that the committee be abolished and that students "participate in the various protests." On the first day of the hearings some students managed to get into the hearing room in City Hall, despite the fact that "over 150 people carrying special white cards were allowed to enter the hearing room ahead of those who had been standing in line." When some witnesses, including Archie Brown, an officer in the International Longshoremen's and Warehousemen's Union (ILWU) and frequent CP candidate for office, shouted "open the doors," twelve were dragged out by the police. Students on the inside began to sing the "Star-Spangled Banner," while those on the outside sang the "Battle Hymn of the Republic." When the sheriff asked the students to leave or be quiet, they complied.[3]

Newspaper coverage of this as a "riot" attracted hundreds more students to the next day of hearings. Their representatives negotiated access to the hearing room on a first come, first served basis. When preferential admittance was once again given to card holders, the neatly dressed students—boys wearing coats and ties and girls in long skirts—sat on the floor outside the hearing room and sang. This time the police turned on the fire hydrants and hosed the students down the thirty-six marble steps; those remaining at the top were dragged down. When the wet, bedraggled students began to sing "We Shall Not Be Moved" at the foot of the stairs, the police attacked them with billy clubs, arresting sixty-four, including thirty-one Berkeley students. The charges against all but one were later dismissed by a judge, and that one (a Cal senior) was acquitted by a jury. On the third day, the student picketers were augmented by several thousand longshoremen. HUAC left town without further incident. Estimating that HUAC had cost the city $250,000, the mayor said never again would it be allowed to use a city building.[4]

This affair became a mythic event for several generations of Berkeley students with the participants elevated to heroic status. They were immortalized by HUAC itself when it commissioned a commercial film company to produce a 45-minute film from heavily edited TV footage subpoenaed from TV stations and private photographers. Made part of HUAC's official report (which protected the producers from libel suits), hundreds of prints of *Operation Abolition* were sold for $100 each. Highly distorted, with commentary that did not match the pictures, the film said the demonstrations were Communist-inspired and -led. The narrator identified known Communists observing the demonstrations from the sidelines without mentioning that these same Communists had been subpoenaed to appear at the hearings the students were protesting. The Berkeley chancellor's office purchased its own copy after receiving much adverse mail about it. Vice-Chancellor Adrian Kragen sent a memo in October that noted that "an especially unfortunate aspect of the film . . . has been the inaccurate impression which it leaves that students constituted the major portion of those involved and . . . [they] were all or largely from the University of California." The Regents asked to see the film at their September meeting. It was also shown to 600 students at Cal's International House on September 30, 1960. Professor Henry Nash Smith of the English Department led the critique and provided corrective commentary.[5]

Operation Abolition put Berkeley on the map as the protest capital of the country. Widely shown to schools, clubs, and corporations as well as to the military, government employees, public utilities, the American Legion, the Daughters (and Sons) of the American Revolution, and a wide variety of patriotic organizations, it was "the Nation's most-talked-about film" by 1961. HUAC claimed it was seen by 15 million people. It also "served as a beacon to advertise radical activity," leading "socially conscious high school and college students [to be] drawn to Berkeley like bees to honey." The film effectively recruited incipient radicals to come to where the action was.[6]

The different reactions to the film revealed the generation gap which would become a gulf in the coming decade. When I saw the film on campus a couple years later, we roared with laughter. It was so bad and the errors so egregious that the message we heard was that these self-styled representatives of American virtue were essentially deceitful and trying to play us, the students, for fools. We learned to see HUAC, and by extension our government, as irresponsible and destructive. Whereas HUAC said the subpoenaed Cal student was a member of the CP, students believed he was called to testify because of his activity for civil rights, peace, and against capital punishment.[7] After "a number of graduate students lost fellowships, grants and jobs [and] at least two foreign students were deported," the politically-minded Berkeley students identified their plight with the students sitting in and being arrested in the South. Harsh treatment by the San Francisco police and the singling out of a few for additional punishment undermined governmental authority in student eyes. Southern cops and California cops did not seem very different in their response to dissent.[8]

While students saw their own political activity as part of their education for effective citizenship, the administration saw it as a public-relations problem. In December of 1960, SLATE published a record called *Sounds of Protest,* on which Kenneth Kitch and Mike Tigar narrated its version of the HUAC demonstrations. Advertised nationally for $2, it wasn't as popular as the film, but it did embarrass the administration and gave it the excuse it was looking for to extract the SLATE thorn from its side. As early as May of 1959, Vice-Chancellor Sherriffs was looking for "the right reason at the right time to get Slate off the campus." On March 30, 1961, Dean Shepard admonished SLATE to stop advertising that its record was produced by an "officially recognized student political party at the University of California." SLATE Chairman Mike Myerson apologized, but on June 9th, a newspaper reporter told him SLATE had been indefinitely suspended and could "neither use the name of the university nor utilize university facilities." Several faculty members asked that the suspension be lifted after one semester, but President Kerr had already modified his directives to eliminate the category that let SLATE have campus privileges. From then on it was exiled to the campus margins, where dwelled the UYDs and other "recognized off-campus organizations"; it could no longer hold business meetings or have an office on campus, but it could sponsor special events. SLATE was permanently put into purgatory.[9]

The next day President Kerr told the graduating class of 1961:

> The 1960s are witnessing another shift in the student scene. There is active and vocal concern about the shape of society, and particularly in the areas of civil rights and civil liberties. . . . We should be, and we are proud to be, associated with today's students. We should preserve for them and for those who will follow them a university environment where they can be free to hear and to read, to talk and to act, within the bounds of responsibility and respect for orderly procedures.[10]

A few days later the California legislature issued the *Eleventh Report of the Senate Fact-Finding Subcommittee on Un-American Activities.* In 1957, its chairman, Senator Hugh Burns, had become the first Democrat to be elected Senate president pro tempore since 1889. His powerful position enhanced the importance of his committee reports, even as his role in producing them receded. "Alarming Red Drive in Colleges Described,"

Headline announcing that SLATE had been kicked off campus by the UC Berkeley administration.

blared the headline in the *Los Angeles Times*. "U.C. Under Fire in State Senate's Subversive Study," said the *San Francisco Chronicle*. "Probers Rap Red Inroads at U.C." announced the *Oakland Tribune*. The *Eleventh Report* devoted half of its 202 pages to "Communist Recruitment of Youth"; sixty-seven pages were on Cal. SLATE was mentioned thirty times, with particular emphasis on its role in the HUAC demonstrations. Because of the timing, few believed the university when it denied that the Burns report had prompted the suspension of SLATE as a recognized student group. Indeed, Burns had predicted that SLATE would lose its campus rights in March,[11] and his committee expressed pleasure two years later in its *Twelfth Report*:

> A few days after our 1961 report, containing a lengthy and detailed exposure of SLATE, was published . . . the organization was banned from the university campus, and has since been compelled to function separate and apart from the university. Whether or not our report played any part in this forthright action on the part of the university administration we have no way of knowing, but in our opinion it was at least a fortunate coincidence.[12]

After the fall semester began, SLATE threw down the gauntlet. In October, SLATE chairman Ken Cloke, who was also an elected representative to the student government, said the Kerr Directives were a direct cause of student apathy. He and another SLATE rep, Roger Hollander, offered a motion in the ASUC executive committee condemning the Kerr Directives. On November 13th, the *Daily Cal* published a column by Cloke and Hollander objecting "to the restriction or limitation of speech at the University" that relegated "social and political action" off campus and protesting "the decisions to eliminate, without precedence, student rights which previously existed." Kerr shot back with an open letter printed on the front page of the student newspaper. He was particularly angry at the accusation that prior student rights had been eliminated. Kerr believed he was slowly but surely removing restrictions that had accumulated during the Sproul years to make the campus more of "an open forum." He called SLATE's claims to the contrary "a good example of the 'Big Myth' technique at work," and offered to return to the old rules and policies. Chancellor Strong accused SLATE of misrepresentation, the *Daily Cal* called it "The Big Lie," and the ASUC voted 11 to 4 to support the Kerr Directives. Cloke and Hollander responded with another open letter and SLATE put out a pamphlet sardonically called "The Big Myth." The semester ended with nothing changed and little clarified for those, like myself, who were new to the campus. We could see that a fight was brewing, but we weren't too sure about what.[13]

This jousting with the administration over rules was not just an academic exercise, because so much was happening in the outside world that students wanted to be a part of. Since the campus was our home, administration restrictions on what students could do and say on our turf chafed. What the students were looking for, and probably the faculty as well, were not rules but inspiration. And our new leaders did inspire us; we quoted them endlessly as we protested their rules.

What we heard was not their admonitions against rocking the boat but their ringing call for freedom and citizen action.

We heard President Kennedy tell an audience of 88,000 at our Spring 1962 Charter Day celebrations: "Nothing is more stirring than the recognition of public purpose. Every great age is marked by innovation and daring—by the ability to meet unprecedented problems with intelligent solutions."

We heard Governor Brown say at a University of Santa Clara commencement speech in June of 1961, "Far from discouraging your students social and public interests, I propose that you positively exploit them. . . . I say: thank God for the spectacle of students picketing—even when they are picketing me at Sacramento and I think they are wrong,

for students protesting and Freedom Riding, for students listening to society's dissidents, for students going out into the fields with our migra-
tory workers and marching off to jail with our segregated Negroes. At
last we're getting somewhere. The colleges have become boot camps for
citizenship—and citizen-leaders are marching out of them."[14]

We heard President Kerr say, at the March 20, 1961, Charter Day
ceremonies, that "the University is not engaged in making ideas safe for
students. It is engaged in making students safe for ideas. Thus it permits
the freest expression of views before students, trusting to their good sense
in passing judgment on these views." And in response to Richard Nixon
in his 1962 gubernatorial campaign, Kerr said: "The University is an
open forum. We have confidence in the judgment, wisdom, and cultural
faculties of our students."[15]

We heard Edward Strong, when he was installed as the third chancellor of the Berkeley campus on March 22, 1962, tell us, "Free universities make for a free society, and a free society, for the sake of the future,
must ever uphold free inquiry within its universities."[16]

These words contrasted with administrative actions, a contrast we
denounced as hypocrisy. Administrative actions emphasized that when it
came to students, free inquiry was not really free. It was regulated.

At the time I arrived in 1961, students who wanted to join religious
or political groups had to do so off campus. If these groups registered
with the dean of students each semester; provided a list of at least ten
members, including all officers, all of whom were affiliated with the university; and had a faculty advisor, they could be "recognized off-campus"
groups. But they could not meet on campus, advocate political action,
collect money, or solicit members. They could put up posters at eight specific locations advertising their off-campus meetings. And they could,
with administration approval three days in advance, use vacant classrooms for panels of qualified speakers on topics intended to educate the
university community, provided the speakers made a "balanced" presentation of two or more views of the issues. Students were not allowed
to gather in the open plazas for any political purpose, with two exceptions. Students, staff, or faculty members could "hold extemporaneous
speeches or rallies without prior registration" in a plaza behind the new
Student Union, which was well off anyone's beaten path. Or we could
schedule them at noon at the more centrally located Wheeler Oak, otherwise known as the "rally tree," at least twenty-four hours in advance.[17]
While we found these rules irritating, we learned to live with them,
largely because the political space at Bancroft and Telegraph made it pos-

sible to preach our many messages to at least some students as they entered the university grounds. Politics might be kept off campus, but it could hang out around the edges.

9 | Summer Vacation in Washington, D.C.

As I ENTERED MY second semester, I decided it would be great to get a summer job in Washington, D.C., where I could see all the politicians I had read about. With three aunts and two cousins in the D.C. area I wouldn't be going there cold. The federal government hired students for summer jobs as a way of interesting them in government service. Helen asked Aunt Leslie to find a job for me and, as a civilian administrator in the Navy Department, she arranged for me to become a GS-3 clerk-typist at an annual salary of $3,760. I had to take the typing test twice before I passed and got a security clearance. I learned that there were three levels of clearance and every employee of the Navy Department had to pass at least the first one. Leslie was cleared for top secret. I don't know what investigation was done, but I had no trouble getting the low-level clearance necessary to be a clerk-typist; at 16 I hadn't done anything yet.

Leslie kindly allowed me to stay with her in her studio apartment at 1629 Columbia Road. As she was a middle-aged spinster used to living alone, I'm sure my mere presence was something of an imposition, but she never let on. Every day we took the Number 42 Mt. Pleasant bus to and from work in temporary buildings built during World War II. I never figured out exactly what Leslie did for the Navy. I typed. I met my first electric typewriter at the Navy Department. Selectrics hadn't been invented yet, nor had White-Out or CorrecType; when I made errors, I had to erase them. Copying machines were in their infancy; the copies created by Thermofaxes were lousy and expensive. Each typo meant erasing an original and fifteen carbons. *Fifteen* carbons. The incentive system definitely favored accuracy over speed.

Some weekends Aunts Peggy and Patsy took me and their daughters, Kathy and Lee, to different tourist spots or entertainments in Virginia, where they lived. The tourist sights in Washington I saw on my own, with a little help from Congressman Corman's office. Leslie wanted me to go out at night; she preferred to stay home and read. My idea of fun was to volunteer at the Democratic National Committee or Corman's office, whichever was open after 5:00 P.M. Here too I only typed, but at least the copy was more interesting than that at the Navy Department and I could pick up some political gossip.

At the DNC I met one other Californian, a senior at Stanford on whom I developed a minor crush. I later learned he was quite the BMOC, already known as Stanford's living legend. He was kind to me; making me feel a little more important than just another typist. I encountered him one more time, in 1975, at Arlie House in Virginia, when we were both finalists in the White House Fellows competition. I remembered him; he did not remember me. In the intervening years, his basic personality had shifted from nice to nasty. I quickly learned what a fine family he had married into and what an important job he had teaching international relations at a major eastern university. He tormented me with caustic asides and cutting public comments on how preposterous it was that we were both finalists in the same competition. After all, I was only an assistant professor at a minor state college. Surprised, shocked, and rather uncomfortable by his public put-downs, I declined to return tit for tat, even though I had inherited Helen's acid tongue and could well defend myself in verbal repartee. Surely politeness was more politic when we were all being closely scrutinized. Since he was chosen as a White House Fellow and I wasn't, perhaps he was right to believe that cruelty got you further than kindness.

The most interesting thing I did that summer was go to the White House Seminars, which was a fancy name for lectures to the summer workers by Washington VIPs. Cabinet members and congressional leaders spoke to us in Constitution Hall, where literally thousands of us filled the corridors and hung from the rafters. Initially the head secretary in my unit would not let me take the necessary time off. She said the government wanted to recruit future professionals, not secretaries, so why should I go? I loved working in Washington and wanted to return, but not as a secretary. I went over her head to Captain Cunare, who said go, so I did, every week.

I enjoyed them all, but the highlight was hearing President Kennedy bid us farewell from the White House Lawn at the end of the summer. I brought my camera and wormed my way to the rope, where I got a shot of him speaking about twenty feet away. After he finished he walked to the crowd of outreached hands and began shaking them. I framed my shot and waited for him to turn toward my end of the line. But he went the other way; all I saw was his back and the heads of other summer workers leaning over the rope to see.

The speech I remember best was by Attorney General Robert F. Kennedy. I was sitting placidly in the audience when I heard him say "I have desegregated every bus station in the South." "What!" I said almost audibly, sitting straight up. Desegregation of the bus stations had been precipitated by the freedom rides which CORE sponsored in 1961 after the Supreme Court extended the prohibition against segregation in interstate commerce to cover restaurants in bus stations as well as the buses themselves.[1] On May 4, 1961, thirteen individuals—black and white, male and female—boarded a Trailways bus in Washington, D.C., and headed south. All the freedom riders deliberately used both segregated restaurants at every station. They made it to Atlanta with only minor incidents in the Carolinas. However, in Alabama they were met by mobs at Anniston and Birmingham, where several were seriously injured while FBI agents watched and took notes. Lack of bus drivers forced cancellation of the rest of the trip, but it took Justice Department intervention to get them safely out of Birmingham via the airport. A group of workers from the Student Nonviolent Coordinating Committee (SNCC) took their place after finding a bus driver who believed the government's promises of protection. Leaving Birmingham on May 20th, their bus was savagely attacked in Montgomery, forcing President Kennedy to send in 600 federal marshals. Massive publicity prompted hundreds of persons, mostly college students and ministers, one-quarter of whom were female, to descend on the South, where almost 400 were arrested before the summer ended. Attorney General Kennedy asked the Interstate Commerce Commission to issue regulations implementing the Supreme Court decision, which it did on September 22, 1961.[2]

Issuing an order is one thing. Enforcing it is another. In June of 1962, Helen and I drove to Alabama to visit the relatives before I took the train from Birmingham to Washington. I checked out the bus and train stations and found them still racially segregated; there were separate entrances to separate waiting rooms with separate facilities. The attorney general's claim that he had desegregated all the bus stations in the South was simply wrong. Birmingham wasn't desegregated, and I suspected it wasn't the only place that wasn't. I headed for the closest mike, from which we were permitted to ask questions at the end of each speech and was second in line. When my time came I said I had just come from Birmingham (which was not quite true; it had been a few weeks) and the station was still segregated. Kennedy's only reply was to repeat his statement, "I have desegregated all of the bus stations in the South." He didn't even say he'd check it out. Many years later Robert Kennedy became something of a cult figure to those on the left of the Democratic Party. In my eyes, he was always the man who didn't know the truth and didn't want to know.

10 | *Crossing the Line*

My room in 804 Davidson Hall was waiting for me when I returned to Berkeley. I placed into the honors courses for Chemistry and Western Civilization, as well as the toughest version of Introductory Zoology. Next to politics, the life sciences were my passion, and I had some vague idea that I might make my career there. I was particularly interested in entomology, having learned to love it from my tenth grade science teacher, Charles Brown, despite the fact that he wouldn't admit me to the highly select high school biology club. When Brown turned me down, I started an entomology project in my local 4-H Club and recruited a couple boys to meet the quorum and Helen to head it. My third and final year I won the Los Angeles County 4-H entomology award. I was also interested in genetics and evolution—my copy of George Gaylord Simpson's *Evolution of the Horse* was tattered from use. However, one could not major in either entomology or genetics, only biology with the expectation of specializing in grad school. I soon discovered that the biology courses were populated by pre-med students who would kill to raise their GPAs by even a smidgen. Majoring in biology would not work if I wanted to do anything in college besides study.

I got a part-time job delivering the new western edition of *The New York Times* to the four high-rise girls' dorms. Boys were not allowed above the ground floor, so the *Times* had to hire girls to put the morning paper in front of the door of every subscriber at 6:00 A.M. Only a few years earlier I had phoned all the newspapers delivered in the Valley looking for a carrier's job but was told that state law prohibited the hiring of girls for such tasks. It was too dangerous for girls. I wondered if the law had changed to accommodate the *Times*. I also wondered why it was less dangerous in Berkeley for me to go from one unit to the other through the large underground parking garage between them, in the early morning hours, than it was to go door to door in tract homes in the Valley, at a time and place where few people locked their doors and I never saw a cop.

Politically, this looked like it would be an exciting fall: Governor Gerald P. (Pat) Brown's bid for reelection was being challenged by Richard Nixon. Helen had infused me with her dislike for Nixon, which dated from his 1950 Senate race and was only enhanced by his 1960 presidential campaign. She was active in Brown's campaign. Between classes I passed out flyers at Bancroft and Telegraph to recruit students to help put Nixon permanently out of politics. As the campus organizer of Students for Brown I developed my connections with local Democratic Party officials, regularly visiting the 7th C.D. party headquarters on Ashby Avenue to use the mimeograph machine.

In mid-October, our focus on local politics was rudely interrupted by the Cuban missile crisis. Despite its official status as an independent country, Cuba had been an American colony since the Spanish-American War of 1898. "By 1956, American companies owned 80 percent of Cuba's utilities, 90 percent of its mining operations, and 40 percent of its sugar plantations."[1] It was run by dictator Fulgencio Batista until he was overthrown in 1959 by Fidel Castro. Diplomatic bungling by the United States led to an alliance between Castro and the Soviet Union, which the United States found to be intolerable. In April of 1961, the United States sponsored an attempt by several thousand Cuban exiles to invade and retake Cuba, a tragedy of errors and ineptness forever known as the Bay of Pigs fiasco. To forestall a future invasion, Castro permitted the Soviet Union to construct missile bases in Cuba, which U.S. reconnaissance aircraft photographed in October of 1962. President Kennedy blockaded Cuba to prevent further missiles from arriving, and both nuclear powers went on full military alert. Many students thought nuclear war was imminent and for several days talked of little else.

After the missiles were removed, Kennedy urged that civil defense shelters be designated everywhere; our campus administration complied. Black-and-yellow fallout shelter signs blossomed in all the buildings. Most of us thought this was ridiculous. Fallout shelters wouldn't protect us; they just gave the illusion that a nuclear strike was survivable and thus reduced the incentive to work for permanent peace. We didn't check to see if there really were fallout shelters where the signs said there were, let alone how many people could survive in them for how long. We did remove the signs. This was not a coordinated effort; it was spontaneous and individualistic. No group said "do it." Yet signs disappeared almost as fast as they were put up, only to reappear as trophies on student walls. I gave one as a wedding present to two Berkeley students who tied the knot. Another I have to this day.

Our anarchistic opposition was mild compared to the paranoia the missile crisis provoked elsewhere.

> Several Nevada communities claimed they were ready to shoot invading Californians who sought shelter over the state border. A Catholic priest published an article entitled "Ethics at the Shelter Doorway," which argued, "I doubt that any Catholic moralist would condemn the man who used available violence to repel panicky aggressors plying crowbars at the shelter door."[2]

Fortunately, President Kennedy agreed with us and began to talk more about peace than war. Soviet leaders were equally shaken by the brief sojourn to the brink of nuclear annihilation. One small step was taken to preserve the human race.

My reaction was to redouble my efforts to defeat Nixon. I figured that if Kennedy had taken us that close to war, Nixon would have gone all the way. If he became governor of California, he would have the political base to run for president again and perhaps be elected. Soon I did little besides go to class, science labs, and meetings while mostly working to "Keep California Brown." I didn't do homework. Relief at his ignominious defeat by the California voters was diminished by the realization that I was flunking three of my four courses. In November, a sharp change of direction salvaged the situation. But while I raised my F in Zoo 1A to a bare A, when chemistry professor George Pimentel decided my near-B was really a C, I was left with the lowest grades of any semester—the only time I didn't qualify for the undergraduate honor society—and convinced that I had no future in science.

In the meantime, some strange change was taking place within me. I was crossing the fine line between childhood and adulthood and simultaneously beginning to rebel at any and all constrictions. It was almost a physiological change, as though new chemicals were coursing through my body. I felt my perspective on the world alter from one of looking up to looking out. Adults were slowly ceasing to be authority figures on whom I could depend but whom I must unquestionably obey. I began to challenge everything—ideas, rules, anyone who wanted to tell me what to do or what to think. This change was mostly internal. The main outward manifestation was that I let my hair grow long. I told people that getting regular haircuts was too much trouble, but that wasn't the real reason. In the fifties, only beatnik girls wore long straight hair. Good girls' hair was either curled or coiffed. The beehive was popular; hair care took hours. Short and straight was neither in nor out. Long and straight symbolized alienation and rebellion. Growing my hair was a way of defying the rules.

Hairstyle was not the only rule I challenged. The dean of women was not impressed when I violated the rule requiring that all girls be in their dorm by 10 P.M. The boys could come and go when they pleased; girls had to be protected. Every girl had to sign in and out in the evening so she could be traced if she didn't return, and dorm doors were locked at ten. I had no problem with this rule except when meetings went late, and since I was now associating with "adult" Democratic Party regulars, this sometimes happened. It was embarrassing to have to leave a meeting early to meet the curfew. I spoke to the housemother and she said the simplest solution was for me to sleep someplace else those nights I couldn't make it back on time. If I rang the doorbell, she would have to let me in, and she wanted to sleep. I had no place else to go late at night and didn't want to wake her up, so I put up with this restriction until election day. I knew there would be a party that night to watch the returns come in, and I wanted to go. It would not be over by ten.

As I left I told the housemother I would be back late, and I was. When I rang the bell, she sleepily opened the door and said nothing. The next day I got a note to see the dean of women, who rapped my knuckles for violating the rules. The administration's justification for all of these rules was its belief that it must act in loco parentis. Like most parents, it believed that girls required more protection than boys. However, with thousands of "children" to parent, it could not accommodate itself to special situations. This did not convince me. I wasn't out late carousing, I was doing serious politics. My own mother knew and approved of what I was doing; why did I have to obey these silly rules?

In January, four of us drove to Sacramento for Governor Pat Brown's inaugural ball. We got back *very* late. Once again I woke the housemother to get in, and once again I was brought before the dean. This time she wanted to punish me; it was my second offense. I don't remember what the punishment was, but I do remember that no one else among the students thought that there was something wrong with these rules. The fact that they applied only to girls because the doors to the boys' dorms were not locked mattered to no one but me. The only solution seemed to be an individual one. Helen wrote a letter asking that I be let out of my dorm contract, even though it cost her the room deposit.

Fortunately I had met someone commuting from the suburb of Walnut Creek who wanted to live closer to campus, so we found an apartment to share on the second floor of 2509 Stuart. Marida was not very political, but she was a good roommate. Our first apartment had one bedroom, a kitchen, and furniture; her parents supplied most of what we needed to set up housekeeping. Unfortunately, there were no hallways and thus no purely private rooms. This became a problem when she acquired a boyfriend who hung around all the time and preferred that I be elsewhere. We survived until the end of the semester and then went our separate ways. The next time I saw her she was standing behind a counter in Sproul Hall, working as a clerk. Visibly pregnant, she had dropped out of school.

11 | *The Speaker Ban*

In the spring of 1963 I paid my $1 dues to join SLATE, encouraged by Allan Solomonow and Ken Cloke. Ken had joined SLATE upon entering Cal in 1959, as did several of his friends from Reseda High School. Allan had pretty much moved on. At the time I joined, SLATE was going through one of its periodic identity crises over whether it should continue and what it should be. The Regents had made ROTC voluntary the previous June, and SLATE's seldom-successful efforts to elect representatives to the ASUC did not bring activists into the organization. SLATE needed a more compelling program. It started a major campaign to eliminate the speaker ban.

By this time I was well on my way to becoming a radical civil libertarian, a process that was completed in the spring semester by taking Speech 123, a course on freedom of speech taught by Jacobus ten Broek. Thanks to intensive reading and debate about the ideas of three apostles of free speech—Milton, Mill, and Meiklejohn—and many Supreme Court cases, I finished the year convinced that nothing was so dangerous to a democratic society as the suppression of iniquitous beliefs— especially by the state. Thus, the idea that a great university, where academic freedom was supposed to reign, should be closed to any speaker seemed preposterous.

The speaker ban had crept into existence over many years but became formalized in the 1930s and flourished in the Cold War paranoia of the 1950s. As a formal policy it can be traced to two rules written by the Sproul administration and endorsed by the Regents in 1934–1936 when student protests were prompting legislative inquiries. Regulation 5 on academic freedom, which was written in response to publicity that Communists were infiltrating the university, included the statement that "the University assumed the right to prevent exploitation of its prestige by unqualified persons or by those who would use it as a platform for propaganda." Regulation 17 said in part that "in no circumstance shall any speaker . . . be invited to address any meeting . . . except upon invitation of the president or his direct representative." From the administration's perspective, the purpose of the rules wasn't so much to guide the students as to guard the university; administrators bent them when they wished.[1]

The application of the university's speaker policy was erratic. In 1947, former vice president Henry Wallace was deemed too controversial to speak at UCLA because he opposed Cold War policies. But in early 1949, UCLA students heard a debate between two professors, one of whom had just been fired from the University of Washington after he admitted membership in the CP. Shortly thereafter, UCLA withdrew an invitation to socialist Harold Laski, a professor at the University of London and Labour Member of Parliament, after President Sproul said his appearance "would not be pleasing to the Board of Regents." All candidates for public office were kept off campus, though that did not stop them from speaking to students. When Richard Nixon ran for the Senate in 1950 and Adlai Stevenson ran for president in 1956, they stood on city property to address students amassed on campus. During Pat Brown's 1958 gubernatorial campaign he spoke at all the state colleges but none of the university campuses; they had different governing bodies and different rules.[2]

Policy on who was and was not a suitable speaker for the university community had less to do with academic judgment than with the political environment. After World War II, as after World War I, a wave of anti-Communist hysteria swept the land. On March 21, 1947, President Truman signed Executive Order 9835 ordering investigations into the loyalty of federal employees; the Civil Service Commission created loyalty boards and a master index of all persons investigated. Dismissal could follow "membership in, . . . or sympathetic association with any . . . group . . . designated by the Attorney General as totalitarian, fascist, communist or subversive, or as having adopted a policy of advocating or approving the commission of acts of force or violence to deny others their rights under the Constitution of the United States, or as seeking to alter the form of government of the United States by unconstitutional means." The "attorney general's list" was used by the university to screen prospective speakers. In 1951, Max Schachtman, a prominent socialist who was not a Communist, was not allowed to speak at Berkeley; at UCLA, nine out of ten prospective speakers for an Anthropology Department forum for Negro History Week were denied clearance by the FBI.[3]

Later in the 1950s, as rabid anti-communism was receding, speaker restrictions underwent several changes that both expanded and restricted their scope. Candidates for political office were permitted on campus provided that they were part of a "balanced program"; off-campus student groups could use university facilities for speakers if and when the administration approved. "Communist" was expanded to mean "controversial." In May of 1961, Malcolm X, an outspoken minister of the Nation of Islam, was not approved to speak at Berkeley, supposedly because he was a religious leader. Instead he spoke at Stiles Hall. That same year evangelist Billy Graham and Episcopal Bishop Pike both spoke on campus.[4]

Even among admitted Communists, exceptions were made. In the spring of 1962, two Soviet nationals, Cosmonaut Gerhman Titov and Professor Troukhanovskii, spoke on the Berkeley campus. But a year later Chancellor Strong personally forbade the participation of Herbert

Aptheker, editor of the CPUSA journal *Political Affairs,* in a graduate student colloquium on Negro history run by the History Department, citing Regulation 5. Aptheker's daughter, Bettina, was a freshman at Cal and as such could speak openly on campus about communism or anything else. Her father, although he held a Ph.D. in history from Columbia University and had published numerous scholarly works on Negro history, could not. The History Department held the seminar at Stiles Hall and passed the hat to pay his expenses.[5]

The Kerr Directives loosened the reins, but by decentralizing decision-making to the chancellors they also created more inconsistencies. In March of 1961, SLATE sponsored a talk by Frank Wilkinson on campus. HUAC had called him a Communist organizer, but he had neither denied nor admitted an affiliation. When he twice refused to testify at HUAC hearings, he was sentenced to one year in prison for contempt of Congress. President Sproul would not have allowed him to speak on campus, but President Kerr refused to cancel his appearance even as Berkeley's assemblyman, Don Mulford, vehemently objected to Wilkinson's presence on campus. As the publicity swelled his audience to 3,500, three dozen carloads of Bay Area citizens went to Sacramento to protest on the capitol steps. Governor Brown told them that "this country has become great because we let everybody speak their piece. . . . To ban them before we know what they're going to say . . . is a very serious mistake." However in 1962, Riverside's chancellor would not let Nobel Laureate Linus Pauling speak about disarmament on his campus, stating that this was not Pauling's area of expertise. Pauling had repeatedly denied ever being a Communist.[6]

Students on several campuses challenged the speaker ban. In 1962 the ACLU filed a lawsuit against the Regents on behalf of DECLARE, a student group at UC Riverside, after its chancellor nixed a debate between Dorothy Healey, chairman of the Southern California district of the CP, and conservative Republican Lloyd Wright. In 1963, SLATE asked to play tapes on campus of a speech by Mickie Lima, CP Northern California district chairman. Permission was denied by Dean Towle. Next, SLATE asked to hold a meeting at which students would read from the works of Communist writers. This was approved. In the meantime, the Berkeley students voted overwhelmingly for a SLATE-sponsored initiative to end the speaker ban, the *Daily Cal* editorialized against it, and the ASUC senate voted to abolish it, as did the campus chapter of the American Association of University Professors (AAUP).[7]

✳ SLATE

BAN THE BAN

The Communist Speaker Ban at Cal cheats the students in two ways: it deprives them of their freedom to hear and it infringes upon their academic freedom.

It is frightening to think that students should have to give up their rights as citizens in order to attend college, but this is the case at the University of California. Though we live in a society which sanctions the voicing of all views, Cal students are prohibited from hearing Communists. If, as President Kerr states, we are to have an "Open Forum," it behooves us to hear all views, no matter how unpopular they are. Students particularly should be allowed this freedom, for they are forming opinions which must guide them for many years. To deny them their right to hear all sides of the issues they must weigh is to cripple their judgement and hobble their minds.

The University, however, has a more telling responsibility to freedom of expression. The commitment to academic freedom is a cornerstone of competent scholarship. In order that a scholar be truly informed and productive, he must have available to him every relevant thought about his subject. The prohibition of Communist speakers denies the students of the social sciences the Marxian view of their subjects. It also, as in the case of Dr. Herbert Aptheker, denies other disciplines their right to hear creative and important men, simply because these men are Communists.

Vote for Freedom of Speech
Vote to Abolish
the Speaker Ban
ASUC PRIMARY ELECTIONS

(over)

Leaflet for a SLATE-sponsored student initiative in May 1963 asking the Regents to end the Speaker Ban.

President Kerr had already decided that the time had come for the University of California to join most of the other prestigious universities in the country which allowed any speaker on any topic. The task was to persuade the Regents, some of whom were rabid anti-Communists. He thought he had sufficient support by the fall of 1962, but Governor Brown said the timing was bad because Richard Nixon would make it a campaign issue. Nixon did just that, saying he would expand the speaker ban to include "any individual who pleads self-incrimination [the Fifth Amendment] before a legally constituted legislative committee or grand jury investigating subversive activities" and "any individual who defies the provisions of the Subversive Activities Control Act of 1951." Not until June 21, 1963, did the Regents abolish the speaker ban, by 15 to 2 with one abstention.[8]

SLATE celebrated by inviting a series of speakers who were too controversial under the previous policy to be heard on the Berkeley campus. The first Communist speaker was Mickie Lima, who addressed 1,000 students in July at a meeting the *Daily Cal* characterized as boring. Herbert Aptheker returned in late October to discuss U.S. foreign policy in Viet Nam. Neither evoked much of a reaction by the students or anyone else.

Our first really controversial speaker was Malcolm X, who gave a speech on October 11th that was definitely not boring. My notes of that day report the following:

> Malcolm X spoke here today. It was one of the biggest things SLATE has done in years. Over 10,000 heard him, and heaven only knows how many classes were unofficially canceled. The crowd was packed as far back as the middle of Wheeler Hall and spilled out at the sides toward Durant Hall on the right and Sather Gate on the left. Students were hanging out of windows in Dwinelle, Durant and Wheeler and sitting on the steps in front of the Podium.
>
> It was almost by accident that we got him to come. When Art Goldberg was in Washington D.C. this summer Malcolm X walked in a coffee-shop where he was eating. The patrons rushed forward to shake his hand and Art resolved that he had to speak at a SLATE forum this semester. He made contact with the Black Muslims thru Reverend Bernard X and Monday Oct. 7 he got a call saying Malcolm would have time Friday at noon to speak on campus. He immediately ran to the Dean's office for the forms, bullied our advisor into signing it without reading it and rushed off to his faculty advisor, Levine, and told him he was going to moderate when Malcolm spoke in a few days. Levine signed just to get Art out of the office, and Art got the papers back in the Dean's office a little before the

Malcolm X finally spoke on the Berkeley campus on October 11, 1963, after being banned in 1961. The Speaker Ban, which was applied to controversial speakers, had been rescinded by the Regents only in June 1963. *Photograph by Jo Freeman.*

5 o'clock deadline. He then asked what was the biggest Hall they had. They replied it was Harmon [Gymnasium]. "We'll take it" he shouted as he ran to tell the good news to SLATE Co-Com.

That night the Dean's Office called Steve DeCanio and informed him that it would cost $150 to rent Harmon: $45 for the P.A. system and $105 to pull the bleachers out from three walls; this was without seats. So that night we all spent a few hours on the phone calling up people to raise money. The next morning we had a table and jar out to collect money and leaflets were out advising the students of our plight and soliciting funds in order that they might be able to hear Malcolm X. We collected $85 that day. The money just rolled in. It was the most we had ever collected for anything; but it was still not enough.

For once, though, luck and the Dean's office was with us. The chairs in Dwinelle Plaza had been put up for Sargent Shriver on Wednesday and had to remain up for Family Day on Saturday. Tuesday night they gave Steve a call and told him that he could use the set up in Dwinelle for Malcolm X. All we had to pay for was the P.A. system and the police, roughly $90. Even so we almost missed again. Tuesday at noon Mrs. Weaver told Art, Steve and myself that Levine was unacceptable as a moderator as he was untenured. She gave us ½ hour to find someone else. Art took off like a flash of greased lightening. Where could he find someone at noon? Again luck was with us. A Viet-Nam rally was being held at Telly and Bancroft and who did he run into there but [Prof.] Sellers. The deadline was made with a few minutes to spare.

Friday morning it was raining. After all this it was raining. As Steve put it "Looks like God is white after all." But lo and behold it cleared up. So I guess she is black. The crowd began pouring in at 10:30 but Malcolm didn't arrive until five til twelve. He had been spotted on campus a couple times and was twenty-five minutes late so we didn't know what was happening. I got the release for the tape recording signed just in time. The recording studio agreed to give me a duplicate of it after I signed a long list of what I wouldn't do with the tape; such as give it to a radio station. Part of the ubiquitous red tape.

Art was so nervous and excited. He was overjoyed at being able to give the introduction and scared silly of the people. It was the first time he had been in a suit in three years and we kidded him so much it will probably be another three before he puts it on again. The program started with Sellers and Art's introductions. Both of which stuck a knife into the Kerr Directives.

It was fascinating watching the reaction of the audience. Malcolm spent most of the time blasting the "so-called white liberals" of which the audience was mostly composed. Being liberals and being used to radicals they couldn't express much disapproval of another radical. But neither could they applaud their own blaspheming. They didn't know when to laugh, when to clap, or what to do. Usually they just emitted some sound or other to show a reaction. And what Malcolm had to say evinced quite a few reactions.

After it was all over the discussion still kept on. The talk was referred to some way or another in all three of my afternoon classes. Just between Latimer and Dwinelle I passed five clusters of from 10 to 50 people in heated discussions of Islam or Civil Rights, the Negro or some aspect or derivative of what Malcolm X had said. People were talking about it all over campus. Most people finally decided that they disagreed with him but everyone was interested and shocked and everyone talked. SLATE was fulfilling its function the highest form this time. Getting the students to think.

As a SLATE vice chairman I was one of four members to greet Malcolm X. Thrilled to shake his hand and exchange a few words, I found him "quiet, good-natured and very unfanatical." I had a different impression a week later when five of us from SLATE shelled out $3 each to go to a banquet given for him by Mosque #26. There were a few other whites sitting in little islands amid a sea of black faces. Malcolm's message to this mostly Negro audience was much stronger than it had been to the mostly white one at Cal. Much stronger. "It was kind of an interesting experience to sit there and hear yourself blasphemed from head to foot; morally, physically, mentally, genetically, psychologically and any other adverb you can think up," I wrote to my mother. I didn't get pissed until he distorted basic genetics. I was taking Genetics 100 that semester, and once I heard him speak authoritatively about a science of which he clearly knew nothing, it discredited the rest of his message, at least for me.[9]

Cal's next controversial speaker was not sponsored by SLATE. Madame Ngo Dinh Nhu, sister-in-law of South Viet Nam's leader Ngo Dinh Diem, was brought to us by Delta Phi Epsilon, the foreign service fraternity. Known as "the Dragon Lady" for her biting tongue, she was touring the United States to drum up support for the regime which our government was in the process of undermining. Viet Nam had been much in the news the previous summer due to the self-immolation of Buddhist monks who objected to the Diem government. SLATE organized a picket of Mme Nhu when she spoke at the Sheraton-Palace Hotel in San Francisco and again in Harmon Gym on October 29th. While 8,000 students inside greeted her with hisses and some polite applause, 150 SLATE supporters picketed on the public street outside. One student was arrested in an otherwise peaceful protest.[10]

By far, our most controversial speaker was Captain Ralph Forbes, leader of the Western Division of the American Nazi Party. SLATE didn't seek him out; we sponsored him because, having campaigned for an open forum, we felt we had to. Early in April of 1964, Allan Solomonow brought to our attention an ad in the *Daily Cal* that said: "AMERICAN NAZI SPEAKER seeks sponsor for campus speech. Write Clyde. . . . " Removal of the speaker ban did not mean anyone could walk on campus and speak at will; some group, student or otherwise, had to provide official sponsorship. This was a challenge that not everyone in SLATE was willing to accept. After extensive and heated discussion in the SLATE Coordinating Committee (Co-Com) on whether our devotion to civil liberties mandated sponsorship of a speaker whose ideas we detested, we decided it did, if no other group would sponsor him. I got the job of writing Clyde. I was no longer vice chair. After being defeated for chairman by Art Goldberg at the beginning of the spring semester, I became editor of the SLATE newsletter.

Clyde turned out to be C. Thomas Irwin, a Cal student who had counterpicketed us with Nazi signs when we demonstrated for civil rights during that year. He replied to me that our "answer is the only one I've received so far. I had suspected that SLATE would be the only group that would have guts enough and true liberality enough to sponsor an American Nazi." He wrote that Forbes resided in southern California and had already spoken at UCLA and USC.[11] At the top of his letter was a sticker with a swastika and the words "WHITE MAN . . . FIGHT" on it. He enclosed a copy of the "Program of the World Union of National Socialists" and "National Socialist World View," where he had circled the section on "The Negro." The American Nazi Party advocated building a "modern industrial nation in Africa" to which American Negroes would be paid to go. Those "remaining in America will be rigidly segregated non-citizens." At the top of this leaflet Clyde had written, "The ANP supports the views of Malcolm X."

Soon I heard from Captain Forbes, bragging about his exploits as a speaker and expressing the "hope that our opposition in Northern California presents more of a challenge than the anemic pinkoes of the Southland." I assured him we would. His next letter was clearly calculated to cultivate my goodwill: "As you know most girls don't express a very strong interest in anything as abstract as free speech, and a girl with brains and wit is as charming as she is rare. Most female participation in politics is emotional, either the motivation comes from a misdirected motherly protective feeling towards an image of helplessness or a compulsion towards masculine attractiveness."

SLATE was willing to provide official sponsorship and do the work, but we weren't willing to raise the money the university required as we had for Malcolm X. Forbes had to pay for Harmon Gym, the PA system, and the police. It still took a lot more work to sponsor Forbes than Malcolm X. For one thing, we couldn't find a faculty moderator. Few faculty would moderate forums they weren't personally interested in attending; while any chancellor could waive this requirement for select speakers, ours wouldn't. The previous October we had had to cancel a rally featuring SNCC field secretary Mike Miller because he was a *former* student and we could not find an available tenured faculty member by the deadline for reserving the space.[12] With Forbes we had plenty of lead time, but none of the prominent faculty members who had spoken out against the speaker ban and on related civil liberties issues would agree to moderate a Nazi speech; they didn't want to be tainted by that close an association with something they abhorred. Dean Towle suggested we ask Van Dusen Kennedy, an obscure professor in the Business Administration Department, to sign the papers and make the formal introductions. After a lot of sound and fury, Forbes's appearance before an audience of 7,000 in Harmon Gymnasium was an anticlimax. Rather than a riot, as some had predicted, students greeted Forbes's speech with silence or laughter. That's all. Nothing happened.[13]

12 | *The* SLATE Supplement

SLATE HAD MORE ON its agenda than just the speaker ban. One of our ongoing concerns was the quality of education at Cal. Personally, I liked most of my classes because they made me think; in high school, rote memorization and repetition was what was required. But Cal *was* impersonal. With most of the introductory courses taught in auditoriums that held up to 1,000 people, it was easy to get lost. I never met most of the professors from whom I took required courses, even in my major; they were just distant figures on a stage or, occasionally, a TV screen. Our high schools did not prepare us for the degree of anonymity we experienced at Cal. Although most of us went to class, it wasn't necessary. To cram for exams one could just buy the course notes from a commercial note-taking service. As for papers, everyone I knew wrote their own, but we heard about "paper files" in the Greek houses to help little brothers and sisters keep their grades up without cutting into party time, and some of the dorms had rudimentary files. It was a little harder to skip section meetings, which had about twenty students in each and were taught by graduate student teaching assistants. Most TAs were inexperienced (though some had been teaching for years). While some were good teachers, and they did know our names, they were mostly concerned with meeting the requirements of their own graduate programs and were, well, inexperienced.

We had come to Cal, with its reputation for excellence, with high expectations about the education we would receive. Not a few were disappointed. Learning was a passive experience in which we read, went to lectures, and read some more. Students wanted more of an active, participatory education than Cal was equipped to provide, at least for those in the humanities and social sciences. We thought it would be better if classes were all taught by professors rather than TAs and that professors should be rewarded for good teaching rather than publishing. After I endured five years of grad school in a university which did not have TAs and four years as a professor learning how to teach with no support or supervision, I concluded that our expectations were naïve and unrealistic. Cal balanced competing needs and utilized limited resources reasonably well. One could get—indeed I got—a very good education. But as undergraduates we did not appreciate what Cal had to offer; we thought we deserved better.

In the spring of 1963 SLATE published a special issue of the *Cal Reporter* on education. Identified as Vol. 4, No. 1, this was the first issue since 1960 (and the last). The headline over the lead article by Brad Cleaveland read "Students Indict Cal!" Other articles were entitled "University Abdicates Social Responsibility," "UC Freshmen Find Idealism Soon Shattered," "The University—A Cog in the War Machine," "Should 'Alma Mater' Be A Foster Mother?" and "Teaching With Television: Fragile—Handle With Care." As one of the six editors, I contributed a piece on "Freshman's First Course: How to Beat the System." The *Daily Cal* described our effort as a "snarling . . . grouchy bear" but did admit that "the professed purpose of the *Reporter* was to stimulate discussion, and that it did, from the Terrace to the Faculty Club to Sproul Hall."[1] That summer SLATE hosted a conference on educational reform.

The following fall we decided to help our fellow students "beat the system" by publishing comments and analyses of all the main courses—and as many minor ones as we could—in order to guide students into taking the best and avoiding the worst. We called this *The SLATE Supplement to the General Catalogue*. Issue Number One was only eight mimeographed pages on "Ways to Get an Education in Spite of the System" featuring a quote from Clark Kerr taken from lectures he had given at Harvard the previous April.

> Undergraduate students are coming to look upon themselves as more a "class"; some may even feel like a "lumpen Proletariat." Lack of faculty concern for teaching, endless rules and requirements, and impersonality are the inciting causes.

Issue Number Two came out at the beginning of the Spring 1964 semester. Its 56 pages (still mimeographed) cost us $950 and sold for 25 cents each. To help recoup our costs, we added some ads. Once again we quoted President Kerr. The chief editor and guide was Phil Roos, a graduate student in sociology, whose abode at 1936 Parker Street became the office, conference room, and warehouse. Jann Wenner was the associate editor; Doug Brown, Bob Pritchard, and I were the assistant editors. We had an editorial staff and a production staff. We thought our masthead made us look very professional. In reality we were earnest amateurs trying to figure out what to do.[2]

What we did was assign departments to different student reporters, mostly undergraduates, not all of whom were in SLATE. The reporters wrote up all the required undergraduate courses and as many others as they could. Having decided to major in political science, I reported on that department, as well as on a couple introductory courses in other departments for whom we had no one else. It was up to each of us to find information and summarize it in a sentence or a paragraph. One source was our questionnaire—covering both sides of one long sheet—which we distributed at the end of each semester outside the largest courses, asking students for their evaluations. In addition to comments, we asked for grades. The idea that students should grade faculty—using traditional letters and not the numbers more frequently found in survey instruments—was a deliberate role reversal, and it grated on faculty nerves. Our questionnaires were not a random sample, and they were rarely representative. We did not—indeed we were not allowed to—pass them out in class.

Publishing the *SLATE Supplement* was like lobbing a grenade into the faculty club. A poorly reviewed French professor wrote the *Daily Cal* denouncing us as "irresponsible crusaders." There were probably more letters I didn't keep copies of and don't remember.[3] No faculty member ever gave me his opinion of my evaluations, but I certainly heard from the political science graduate students when they thought my write-ups were wrong or my comments too caustic. I particularly remember being chastised by Sara Shumer, whom I knew from the YDs. Their criticisms compelled me to read the questionnaire responses more analytically and also to visit those classes and professors of which I had no personal knowledge. Over time I developed a network of informants who reported on the poli sci classes they took; Jerry Fishkin was one of the best. I became a critic and interpreter of courses rather than just a reporter of questionnaire responses.

The reviews I wrote during my last three semesters as an undergraduate were an invaluable educational experience. I learned there was no such thing as a good professor or a bad professor, though there were good courses and bad courses. Some professors were good for some courses and some types of students and not for others. Some faculty were stimulating in seminars but lousy lecturers; some were the reverse. Some taught over the heads of those looking for "mickey" courses; some taught under the capabilities of serious majors. Since required courses had to be taught every year, some faculty—particularly new and inexperienced professors—were assigned to teach topics which were not really their forté, generating large numbers of negative evaluations. I learned to read the questionnaires skeptically, even when we had returns from most of the students enrolled. We asked for personal data, including GPA and major; I could see how different types of students rated the same course very differently. I also learned that students who really liked or hated a professor were the most likely to say so. We got more skewed response patterns than bell-shaped curves.

Writing for the *SLATE Supplement* was one of the few things I did as a student which had a real impact on other people's lives. It particularly taught me that writers had to be responsible for their words. I learned to think about how my words would be read by both faculty and students when I was writing them. Words could hurt. How could I make my point without causing undue pain?

As course evaluations became institutionalized over time at many other colleges, the original purpose was ultimately lost. We were one of the first schools in the nation to evaluate courses, but it was hard to sustain the project with student volunteers. After I left, funding for the *Supplement* was taken over by the ASUC, though the work was still done by volunteers. When I went to graduate school at the University of Chicago a few years later, there were no student evaluations, but by the time I started teaching in 1973, they were mandatory at my institution. These questionnaires were prepared by the administration and did not ask for the characteristics of the students filling them out. Nor were they evaluated in any way. They were simply collected and stored. While they were available for viewing, the time needed to read and understand all of them for any given course or professor was prohibitive. Not a single student I asked had ever read any of them; they all relied on the grapevine and the catalog for their information on what to take.

When I entered New York University School of Law in 1979, I read an article in the student paper on the dismissal of a clinical professor for "poor teaching" based on his class evaluations. From a little inquiry I learned that he was not a bad teacher but was a bit unconventional. As best I could tell, the real reason for his dismissal had to do with internal politics, not teaching skills; these were merely an excuse. The next year I located and read the mandatory questionnaires for some courses I was considering. Deciphering them was a waste of my time. During my three years as a law student, these questionnaires were passed out to students in every class at the end of each semester, ostensibly to aid student choices. I refused to fill them out. In becoming institutionalized, the purpose of student evaluations had become perverted.

The aim of the *SLATE Supplement* in evaluating professors at Cal was to help students make informed choices about their education and to a lesser extent to give the faculty feedback that might help them improve their teaching. Because Cal was so big and impersonal, students were responsible for planning their own learning experiences. We tried to make this easier. We never intended, or expected, our reviews of courses and professors to be used to fire anyone.

13 | *Fair Housing*

Until 1963, housing segregation was the only issue which put Californians on the same moral plane as southerners. Indeed, housing segregation was more of a northern problem than a southern one. In the South, neighborhoods were interlarded with streets of houses occupied by whites alternating with streets inhabited by Negroes. This pattern was left over from the days before motor vehicles when domestic workers had to live within walking distances of the homes they worked in. It also reflected a different cultural attitude toward race, which I heard Negro comedian Dick Gregory explain: "In the South you can get as close as you want as long as you don't get too big. In the North you can get as big as you want as long as you don't get too close." By the time of massive Negro migration to northern cities in the 1920s, public buses made a different housing pattern possible. Neighborhoods were designated for one race or the other and these decisions were enforced through racially restricted covenants in land deeds.

Negro migration to California jumped during World War II; prior to that, the percentage of nonwhites had *decreased* every census. Between 1940 and 1960, nonwhite Berkeley residents went from 6.2 to 26.1 percent and Negro residents from 4.0 to 19.1 percent.[1] As the growing Negro population concentrated in the southern and western sections of the city, the housing units in those sections become more and more overcrowded. California had encouraged racial separation of neighborhoods earlier than most states in an effort to discourage Chinese immigration in the nineteenth century.[2] After World War II, the law no longer sanctioned racially separate housing patterns, but the practice had become customary. A variety of federal programs to facilitate homeownership supported and even encouraged segregated housing in the belief that homogenous neighborhoods enhanced stability and maintained property values.[3] Indeed, Rule 5 of the National Association of Real Estate Boards specifically listed Negroes among the "undesirables" who should not be brought into good neighborhoods. Even when this custom was denounced by political and civic leaders in the 1950s, it was so pervasive that real estate brokers were punished by their peers for breaking it; they in turn enforced the proscription among their sales force. In 1961, it was not illegal to refuse to sell or rent because of race.[4]

I saw a small sample of how this custom worked in the late 1950s after Helen began selling real estate to supplement her teaching income. Before moving to the Valley in 1952, we lived in Baldwin Hills. Helen taught in several East L.A. schools where she had many friends among her Negro colleagues. A few years later, one of them asked her to find a house to buy in the Valley, which was almost all white with a scattering of Mexicans. She found a house that her friend wanted to buy with a willing seller. When her broker found out the buyer was Negro, he told Helen to take her license off the wall—that is, he fired her.

The City of Berkeley had only 110,000 persons, but it was not as progressive as the campus. A minimum voting age of twenty-one plus residency requirements to register kept most students out of the local electorate. Until 1961, "conservative Republicans routinely won nearly every race in city elections. . . . Conservatives controlled politics through the *Berkeley Daily Gazette* and meetings at the Elks Club." After elections that year, a "liberal white-black coalition claimed a five to four majority on the council."[5] One of the problems they attacked was racial discrimination in housing. By 1963 there was ample evidence that white owners and landlords routinely kept minorities out of white neighborhoods. Even when property-owners did not want to discriminate, real estate agents enforced what they saw as community norms. In August of 1961, the city council appointed a Citizen's Committee to Study Discrimination in Housing, which interviewed landlords and brokers. Many realtors readily admitted that applicants for business space as well as homes and apartments were steered to what they thought were the appropriate neighborhoods. The widespread belief was that when minorities came into "good" neighborhoods, property values went down.[6]

In 1961, the Berkeley Law Students Democratic Club tested real estate practices by dispatching white and Negro women to tell realtors they wanted to purchase homes. They found that "attempts of negro interviewers to purchase houses in parts of this area which are predominantly caucasian were frustrated, and white interviewers were steered away from the negro areas. . . . Much of the discrimination leading to segregation in East Bay housing stems from the realtors *themselves,* to the end that most negro home-buyers do not get the opportunity to deal with a homeowner who might otherwise be willing to sell to them."[7]

The pattern was the same for rental housing. Most minority students at Cal were foreign students; they complained that they could not find housing in the neighborhoods closest to campus. In the fall of 1958, the *Cal Reporter* ran a series of articles on this problem. It reported that when interracial roommates looked for apartments separately, not only did the whites find many more units available, but when they brought their nonwhite roommates for an interview the apartments were already taken. By 1959 the university was beginning to pay attention. A private residence for women that the *Cal Reporter* had identified as discriminatory was removed from the university's list of approved accommodations. In January of 1960, at the urging of the Berkeley NAACP, the University Housing Office required all landlords listing with it to certify in writing that they would not discriminate.[8]

The worst offenders were the Greek Houses, which continued to follow the rules of their national organizations to restrict membership by race, religion, and sex. The university continued to ignore this practice until Pat Brown, in his last act as attorney general before moving into the governor's mansion, issued an opinion on January 5, 1959, that the university was acting unconstitutionally by recognizing racially discriminatory fraternities and sororities. This was publicized widely, and at their regular July meeting the Regents voted that recognized student organizations could not have rules requiring discrimination based on race, religion, or national origin. They gave the Greeks until 1964 to effect changes in their national charters or to disassociate themselves.[9]

After many months of hearings and debates, the city council passed an ordinance in January 1963 prohibiting discrimination on the basis of race in both real estate sales and rentals. The reaction of Berkeley residents was almost hysterical. It took only three weeks for 10,000 voters to sign a petition putting repeal of the ordinance on the ballot in time for the April municipal elections, in which it became the main issue. The liberal candidate for mayor was Dr. Fred Stripp, a professor in the Speech Department and our debate coach. The Young Dems turned out in force to elect Stripp and defeat the repeal measure. After long hours of phoning and canvassing voters, we learned the meaning of the phrase "I'm all for civil rights, but not next door." Municipal elections in California are officially nonpartisan, but in fact the major parties often support candidates and ballot measures. They signal their preferences to the voters. Local Democratic Clubs officially endorsed Stripp and fair housing; local Republican Clubs unofficially opposed both. An unprecedented 83 percent of the voters came to the polls to repeal the fair housing ordinance by 22,750 to 20,456. Stripp lost by an even narrower margin. The voter surveys showed just how partisan that election was: 70 percent of Democrats voted to keep the city council ordinance; 84 percent of Republicans voted to revoke it.[10]

All of us were gloomy the day after the election. Mike Schwartz, my colleague on the *Cal Reporter,* wore a little badge made from cardboard on which he had written, "I'm *STILL* for Fair Housing." He said we needed a post-campaign button. Jerry Fishkin had started collecting campaign buttons, so I asked him how to buy some made to order. He told me to look in the yellow pages under "badges." I phoned the companies I found listed, collected some money from various UYD and SLATE activists, and ordered my first thousand buttons. They weren't very pretty, sort of rusty brown on bluish white, but for the rest of the semester "I'm *STILL* for Fair Housing" became a solidarity symbol for a small cadre of students. This act also initiated what became my longest-running career—as a button-seller.

Ignominious as it was, the defeat of the Berkeley fair housing ordinance was only a small battle in an ongoing war that was already being waged in the state legislature. Assemblyman Byron Rumford had introduced a fair housing bill in February. It had the support of Governor Brown and Assembly Speaker Jesse Unruh and easily passed the Assembly on April 25th in a highly partisan vote. In the Senate, whose Democratic chairman opposed it, it was bottled up in committee. The endless delay prompted members of several CORE chapters to hold a continuous sit-in in the state capitol. On the sixteenth day, the demonstrators blocked the entrance to the Senate. Despite the staunch opposition of Senator Hugh Burns, the powerful president pro tempore, on June 21st the Rumford Fair Housing Bill became law.[11]

This, unfortunately, was not the end. The California Real Estate Association and the California Apartment Owners' Association formed the Committee for Home Protection and circulated a petition for what became Proposition 14 on the November 1964 general ballot. It stated that "neither the State nor any subdivision or agency thereof shall . . . limit or abridge . . . the right of any person . . . to decline to sell, lease or rent [real] property to such . . . persons as he, in his absolute discretion, chooses." Over 600,000 qualified signatures were collected within ninety days, initiating a bitter battle that made the Berkeley fair housing controversy look tame. As in Berkeley, Democratic officials and Democratic Party organizations opposed Proposition 14. But, unlike those in Berkeley, Republicans were divided. Party affiliation also divided the voters, but only slightly. Even though California registration was predominantly Democratic and 60 percent of the voters supported the Democratic presidential ticket, only 34.6 percent opposed Proposition 14. Almost two-thirds of the 84.6 percent of registered voters who came to the polls in November of 1964 amended the California constitution to prohibit fair housing laws.[12]

This too was not the end. Federally funded urban renewal projects in California cities screeched to a halt as the Johnson administration sought to discourage opponents of fair housing in other states from pursuing a similar course. Several lawsuits were filed, and on May 10, 1966, the California Supreme Court, by 5 to 2, declared that Proposition 14 violated the "equal protection" clause in the Fourteenth Amendment to the U.S. Constitution. The Rumford Law quickly became a hot issue in the 1966 gubernatorial election, as Republican candidate Ronald Reagan urged legislative repeal. Although Reagan won, the Democrats retained control of the legislature by a hair, and fair housing remained the law. On May 29, 1967, the U.S. Supreme Court upheld the California Supreme Court by 5 to 4.[13]

There were multiple meanings in these events, some of which I saw, and some of which escaped me and probably most of my fellow activists as well. The ones I saw were the ones which my political science courses prepared me to see. In Poli Sci 1, John Schaar had lectured extensively on how the Constitution attempted to balance minority rights with majority rule—the former protected more than the latter by the founders, the latter slowly increasing at the expense of the former during the nineteenth century and ballooning in the twentieth century. The minority rights the founders were concerned about were those of political minorities, not racial minorities, but it was a principle which could be readily transferred by the Supreme Court. Schaar interpreted the Supreme Court as an essentially antidemocratic institution whose function was to protect minority rights from, to borrow a phrase from de Tocqueville, "the tyranny of the majority." Having absorbed the idea that democracy was a universal good, we were shocked to hear this. But the referenda votes showed me what he meant. We worked for fair housing because we thought it was the morally right thing to do; the voters in Berkeley and in the state of California taught us that what was right and what the people wanted were not always the same.

Among the things that we did not learn from this vote, but should have, is the basic lesson all elected officials learn with experience: it is dangerous to get too far ahead of public opinion. In the vote on the

Berkeley fair housing ordinance and on Proposition 14 one could see the seeds of future racial conflict. Proposition 14 presaged a white backlash even while the frontal assault on white privilege in the North was just beginning.

14 | *Mexico and Central America*

A LOT OF SLATE activity took place during the summer, when the organization held an annual conference where activists often met with students from other campuses to share experiences. Because I missed these conferences I was not plugged into the national network that student activists were building in the early sixties. I spent the summer of 1962 in Washington, D.C., earning money and the summer of 1963 in Mexico and Central America spending it. Since my only expense while working in Washington was transportation and entertainment, I accumulated a small nest egg and used it to indulge in a summer program in Guadalajara, Mexico, sponsored by the University of Arizona. I hoped that immersion in a Spanish-speaking environment would teach to me to speak the language I had studied formally for four years. I didn't learn Spanish as well as I had hoped, but I learned a lot of other things.

On June 25th, Helen drove to Tijuana and put me on a bus for Guadalajara. I took the front seat opposite the driver, thinking only of the great view from the front window. But two days in a seat where I could not stretch my legs wreaked havoc with my knees. I learned not to do *that* again. For six weeks I lived with three other girls from the States in the home of a Mexican family, rode the bus to school and around the city, and took numerous side trips. The family we stayed with was relatively prosperous—Dr. Carlos Valle was a physician—residing in a large and lovely house, so I was always puzzled about why they took in paying guests. Although Sra. Valle was not employed, she had two live-in maids to do the cooking and cleaning. This was new to me. I knew no one in the United States who had one maid, let alone two. They lived in a small room off the kitchen. I tried to talk to them, but they wouldn't tell me much about their lives or what they earned, or perhaps my Spanish wasn't proficient enough.

What impressed me most about Mexico was the abysmal poverty I saw all around. This too was new. I *thought* I had seen poverty in my trips to Alabama, in some places around Los Angeles, and even in Tijuana, a growing city right across the Mexican border. But I hadn't; I had just seen poor people. Being poor is a relative condition, and not strictly an economic one. One is poor compared to the others around you; you can eat well and sleep warmly and be poor. One can be poor in many ways; you can be rich in material things and still have poor health or lack family or friends or peace of mind. Poverty is an absolute lack of the minimal necessities for a decent life.

Once I saw the pervasive poverty of Mexico I understood the *braceros* who came to California to work in the fields for low wages. As bad as it was, it was better than what they had at home. I also better understood why U.S. labor unions opposed these workers; the standard of living that American workers were trying to escape from was what Mexican workers aspired to. Mexican goods were cheap because labor was so cheap. In Mexico I also learned to see the United States not as America the Beautiful but as El Coloso del Norte—the Colossus of the North, the 800-pound gorilla who could sit where it pleased without regard for others. I wrote Helen long letters describing what I saw and the people I met.

Guadalajara was a charming city whose virtues I appreciated more when I visited Mexico City with another girl after school ended. We stayed in a pensión (small, dorm-like hotel) for students on Callé Ignacio Mariscal and spent our days walking and riding all over la Ciudád. After a few days, she said it was time to go home to L.A. I had about $50 left and at least three weeks before Cal classes started. I didn't want to go home. Percolating in my mind was one of those crazy ideas I sometimes get; ones that on the surface seem irrational but have a certain compulsion to them that drives me to fulfill their promise.

I wanted to go to Panamá.

One of my Davidson Hall dormmates, Natasha Súcre, lived in Panamá City. I decided to visit her. Of course, we were merely floormates, not friends, and I didn't have an address or phone number for her. Nor did I know how to get to Panamá or what I would do when I got there. I had heard about a PanAmerican Highway; there had to be a bus from Mexico to Panamá. I did realize that my $50 might not be enough to take me there and back to L.A.; I figured I'd solve that problem when I had to. And I didn't have a passport; entering Mexico from California only required a tourist card which was good for three months. I did have two heavy suitcases, full of six weeks of clothes, books, and gifts.

Armed with little but naïveté and youthful enthusiasm (and the suitcases), I hopped on a bus going south. In each town on the way to the Guatemalan border I found out how to take the next leg of the trip. When the border guard asked for my passport, I pulled out my birth certificate. It said I was born in the U.S.A. I showed it to the guard; he stapled it to a white piece of paper on which he put the Guatemalan entry stamp. That became my passport. I used it all the way down and to get back into the United States.

The PanAmerican Highway turned out to be dirt road. The buses were jitneys, about the size of a minivan. I rode them from Mexico to Guatemala City to San Salvador to Managua to San José. I never knew until the next city what bus to take or how much it would cost. Each leg took about one day of bouncing along the rocky road at a snail's pace. In each city I stayed two nights in a pensión and spent the day in between walking around. The pensiónes were a few cuts below the one in Mexico City; several beds per room, each with a thin mattress on a narrow cot. I left my suitcases in the bus stations. The only time I had to carry them was when we found the road to Guatemala City washed out. The driver waited for the bus from the other direction to arrive and the passengers switched buses, carrying our luggage about a quarter-mile down a steep ravine and back up again.

I ran out of money in Davíd, at the Panamanian border. It was time to find a ride. The bus driver dropped me off at the gate. I told the border guard what I was going to do so he wouldn't get the wrong idea when I stopped cars to talk to the drivers. Stand over there, he said. *He* would find me a ride to Panamá City, and he did. For about an hour he scrutinized each car that came through, occasionally asking the driver some questions. When he found a suitable family, he introduced me. The Wymans had worked in the canal zone for seven years as civilian employees of our military forces. They had an 18-year-old son, which is probably why they were willing to give a lift to a 17-year-old girl a long way from home. They had driven to Costa Rica for a few days' vacation. They spoke no Spanish. I did not understand how anyone could live in a

Spanish-speaking country for seven years and never learn the language, but since they mostly stayed in the zone, they never felt the need. I translated for the rest of the trip. I told them I was going to visit my friend but I didn't have her address. They recognized the name Súcre, confirming what Natasha had told me about the prominence of her family. Since they weren't sure how to get in touch with this family, they invited me to stay with them until I could do so. Although it only took a couple of days to find Natasha, I stayed with the Wymans for a week.

I told neither Natasha nor the Wymans that I had less than $5 and no ticket home. I said I was expecting my mother to send money for me to the American Embassy. In fact, she probably didn't know I was in Panamá until right before I left, since I wrote her that I was on my way only when I reached Managua. Besides, I wouldn't ask her for money to get back. One of her most frequent admonitions was "Don't ask others to pull your chestnuts out of the fire." I went to Panamá without her help, and I would get home without her help. Since Panamá City was a port, I decided to get a job on a ship going to California and work my way back. I went off to the harbor to find someone who could help me do this. The harbormaster told me not to get my hopes up. Not many ships going to California stopped there, he said. Those that did had a full crew complement, and those that needed extra help required seaman's papers, which I surely didn't have. And besides, who needed a girl to work on a ship? Maybe a private yacht might take me, he said, but it might be months before one appeared. I also dropped this idea on someone at the American Embassy, who laughed and said "good luck." The Embassy provided a mail drop for traveling Americans, not employment opportunities or financial rescue.

I returned to the port three times to see if my ship had come in. The third time the harbormaster told me he had a better idea. He was the treasurer for the local Red Cross; the chapter would loan me $80 with which I could fly to Miami and take a bus to Birmingham. "Why Miami?" I said. "I need to go to L.A." He told me that the policy of the Red Cross was to loan only enough money to send stranded Americans to the nearest port of entry, and that was Miami. When I had taken the bus south, I was also going east. Panamá City was east of Miami. Normally, he said, that was as much as the Red Cross would provide. But since I had told him I had relatives in Birmingham, he had prevailed upon them to add another $20 to get me that much farther. After that I was on my own. "I'll think about it," I told him.

I really didn't want to borrow money from anyone, not just my mother. It was more honorable to work my way back. But I was running out of time. I needed to return to Berkeley before the semester started, and I couldn't impose on the Wymans's hospitality too much longer. Pragmatism trumped honor. I arrived at the Birmingham bus station Labor Day morning, having paid $62.50 for a one-way plane ticket to Miami and $20.90 for one-way bus fare to Birmingham. Two Mitchell children had homes on the outskirts of the city. I alternated phone calls to Uncle Webster and Aunt Ruth. Neither were home.

In between phone calls I wandered around the bus station and soon discovered that it was still racially segregated. I decided to wait in the Negro waiting room, which was small and out of the way. I sat and read. After a couple hours two Negro women asked me what I was doing there. I don't believe in racial segregation, I said. I'll go into the white waiting room if you will go with me; otherwise I'll wait here. They both left shaking their heads in astonishment. I half expected someone from the bus company or the police to tell me to leave and thought about what to do if that happened. It didn't.

I finally reached Uncle Webster when he returned from a family barbecue late in the afternoon. I asked him to loan me $50 to take the bus to California, but he insisted on phoning Helen. She insisted that I fly, adding another $107.21 to my indebtedness. I thought I'd catch hell from Helen when the plane landed, but all she did was take me out to lunch and listen enraptured for two hours while I told her about my trip.

It took me a couple months to repay all my debts, but overall I thought the trip was worth it. It opened my eyes to so many things.

Traveling through Central America opened a little window through which I saw U.S. imperialism. Before, it was just a word, used mostly by leftists in a litany of phrases regularly used to denounce the United States. It had no meaning for me until I saw Central America. Most impressive were the U.S. marines in Guatemala City. After the Cuban revolution established a Communist beachhead in the Western hemisphere, our government wanted to ensure that there were "friendly" regimes running the other states in the Caribbean. That often meant helping conservative oligarchs and dictators oust reformers, and sometimes it meant installing military governments. I did not know enough about Central America to understand what I saw, but all those U.S. soldiers in someone else's country shook me up. In San Salvador, I met a young teacher who invited me to spend the night in her home. It was a hut with a dirt floor.

We talked until late. Even education was not a ticket out of poverty. Natasha showed me more in Panamá. Her family was well off and she drove a sports car but was duly appalled at the "casas brujas" (witch houses), or shanty towns, where the bulk of the urban population lived. She saw her country's poverty as a consequence of U.S. imperialism and made me reevaluate my assumptions about our foreign policy.

I also reconceptualized race. My epiphany came in Costa Rica, which had advertised itself as the only majority-white country in Central America. The day I walked around its capital most of the people I saw on the streets didn't look white to me. By the end of the day, I realized that that was because I had internalized the U.S. definition of race as a bright line between pure white and nonwhite. In Costa Rica the line was drawn elsewhere; indeed, it was more blur than line. While I was not sure where it was drawn, I finally understood that race was a social construct. It was not genes or color or physiognomy but society that decided what race meant and what label each person wore. If society could define what race meant, it could redefine it as well.

There were also personal lessons. One was: Don't do things like that. Going off to a foreign country with no way to get back and no money was really stupid. Not that I stopped doing wild and crazy things; I was still young. What Panamá taught me was to have a backup plan; two or three backup plans if possible. The second lesson was more subtle, and I didn't fully appreciate it until years later when in graduate school I read the scholarly literature about low self-esteem in teenage girls. I realized that self-esteem was not inborn; it came from two sources. One was actual achievement, handling problems, proving one's worth. The other was being told one was worthwhile. Boys got more praise for lesser achievements than girls, but they also did things girls were not allowed to do, or if allowed, not compelled to do. Indeed, boys were expected to prove themselves by showing that they could handle difficult situations and solve problems. Girls, on the other hand, were more likely to be protected from the real world. They were not expected to handle problems, they were not taught to handle problems, and it took a lot longer for them learn how to do so—if they learned at all. By going off to Panamá, I'd acted like a boy. And by extracting myself from that situation, however inelegantly, I'd proved my competency at a young age. Knowing this steadied me. For many years when I found myself in a sticky situation I would tell myself: "You got out of Panamá, you can get out of this." And I did.

15 | *The House on Parker Street*

A FEW DAYS AFTER my return, Helen and I drove to Berkeley to look for an apartment for me to share. Her car was full of stuff to set up housekeeping. It was late for apartment hunting, and for three days we found nothing. It seemed I might be back in the Berkeley Inn. Then Helen spotted an ad in the *Daily Cal* for an entire house for only $135 a month plus utilities and insisted that we look at it. That was three times my budgeted room rent; what did I want with a house? The small, plain house at 2032½ Parker Street was one of many built behind a main house to accommodate the exploding student population after World War II. In the front of the lot was the standard Victorian, where the owner, Mrs. Roberts, lived and rented rooms. She had no vacancies in her home and didn't want to rent single rooms in the one out back. Helen persuaded her to rent the whole house to me by assuring her she'd be responsible if I failed to meet my obligations in any way. That was a safe promise. Helen didn't believe in failure, at least not of responsibility, certainly not by me. She paid the first month's rent and the refundable cleaning fee, told me to run ads in the paper to rent out the rooms, and got in her car and drove home. At the age of 18 I became a landlord.

From Helen's perspective, this was a reasonable solution to my housing problem because she too rented out rooms once I left home. Actually, she rented out my room even before I left home; as soon as I graduated from high school, I moved into the den and a strange man took over my room. After I left, Helen moved into the den and rented out her room as well. Our former bedrooms went for $55–$60 a month, including cleaning, linen, and kitchen privileges. Since she sent me $100 a month and claimed she saved at least $50 a month by not having me live at home, I sometimes joked that she was the only parent I ever heard of who made money by sending her kid to college.

My new house had a nice-sized bedroom, kitchen, bath, and living room on the ground floor with a screened porch on the side. Upstairs were three attic rooms, strung together. The floor space was the same as below, but the sloping roof cut the headroom considerably. I took the last room on top, so no one would walk through my space to get to theirs. There was a skylight window in the roof over my bed which occasionally leaked. I rented the downstairs bedroom to a Sikh graduate student and the upstairs to two women who were not students. Berkeley rentals were aimed at a student population; they were generally furnished and leased for the nine-month academic year. Mrs. Roberts had not adequately furnished my house—there were no desks—but prospective tenants expected to find all the basics, so I had to scramble for furniture as well as roommates. Helen had convinced me that I should not split the rent but rent out the rooms at market value to cut my costs. After all, I was paying for the ads, doing the work, and taking the risks. I got $50 for the downstairs room and $80 from the two women with whom I shared the attic. Allan occupied the screened porch for two weeks while waiting for his new apartment in the city to become available. He had left Hastings Law School and wanted to work while trying to decide what to do next. I didn't charge Allan, but he said it was comfortable enough to rent as a room, so when he left, I rented it for $20 to a recent graduate from Georgia Tech who was bumming around until he went into the service in January. Because it would eventually get cold, he wasn't sure how long he would stay, but I was happy to get the extra $20 a month as long as I could. We shared the kitchen, bath, and utilities; unlike Helen, I didn't clean or provide linen.

The five of us never gelled as a group; each went his or her own way, with me acting as house administrator, utility bill collector, dispute resolver, and negotiator. In December and January the others moved out and there was some shuffling of housemates for several weeks. My first new permanent tenant was Antoinette Toms, a Wayne State University dropout who wanted to experience California. She worked as a secretary in the Student Activities office. Toni was a few years older than I and had lived a lot for her age. The oldest of eight children of a Detroit policeman and a homemaker, she told me she was a constant disappointment to them. Her family was Irish and Polish and devoutly Catholic; Toni was not. Born the day after Christmas in 1941, she birthed a son on her sixteenth birthday, which she gave up for adoption. She found that so traumatic that her next two pregnancies were aborted.

Toni described to me in graphic detail her first abortion, which she had only two months after giving birth. Her boyfriend took her to a flat in the Negro section of town that was full of battered furniture and screaming children. She paid $25 to get in the door and spread her legs on the dining table. For fifteen minutes the woman pushed a hard rubber rod into her vagina while Toni drank gin mixed with Kool-Aid to dull the pain. The woman told her to go home and put on a sanitary napkin; it would take about 24 hours for the rod to work its way out and then she would have her period. The following day Toni went to school and work until "menstrual cramps" drove her home in the middle of the afternoon. This was just the beginning. The cramps became painful uterine contractions which slowly expelled the fetus, along with a lot of blood. For the next week the pain and blood clots were unrelenting. Toni's experiences with pregnancy and abortion and her boyfriend did what the nuns in her Catholic school could never do: scared her into several years of celibacy. Her mere descriptions were enough to scare me.

The polite Sikh was replaced by an impolite Persian who thought that the three women living upstairs were his for the taking; he didn't understand the word "no." I got rid of him and rented the bedroom below to a young man named Ron who was recently discharged from military service. Ron wasn't sure what to do next. He came with two huskies, one of which, he claimed, was half wolf. Mrs. Roberts wasn't thrilled about the dogs, but the back yard was fenced so she didn't kick them out. The porch stayed empty until Ron asked if his friend Tom could rent it. They had decided that an electric blanket would make it possible to sleep in the cold and Tom could spend his waking hours in the kitchen or living room. Since we three women upstairs didn't spend much time downstairs, I said okay. After a few weeks, the four of us did gel as a group, a strange one to be sure, with the third woman remaining something of a fifth wheel. I was the youngest and the only student.

We had a few good times together even though our lives were very different, especially when Allan showed up to cook dinner. Allan and Ron had some major arguments, since Allan was antimilitary and Ron was pro. Toni and I were more ambivalent, having grown up on patriotism and Saturday-matinee war movies. Despite, or perhaps because of, our radically different backgrounds, we grew to be good friends. Toni had taken Russian in college and was enamored with the language. She called me Tovarisch (Comrade) and taught me a smattering of Russian. From Allan we both learned some Yiddish, as well as how to sing "Hava Nagila" and to dance the hora. I contributed my Spanish, and we all used the phrases of local studentspeak—mostly epithets and expletives such as "you fucking broads" and "damned prick."

Our conversation was probably unintelligible to most others. Having grown up in the isolated and sheltered environment of the Valley, I did not know what words like "fuck" meant. I finally asked, amusing everyone with my ignorance. I could use the words without knowing exactly what they meant because they were so prevalent; one absorbs language patterns even when the meaning is obscure. Helen would have blanched at my copious use of such terms (and probably washed out my mouth with soap); her strongest expletive was "hell's bells." Once I learned the local usage and got over their novelty, the words lost their sense of shock and became ordinary. When used constantly, words deemed dirty by most become merely forms of emphasis. But when I took Toni home to Northridge with me during spring break, we held our tongues around Helen.

Toni was a solid sleeper. Once when she was sacked out on the couch I tried to wake her by banging pans over her head, but she merely grimaced and slept on. I put ice cubes on her feet, but she kicked them off. It took about half an hour of work to get her up and running; if there were a fire, she'd be dead. Her deep sleeps could be entertaining. In the late spring, Ron, Toni, and I spent an evening in the city and slept over on Allan's floor. When we woke the next morning, Toni was still out of it. Allan's sense of mischief was contagious. At his instigation we rolled Toni up in a blanket and put her out on the sidewalk. We watched through the windows as the morning go-to-work crowd walked around this sleeping hulk with long auburn hair trickling out from under the blanket. No one stopped. A lot stared, but no one stopped. Finally Toni woke up to a bright blue sky and found herself in the middle of the sidewalk. She got up and looked around, clearly disoriented, while we laughed uproariously inside. After a few minutes she figured it out and pounded on the door to be let in. Was she mad! We laughed so hard that she started laughing too, but I'm not sure she ever forgave us.

I occasionally brought my housemates to SLATE and other activities, but, not being students, they were more interested in the parties than the politics. SLATE, like other organizations, raised money by running beer busts. Pot was creeping into the student subculture but was still rather rare. Booze was the drug of choice, its enjoyment enhanced by a tinge of illegality. California law prohibited the selling of alcohol within one mile of a college campus, so there were no local watering holes. To get around the law, sort of, liquor was not sold by the drink at parties. Instead there was an admissions fee, usually $2, with a basket for "contributions" next to the keg. Beer parties were openly advertised in the student newspaper without concern for the cops. I did not drink, and watching other people get drunk was not my idea of fun, but I was sometimes drafted to be SLATE's doorkeeper. Although still a minor, I was always sober. Fortunately, I missed the one party raided by the police. No one knew who called the cops, but they confiscated the bar, the keg, and the money. When SLATE members Steve DeCanio and Jeff Grobart went to pick them up from the police station the next day, they were arrested for selling liquor without a license; DeCanio was sentenced to six months' probation while the charges against Grobart were dropped. The next SLATE party was advertised: "Milk and crackers served. Bring your own bail, etc."[1]

16 | *The Assassination of JFK*

ON NOVEMBER 22, 1963, I was in Professor Sheldon Wolin's History of Political Theory class, listening to his elegant exposition of early Greek thought. A young man walked up to the podium and handed him a note. Wolin read it and paused for a very long time before telling us that President Kennedy had been killed. Class was dismissed. That night Professor Fred Stripp spoke at a candlelight vigil where we mourned what seemed the loss of the ideals that JFK represented.[1]

Thanksgiving was very bleak that year. I stayed in Berkeley and listened to the funeral on my radio, since I did not have a TV set. Cousin Linda, by then a senior in high school, wrote me on November 25th:

Dear Jo:
Today we watched President Kennedy's funeral. It was very beautiful. It was hard to conceive that Mr. Kennedy could be dead. He was so young and had so much he wanted to do. Everyone that I talked to said that it would have been different if he was old and ill. When we heard about the shooting we were in 3rd period and I can remember feeling chilly and that my heart started to beat hard and fast. Right then I prayed that he would live, but had a feeling that he wouldn't. Our principal came on the PA and said the Presi-

dent was dead. Some girls started crying and the teacher kept saying "Not the President."

If it was any time in my life so far, I wanted to cry so hard, but I just sat there staring at the floor. Only the colleges were closed, the high schools were left to individual principals. We stayed in school.

While watching the TV, I couldn't help but admire the way Mrs. Kennedy had controlled herself. Comparing Mrs. Johnson to Mrs. Kennedy, it seem all lop-sided. She spoke all those languages and could speak right to the people. I was amazed that most of the funeral arrangements were made by her.

You must feel proud to have seen the President. I had hoped someday to see him before his term ran out. After this I just may become a life long Democrat. I remember the fights we had over Kennedy and Nixon, but just a few months ago I really liked President Kennedy and I will probably think of him as the greatest President. When we stopped in Okla. in 1960, we watched the Democratic Convention, and William wanted to see Lyndon Johnson become the candidate for Pres. Now he is. Right now we are watching a special called "Four Dark Days—From Dallas to Arlington."

When they told that he was going to be buried in Arlington by the Custis-Lee Mansion and I knew exactly where it would be. I'm glad that there will be a light by his grave, because it symbolizes the kind of man and President he was.

Please write me soon. We have kept papers from these days. If you were unable to purchase them. I'll send them to you so that you can read them.

Love
Linda

17 | The Bay Area Civil Rights Movement

THE CIVIL RIGHTS MOVEMENT came to the Bay Area with a bang in the fall of 1963. Until then, it was mostly a southern movement. We read about it, we sympathized with it, we raised some funds for southern projects, we applauded speakers from southern schools who described their experiences to us, but we were not participants. There was a brief flurry of activity in the spring of 1960 when the Greensboro, North Carolina, sit-in prompted sympathy pickets of Woolworth and Kress five-and-dime stores. The Berkeley pickets only lasted until summer sent the students packing. In Oakland, several dozen Negro residents continued picketing until March of 1961. In 1962, the Cal student government collected money, food, and clothing for the southern students, but the administration curbed this as prohibited "off-campus" activity. The SLATE summer conference "The Negro in American Society" brought three to four hundred persons together in July of 1962, leading to the formation of Bay Area Friends of SNCC, but it too was primarily concerned with support for southern activists.[1] We did work for fair housing, but except for the brief fight against the Berkeley repeal ordinance, that did not require mass participation.

The civil rights cauldron had been bubbling in the South for almost ten years; in 1963 it boiled over. During that year almost 1,000 civil rights demonstrations occurred in at least 115 cities, more than 20,000 people were arrested, 10 persons were killed, and there were 35 bombings.[2] Not all of these penetrated the consciousness of Cal students, involved as we were in our studies and in local issues. But there were so many demonstrations, and some were so important, that few of us could remain unmoved.

In the spring of 1963 the Southern Christian Leadership Conference (SCLC), led by Dr. Martin Luther King, Jr., launched a campaign to end segregation in Birmingham, Alabama, reputed to be the most segregated city in the United States. The city fathers had shown a determination to keep the races separate matched only by the willingness of the white population to use violence against the 40 percent who were black. For days, SCLC led Birmingham Negroes in marches to which the police responded with snarling dogs, electric cattle prods, and fire hoses. The scenes of schoolchildren and ministers trying to pray while snapped at by police dogs and knocked down by streams of high-pressure water were nightly fare on the TV news and daily headlines in the papers.[3] Two days after SCLC reached agreement with civic leaders, the city was rent with bombings and riots. Public Safety Commissioner "Bull" Connor, who ordered the heavy-handed tactics, was the perfect poster boy for what was wrong with America, while Dr. King, who authored his famous "Letter from Birmingham Jail" after his arrest during these demonstrations, articulated our highest ideals. The contrast shook up even those who thought civil rights was a southern problem and none of their concern.

Birmingham was just one such shock to our national conscience in 1963.

- On April 23rd, William L. Moore, a white Baltimore letter carrier and member of CORE, was murdered in Alabama soon after he began a one-person walk against segregation. Other CORE members were threatened and arrested when they tried to complete his walk.
- On June 11th, Alabama governor George Wallace carried out his threat to "stand in the door" to prevent two Negro students from enrolling in the University of Alabama.
- On June 12th, Medgar Evers, Mississippi field secretary for the NAACP, was murdered by a sniper in front of his home in Jackson, Mississippi, while President Kennedy was making a televised speech promising major civil rights legislation.
- On August 28th, Dr. King led almost a quarter of a million people—about one-third of whom were white—in a March on Washington to demand passage of a comprehensive civil rights bill.
- On September 2nd, Governor Wallace stationed National Guardsmen in front of formerly white public schools to keep out Negro children admitted by court order.
- On September 15th, four little girls were killed when a Negro church was bombed in Birmingham, Alabama.

As these events grabbed the headlines, important Negro spokesmen came to campus to seek our support. Author James Baldwin lectured to 9,000 during the May Birmingham confrontations. James Farmer, national director of CORE since 1961, addressed 1,000 students the day classes began in the fall and another 5,000 in San Francisco a few days later.[4]

CORE was the most active civil rights organization in the Bay Area. Founded in Chicago in 1942 by "a small band of dedicated young pacifists and members of the Christian pacifist Fellowship of Reconciliation (FOR)" who wanted to apply the Gandhian principles of nonviolent direct action "to the resolution of racial and industrial conflict in America," it primarily worked in the North. Its director, James Farmer, had been race-relations secretary of FOR. Gandhian tactics were very compatible with Christian beliefs, as both emphasized goodwill and reconciliation. An early CORE leaflet urged members to "Remember technique! . . .

Gather facts. Negotiate. Rouse public opinion, and then, if absolutely necessary, and only as a last resort, Take Direct Action."[5]

For two decades, CORE was a loose federation of local groups with only a handful of members, mostly in midwestern cities, largely run by volunteers. It sponsored a small interracial bus and train trip to southern border states in 1947 and a few nonviolent sit-ins to desegregate northern restaurants and other public facilities, but it was largely unknown until the 1961 freedom rides brought national publicity. In the next four years, CORE expanded to several thousand members in 140 chapters with a staff of over 100. Begun as an integrated organization, often with whites in leadership positions, by 1965 it "ceased simply serving Negroes and [became] a Negro organization," shifting "its emphasis somewhat, focusing less on desegregation and more on political action, economic discrimination, and problems within the Negro communities."[6]

CORE was in the midst of this transition in 1963. A Berkeley (non-student) chapter formed in 1959, declined, resurrected to picket Woolworth's after the 1960 Greensboro sit-ins, and then declined again. It was largely white. When it first demanded that local employers hire more Negroes in 1961, it "advertised in the press for Negroes willing to fight discrimination" by asking for jobs. Birmingham catalyzed a response all over the country. CORE chapters formed spontaneously throughout the north, especially in California and New York. Money in CORE's coffers and warm bodies on its picket lines grew as well. Before Birmingham's dogs and fire hoses, only a handful showed up for Berkeley CORE's picket of the Montgomery Ward department store to demand that it hire more Negroes. Afterward hundreds came, and the store signed an agreement to hire aggressively. "Montgomery Ward hired about seventy-five blacks within several weeks, about half in sales positions."[7] Whatever Bull Connor did for Birmingham, he was a great help to the Civil Rights Movement in California.

Campus CORE held its first meeting of fifty new members in October of 1963. Civil rights had become a student issue in September when the vice president of the junior class was asked not to escort one of the girls competing for queen of the annual football festival sponsored by the Berkeley Junior Chamber of Commerce. Light-skinned Lynn Sims was one of the few Negroes among the Cal student body and only one of the six escorts chosen by the university honorary men's society. The Jaycee Queen chairman told reporters that four of the six queen candidates were from southern schools and "We had to protect the mental and physical well-being of the girls no matter what." After a four-hour meeting pick-

At the beginning of the fall 1963 semester SLATE organized a picket of the
Berkeley JayCees to protest its exclusion of the vice president of the junior class
from escorting a football festival queen candidate because he was a Negro.
Photograph by Jo Freeman.

eted by SLATE, the Jaycees apologized, but the university still withdrew
its support. The meeting was still underway when three of us left the
picket line at 11:40 P.M., casually walking across the empty street as we
always did. As we were getting into our car, a Berkeley police officer
came over and issued us all tickets for jaywalking. My fine was $2. It was
my first political offense and my first realization that when ordinary acts
became political, you often pay a price.[8]

Campus and Berkeley CORE worked together to pressure local merchants to hire more Negroes. Jobs were the issue, more of them for Berkeley Negroes was the goal. That there was a problem was already established. In 1960, the U.S. Civil Rights Commission held hearings in San
Francisco on discrimination throughout the Bay Area. It included in the
record a 1958 report on "Employment Opportunities for Members of
Minority Groups in Berkeley," which found that

> In grocery stores, for example, only 1.5 percent of a total of 269
> employees observed working in a representative sample of 35 stores
> were Negro. Similarly, in 20 banks, the only Negro employee ob-

served was 1 maintenance man. Only 2 Negroes were observed in sales positions in a representative sample of 24 department, variety, and specialty stores, although an occasional Negro was seen working as a porter, maid, dishwasher, or stock clerk.[9]

CORE went after the merchants on Telegraph and Shattuck Avenues, the two main commercial strips. Agreements were reached, then canceled, then reached again. Race and civil rights issues were on the front page of the *Daily Cal* three days out of five during the fall 1963 semester.[10]

The biggest blast came when the Ad Hoc Committee to End Discrimination closed down Mel's Drive-In, one of whose owners was running for mayor of San Francisco. The first pickets appeared in front of Supervisor Harold Dobbs's San Francisco restaurant on October 19th, switching on succeeding days to his Oakland and Berkeley eateries. The style of the Ad Hoc Committee was not that of CORE. There had been no negotiation. Direct action was the tactic of first resort, not the last. Gone was CORE's concern for image, with proper dress, disciplined picketing, and monitors to prevent even a semblance of violence. The Mel's picket was more like a labor action than a civil rights demonstration.[11] As described by Jack Weinberg, soon to be chairman of Campus CORE:

> This action . . . changed the entire mood of demonstration. The notion of trying to maintain a respectable image was almost entirely demolished. The first Mel's lines did not even pay lip service to nonviolence. The policy was, "We'll defend our line." There was singing, shouting, clapping, smoking, talking, walking two abreast, dancing, and all types of dress on the line. "Experienced" civil rights demonstrators didn't know what to think. Some stayed away; some tried to instruct the line in proper conduct; some joined in. Never before were there such large civil rights picket lines.[12]

The climax came the weekend before the election. On Saturday the Ad Hoc Committee picketed Dobbs's home. That night, and again on Sunday, the demonstrators conducted the first mass sit-in of the Bay Area Civil Rights Movement. They occupied all the seats in one restaurant and refused to order food. Fifty-nine were arrested. When Dobbs lost the election to Jack Shelley, many said the picketing was politically motivated. Dobbs signed an employment agreement with the Ad Hoc Committee the next week to hire Negroes in "up front" positions. Soon thereafter another agreement was signed with the Doggie Diner chain without demonstrations.[13]

Most of us did not know where the Ad Hoc Committee came from or why Mel's was singled out for action when there were so many employers who did not hire Negroes. Frankly, we didn't care. The action attracted us; the opportunity to act for a good cause made it all seem so right that who organized what for what reasons was irrelevant. Years later Mike Myerson, co-chair of the Ad Hoc Committee, claimed credit for the W. E. B. DuBois Clubs. He said that club members worked with Negro youth in San Francisco and from them learned that the kids could eat at Mel's but not work there. They decided to organize a picket. Two San Francisco State students, William Barlow and Peter Shapiro, gave credit to a student group formed at their college. San Francisco attorney Terry François, president of the San Francisco chapter of the NAACP from 1959 to 1962, later said he had targeted Dobbs many months before the demonstrations. François had pressured businesses practicing racial discrimination for many years; Mel's was one of those who had refused to negotiate its hiring practices. Recognizing that Dobbs's desire to run for mayor made him vulnerable, François encouraged students to form the Ad Hoc Committee specifically to picket his restaurant. Whoever was responsible, the Ad Hoc Committee put civil rights protest on a different level. For the first time, we had to think about civil disobedience.[14]

18 | On Civil Disobedience

I DID NOT HAVE to think twice about participating in civil rights demonstrations, but getting arrested was another matter altogether. Supporting the Civil Rights Movement was easy because I was raised on civil rights. Precisely because Helen was from Alabama and the movement started in Montgomery late in 1955, what it was doing and what it meant was dinner-table conversation. Although she didn't like everything it did, by and large Helen supported the movement. She believed that the time had come for the South to change its ways and that it wouldn't do so without pressure. How Helen got "right on race," to use the southern expression, I do not know. We never discussed it. I took her views for granted and made them my own. I did not become curious about why she differed so significantly from the rest of her family until after I had left the movement. By then she was sick and dying and didn't want to dwell on the past. But since I am her daughter, I can make an educated guess.

Marion County, where she grew up, was a white county; less than 3 percent of the population was Negro. I've seen nothing in her early correspondence with her sisters to indicate any awareness of race before she left the South to join the Women's Army Corps in 1942. While she never mentioned race in connection with her service, she did tell me that her years in uniform was the most profound experience of her life. Afterward, she became something of a World War II buff; our shelves were lined with books on the conflict. She kept her army memorabilia, including her uniforms, safely in a trunk, never parting with them the many times we moved even though their only use was as playthings and dress-up clothes for my childhood games.

The war changed the attitudes of many Americans on race; indeed, it made the Civil Rights Movement possible. Or more exactly, it made a critical mass of whites receptive to the movement's message of equality and justice which they had not been willing to listen to before.

After failing to find a professional position with her home economics degree, Helen became a teacher in the L.A. public school system. She had taught high school in Alabama for six years during the Depression until the school ran out of money and closed. She once told me that all L.A. teachers started in the Negro schools on the east side; if successful, whites could move to white schools in other neighborhoods; Negro teachers stayed. In January 1952, we moved to Van Nuys, a large neighborhood of small tract homes in the middle of the Valley. Until then, most of her friends that I can remember were Negro teachers in the different schools where she taught. I suspect her choice of friends was due to a greater cultural affinity with the Negro teachers than with the white; southern roots were a stronger bond than skin color. Helen would often tell me she was going over to so-and-so's house to eat ham hocks and black-eyed peas.

Her best friend was Lois Rabb, a pleasant light-skinned woman whose husband died when her two daughters were just entering their teens. Helen and Lois hung out together; we spent many, many days at her comfortable house with its small yard. Her daughters, Joyce and Jeannie, were several years older than I—too old to be friends but about right to be surrogate cousins. They carried me on their bikes, taught me to play chopsticks on their piano, and engaged me in endless games of fish. The year before we moved to the Valley, Helen taught at Mount Vernon Junior High School. She took me out of my neighborhood school and enrolled me in the abutting Arlington Heights Elementary School. The simple solution to the perennial after-school child care problem was for me to walk around the block to her classroom. Both schools were Negro. I may have been the only white child in my school; if not, there weren't many others. I have only pleasant memories of Arlington Heights Elementary School; I was not aware of race as a great divide or even of being particularly different from the other kids. Skin color was an individual characteristic, just as height and hairstyle were, not a chasm. Indeed, when I came home from my first day at all-white Lemay Street School in 1952 I complained to my mother that all the kids in my class looked alike.

Her Negro friends drifted away after we moved to the Valley (though she stayed in touch with Lois until she died), but I think those relationships as well as her army experience explains her ready acceptance of the Civil Rights Movement as well as my own eagerness to participate. The idea that her friends and colleagues—and my teachers—should be kept legally separate, or even discriminated against, made no sense. It was blatantly unjust.

To demonstrate was one thing; to get arrested was another. Violating the law was something good kids just did not do. Some readily sat in and courted arrest, but I had to think this one out, and I know many other students did as well. Dr. King had justified massive disruption and arrests in his "Letter from Birmingham Jail" as necessary to combat segregation. He repeated the classic argument that one should only obey just laws. "All segregation statutes are unjust because segregation distorts the soul and damages the personality," he wrote. Laws "inflicted on a minority that [was] denied the right to vote" were also unjust. But what about laws that were neutral, such as parading without a permit, for which he had been arrested? To answer this, Dr. King had to take the classic justification of civil disobedience a step farther and argue that "such an ordinance becomes unjust when it is used to maintain segregation and to deny citizens the First-Amendment privilege of peaceful assembly and protest."[1]

But the sit-ins at Mel's, and the ones likely to be held in future demonstrations, were not in violation of laws used to maintain segregation or to deny the right of peaceful assembly. We had no quarrel with laws against trespassing or disturbing the peace. Legal segregation was not practiced in California. Nor does the right of peaceful assembly extend to raucous occupation of someone else's property and disruption of their business. How could someone in good conscience deliberately court arrest in this manner? The obvious answer is that laws were broken in pursuit of a good cause: compelling employers to cease informal, and illegal, racial job discrimination. But this answer only led to another question: If one could guiltlessly violate a neutral law in pursuit of a good cause, did that mean that one could violate all neutral laws? Did intent alone determine the meaning of, and the proper response to, public behavior? Did the nature of the act change solely by the intent of the actor? If so, should society's response to that act, in particular the punishment of it, be determined by that intent? Should good people pursuing selfless goals be punished less or not at all while society's wrath was limited to bad people acting solely in their own self-interest? Did whether or not one could vote, and thus participate indirectly in changing the laws, make a difference?

Confronting these issues provided me with one of the most intellectually challenging experiences of my life. I was fortunate that so many others were facing them at the same time so we could talk about it. I was also fortunate to be taking some courses which bore directly on these issues and to have professors in other courses willing to incorporate them into their regular curriculum. Sheldon Wolin touched on this in his Political Theory course, which was actually the history of political philosophy since the early Greeks; his TA, Peter Euben, led us in a discussion of civil disobedience after the demonstration at Mel's. Joseph Tussman engaged a 50-person seminar in Political Philosophy extensively on the issue of "political obligation," a topic on which he had published a major book. The Y held a retreat on civil disobedience with readings and discussions which let me probe even more deeply into it. The sit-ins made our education meaningful in a way it had not been before.

It was Socrates who finally convinced me I could, indeed should, get arrested. As rendered by his disciple, Plato, in the *Apology*, he clarified the confusing impulses in my head. The issue was not whether or not one should break the law. The issue was whether breaking the law could achieve a larger social good. There are many laws, some good, some bad, a lot silly. All of us break many laws, many times, usually without either bad or good intention. I had jaywalked many times; only once did I get a ticket for it and that unintentionally. Socrates was charged with "corrupting the youth," a pursuit he not only denied but had no wish to do. He saw himself as a "gadfly to a horse that is large and well-bred but rather sluggish because of its size, so that it needs to be aroused. It seems to me" he said, "that the god has attached me like that to the state, for I am constantly alighting upon you at every point to arouse, persuade, and reproach each of you all day long." I saw those who courted arrest not as the enemies of social order but as gadflies who, by sacrificing some of their own benefit and comfort, made the world a better place for everyone. Like Socrates, I felt it was the highest calling to "go about and persuade you all to give your first and greatest care to the improvement of your souls, and not till you have done that to think of your bodies or your wealth. Wealth does not bring excellence, but that wealth, and every other good thing which men have, whether in public or in private, comes from excellence."[2]

When I went to Northridge during semester break I tried to discuss some of this with Helen. I was moving toward the belief that it was neither good nor bad to deliberately break the law for selfless ends. If breaking the law woke people to an injustice that they would otherwise ignore, if it compelled them to treat a festering sore, it was a necessity. She would have none of this. Breaking the law was something one just did not do. Period.

19 | *The Sheraton-Palace*

AFTER THE ARRESTS at Mel's, things were quiet for a while. Then CORE took the lead again by organizing a "shop-in" at Lucky's supermarkets. Lucky's was an old adversary, having been picketed successfully by CORE as long ago as 1948. CORE had negotiated another agreement the previous summer, but no additional jobs for Negroes appeared. In February 1964, CORE set up picket lines at several markets. A week later it started the "shop-in." Although new to us, it was a classic form of nonviolent disruption; all our actions were legal, but they significantly interfered with the ability of Lucky's stores to conduct business. Basically, we went shopping, piled our carts with goods, and changed our minds at the check-out counter. Since we looked like ordinary shoppers, the cashiers had no way of knowing that they would be left with ringing cash registers and a counter full of unwanted goods. The managers had no way of separating the real shoppers from the ringers. And the real shoppers didn't want to stand in lines forever waiting for cash registers to be cleared and goods to be returned to the shelves. After a few days of this, the new mayor of San Francisco, John Shelley, negotiated an agreement; the parent company promised to hire at least sixty Negroes. We left. A few months later our local Lucky's, on the corner of Haste Street a few blocks from campus, closed forever.[1]

The week the Lucky's agreement was announced, a picket line appeared outside the Sheraton-Palace Hotel in San Francisco. This was another Ad Hoc Committee action, but unlike Mel's, negotiation was tried first. According to co-chair Mike Myerson:

> In Birmingham hotels, black bartenders and waiters are commonplace, but in San Francisco that year there were none. The city's hostelries were in a vulnerable position, all of them booked several months in advance to play host to the Republican National Convention. The Sheraton-Palace, soon to be Rockefeller headquarters, employed nineteen blacks, all in menial jobs, of a work staff totaling 550.[2]

The Urban League and the NAACP had begun negotiations with the hotel industry in March 1960 because so many local Negroes complained that they could not get jobs in San Francisco that they had held in southern cities. These talks sometimes led to promises but rarely to actual performance. After the successful Mel's action, demonstrations seemed like a quicker route. The most logical targets for action were the three oldest and most elegant hotels in the city: the Sheraton, the Mark Hopkins, and the Fairmont. If one of them agreed to hire more Negroes, the other hotels would follow. Of these three, the Sheraton was the most accessible. The Ad Hoc Committee met with the Sheraton management on December 11th to ask for the racial composition of its employees and followed this with a letter on January 13th. The hotel finally disclosed that only

19 of its 550 employees were Negroes. Two more meetings did not persuade the hotel to commit itself to actively recruit more Negro employees. Picketing began on February 23rd. The Sheraton responded with a court injunction limiting the number of pickets to nine and slapped the Ad Hoc Committee and its leaders with a $50,000 lawsuit.[3] Later that spring I wrote about what happened next:

> It was the suit which fomented the demonstration of about 500 people of February 29; the first big demonstration. Here again they started with quiet picketing, then singing and chanting. After an hour or two of this the monitors started sending groups of ten people into the Hotel, without signs, to just stand along the walls or sit in the lobby chairs. The next step was to cautiously add signs; this occurred with about the fourth group of ten people. Gradually getting bolder, the whole picket line went in, quietly through the Market St. door and out the New Montgomery entrance, forming a circle in, out and around the Hotel. To this was added singing, chanting, and clapping hands, and toward the end of the afternoon the line walked in the Market St. door and instead of turning the corner toward New Montgomery kept walking along the corridor paralleling New Montgomery. This essentially moved the whole picket line inside the Hotel.
>
> The result of this was two hours later the court issued an injunction prohibiting picketing inside the Hotel and limiting the number of pickets outside to nine. The monitors read the injunction to the demonstrators and they were asked to leave and disperse, which they did. The next day, however, they assembled again to picket outside the Hotel, in excess of the number allowed, and 81 were arrested. As a result of this there was a demonstration held late that night outside the Hall of Justice and several people marched over to the Sheraton-Palace to resume picketing, and were promptly arrested. This brought the total to 123. (The charges were later dropped as the injunction was declared to have been improper and invalid.) Negotiations resumed that week in a heightened atmosphere of tension. On Thursday, March 5, the Sheraton-Palace Hotel hired its first Negro waitress, but refused to sign an agreement insuring that this was not just tokenism. Hence the big demonstration of about 3,000–4,000 people of March 6 and 7.[4]

The Ad Hoc Committee spent the week leafleting the local campuses. It invited students to come join the picket line next Friday, March 6th. Thousands of us came from all over the Bay Area—but mostly from Cal and San Francisco State—to put our bodies on the line to show our commitment to civil rights. The usual procedure at Cal was for us all to congregate in front of Stiles Hall, on Bancroft south of Telegraph. Those with cars drove up, like an airport taxi line, for those waiting to pile in. Leftovers or latecomers took the bus across the Bay. By then the Ad Hoc Committee had a lot more support from the other civil rights organizations, which no longer held their noses at the raucous nature of the demonstrations. The hotel got another court injunction to limit the pickets to 100; far from stopping us, it egged us on. During the day, Mayor Shelley brought representatives from all parties together and they reached an agreement. However, the Sheraton was unable to get the approval of the Hotel Employers Association, so it would not sign. A joint press conference in support of the demonstration was held by Dr. Thomas N. Burbridge, the recently elected head of the NAACP chapter; CORE head William Bradley; and the three leaders of the Ad Hoc Committee: Mike Myerson, Tracy Sims, and Roy Ballard.[5]

We started quietly enough around dinnertime. As the night wore on, we became louder and louder, singing freedom songs and chanting. Our numbers surged and then thinned to about 1,500 as picketers grew cold, tired, and bored. Around 10:00 P.M. we moved inside. The hotel secured another injunction but did not enforce it while continuing to negotiate. Instead we were invited to "sleep-in" right where we were. We sat down, occupying the entire lobby, except for a pathway left for hotel guests, police, and other notables—including ten African VIPs booked into the hotel by the State Department.[6] The leadership went upstairs to negotiate with the Hotel Employers Association. Negotiations dragged on while we were entertained by comedian Dick Gregory and led in songs by songwriter Malvina Reynolds. Thrice we were told that agreement had been reached to hire more Negroes in thirty-three hotels. Thrice lawyers for the Hotel Employers Association said they could not sign. First they wanted the unions to agree, then other Negro leaders; finally they insisted that all thirty-three hotel owners had to be consulted.

Sometime between 3:00 and 4:00 A.M. we were instructed on how to be arrested. We were told that those willing to be arrested should cluster at the three main doors, while the rest should stay out of the way. Juveniles, that is, those under age 18, were explicitly asked not to be arrested, though no one checked IDs. Fortunately, I had turned 18 several months earlier. In order to lengthen the process, we were told to link arms and legs until we were separated and then go limp so we would have to be carried out. This also made good camera copy for the TV stations and newspapers.

It was all very orderly. A large group sat down and linked themselves together. The police waded in and tore them apart. Line after line of protestors walked to the front, sat down and linked up. We could see the zeal on the faces of the cops as they pulled us apart. They could see the stubborn resistance on ours. Those who had chosen not to get arrested began to sing.

> After six arrests, Willie Brown made a speech in which he asked the demonstrators to leave the doorway and simply hold a sleep-in. The demonstrators did not move until the members of the Ad Hoc Committee had had a chance to vote on this proposal and cheered when it was voted down. However, after about 40 arrests, Tracy Sims announced that bail had been set at $600 (this later turned out to be a false rumor circulated by the police to scare us into leaving) and said that those who could not afford to remain in jail until Monday should hold a sleep-in, but asked as many as could, to let themselves be arrested. Self-sacrifice flew out the window once it required a very heavy sacrifice and other, less drastic action would also be sanctioned by the group. The decision was left up to the individual then, not the group. Three-fourths of the remaining demonstrators got up and moved. Many of them later sat down again after the rumor was exposed for what it was, and they saw many of their fellows being dragged off.[7]

My turn came around 5:00 A.M. Along with others I left my spot on the side, sat down in front, and looped my arms and legs into those on either side of me. When the police grabbed the person next to me, I held on. Despite my belief in nonviolence, I had no compunction about this form of resistance. We got a certain pleasure out of "fighting" the police without actually fighting. And the cops got a certain pleasure out of giving us as hard a time as they could without drawing the attention of the press. They didn't do anything to me worthy of coverage, but once outside I was tossed hard into the paddy wagon, landing with a resounding thud, and some pain, on my tailbone. In my mind this police "retaliation" removed whatever doubts I had about my initial "resistance." I felt like I'd given as good as I'd got, given that I had to be nonviolent.

The booking process was slow and tedious. I'd never been inside a jail before and had no idea what to expect. It did make student complaints about assembly-line processing during registration seem unfounded. The clerks were rough; they told us they were just doing their job, but it was obvious that many were on overtime and grouchy from lack of sleep. We thought we had acted in a noble cause; they thought we were a pain in the butt. After processing, I and the other thirty-three women were locked up in a large room with metal tables and benches and open toilets.

HOTEL PICKET BEDLAM

200 Jailed, Hundreds Jam Lobby

News Call Bulletin

SAN FRANCISCO'S EVENING NEWSPAPER

Volume 5, No. 181   SATURDAY, MARCH 7, 1964   Price 10c

9 STAR FINAL

WEEKEND TV GUIDE

Hiring Talks Broken Off

By Hadley Roff

Bedlam in the Sheraton-Palace Hotel mounted explosively this afternoon as spokesmen for the major hotels said they'd no longer deal with the demonstration's collegiate leaders.

Joseph Sullivan, executive secretary of the San Francisco Hotel Employers Association, said the leaders are "irresponsible" and their demands "impossible."

Two hundred or so youthful demonstrators were carted to paddywagons before dawn in the largest mass arrest in San Francisco history.

Another 450, recruited mostly from Bay Area colleges, remained behind. At first, they stretched out on chairs and squatted on the floor in the lobby in a "sleep in."

But within an hour young agitators exhorted them to demonstrate again. "One group has gone to jail. Why not us?" they said.

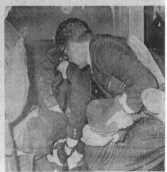

Limp and dragging her feet, this girl is taken from lobby by policemen.

The second civil rights sit-in at the Sheraton Palace Hotel made headlines in all the Bay Area newspapers. 167 were arrested early the next morning and an agreement with the San Francisco hotels to hire more Negroes was signed later that day.

No one could sleep; we mostly sat on the floor, talked and sang. Sometime that afternoon, bail bondsman Jerry Barrish paid the bond on our bail of $56 each.[8]

After I returned to the Sheraton, I found out that 167 of us had been arrested and charged with disturbing the peace while another few hundred had stayed and continued to picket. We cost the city over $10,000 for 186 police. While we were still in jail, leaders in the ILWU had phoned Mayor Shelley, who had enjoyed major union support for his recent election, and urged him to resolve the conflict. Several children of the ILWU leadership were in the Sheraton demonstrations, and many Negroes were among its members. The mayor called all parties into his office and kept them there until they signed an agreement. It required affirmation of a nondiscrimination policy by thirty-three hotels, regular "statistical analysis" of job categories, a goal of 15 to 20 percent minority employees, inspections to determine compliance, and amnesty. It was signed by Myerson, Sims, and Ballard, and a lawyer for the Hotel Employers Association and was "endorsed, ratified and approved" by four Negro leaders in San Francisco. We cheered and sang after the agreement was read to us. Dick Gregory asked us to clean up the debris in the lobby. We did so, and then we left.[9]

The names, addresses, occupations, and ages of those arrested were published in the newspaper and tell something about who we were. Men significantly outnumbered women among the arrestees. There were 127 men, thirty-four women, and six juveniles (four boys, two girls). The *Chronicle* reported that eight arrestees were Negro, half the demonstrators were women, and 60 percent were white. I estimated that 70 to 80 percent were white but didn't do a sex count of the demonstrators. I did analyze the arrestees by age and occupation. They seemed slightly younger than the demonstrators. Two-thirds of the men and three-fourths of the women were between the ages of 18 and 23; ninety-three men and twenty-two women said they were students. Of the rest, a handful of the men said they were laborers, clerks, or unemployed. Most of the remaining women were clerks or secretaries. There were very few professional workers (teachers, attorneys). The *Berkeley Daily Gazette* identified seventy-eight local residents.[10]

Tracy Sims was the first and only woman I saw in the leadership of a Bay Area civil rights group. At 18, she was the youngest of the three leaders of the Ad Hoc Committee. She and Roy were Negro; Mike was white. As the main spokesperson throughout the Sheraton-Palace demonstration, she did a great job. Tracy told reporters that she had been involved in the Civil Rights Movement since the age of 14, when she picketed the local Woolworth's in sympathy with the students in North Carolina. She had graduated from Berkeley High the year before and had dropped out of San Francisco State after only one semester to devote herself to the movement, serving as chairman for Youth for Jobs and secretary for the San Francisco DuBois Club. Her fourth and fifth arrests were at the Sheraton-Palace. The newspaper reports implied that it really stuck in the craw of the hotel association and city leaders to have to negotiate with an 18-year-old girl. After serving her sentence for the demonstrations, she dropped out of sight.[11]

20 | *Auto Row*

I DID NOT TELL Helen I had been arrested. I knew she would not approve and hoped she wouldn't find out. That was wishful thinking. The newspapers had published the names of those arrested. A daughter of a teacher at her junior high school who was a freshman at Berkeley read the fine print in the newspapers and recognized my name. She told her mother, who told my mother, who phoned me. The outrage and anger in her voice still rings in my ears. She was not sending me to college to get arrested, she said. That was not the return she expected on her investment. Picketing was one thing, but if I ever got arrested again, I could forget about more financial support from her. I was pretty angry myself. It was my life and my decision, I told her. The phone lines crackled for about twenty minutes before she hung up, having gotten no promise from me to stop. Socrates had a greater hold on my mind than Helen did on my pocketbook. Five weeks later I was arrested again.

Helen was not the only one who disapproved. We were denounced by almost everyone in authority. Governor Brown said we endangered people's lives by blocking entrances at the Sheraton-Palace, set back the civil rights cause, and made it more difficult to defeat Proposition 14, which would void the Fair Housing Act. Mayor Shelley said we were "wild, irresponsible and thoughtless." On March 12th, prominent churchmen issued a statement saying that "the hope that these tactics have produced a victory for the Negro is a dangerous illusion." Our elders came up with a litany of reasons to discredit us, the most frequent of which was that the demonstrators were mostly white, even though the leaders and spokespeople were Negro. The clergymen said, "To the credit of our Negro fellow citizens, let it be noted that their part in these unfortunate events has been minimal." The *Examiner* quoted one "Negro leader" saying that we "had no more concern about the negro than [Governor] Bilbo [of Mississippi]." Columnist Charles Denton asked how "do responsible Negro leaders really expect to be taken seriously when they allow themselves to be represented in their struggle by an 18 year old girl in the full flush of adolescent arrogance, some students who figure getting their heads cracked is easier than cracking a book and a few retired beatniks who think anything at all beats working?" And of course the DuBois Club connection with the Ad Hoc Committee exposed us to redbaiting. All the daily newspapers denounced our outrageous tactics, including the student newspapers at Cal and San Francisco State. Our only press support came from two *Chronicle* columnists: Herb Caen and Arthur Hoppe. Hoppe normally wrote in a humorous vein, but he was quite serious when he compared us favorably with the "firebrands" of the Boston Tea Party. "One man's heroes are another man's bums," he wrote. "It just depends on which side you're on."[1]

I had no specific plans to be arrested again, but it was already in the cards. A newly militant NAACP set up picket lines on Auto Row on February 21st after a futile month trying to find someone willing to even discuss hiring more Negroes. (Auto Row was Van Ness Avenue, on which a plethora of car dealers had their showrooms.) On March 9th, Dr. Burbridge, a pharmacology professor at the University of California Medical School, told reporters that "out of 260 employees, San Francisco Cadillac has hired only seven Negroes." On March 14th, 107 people were arrested in front of the Cadillac agency, including twenty Cal students and/or Berkeley residents. The mayor negotiated a moratorium on civil disobedience while picketing continued and discussions began.[2]

Other employers were also under investigation and on the agendas of different civil rights organizations. CORE was looking into the Bank of America, which had 29,000 employees in California. CORE had found that minorities were only 2.4 percent of its employees and Negroes only 1.9 percent, with none in executive positions. Of course Bank of America disagreed, but the bank's general counsel said, "We are always ready at any time to sit down and discuss the problems with responsible representatives of any minority group."[3] It did seem like the demonstrations were having an effect.

One consequence of my arrest was that I became part of an identifiable group of civil rights activists. We saw each other at meetings and on campus, where we reinforced each other's commitment to the movement. If the charges had been dropped, I think a lot of the students who had been arrested would have thought twice about doing it again. But because they were not, and because our actions generated so much discussion, we had to defend ourselves time and time again. The more we argued, the more committed we became. I had doubts about the desirability of getting arrested before my first arrest; by my second I had none.

As my commitment to the Civil Rights Movement grew, I realized that I should take Helen's threat to disown me seriously. The house I ran and the rooms I rented kept my expenses down, but not nonexistent. I needed a more reliable income, so I got a job.

It was the perfect job.

State Controller Alan Cranston was running for the U.S. Senate seat occupied by Clair Engle, who had an inoperable brain tumor. No one was surprised that Cranston wanted to be our senator; he was the "most eligible" candidate in the state. We were surprised when Pierre Salinger, who had served as President Kennedy's press secretary, made a last-minute decision to run for the seat. Although born in California, Salinger lived in Virginia and wasn't even eligible to vote in California. After CDC endorsed him in February, Cranston opened a northern California campaign office in Oakland, run by Democratic Party stalwart Joe Close. I was hired to work there twenty hours a week for $1.15 an hour, plus bus fare. It was only minimum wage, but I could work any twenty hours I wanted in an office that was open twelve to fifteen hours a day, seven days a week. This was a compatible schedule with going to class and to demonstrations, and eventually to court.

I told the UYDs that I was in charge of literature distribution for northern California, but it was only political puffery. In reality I was a shipping clerk. But it was a political job that I expected to last through the summer and to lead to greater things if Cranston beat his Republican opponent in November. Shortly after I started, Toni lost her job as a secretary at the Student Activities office, so I introduced her to the campaign. She was hired for more money than I got but with less flexible hours.

For two weeks, picketing and negotiations continued between the NAACP and the Automobile Dealers Association. Then they broke down. The dealers published their own "Declaration of Policy" that emphasized that they were already equal opportunity employers. They asked the NAACP for a list of qualified applicants seeking jobs in their showrooms, but the NAACP replied that it was not an employment agency. Unlike the South, which wanted to keep Negroes in their place, what was at stake in the North was whose responsibility it was to rectify the consequences of decades of oppression and discrimination. The civil rights organizations wanted more than passive "equal opportunity." They wanted San Francisco's employers to actively recruit Negroes for good jobs and train them if necessary. The NAACP asked the auto dealers to agree to a goal of "16 to 30 percent employment of minority group persons in future job turnover openings." The employers were concerned about their bottom line; they didn't want costly training and recruiting responsibilities. And they didn't want anyone telling them how to conduct their business.[4]

On April 6th, representatives of the United Freedom Movement held a press conference. CORE chairman Bill Bradley stated that Auto Row "will receive what it justly deserves" if a hiring agreement was not reached soon. "What it justly deserves" was a veiled reference to more sit-ins and civil disobedience. A mass demonstration was announced for Saturday, April 11th, at 11:00 A.M., and volunteers were invited to paint signs in preparation.[5]

I was in the basement of Cranston headquarters packaging and labeling on April 11th while the second Auto Row sit-ins were going on. I wanted to be there, but duty compelled me to go to work. In the afternoon, Joe Close said he was driving to the City and did I want to go along? Did I! Toni decided to come as well. Joe dropped us off near Van Ness Avenue, which was closed to traffic, and went about his business. We joined the line outside the Cadillac agency. Most of the arrests had already happened. Several hundred people had picketed three auto agencies for a couple hours before half went inside. In one showroom, they crawled into and under the cars and sat in the offices. In the rest they just sat on the floor.

The police started at the Lincoln-Mercury dealer and, after cleaning it out, went on to Chrysler and Cadillac. The paddy wagons were backed into the showrooms, which conveniently had doors big enough for vehicles to enter. Although no one said so, there appeared to have been an agreement worked out with the cops to minimize everyone's discomfort. Demonstrators were not told to link arms and legs, and while going limp was still encouraged, no one was hassled for walking to the paddy wagons. The police had received special instructions on handling protestors and were almost gentle. Four at a time, one for each limb, they carried the limp bodies and hoisted them feet first into the paddy wagons. There was no tossing, no dragging, no dropping.[6]

There were only a few dozen pickets left when Toni and I arrived. Someone announced that this was our last chance to be arrested, as the Cadillac agency would close at 5:00 P.M. I asked Toni to come with me, but she declined. She had become more political during her months in my house, but she wasn't ready to get arrested. She was not a student and not part of the student subculture. Social and parental disapproval still loomed large in her mind. I gave her my purse to take home, since I now knew what happened in booking and didn't want to consign it to the property clerk.

Ten of us went inside, dispersed, and sat down on the floor, neither singing nor chanting. "Six youths and five adolescent girls invaded the showrooms" the *San Francisco Examiner* said.[7] A few cops stood nearby along with a dozen other people just watching or taking photos. A plain-clothes officer recognized me from previous demonstrations and came over to say hello. After we chatted for a few minutes, a captain appeared and ordered our arrest. No one even asked us to leave. A boy standing to the side, adorned with a beard and a CORE button, was also arrested, despite his protestation that he had just come in to watch. No other watchers were arrested. I lifted my arms and uncrossed my legs to give the cops an easy grip. Fifteen seconds later I was in a paddy wagon. A few hours after that I was out of jail and back home.

This time 226 were arrested. The newspapers didn't list us separately by sex and I didn't try to figure out how we divided up from the names. We were charged with disturbing the peace, trespassing, unlawful assembly, and remaining present at a place of riot.[8] Bail was $78, or $35 more than was usual for these minor misdemeanors. The NAACP raised the money to pay the bail bondsman, who gave us all ballpoint pens imprinted with his ad: "Don't Perish in Jail. Call Barrish for Bail." Based on information published about arrestees and observations by myself and others, I concluded that the Auto Row sit-ins had more adults and fewer students than those at the Palace, and many more Negroes. While the papers described the pickets as "predominantly white," we thought it closer to 50 percent. More Negroes were also arrested, though I don't have an exact count. Sixty percent of the arrestees gave their occupation as "student"; those listed as "teacher" were probably grad student TAs. As before, "laborer," "clerk," "secretary," "printer," and "unemployed" were the only other occupations listed by more than one or two people. Only 65 percent were between the ages of 18 and 23.[9]

Once more we were condemned. Once more the demonstrations had their intended effect. The pickets continued. On April 13th, the national NAACP announced it would hold demonstrations against auto dealers in fifty cities, beginning on May 4th with a protest at General Motors headquarters in Detroit. The Lincoln-Mercury dealer who had received the worst of the April 11th sit-in settled on April 17th. That same day Bill Bradley promised there would be 2,000 demonstrators on Saturday and possibly "creative destruction." With thousands of people massed on

Auto Row ready to go in again, a sit-in was avoided at the last minute when both sides made pledges to the Mayor's Interim Committee on Human Relations, created because neither side would negotiate with the other. The NAACP got the promises it wanted, and the auto dealers got peace.[10]

This ended the massive sit-ins in San Francisco for civil rights and jobs for Negroes. CORE began picketing the Bank of America around the end of May but could do little more than inconvenience some of the local users of its 900 branches throughout the state. Pickets rarely numbered more than thirty to fifty and could only hit a few branches at a time. In June, CORE began a version of the shop-in. Protestors dressed like normal bank customers lined up to request change from tellers, then lined up again to turn it into bills. Those with Bank of America accounts withdrew and redeposited the same money. Nothing illegal, but definitely disruptive. When the bank got an injunction against the "stall-in," instead of negotiating, Bill Bradley asked the governor and the mayor to intervene. They did. While insisting that its hiring of minorities was ongoing and laudable, Bank of America signed an agreement with the California Fair Employment Practices Commission which provided for regular reports of its recruitment activities and success rates. CORE wasn't mentioned, and the bank's general counsel said he didn't care if CORE approved. The San Diego CORE chapter held a sit-in, but nothing came of it. In late summer, Bill Bradley announced that the Bank of America action was suspended; nearly 240 Negroes had been hired in white-collar jobs between May and July.[11]

The demonstrations had spillover effects on other employers. These didn't make the papers because they weren't spectacular, but were highlighted in organizational newsletters. An *S.F. CORE-lator* mailed in April 1964 reported that "during the past four months the Employment Committee, . . . has negotiated and signed over 375 agreements with major corporations in the San Francisco area." These had "measures designed to affirm within the employer's own organization an equal opportunity hiring policy, assurances that the management will encourage and seek job applicants from minority groups, and the right of CORE to make regular evaluations of the progress made by management in its hiring policy and in the actual number of minority group employees."[12]

Once again I did not tell Helen I had been arrested. Once again she found out. This time it was ice and not fire in her voice when she phoned. I had disobeyed her. She was serious about her threat to cut me off, she said. She would teach me a lesson. I didn't ask her to reconsider; I was ready, I had a job. At 18, I had come to the conclusion that it was time to cut the apron strings and this was as good a reason as any. I've been self-supporting ever since.

21 | *Clogging the Courts*

THERE WERE MANY reasons that the sit-ins ceased. Employers were more amenable to negotiation with civil rights organizations once they assessed the alternative consequences. The mayor of San Francisco encouraged employers to do a better job of recruiting Negroes and arranged agreements with them to do so. CORE was torn apart by racial strife as more Negroes joined what had been a heavily white organization. The NAACP was rent by factionalism over its role in the sit-ins; taking the lead in fostering militancy was not consistent with its tradition of responsible leadership of the Negro community. The Ad Hoc Committee shifted to Oakland, where it picketed the *Oakland Tribune* and the restaurants around Jack London Square until it fell apart from exhaustion and internal acrimony in the fall of 1964.[1]

Another reason was that the time and energy of those people willing to sit in was siphoned off by the trials. Although the Hotel Employers Association agreed to drop its civil suit as part of the Palace settlement, only the district attorney's office could dismiss the criminal charges, and it declined to do so. The sit-ins had been blasted by so many public officials and respectable community leaders that leniency was not politically wise.[2] Quite the opposite: they wanted to teach us a lesson. I'm not sure that we learned what they intended to teach us, but we did spend a lot of time in court.

The Sheraton and Auto Row arrests created the potential for 500

trials at a cost of hundreds of thousands of dollars—perhaps millions—
for judges, prosecutors, court officers, police, and courtrooms. Quite a
few attorneys, most recruited through the National Lawyers Guild, volunteered to handle our cases, at considerable cost to them of time away
from their private legal practices. The attorney who coordinated the legal
work, Beverly Axelrod, worked almost full-time on it for three months.[3]
To comply with the constitutional requirement for a speedy trial for
criminal defendants, the San Francisco city courts suspended all civil trials for several months. As a ploy, our attorneys asked for individual trials, knowing very well that "this sort of thing could mean a complete
breakdown in our judicial system," as one judge said. Then they asked
for a mass trial of those arrested at each sit-in. Although the DA was
willing, this was rejected by the administrative judge as impractical and
unfair to the defendants. The court decided that we would be tried in
groups of ten to fifteen, alphabetically, except for juveniles. Some trial
groups were all women, while most were all men. The thirty-four women
in Sheraton II were tried in two groups, except for a few, including Tracy
Sims, who were tried with some of the men. Six ministers arrested at
Cadillac II requested and were given a separate trial, before deciding to
plead nolo contendere—no contest.[4]

The defendants had several meetings to decide whether we should go
to trial or plead nolo contendere. The latter has the same legal effect as
a guilty plea, but one doesn't have to admit guilt under oath or endure
the burden of a trial. To persuade us to do this the DA offered us sentences of 30 days suspended, a $25 fine, and six months' probation. Our
lawyers said this was a lighter sentence than was likely if we were found
guilty after a trial. They also said there was a passable chance a jury
would find us not guilty because of the free speech issues raised by what
we were doing. But to us, guilt or innocence wasn't the issue. We knew
we were guilty of something; would a trial, which was available only
if we pled not guilty, achieve any larger social good? Some argued that
if all of us insisted on trials it would clog the courts and this would
make the city more reluctant to arrest future demonstrators. Others said
this would adversely affect the normal court population, including other
criminal defendants who might stay in jail longer before their trials.
Some argued that we could use the trials for further education of the
jurors and the public, others that the audience was too small and too
remote for this to be practical. Some felt that we would waste our time
sitting through trials; others felt that any opportunity to talk about the

evils of discrimination should be used. In the end, we voted overwhelmingly to go to trial. Of course, each individual could plead as she or he wished, but once the vote was taken there was a certain social pressure to comply.[5]

I was one of many who had real doubts about what was the right thing to do. I reread the literature on civil disobedience, but it didn't resolve my conflict. If I knowingly and willingly broke the law to attract attention to a social evil, what right did I have to then plead not guilty before a court? How could I ask a jury to find me not guilty, especially when I didn't challenge the law itself as unjust? Those who had written about civil disobedience did not face the same situation. Gandhi, who was held up as the most exacting theorist of nonviolent civil disobedience, had declined to plead or participate in his trials at all. He held the British courts in India to be illegitimate and denied that they had any jurisdiction over him. Thoreau was no help. His famous essay "On Civil Disobedience" was originally given as a lecture entitled "On the Relation of the Individual to the State" to explain his refusal to pay poll taxes in 1842 to a government that supported slavery and condoned a war against Mexico. His was an isolated act of an individual against a state he felt was acting illegitimately, for which he spent one night in jail. Our protests were part of a collective action against private businesses in which we violated laws that were not improper or unreasonable in themselves. We violated the law not as an act of conscience to protest unjust actions by the state but to pressure private business owners to act according to our own values and to gain attention for our cause. Why should we now ask the community to acquit us?[6]

In the end, it was Socrates whose example I followed. He defended himself before the jurors of Athens. He was found guilty by a bare majority, but, unlike Gandhi, he acknowledged the right of the state to try him. In ancient Athens, the prosecution and the guilty defendant each proposed penalties and the jury chose between them. Socrates initially said that a person like him was so useful to the state that it should give him free meals; then allowed that perhaps he should pay a small fine. The prosecution asked for his death, and that is what he got. As related by Plato in the *Crito,* Socrates' friends arranged for him to escape and live his life out in exile, but when presented with that opportunity, he refused. To reject the decision of the judges would be impious. Exile would be worse than death. The state is my father and mother, he told his friends. It gave me life, and it can take it away. He would defy the state to satisfy his conscience but not to protect his life. Socrates drank the hemlock and died in 399 B.C., but it was a noble death. Twenty-four hundred years later it influences us still.

22 | On Trial

THE TRIALS WERE more of a circus than the sit-ins had been. When picking a jury, each side can challenge prospective jurors, some for cause and some without cause. The DA's office systematically challenged all Negroes in the jury pool, either by getting them to admit sympathy for us during voir dire or with a preemptory challenge. On some days "the challenges were so thick and fast" that the jury pool became depleted. Some of the Negroes who were left on the juries complained of being browbeaten by their fellow (white) jurors during deliberations. We became a political football tossed between judges running for office, some playing to the liberal element in the city by being lenient toward us and some appealing to the less liberal by being severe. One judge increased bail to $500 each; another lowered it. The presiding judge ordered all defendants to be in court every day, including jury selection. Our lawyers protested that California law did not require this for misdemeanor trials, that the students would miss class and the workers would miss jobs, and that being present for the often-lengthy jury selection served no purpose. It was up to individual judges to issue bench warrants for missing defendants; some did, some didn't. I missed the first day of jury selection in my second trial because I wasn't notified until that evening that it had begun. The judge issued a bench warrant for my arrest but it was rescinded when I appeared the following day. One of our lawyers, Vincent Hallinan, had four sons and his wife among the defendants. Terrance, nicknamed Kayo, a third-year student at Hastings Law School, was in his father's trial group. The father told the son to go to class during jury selection for his trial. By the end of the first day, Kayo was in jail for failing to appear in court, even though he came for the afternoon session. Hallinan, known for his leftist politics and flamboyant trial technique, subpoenaed Mayor Shelley, who, to everyone's surprise, came to court. Judge Elton Lawless wouldn't allow him to testify.[1]

My first trial began on April 16th, the week after my second arrest. It ended a month later, on May 12th. There were fourteen of us, all women. Our two attorneys, Beverly Axelrod and Alex Hoffman, would become much better known in a few years as legal counsel to the Oakland Black Panthers. Our judge, Fitz-Gerald Ames, was sympathetic to our cause but not to our personal schedules. He conducted our case only four hours a day to allow time for other court business. Jury selection lasted a week, during which we had to be in court every day. Judge Ames let us put into evidence pretty much everything we wanted, in particular information on *why* we were at the Sheraton-Palace and refused to leave. Roselyn Leonard, the one Negro in our group, sang "The Lord's Prayer" for the jury (to show how we disturbed the peace). Only three of us were supposed to give extensive testimony about our motives, and I wasn't one of those selected. The rest of us were just supposed to testify briefly about where we were when arrested. But when my time came, the prosecutor asked me *why* I was there, and I told him. He probed more and more. I warmed to the task. For two hours we played verbal volleyball. He lobbed me hard questions, trying to get me to admit that I wanted to harm the hotel financially in order to force it to do something I had no right to force it to do. I bounced them back. I don't remember quoting Socrates to him, but I did quote Edmund Burke and President Johnson to explain what I was doing there, as well as the statistics on how few Negroes were employed by the Sheraton-Palace hotel.[2] All of this was part of our strategy to put the Palace on trial. Thanks to the judge who let everything in, the assistant district attorney couldn't stop us. The indictment of race discrimination that came out in our testimony was summed up and synthesized in Axelrod's brilliant closing argument. After our acquittal, the defendants and the jurors held hands and sang "We Shall Overcome" while the judge bowed his head.

The results of the trials were as erratic and inconsistent as what happened in the different courtrooms. Although there was no final count, a preliminary count of roughly forty trials over four months found that about half of the defendants were convicted, though it sometimes took two or three trials to do so. About a quarter got jail time (not suspended), with or without fines. The average jail sentence was 30 days. The heaviest went to Dr. Burbridge. When a second jury convicted him, he was sentenced to 90 days on each of three counts, to run consecutively for nine months in the county jail. After he served 30 days when he lost on appeal, Governor Brown commuted his sentence to time served.[3] None of the women in the Sheraton II trials were convicted except Tracy Sims. All of the codefendants in her trial group, men as well as women, were acquitted. She was sentenced to 90 days in jail and fined $200. Even the *San Francisco Examiner* was distressed by this. It editorialized against the "singling out of Miss Sims" because "it was not right to pick one defendant and make her a symbol of the guilt of all."[4] That the other women escaped conviction didn't mean they got off easy. Jackie Goldberg had two trials, with two hung juries, lasting three to four weeks each. Jackie was appalled when she did not recognize the cop who testified he had arrested her. At the Palace she was linked between two large longshoremen who did not let go. After futile attempts to pull them apart the cops lifted them as a group and put them in the paddy wagon. This took a long time, during which she watched the cops closely; the cop who claimed her at trial was not one of them. Her brother Art was acquitted after a one-week trial, as were the other men in his group.[5]

I too found my trial very costly, despite the acquittal. The bus fare over the Bay was fifty cents each way. A dollar a day was a lot of money —almost an hour's work as a shipping clerk. There were no car pools. To save money, I hitched from Shattuck Avenue. Every morning I stuck out my thumb and waited for a driver to pick me up. Fortunately, this trial was in a courtroom at City Hall, located at a popular freeway exit, instead of the Hall of Justice, which was farther away. Each afternoon I went to the entry ramp and hitched back across the Bay. In the two-hour lunch break I studied. After court I went to work. I didn't go to class for a month. Educationally, the trials were both a benefit and a burden. I wrote the best term papers of my college years about my participation in the Civil Rights Movement, trying to synthesize what the great minds thought about civil disobedience and civil rights with my own experience. That year was the first time I was able to meld thought and action—to think out what I was doing and act on what I thought. I had never learned so much and thought so deeply as I did then. And I had never been so exhausted. I got As on the term papers, but those courses for which comprehension required class attendance more than reading, which graded on exams not papers, were a disaster. My GPA was lousy, but I did pass all my courses and didn't drop any of them. So many students requested incompletes (which weren't given for the asking) that President Kerr discussed it with the Regents at their May meeting. What to do was left to the good judgment of Dean Towle.

Denying incompletes to arrested students was not the only punishment debated that spring. Assemblyman Mulford (R-Berkeley/Oakland) demanded that the Regents expel or suspend students with two or more arrests, even before conviction. In April, he told the press that "there can be no room for those who repeatedly violate the law" when there were so many "law-abiding students" deserving admission. He released a list of 412 people arrested at eight Bay Area demonstrations from the May 13, 1960, anti-HUAC protests at San Francisco's City Hall through the first Cadillac picket on March 14, 1964. Of those whose academic affiliations could be ascertained, 107 were from Cal. This "included 22 graduate students, 84 undergraduate students, 1 professor." Mulford also called for a special legislative investigation of student protestors. President Kerr rejected these demands on May 5th in his Charter Day address at the UC Davis campus, when he said that what we did off campus we did as citizens, "outside the sphere of the University." This did not end the debate inside the administration. Vice-Chancellor Sherriffs sent a confidential memo to Kerr on May 19th with his own analysis of the Mulford list. He found that 108 current and 50 former students had been arrested and noted that they were disproportionately from the Departments of History, English, Sociology, Anthropology, and Political Science. He recommended that incompletes not be given unless a student was in court during an exam.[6]

My second trial began on July 13th and ended July 21st. Four of us arrested in the "rump" sit-in at Cadillac II were tried together, one in absentia because he went home to Philadelphia for the summer. Charges were dropped against the boy who had stood on the side merely observing us sit in the showroom. Of the other six, some were juveniles and others pleaded nolo. Since there were only three of us to face the jury, two girls and a boy, we sat at the defense table with our attorney, Arthur Brunwasser, rather than in the courtroom as did the defendants in the larger trials.

During jury selection the prosecutor systematically excluded all Negroes and objected to anyone with a college degree. Jury selection took a little over four days, the trial less than two, and the jury only two hours to convict us. I was the only defense witness and only testified for forty-five minutes. Judge Andrew J. Eyman was not Judge Ames. He sustained every prosecutorial objection to anything I tried to say other than that we were indeed in the Cadillac agency on April 11, 1964. He would not let me testify about why we were there or tell the jury that no one told us to leave. He signaled to the jury his own opinion of our actions through repeated references to "participation in illegal or unlawful demonstrations." The jury got the message. The prosecution dropped three of the counts, but we were all found guilty of trespassing.

The following day Judge Eyman sentenced us to 15 days in the county jail and fines of $29 and gave us a lecture. We didn't go directly to jail. Our attorney thought the judge's conduct at trial and insufficient evidence presented by the prosecutor gave us a basis for an appeal on technical legal grounds. We went with him to post the appeal the next day and were fortunately released on our own recognizance; that is, without having to post bail. It would be almost two years before our appeal was denied and we had to serve our sentences.

Although a guilty verdict certainly seems worse than an acquittal, it wasn't worse by much, at least not in the short term. Each arrest cost me a month of my life; the first in trial and the second split between trial and jail. Fortunately I didn't have to pay my attorney, or the month-long trial that led to an acquittal would have cost more than the six-day trial with a fine of $29. Guilty verdicts do give you a permanent record, but so do arrests. For many years every time I filled out an employment application, I had to answer yes to the question "Have you ever been arrested?" After ten years or so, this changed to "Have you ever been convicted?" to which I still had to answer yes. By the mid-1980s, it was "Have you ever been convicted of a felony?" and I could finally answer no. Whenever a government agency takes your fingerprints, whether for an arrest, a job, or some other purpose, a copy goes to the FBI. This record does not always include the trial outcomes. Anyone with access to that file—and a lot of institutions have such access—knows how many times I was arrested, but not that the arrests were for demonstrations or the verdicts. Criminal convictions have other consequences, even when just for misdemeanors; some plague me still. It is never the case that one "pays one's debt to society" and that is the end; a criminal record lasts forever.

Did we get fair trials? That is hard to say. In the 1980s, after I became a lawyer and even an assistant district attorney for a couple years, I retried my own cases in my mind. I concluded that I was legally guilty the first time, when I was acquitted, and legally not guilty the second, when I was convicted. The main lesson I learned from these trials was that neither judges nor juries reach verdicts based on the law and the facts as much as they do on their own gut-level sense of right and wrong. Juries pay more attention to the accused and the circumstances than to what the law says about the act. They add to the equation their feelings about whether this particular defendant *deserves* to be convicted, and on the same facts sometimes reach different conclusions for different defendants. Judges don't let juries think alone. Judges influence the outcome by controlling what evidence the jury considers and by signaling to the jury their own opinion. What I learned from the cases I tried as a criminal prosecutor reinforced the lessons I learned from my trials as a criminal defendant.

Should we have pled nolo? If we wanted to reduce the costs to us of our actions, the answer is clearly yes. We asked to be arrested; we knew we were breaking the law. We did not insist on trials in order to "prove" our innocence but to use the courtroom as a forum to continue publicizing our cause. The immediate personal costs of the guilty verdicts weren't much higher than the acquittals; the price of a nolo plea would have been much lower for us and even more so for the judicial system and the taxpayers. But if we wanted to make still more personal sacrifices for the cause, insisting on full trials was a good strategy. They got as much press coverage as did the sit-ins; if the former were a means of educating the public, so were the latter.

Was the city wise to try us? I'm sure the authorities thought that if they dealt with us harshly it would prevent future illegal demonstrations. Their actions probably discouraged some people and did have a dampening effect on the movement. But the trials also became a badge of honor which attracted others to the cause. In the next year, students at both Berkeley and San Francisco State went from civil rights sit-ins to occupying campus buildings. Over the next few years, authorities in most states concluded that it was not a good use of their budget to arrest, or to try, those who commit civil disobedience. The deterrence was minimal and the expense was great. I've been in and/or watched many demonstrations and mass arrests since 1964. Now police try to avoid arrests, and prosecutors often dismiss those that do occur. Civil disobedience has become institutionalized as a protest technique—much as striking, picketing, and pamphleteering were before it—and law enforcement agencies no longer view suppressing it as part of their job.

The difficult issue is not whether we should have demanded trials—they served a purpose—or whether we were guilty of breaking the law—we were. The real issue for a democracy is the proper sentence for those who violate the law for political purposes. Should crimes committed for a social good be punished more, the same, or less than crimes committed for personal gain? One can argue this either way. Indeed, the criminal law itself acknowledges the importance of intent.

While intent is a crucial issue in most criminal cases, I do not think that a selfless motive justifies an acquittal, though there may be some circumstances in which that is the most appropriate response. Those who deliberately and knowingly break the law for a political purpose to achieve a social good should not expect the act itself to be judged by a different standard than those who do so from personal motives. But sentencing is a different matter. Sentencing is where the judge, as the embodiment of society, assesses the person and the circumstances, not just the crime. Sentencing is where society weighs the importance of an act and the context in which it occurred against the harm it caused. In sentencing, motive should matter a great deal. In our trials it did matter. Those who were convicted were sentenced far more severely than those breaking the same law whose purpose was "only" criminal.

Our sentences reflected the fact that there is a hidden court in back of every trial, though this is more true of political trials than those that are strictly criminal. It is the court of public opinion. Like it or not, sentences illuminate popular attitudes toward laws and the people who break them. Laws, people, and purposes that are disapproved of are treated more severely than those on whom society smiles. Civil disobedience became institutionalized—with arrests but no trials—largely because the causes of most demonstrators were on the winning side of history. People who are arrested for causes which do not acquire a righteous aura continue to be tried and sentenced harshly.

Socrates found death noble when done for speaking the truth, and far preferable to exile. If I had paid more attention to de Tocqueville, I would have learned that in our society political dissidents and social heretics are not punished with death as they were in ancient Athens. They are condemned to internal exile. "In America," he wrote in the 1830s, "the majority raises formidable barriers around the liberty of opinion; within these barriers an author may write what he pleases, but woe to him if he goes beyond them." Those who offended with their views might remain at liberty, but "your fellow creatures will shun you like an impure being; and even those who believe in your innocence will abandon you, lest they should be shunned in their turn."[7] Ensconced as I was within a community which supported my actions for civil rights, it would be a long time before I understood these words. Those on the cutting edge of social change are always shot at and sometimes shot down.

It's those who come after—if they ride the winning horse of history –
who are heralded as heroes. "Speech" in America is "free" only within
limits; those who "speak" outside those limits inevitably pay for the
privilege.

But even knowing what I know today, I would still have done what
I did. And I still think Socrates was right. Those who commit civil disobedience are deliberately breaking the law, good or bad, for a social
good. However noble our motives, the state can and should judge us.
And as long as we accept the legitimacy of the state—and I did—we
must comply with that judgment, even when we think the punishment is
unreasonable. I also think Socrates was guilty as charged. He did corrupt
the youth. He certainly corrupted me.

23 | *Freedom Summer*

ON THE SECOND of June, the sky fell. Alan Cranston lost the primary
election for the Democratic Party nomination for U.S. Senate to Pierre
Salinger.[1] This not only poked a big hole in my political hopes but portended economic disaster for me. I no longer had a job, or much hope of
getting another one. The few summer jobs around were already taken,
and I knew I would have to go to court again sometime that summer,
which made it hard to work regular hours. My lease ended June 15th.
Berkeley partially depopulated during the summer, so it wasn't feasible
to keep the house and rent it out, even though rents went down between
June 15th and September 15th. Toni and I moved down the block to
2006 Parker, where we rented the entire first floor for only $90 per
month for the summer. The rent was cheap, but since neither of us had
a job we weren't sure how we were going to pay it after the first month.

My head was filled with thoughts of Freedom Summer, the voter registration project in Mississippi which invited hundreds of northern students to break the back of white supremacy in the worst of the southern states. The Kennedy administration had been urging civil rights organizations to concentrate on voter registration of Negroes for some time. After Reconstruction ended, the southern states had slowly disenfranchised Negroes through intimidation and voter restrictions such as the white primary, voter registration, literacy requirements, and the poll tax. In 1960, only one-fourth of the eligible Negroes in the South were registered to vote, in Mississippi only 4 percent, and in some counties none at all. With financial assistance from private foundations, the civil rights organizations created a Voter Education Project in 1962 to register Negroes to vote in the southern states. Civil rights workers, whether outsiders or locals, met stiff resistance through harassment, arrests, and beatings. Particularly in Mississippi, the federal government seemed unable or unwilling to protect citizens trying to exercise the simple right to vote. In November 1963, the Voter Education Project withdrew its funding from the state because the results were so meager.[2]

The most active civil rights organization in Mississippi was SNCC. The Student Nonviolent Coordinating Committee had formed in 1960 to coordinate sit-ins and other direct-action projects. Ella Baker, executive secretary of the SCLC, invited activist students from the Negro colleges to a spring conference at Shaw University, where she midwifed the birth of a new organization. For a while SNCC's home was a desk in the SCLC office, but it wanted to be free of "adult" interference and soon moved out on its own.[3]

In 1961, SNCC staffer Robert Moses began a voter registration campaign in McComb, Mississippi. Registering to vote in Mississippi was no simple task. Each applicant had to appear before the county registrar, fill out a long application, and interpret a section of the state constitution selected by the registrar, who then decided if the applicant was qualified to vote. When Moses organized classes to teach Negroes to pass this exam, he and other SNCC workers were repeatedly beaten and jailed; one local farmer was murdered. In 1962, Moses joined with Aaron Henry of the NAACP and David Dennis of CORE to create COFO—the Council of Federated Organizations. COFO became the umbrella organization for the 1964 summer project, though it was mostly an SNCC endeavor.[4]

SNCC was unique among the major civil rights organizations. Created by students, it was run by its field staff, whose daring, dedication, and commitment created a mystique. SNCC was a "redemptive" organization, more akin to a holy order whose members lived their beliefs as well as sought change in the wider society. They lived in the communities in which they worked on only subsistence pay. Overalls, not suits, were the SNCC uniform. When SNCC asked northern students to come south for the summer, it was a summons to virtue.[5] SNCC's decision to do this had not been easy. Its voter registration efforts were met with increasing violence by Mississippi whites toward Negroes, culminating in the assassination of NAACP leader Medgar Evers on June 12, 1963, in the driveway of his home in Jackson, the state capital.

Believing that outside intervention and national publicity were the only means of securing for Mississippi Negroes the right to vote, Moses decided to organize a parallel election, at which anyone of eligible age and residency could vote. If large numbers of Negroes turned out for a symbolic election, it would dramatize to the nation that they were not allowed to vote in the real one. SNCC needed a larger temporary staff to do this, so Allard Lowenstein, a white attorney working with the southern movement, asked friends at Yale and Stanford for help. About 100 white students spent two weeks in Mississippi before the November 1963 general election mobilizing 83,000 unregistered Negroes to vote in a mock gubernatorial race. While Berkeley and San Francisco State students were picketing Mel's Drive-In, Stanford students were raising money, writing letters, and working for the Freedom Vote. This success convinced COFO to formally sponsor the Mississippi Summer Project, which would bring several hundred northern students to the state to work on voter registration, freedom schools, and community centers. When John Lewis, chairman of SNCC, spoke on campus in December, he told us we might be needed in the South, but the actual summer project wasn't announced for many weeks.[6]

As the civil rights organizations prepared for the students, so did advocates of white supremacy. In the spring of 1964, Ku Klux Klan klaverns were organized in twenty-nine Mississippi counties. The Ku Klux Klan was not a single organization but a label claimed by many separate groups; it applied to most of those who used violence to maintain the racial status quo. The original Klan was formed during Reconstruction by Confederate veterans to keep by stealth and intimidation the power whites had lost in the war. It disbanded as southern whites recaptured control of state and local governments, which then passed laws to keep Negroes from voting. A nativist organization that formed in Georgia in 1915 adopted the name and used the Klan's aura to grow throughout the

South and into many northern states; it was particularly strong in Indiana. Boasting 4 million members at its peak during the 1920s, its targets were mostly immigrants, Catholics, and Jews. By the 1950s it had shrunk to a bare 10,000 members, concentrated in the Deep South, with a headquarters in Tuscaloosa, home of the University of Alabama. The Civil Rights Movement revived the Klan. Indeed, the Klan divided and multiplied into several separate organizations, all claiming to be the one true Ku Klux Klan.[7]

The Klan was credited with the deaths of three civil rights workers early in the summer. CORE staffers Michael Schwerner and James Chaney and volunteer Andy Goodman weren't the first to die for the movement, but they were the first to die in the glare of national publicity sufficient to force a major FBI investigation. President Johnson sent 200 feds into the state to look for them upon their disappearance. On June 21st, the day after the first group of summer volunteers entered the state, the three workers had been arrested for speeding in Philadelphia, Mississippi, while investigating the bombing of a Negro church. Once released, they were not seen again until their bodies were dug up on August 3rd. All three had been shot; Chaney, the one Negro, had been badly beaten.

When their disappearance was announced, Campus CORE organized a sit-in at the U.S. attorney's office in San Francisco. With thirty-five students blocking his door, U.S. Attorney for San Francisco Cecil Poole allowed campus CORE chairman Tom Miller to phone Assistant Attorney General Nicholas Katzenbach from his office and read a statement. At closing time, the demonstrators were physically thrown out of the building but not arrested.

Chaney, Goodman, and Schwerner, plus a volunteer who died in a car crash, were the only deaths from the summer project, but there were many more victims. SNCC documented 1,000 arrests, eighty beatings, and the bombings of thirty-seven Negro churches and thirty Negro homes. Reports from Mississippi were big news for months, especially among civil rights activists in Berkeley. It was a long hot summer.[8]

24 | *Summer Session*

THE SECOND WEEK in June, after the semester ended, Helen came to Berkeley to make sure that my house was left clean and to get her deposit back from Mrs. Roberts. She was in a foul mood, angry about my forthcoming trial and angry that I intended to complete my last fourteen units in summer school and earn my degree in August, a decision which would deprive her of seeing the traditional graduation ceremony. After a couple hours of cleaning house and enduring her growls, I left on a pretext. While I was gone, Allan stopped by and entered without knocking. We often left the door unlocked as burglaries were not common and there was usually someone in the house. I returned to see Helen chasing him out the door with a broom. Someone called the police. After the dust settled, Helen packed her car with my encyclopedia, hi-fi, and some other household stuff brought from Northridge the previous year and drove home.

Helen should have been thankful that my second trial kept me in Berkeley; otherwise I would have gone to Mississippi for Freedom Summer. Only my obligation to appear for trial kept me from applying to COFO. Once I faced the fact that I could not go south in June, I began to think long term. I did not want to work for civil rights in the South for only a summer, I wanted to stay as long as necessary. I figured I could afford to wait a couple more months and finish my degree first. This plan was undermined by the loss of my campaign job and faded when I couldn't find another one. UC charged tuition for summer sessions. I had paid for the first session but couldn't afford to pay for the second or even for textbooks for the first one. Toni picked up temp work as a secretary while I did odd jobs such as store inventory and guinea pig in psych experiments. We scraped together enough for the second month's rent, but not much more. Our food budget was, to put it mildly, meager.

The need to economize challenged our cooking skills. Stale bread at twenty cents a loaf and lettuce at ten cents a head made lettuce sandwiches our staple. Our diet improved considerably when a passing friend suggested we scavenge in the bins behind the grocery stores. They throw lots of good stuff in there, she said. She was right; the bins were full of fruits and vegetables with only a few blemishes on them. We only had to wash them and cut out the rotten spots. Some of the things we found, like eggplant, I had never cooked before. Between the discount bread and regular nighttime scavenging trips we ate okay, except for protein. Toni and I created an informal competition over who would eat our "weekly meat" first. I got mine by arranging invitations to the co-op eating units, whose members could invite one guest a week to dinner. Toni got hers by getting her various boyfriends to take her out. She usually won our contest, but then she had to deal with the boys who generally expected her to sleep with them in exchange for her meals. After a while she just refused to answer the phone and insisted that I handle yesterday's boyfriends.

By the end of my second trial and the first summer session, I had had enough of school and of Berkeley. I chafed to be free of classes and desperately wanted to go to work in the South. I told everyone I was going to drop out and split. There was important work to be done; history was happening right under my feet and it wouldn't wait until I could finish school. That I did not do this is due solely to the personal intervention of James Townsend, the professor in charge of the Political Science Honors Program. This program allowed a small group of us to meet weekly for two years to discuss interesting books and ideas with one professor. It was a striking contrast to the impersonality that was typical of a Cal education. Professor Townsend heard I wanted to drop out and invited me to his home to discuss it. We talked for three hours. By the time I left, he had not only convinced me to stay in school but had suggested a suitable topic for my senior honors thesis (the lack of which was one more reason for leaving). He recommended that I write on civil disobedience.[1]

It was too late to go south, but not too late to join another Freedom Summer project—the demand by the Mississippi Freedom Democratic Party (MFDP) to be seated in place of the regular Mississippi delegation at the Democratic Convention which would be held the last week in August in Atlantic City, New Jersey. The MFDP was another product of the parallel voter registration drive. Officially founded on April 26, 1964, in Jackson, its members tried to attend regular Democratic Party precinct and county meetings; when rejected, they held their own. Its candidates for senator and three congressional seats in the June 2nd Democratic primary were resoundingly beaten. (In the November general election, the MFDP sought and was denied a ballot line as a separate political party.)

SNCC/MFDP decided to challenge the right of the Mississippi Democratic Party to seat its delegates at the national convention and recruited a few white Mississippians into the MFDP so it would be an integrated delegation. Summer volunteers simultaneously brought 17,000 Negroes to register as voters, of whom 1,600 succeeded, and informally registered 80,000 into the MFDP in their homes and churches.[2]

The most prominent spokesperson for the MFDP was Fannie Lou Hamer. Born in 1917 and raised in the Mississippi Delta, she was one of SNCC's earliest local recruits, its most persistent, and eventually its most famous. Her sonorous voice and eloquent speeches, as well as her courage in the face of beatings, evictions, and death threats for registering to vote made her a symbol for young people all over the country, black and white, who thought that politics should be about the pursuit of justice rather than pure self-interest. Hamer finally registered in January 1963 and cast her first vote for herself in 1964 when she ran for the Democratic Party nomination for Congress. Although the best known, Hamer was just one of several women who were at the core of the MFDP. Victoria Gray, who also ran for Congress in 1964, Annie Devine, and Unita Blackwell were all members of the 1964 MFDP challenge delegation who played key roles in the Civil Rights Movement in their communities. These women made lasting impressions on those who met them or even just heard them speak and watched them work.[3]

MFDP leaders recruited northern support long before the summer began or the party was officially founded. The California Democratic Council voted its approval at its February endorsement meeting. In March, Joseph Rauh, longtime liberal Democratic Party activist with ties to the Americans for Democratic Action and the United Automobile Workers, agreed to be the MFDP's lawyer and present its case to the convention credentials committee. On August 6th, the MFDP held its state convention, where 800 people chose sixty-four Negroes and four whites to represent it in Atlantic City. By then "nine Democratic state delegations and twenty-five Democratic congressmen had expressed support for the challenge."[4] The challenge would take place not just inside the convention but outside as well with a vigil on the Atlantic City boardwalk.

I had already demonstrated at the Republican Convention, which was conveniently held in San Francisco the same week as my trial. CORE picketed the convention headquarters hotel during the day and the convention itself during its evening sessions in the Cow Palace, an arena built just south of the city limits.[5] Although the Republican members of Congress had traditionally been more supportive of civil rights than the

Democrats, whose committee chairmen were usually southerners, this was changing. When the Civil Rights Act passed the Senate on June 19, 1964, Arizona senator Barry Goldwater, soon to be the party's nominee for president, was among the twenty-seven senators voting no. This was reason enough for CORE to demonstrate.

During the day, when not in court, I wandered through the convention hotels, picking up literature and sampling the buttons. Jerry Fishkin had asked me to pick up buttons for his collection, and I was starting to collect for myself. I already had Democratic campaign buttons, but that was because I wore them. Picking up opposition buttons in order to put them on a bulletin board or in a box required some attitude adjustment. I had never been surrounded by so many Republicans, and they seemed like a strange breed. I was in enemy territory.

One evening I even got inside the convention hall for half an hour. Traditionally, delegates demonstrated on the floor after their candidate's name was put into nomination. This convention was so dominated by Goldwater that the plethora of also-rans didn't always have enough delegates for a respectable demonstration in front of the all-seeing TV cameras. Michigan governor George Romney's convention managers came to the gate where we were picketing to solicit warm bodies to demonstrate on his behalf. Toni and I both ran to get in. While she was frantically showing her Michigan driver's license to prove her bona fides as a Romney booster, I slipped through the human barricade. Although I went in in good faith, I found it hard to scream and yell for Romney, about whom I knew little and cared less. As a dedicated Democrat, I was so overwhelmed by the Republican signs and slogans that my usual curiosity and desire to explore new political territory was quickly extinguished. I left.

So focused were we on civil rights for Negroes, both during and before the Republican convention, that we barely knew new ground was being plowed for women. None of us learned from the press that in February the word "sex" had been added to Title VII of the 1964 Civil Rights Act which prohibited discrimination in employment. None of us knew that the President's Commission on the Status of Women had issued its report the previous fall. I did know that Senator Margaret Chase Smith of Maine was running for the Republican nomination for president, but only because I picked up several of her unique oval rose pins. I didn't know that her candidacy was even more unique. Smith was the first woman to pursue a major party nomination; one of her reasons for doing so was "to break the barrier against women being seriously considered for the presidency of the United States." I didn't listen to her nomination while exploring the convention and was completely oblivious to the new awareness about women that all these things indicated. In this I was typical of female students.[6]

As plans for the MFDP challenge were aired in the press, Toni and I decided to go to the Democratic convention together. Since we couldn't afford bus fare, we would hitchhike. We had hitched together a couple times, but never so far. During spring break we hitched to Northridge; Helen picked us up after we got to the Valley and drove us to a good pickup spot on the highway north when we were ready to leave. One weekend in June we hitched with two other girls down the coast to Big Sur, camping out at night. Toni had also hitched a lot with boys; neither of us had hitched alone. In preparation, we talked with others who had hitched long distances to benefit from their experience. I went to the law library and looked up all the statutes on hitchhiking in the states we might pass through so we could avoid those with severe punishments. All the statutes had pretty much the same language—"no person shall stand in the roadway for the purpose of soliciting a ride from a private vehicle" —but neither words nor penalties correlated with what others told us about how local police and highway patrol officers dealt with hitchhikers. Picking our route would be a gamble, though we figured cops would go easier on girls.

The last week in July, Toni learned that she would not be able to attend San Francisco State in the fall because Wayne State hadn't sent her transcripts in time for her to be admitted. Then she ran into some friends who were driving to New York. They offered to drop her off in Detroit, so she packed up and went back to her parents. I was pissed at her for deserting me. How would I get to Atlantic City by myself? I asked around for other students going to the vigil, but the only one with a car was Art Goldberg and his roommate Sandor Fuchs. Art told me they didn't want a girl along. I looked for someone else to hitchhike with me but found no takers. I told people that if I couldn't find a ride or a hitching partner, I'd go by myself. Everyone said I was crazy; it was too dangerous for girls to hitchhike alone.

Except Allan.

He said, "Sure, you can do it. I'll take you to the highway when you are ready to go."

He'd already told me how to finance the trip, not that hitchhiking cost very much. Allan worked in a San Francisco restaurant called the Spaghetti Factory. On the wall was a poster with a mushroom cloud sur-

rounded by the words "GO WITH GOLDWATER." It was very popular. He suggested I have some buttons made up like the poster and sell
them at the Democratic Convention. He offered to finance their manu-
facture and keep a few hundred to sell himself. I could pay him back
when I returned. When Toni finked out, I had several hundred pink buttons waiting to be sold.

Other arrangements were in the works. Allan was going to sublet our
apartment. He expected to go to Ohio in the fall to attend graduate
school in education at Antioch, but he wanted to stay in San Francisco
and earn money as long as possible. His lease was ending, and he didn't
want to sign for another year when he only needed another month. I had
made deals with two local media in exchange for press credentials so I
could get inside the convention itself. The *Daily Cal* gave me a press card;
it didn't want a story on the convention but asked me to stop off in Arlington, Virginia, on the way and interview George Lincoln Rockwell,
head of the American Nazi Party. I had an address from an ANP leaflet
I picked up when Forbes spoke on campus. Radio station KPFA gave me
a letter of introduction for the convention itself. One of three affiliates of
the Pacifica Foundation, it was a center for alternative culture and politics. I'd done a little volunteer work for them, and the station manager
was happy to reciprocate. He told me that WBAI, the New York City
affiliate station, would be handling all coverage of the convention and I
should offer my services to it (though I'd have to get a convention credential on my own).[7]

I bit the bullet and told Helen of my altered plans. She was cool
about it, having learned that angry opposition didn't deter me from anything I seriously wanted to do. She told me to mail her a postcard every
day I was on the road so she'd know I was still alive. Perhaps because she
taught those in their early teens, she recognized more than I that a penchant for risky behavior was the adolescent impulse; no doubt she had a
few stories from her own youth that she did not wish me to know. So
instead of a lecture, she made a reasonable request. On Wednesday morning, August 12th, I bought stamps and postcards. At noon, Allan drove
me to the highway and let me out on the shoulder.

25 | *Hitchhiking*

I STOOD ON THE shoulder of the highway with my thumb out, half frightened of and half excited about what promised to be a great adventure. I lugged a large plaid suitcase, the only one I owned, which was much too large for a 5,000-mile trek. I had filled it with everything I could think of that I might need—buttons, camera, film, and clothes. It weighed about fifty pounds. I also carried a large purse and a coat. I had thought long and hard about what to wear, one of the very few times in my life that clothing concerned me at all. Personally I preferred pants. But the dress code of the day required respectable middle-class girls to wear skirts in public. In all my years at Berkeley, I never saw a girl go to class in pants or shorts; they were prohibited at dinner in the dorms. I knew girls got rides quicker than boys. Despite my long hair, from a distance a driver might think a hitchhiker in trousers was male and pass me by. On the other hand, I didn't want drivers to get the wrong idea. I had heard that girls who dressed provocatively invited assault. And while I did not personally know anyone who had been sexually assaulted (it wasn't something good girls talked about), I believed the conventional wisdom that you ask for what you get. I finally settled on a blue pleated skirt hanging a few inches below my knees and a plain blue striped blouse as the best compromise between attracting a ride and deterring assault. I had not yet thought about who would stop to pick me up and who I should refuse. I soon found out.

Men.

When I hitched with Toni and the other girls, the drivers who stopped for us varied. Most were men, but there were also families and even single women, and the guys were often young like us. Ninety percent of the cars which stopped for me when I hitched alone were occupied by single males, mostly middle aged. Initially I turned them down. Soon I realized that if I kept refusing rides from men, I'd never get anywhere. I changed my rules to include cars with only one man, but never more than that. Offers from men were not in short supply.

Neither were problems. For a young California woman of the early sixties, I was relatively naïve and innocent. I knew little of the animal side of men from direct experience; most of what I knew I had learned from Toni. The first truck that stopped to pick me up had two men in the cab. When one eagerly leaned out his window to invite me in I could see lust contorting his face. It scared the shit out of me. It was a long time before I would accept a ride from a trucker, though they were the most likely long-distance drivers. I was wiser when I returned a month later. I calculated that roughly 90 percent of my rides were with single males, and about 90 percent of those propositioned me. Initially I tried to figure out which men were safe, based on the few seconds I had to size them up before deciding whether to get into a car. I avoided those who seemed too happy to see me, any car with more than one male in it (most of the time), and anyone not going a long distance. I also refused anyone who wanted to make a short stop, anyplace, or take a short detour. "Just let me out," I would say, "and I'll find another ride."

I quickly figured out that a good story was crucial. The first ride I accepted took me onto Highway 40 past Vallejo. He asked my age, and I truthfully said 18. He then asked why I was hitching, and once again I was too truthful—no money, I replied. "How would you like to earn a couple dollars?" he asked. I didn't need to ask how. I just said NO definitively, and that ended that. This taught me my first two mistakes: I admitted to being of legal age and implied I might need money. After that I lowered my age to 17, sometimes to 16, and talked about a need to go see my boyfriend or my brother who had suddenly become ill, was conveniently located several hundred miles away, and would be concerned if I didn't show up soon. Someone had told me to hint that I had VD—that would be the best deterrent—but I just couldn't do it. Saying NO early and often was generally my best defense. I was often surprised at some of the men who thought a girl in his car was sexually available. In the Midwest I was picked up by a 40ish man who said he had just dropped his daughter off at college and I reminded him of her. Ten minutes later he asked if I would go to a motel with him. By the end of my trip I had learned that it was neither provocative dress nor physical attractiveness that turned a female into potential prey; it was vulnerability. As one guy told me: "A piece of ass is a piece of ass is a piece of ass." All he cared about was could he get some.

Most of the men wanted to talk, and conversation was the one thing I was willing to provide. Some of the guys were interesting. Outside Sacramento an immigrant from Holland picked me up and told me about all the people who called him a "damn foreigner" because of his accent. I spent the first night in a bus station someplace in Nevada; I wasn't willing to hitch at night. The second night I lucked into a driver doing an all-nighter. I dozed but was reluctant to sleep. I carried maps—available free from gas stations, planned my route, and if a driver wanted a different one, checked to be sure it would get me where I wanted to go. I had been told to avoid Utah—the cops were merciless—so I turned north at Highway 93 before Highway 40 entered that state and picked up Highway 30 near Twin Falls. Superhighways were just being built; these western roads were generally two lanes. From there it was a straight drive to Chicago. I had no reason to go to Chicago, but I needed some sleep and had the address of the CORE Freedom House where I expected, and got, a warm welcome and a comfortable pad on the floor.

August 15, 1964

Dear Mom:
Made it to Chicago. This is a BIG city. And it has subways, though I think they call them "els." It feels so crowded here. The buildings are tall and they are so close together. Have you ever been here?

Hitching out of a city was often harder than hitching in, but Chicago made it easy. Just south of South 61st Street a ramp rose from Michigan Avenue into the Chicago Skyway, which took you to the turnpike. I waited on the block before this entrance until someone stopped who was going well into Indiana and would let me off at a rest stop. I didn't want to stand with my thumb out on an exit/entry road where toll takers might look askance on my solicitation of a ride from a private vehicle. The rest stops were a challenge. I tried standing at the exit lane, but cars were accelerating and didn't want to stop. Eventually I moved to outside the restaurant and just asked those departing where they were going and could I have a ride. A lot of people looked at me strangely, but it worked. The turnpike went to New York; I was going to DC. I had to find just the right car taking the US 70 turnoff. When I arrived it was late, and all I had was a phone number. I didn't phone the aunt I had lived with two summers before or the two that lived in Arlington because I knew that they would disapprove of what I was doing and my mother would catch flak for "letting" me hitch (as if she had a choice). Fortunately someone answered for CORE and gave me the name of a CORE couple who housed civil rights workers. I ended up in a large house in northwest Washington with four times the number of rooms as people.

August 18, 1964

Dear Mom:
    I'm in DC. No, I didn't call Leslie. Don't think she really wants to hear from me. Besides, I found a great place to stay. I've got an entire room, not just a couch in a crowded studio. I'm trying to get press credentials; will see if my local pols can help.

It was one week before the Democratic convention began. I went to the MFDP/SNCC office to tell them I would be in Atlantic City and available for whatever was needed. The staffer gave me an address to go to when I got there but didn't know of anyone driving I could ride with. I showed her my anti-Goldwater buttons and said I was going to finance the trip by selling them. Someone in the office was fascinated by them (maybe another collector?) and offered to make a large poster replicating the button, as advertising, in exchange for a few. I returned two days later to pick it up. I also visited all the campaign headquarters to collect more buttons. My largest finds came from the Goldwater headquarters; Republicans seemed to have more of everything and were eager to give it away.

My primary task in Washington was to get press credentials so I could get inside the convention hall. The Democratic National Committee told me that all media credentials were given out by the congressional press galleries, and it was really too late to get anything. I went to see Joe Beeman, now working as Congressman Philip Burton's administrative aide, whom I knew from CFYD. He made a couple phone calls. The bad news was that my *Daily Cal* press letter was useless; college publications were not given credentials to the Democratic convention. The good news was that my letter from KPFA might get me something. Joe sent me to the radio/TV press gallery, and the man I showed my letter to told me to see him in Atlantic City and he'd see what he could do; while all the press passes had long since been allocated, not all would be claimed.

Despite the fact that my *Daily Cal* letter was of no use, I still felt obligated to interview the ANP leader as I had promised or at least to make a good-faith effort. The leaflet I had picked up when Forbes was on campus gave the address of the National Headquarters as 928 North Randolph Street in Arlington. I hopped on a bus and went looking for Nazis. At that address I found a small house on a large but bare lot on a nondescript street lined with other small houses. A sign over the porch said "WHITE MAN . . . *FIGHT!* SMASH THE BLACK REVOLUTION NOW." I knocked on the door not knowing what to expect and was rather surprised when a polite young man answered the door. He was dumbfounded when I said I was from the *Daily Cal* and had come to interview Rockwell. After asking me to wait, he brought the "duty officer" to see me. Frank Mengele said that Rockwell was not there and only gave interviews by appointment, but if I wanted to come in and talk to them, I could do so. I did.

Inside were four rooms: one had an offset press and printing paraphernalia; another was a wood-paneled office with a shrine to Adolph Hitler. Pictures of Hitler, Rockwell, and George Washington stared from the walls. I interviewed four men ranging in age from 22 to 36. Two were high school dropouts; one had served in the Navy and then gone AWOL; all had been in jail. The one who had gone AWOL was recruited to the ANP while in jail. He said the party gave him a sense of purpose in life; he no longer fought the cops, he fought for the white race. Most of them said they had stopped drinking, smoking, and brawling after joining. While the ANP tried to distinguish itself from the German variety of Nazis, the ones I spoke to made no distinction between "kikes" and "niggers"—terms they used as though they were names rather than epithets. As for the whites who supported "race mixing," they were all dupes. Mengele told me that the ANP had 700 members nationally, twenty working full-time, seven in jail, and a mailing list of 15,000. I took several photographs with my Brownie Bull's-Eye camera and left. Back in Berkeley, I took my notes to the *Daily Cal* and offered to write a story, but there was no interest in anything but an interview with the ANP's main man, and that I did not have.

Saturday I hitched to Atlantic City. I thought it would take a couple hours, but it took all day. I caught a bus to the Beltway, the large expressway which surrounds Washington, but while I got a ride onto it with no trouble, it was a long time before a car stopped that was going to Baltimore, and he wasn't going all the way. Although the expressway had shoulders, the cars were going so fast and were so close that it was somewhat dangerous for drivers to stop. After two hours I was only on another beltway outside of Baltimore. The next car that stopped had lights and sirens; it was the Maryland Highway Patrol. My heart sank. I had visions of being arrested or at best driven far from the expressway and dumped. I told the officer that I was going to New Jersey where my sick brother was anxiously awaiting me. He noted the CORE button I had forgotten to remove, and said, "This is the South, you know." I quickly removed the button. "Get in the car," he said, opening the door to the back seat. He drove off, with me quaking in the rear, but didn't get off at the next exit. I heard him talking on his radio phone to another officer about me but wasn't sure what he was saying. Many minutes later he pulled up under an overpass where another highway patrol car was waiting. I was moved from one car to the other, and the second one drove off. The officers didn't tell me what was going on, but at least we were going in the right direction. Miles later I was transferred again; the third officer let me out at the Delaware border. The Maryland Highway Patrol solved the problem of what to do with an errant female hitchhiker by ferrying me out of their state. I should always be so lucky.

I wasn't. Getting to Atlantic City took the rest of the day, many, many rides, constant consultations with my map as drivers took local routes to their destinations, lots of waiting with my thumb out, some walking with my 50-pound suitcase, and a fair amount of trepidation. It was like tacking against the wind. I couldn't get there directly, but I did get there eventually. When I checked in at the CORE/SNCC headquarters, I was even given a place to sleep. Local families housed those who came early; those who came later would sleep in a church. For the next week, I shared the home of Mrs. Evelyn Moore on North Ohio Street.

26 | *The Democratic Convention*

THE MFDP WAS pursuing a legal strategy separate from the vigil on the boardwalk, which was organized by CORE and SNCC. From its headquarters at the Gem Hotel on 505 Pacific Avenue, it lobbied the credentials committee and the delegates to replace the regular Mississippi delegation with its own. It made three arguments: 1) The Mississippi Democratic Party was not democratic because Negroes were systematically excluded from the political process. 2) It was not deserving of seats at the convention because it was not loyal to the national party or its candidates. In 1948, the national Democratic candidate, President Harry S Truman, had not even been on the ballot in Mississippi because the Democratic state central committee listed Strom Thurmond as its candidate instead. In 1960, a state party convention held after the Los Angeles convention had specifically repudiated the national Democratic Party platform and its candidate. 3) Mississippi was too much of a "closed society" to reform itself and "hence can only be brought into the mainstream of the twentieth century by forces outside of itself."[1]

While I was hitching to Atlantic City, Fannie Lou Hamer was telling the convention credentials committee what had happened when she tried to register to vote in Mississippi. The live broadcast was replayed that evening. Soon the entire country knew Hamer's story and what Mississippi did to Negroes who wanted to vote. When the right to represent a state party was challenged, the convention rules called for the credentials committee (composed of one man and one woman each from fifty-five states and territories) to hear testimony and to vote. If 10 percent of the committee signed a minority report, the matter would be brought to the convention for a final decision. Joseph Rauh, who presented the MFDP's case to the credentials committee, didn't expect to win there but did expect enough support for a minority report and a chance to present the MFDP's case before the assembled delegates. Despite the fact that the national party normally deferred to state party law and rules in selecting a state's delegation, Rauh said there was precedent for seating both delegations and for splitting Mississippi's allotted votes.[2]

Sunday I tracked down the man I had spoken to in the radio/TV press gallery. As promised, he gave me a press credential in exchange for my KPFA letter. "Perimeter" was stamped on it and I soon found that this only got me into the convention hall, not to the bowl where the delegates sat. There were three levels of press passes: floor, seat, and perimeter. The latter were given out to flunkies and runners, which at best was what I was. My fantasy of watching the convention firsthand was dashed, but the pass got me inside and I was happy to have anything at all. He also gave me a railroad-lounge pass, which turned out to be invaluable. For decades, the nation's railroads had sponsored press lounges at both parties' conventions where members of the press could sit, drink, eat, read each other's newspapers, and now, watch TV. During the day, if I needed a Coke or just respite from the heat, I could find it there. During the evening convention sessions, if I wasn't on the boardwalk, that's where I could watch the proceedings. It was also a good place to hear the "other side" of the ongoing debate about the credentials challenges.

The main use the MFDP had for someone like me was to lobby my state delegation to support the challenge. However, the California state convention had endorsed it on August 16th, and only when the delegation leaders began to waver was there any lobbying to do. My perimeter pass let me carry in press releases and literature and distribute them in the warrens of press cubicles and tables laid out underneath the arena. Once a day I reported to KPFA's sister station, WBAI, but I was never given an assignment. Most of my time was spent sitting on the Atlantic City boardwalk with the other vigilers, holding my sign as a shield from the heat, watching the people go by, and memorizing the patterns in the wooden planks at our feet.

The boardwalk was often crowded, but not with us; sometimes our 50 to 100 vigilers were lost in the swirling crowds. The neo-Greek decorations of the convention hall provided a symbolic entry to the Democratic convocation inside and an ironic backdrop to the democracy in action outside. A temporary fence had been erected from the front doors to create a path past us to the street at the side. Opposite, across an acre of herringbone boards, was a covered walkway, below which was the beach. We sat in-between, rain or shine, usually facing the convention center so press and delegates would see our signs. When it showered we huddled under blankets, and when the sun beamed we ducked into the small patch of shade created by each sign. Our signs had drawings of Schwerner, Cheney, and Goodman and slogans such as "Help Produce Democracy," "One Man, One Vote," and "Seat the Freedom Delegates." A flatbed truck with a burned-out car that SNCC had brought from Mississippi was in a nearby parking lot. "Miss. Klan Response to Negro Vote Drive," said one sign on the side. "Talk About US on the FLOOR," said another. A burned-out cross and several American flags decorated the vehicle.

We weren't the only demonstrators. Shortly after noon on Monday, eight American Nazis showed up in uniforms with swastikas. I recognized the "duty officer" I had interviewed a few days before, but not the others. We sat there nonviolently while the YDs attacked the Nazis. The ANP fought back until the police arrived to arrest them (the Nazis, not the YDs). At different times there was picketing from Women's Strike for Peace, the American Taxpayers Union, and a group protesting busing of schoolchildren for integration.

If President Johnson had let the process work, the MFDP might, or might not, have been seated. But he was determined to stay in control; nothing would happen at *his* convention that he did not want to happen. After hearing testimony, the credentials committee created a sub-committee to find a solution. But LBJ was really running the show; he decided to give the votes to the regular delegation and seats in the bleachers as honored guests to the MFDP. Johnson operatives began twisting arms, telling delegates what would happen to them if they supported the MFDP challenge. LBJ told Minnesota senator Hubert Humphrey that if he wanted to be vice president he had to persuade the MFDP to accept the inevitable and not cause trouble. After two days the offer was sweetened; MFDP chairman Aaron Henry and vice chairman Ed King, the white chaplain from Tougaloo College, were invited to be delegates-at-large, with Mississippi's votes going to whomever among the regulars would swear an oath to support the national party ticket. LBJ vetoed Hamer, also an MFDP vice chairman, as a voting delegate because he didn't want "that illiterate woman" to speak from the floor. She was even excluded from most of the back-room meetings. For three days there was a lot of talk about negotiation and the need to compromise, but in reality neither occurred. Johnson made his offer; the MFDP could take it or leave it.[3]

Inspired by Fannie Lou Hamer, the MFDP chose to leave it.

"We didn't come all this way for no two seats," she told anyone and everyone. After hearing several speeches, pro and con, the MFDP delegates voted 64 to 4 against the proposal. But what it wanted made no difference. The motion to seat the regular delegates was rushed through the credentials committee so fast that it was announced as unanimous even though Rauh (who was a voting member from the District of Columbia as well as MFDP's counsel) and several others voted no. I was one of hundreds waiting outside. When word reached us, I could feel the anger flood the crowd. It's the closest I've ever been to being in a riot. Someone began marching us down the street, singing and chanting. By the time we got to the convention hall, our anger had been diffused, but the sense of betrayal was still palpable. Back at the hotel, MFDP staff were phoning members of the credentials committee looking for the eleven signatures necessary for a minority report; only nine could be found in the short time remaining before the official recommendation was submitted to the convention that evening for its rubber-stamp approval.[4]

The Mississippi regulars were just as unhappy as the MFDP with LBJ's solution. Only four signed the loyalty pledge; the rest went home. The MFDP borrowed delegate credentials from friends in other states and sat in the vacant seats assigned to Mississippi. Their silent protest was captured on nationwide TV. Brian Turner, who had just finished his freshman year at Cal, was one of those who helped them do this. He had come to the convention from Washington, D.C., with his father, who was president of Local 77 of the Operating Engineers, vice president of the International, and co-chair of the D. C. delegation. From him, Brian got a couple floor passes and ferried in MFDP members by recycling the passes to bring in several "delegates." Johnson was nominated by acclamation without a vote; none of the Mississippi votes were cast by anyone.

The convention vote was an anticlimax, but the consequences of the conflict would reverberate for years. For several days, three struggles had been waged in Atlantic City. The political contest—who had the power—went to LBJ. The legal fight was a tossup; the MFDP had persuaded many that it had a tenable claim to Mississippi's votes. The moral victory—who was *deserving*—went to the MFDP. While the principles the MFDP represented would carry greater weight in the long term, initially it was the heavy hand of power politics that won. LBJ *claimed* victory; the MFDP *felt* defeated. The treatment its delegates received from the national Democratic Party reminded them of life in Mississippi: power at the top dictated the outcome, the voices of ordinary people were ignored. Power even decided who among the grassroots would speak for them. If LBJ had let the credentials committee and the convention delegates vote as they saw fit, all would have seen the democratic process in action. Because he acted like a powerful politician concerned only with imposing his will, he tainted the entire Democratic Party in the eyes of the most active and dedicated civil rights workers, especially the young. He made it harder for them to see "working through the system" as a viable avenue for social change.

Among the MFDP supporters I saw that week were a dozen Cal students, most of whom had come from their homes in New York. The ones I talked to after Tuesday were outraged at the callous treatment received by the MFDP. I was more sad than outraged, primarily because my sojourns inside the convention hall had exposed me to so many with alternative views. The reporters and the delegates I spoke to thought that the concessions made to the MFDP were major ones and emphasized that its professed goal of an integrated delegation would be met by the new requirements for the 1968 convention. To the practical politicians who had obtained their seats from whatever means were used in their states, a late-term transfer of votes from one Mississippi group to another outside that state's process was not the right response to disenfranchisement of a class of voters; the remedy was new rules for the next convention. They saw the world through different eyes than did the MFDP and its supporters.

My fund-raising activities gave me still another example of how perception shapes response. For a few hours each day I sold my anti-"Go With Goldwater" buttons. I moved a couple hundred feet down the boardwalk in order to keep my roles separate, put on a straw hat sporting large LBJ buttons, and held up my poster, which replicated the pink buttons that lined the top. I was quite amazed at how many people thought I was demonstrating *for* Goldwater. Roughly 20 percent of the people who stopped spoke to me harshly—until I pointed to the mushroom cloud between the words and the LBJ buttons on my hat. Then they apologized and often bought a button, or two, or three. Business was very good. I sold out and had the problem of turning the coins into bills so I could carry them and keep them safe. I gave $50 to the MFDP and a few bucks to Mrs. Moore for the breakfasts she had fed me and left on Thursday while President Johnson was accepting the nomination.

27 | New York City

Aug. 31, 1964
Dear Mother:
    Since I was this close I had to go to New York. Went to the UN and couldn't very well miss the World's Fair. I'm staying with the daughter of a woman I met in Atlantic City. She was in charge of feeding us and finding places for the 100 odd people to sleep. Starting from scratch with no money and no promises she did a remarkable job. In fact it was the only well organized part of the whole demonstration.

The previous spring, CORE had focused several demonstrations on the World's Fair. Three hundred were arrested for blocking the New York City Pavilion. A brief sit-in on the Triborough Bridge halted traffic for a while. Brooklyn CORE, which regularly broke new tactical ground, threatened to block access to the Fair for the opening ceremonies on April 22nd by having hundreds of cars run out of gas on the access roads. However, it only had a dozen vehicles and the advance publicity kept most of the public away.[1] After weeks of boasts, threats, and counter-threats, demonstration day was wimpy. But the publicity it generated was mammoth; hundreds of column inches and equivalent TV time educated the public about CORE's concerns. By the time I got to the World's Fair, all signs of protest had faded. In fact, the movement was shifting from organized nonviolent direct action to unorganized violent direct action.

New York City had had its own long hot summer. The morning of July 16th, an off-duty police officer shot a 15-year-old boy who lunged at him with a knife. That night Senator Barry Goldwater told the Republican convention that "extremism in the defense of liberty is no vice. . . . Moderation in the pursuit of justice is no virtue." Two days later, CORE turned a Harlem rally that was called to protest the disappearance of the Mississippi civil rights workers into one on police brutality. After a march on the local police precinct became unruly, all hell broke loose. By the next morning one person was dead, scores were injured, hundreds of windows had been broken, and dozens of shops had been looted. The riot spread to Brooklyn and was followed by sporadic disruption until rain drenched the city the following Thursday. Whites in the neighborhood around police headquarters made their own protest—hurling rocks and rotten vegetables, damning the Negroes, and rooting for Goldwater.[2]

One casualty of the New York City riots was leadership, or, more accurately, the belief that established Negro leaders spoke for the masses. The people who stormed the streets acknowledged no one as their representatives, either Negro or white, whether elected, organizational, or appointed. Throughout the week black leaders called upon the rioters to cease, while other, less well known, personages told the cops to get out of their community. "Law and order" competed with "self-defense" as rhetorical themes. The people who came to the streets at night to throw bottles, break windows, carry off merchandise, and yell obscenities at the police ignored all pleas. Seeing this, New York City's white establishment wondered if there was some organized conspiracy promoting the riots. Nationally, Democratic leaders worried more that a white backlash would give the election to Goldwater than about the grievances that Negro leaders said were the real impetus behind the riots. After the riot ended, national spokesmen—Martin Luther King, Jr., for SCLC; Whitney Young for the Urban League; A. Philip Randolph for the Negro American Labor Council; and Roy Wilkins for the NAACP—called for a moratorium on demonstrations until after the November elections. This had no effect on the plans of the MFDP, CORE, and SNCC for the Democratic convention in Atlantic City. And, as LBJ and his minions soon discovered, the civil rights establishment could no more bargain on behalf of the sharecroppers who rode the bus from Mississippi than they could persuade the rioters in New York City to stay inside. The disconnection between leaders and masses led everyone to ask, "Which side are you on?"

In between playing tourist, I visited numerous political organizations in New York City, collecting literature and buying buttons, in quantity, at discount. Some groups had offices in lower Manhattan within walking distance of each other. CORE was at 38 Park Row, across the park from City Hall. Several peace organizations, including the SPU and the War Resisters League, were around the corner at 5 Beekman Street. Much farther away I found the ACLU, the Citizens Committee for Constitutional Liberties, the American Committee on Africa, the National Committee for a SANE Nuclear Policy, and a new organization which called itself the Students for a Democratic Society (SDS). My success in selling buttons on the boardwalk had given me an idea of how to support myself my senior year without getting a steady job. I would sell buttons at Bancroft and Telegraph.

On Wednesday, September 2nd, I took a local bus into New Jersey and began the long trek home. Remembering how many drivers had stopped who were only going short distances, I stapled to my suitcase a sign saying "Student to California." With this I hoped to attract only long-distance travelers. I was successful in getting all-night rides, so I didn't have to camp in any more bus stations; all-night drivers wanted conversation to keep them awake. I had the usual hassles and one that was unusual. Standing on the shoulder of Route 66, someplace in New Mexico, I watched in amazement as four taxis pulled up. A middle-aged man with curly hair unrolled the passenger window and asked if I had a driver's license. Yes, I said, and showed it to him. He explained that he was caravanning the taxis to Los Angeles and could use a relief driver so the others could sleep. It sounded good to me, so I hopped in. I assumed they would do an all-nighter, but long after dark the cars pulled over and all the drivers crawled into their back seats to sleep. I slept in the front of my taxi, using my purse as a pillow and my coat for cover. At first light, the curly-headed man awoke and in a groggy voice told me to come visit him. When I said "No thanks," he growled, "Put out or get out." I got out. He removed my suitcase from the trunk, and the taxis drove off, leaving me by the side of the road. It wasn't too long before I got another ride, and this one did go all the way to Los Angeles. The driver left me at a gas station in North Hollywood around 2:00 A.M. on Sunday. I phoned home and told Helen where I was. A half-hour later her car pulled up. She was wearing a robe over her nightie and was only half awake. Saying nothing, she drove to Northridge and put me to bed.

28 | First Week of the Fall Semester

THE DAY AFTER Labor Day I returned to Berkeley. Allan was packing to leave for Ohio. My landlady had rented our floor to four students at double the summer rent. I had a week to find a place to live. I looked for another house and found three which I could have rented out for enough to cover my own room, but the landlords turned me down because I was only 19. Without my mother's backing, my financial credibility was weak. Not that I was broke; from my button money I gave $50 to CORE, paid Allan my share of the cost of the buttons, and still had plenty for a first month's rent and the cleaning fee.

I found a house at 1601 Milvia Street, northwest of the campus, for $215 a month. It was a trek from the student haunts on the south side, but I couldn't afford to be picky. The owners had recently purchased it as an investment and were having trouble finding tenants because one room was occupied by a little old lady whom they did not wish to evict; few students wanted to share their space with an adult. The first floor had two bedrooms with a bath in between on one side of a hallway and a living/dining room and kitchen on the other. Upstairs was another bath plus one large and three smaller rooms with sloping ceilings surrounding a central staircase. No one had to go through anyone else's room to get to their own. I took the large bedroom downstairs that shared a bath with the other tenant and rented out the rooms upstairs. When fully occupied, the rooms paid $210 a month, reducing my living expenses to a manageable amount. My first housemate was Victoria Blickman, a junior from upper New Jersey who would become my political comrade for the year. The other roomers—mostly boys plus one couple—came and went over the months; some may have bonded at times, but I was never part of their group. Much more than the year before, I was just the landlady and house manager.

The following week I registered for classes, paying the "incidental fee" of $120 for the semester. I took the minimum load of twelve units since I only needed eight to graduate and wanted time to write my senior honors thesis. At Bancroft and Telegraph, SLATE was selling the fall *Supplement to the General Catalog,* now grown to sixty-four pages stapled between a spiffy gray cover labeled "Volume II, Number I, Twenty-Five Cents." Due to popular demand, we had enlarged our print run; this issue cost $1,850. Although I had little to do with its production beyond course evaluations, I was listed on the editorial staff, so I caught some of the flak that came from including "A Letter to Undergraduates" by Brad Cleaveland.

Brad was one of those ex-students who were wedded to Berkeley. After graduating in 1959, he continued as a grad student until he received his M.A. in 1962 and was still around in 1964. Born in 1932 and raised in Washington, D.C., Brad had spent four years in the navy between high school and college, where he decided his calling was to be a Presbyterian minister. Brad went from religion to radical politics via the study of political science, serving as SLATE's first treasurer and occasional inside agitator along the way. His many years in the classroom gave him a particular interest in reforming collegiate education. He thought classes and grades were oppressive. Son of a junior high school shop teacher, Brad earned his bread as a union carpenter while writing tracts and working for those causes he believed in. His 12-page call for an "educational revolution" by "open, fierce, and thoroughgoing rebellion on this campus," with demands on the Regents "in which the final resort will be CIVIL DISOBEDIENCE" was largely ignored by the students but read by some faculty and administrators as SLATE's call to arms. Vice-Chancellor Alex Sherriffs wrote President Clark Kerr that it was "deceitful, slander-

SLATE

SUPPLEMENT

TO THE

GENERAL CATALOG

VOLUME II   NUMBER I

TWENTY-FIVE CENTS

The fall 1964 SLATE Supplement published the usual course reviews. Stuck inside were leftovers from a special report published the previous summer, featuring a call for "educational revolution" by Brad Cleaveland (*at right*). Some administrators later claimed this caused the student revolt that fall.

A LETTER TO UNDERGRADUATES

from Brad Cleaveland

Dear Undergraduates,

On May 13, 1963, SLATE published the "Cal Reporter," a newspaper which charged this University with a total failure to educate undergraduates. The paper said that the University pushed the myth that you, as undergraduates, are "training for leadership," when in reality you are training for obedience; that you leave the University with a basic suspicion for intellectuals, and fear of the kinds of thought necessary for you to meet the 20th century world-in-revolution. The theme of a quote from Bertrand Russell ran through the paper:

> "We are faced with the paradoxical fact that education has become one of the chief obstacles of intelligence and freedom of thought."

This is not a minor charge. The charges were clearly focused upon your situation as an undergraduate, and not the graduate schools. The response to the newspaper was astonishing. The Daily Cal made the coy comment that SLATE had again emerged like a "grouchy bear," but that it offered no "constructive solutions." This casual and inappropriate response represented the views of a great many of you, and your professors, and administrators. But those charges were not minor, they were seriously radical, and for the Daily Cal to suggest that we all sit around picking our noses while asking for "constructive solutions" is astonishing!! If the rising waters of a flood threaten to immerse you in death and suffocation, it would be more than ridiculous to reflect on "constructive solutions." Or:

THERE IS NO BLUEPRINT FOR AN EDUCATIONAL REVOLUTION!!!

It was like this: on the one hand there was substantial agreement that the University stamps out consciousness like a super-madison-avenue-machine; on the other, people saying, "So what?" or "Bring me a detailed and exhaustive plan." But there is no plan for kicking twenty thousand people IN THEIR ASSES! No plan will stop excessive greed, timidity, and selling out. At best the University is a pathway to the club of "tough-minded-liberal-realists" in America, who sit in comfortable armchairs talking radical while clutching hysterically at respectability in a world explosive with revolution. At worst the University destroys your desires to see reality, and to suffer reality with optimism, at the time when you most need to learn that painful art. In between those two poles is mostly garbage: Bus Ad; PhD candidates "on the make"; departmental enclaves of "clever and brilliant" students who will become hack critics; and thousands of trainees for high class trades which will become obsolete in ten years.

The first page of Cleaveland's 14-page "Letter," which was published in the summer of 1964 as Vol. I, No. IV of the *SLATE Supplement*.

ous and incredibly hostile." Its "call for revolution" had the "purpose of removing you and Chancellor Strong from office."[1]

What the vice-chancellor thought was a dangerous document was in fact a marketing failure. In order to avoid the bureaucratic hassle of collecting the California sales tax, the *SLATE Supplement* had to qualify for a third-class mailing permit. This required publishing five issues a year. There were only two semesters and thus two occasions to publish course comments. Therefore the "other issues are open to any articles on higher education, ranging in scope from teaching practices to the call for revolution in this issue." Editor Phil Roos carefully disclaimed any responsibility for the views of the author; certainly SLATE as an organization had not officially pronounced its support of Cleaveland's proposals. But given SLATE's history of challenging the university whenever it could, many administrators, some faculty, a few Regents, and eventually newspapers, legislators, and the California Senate Subcommittee on Un-American Activities assumed that "Volume I Number IV" was our revolutionary manifesto.[2]

This issue had been printed earlier in the summer but had not sold well, even for fifteen cents, partially because no one was around to sell it but also because purple prose set in small type didn't command much of an audience unless it was required course reading. At some point the production staff decided to clear the shelves by inserting copies of "Volume I Number IV" inside "Volume II Number I" at no extra charge.

29 | *Eviction!*

ON SEPTEMBER 14TH, Dean of Students Katherine Towle mailed a letter to the heads of recognized off-campus student organizations registered with her office. It said that beginning on September 21st these groups could no longer set up tables, put up posters, distribute literature "to support or advocate off-campus political or social action," or collect money in "the 26-foot strip of brick walkway at the campus entrance on Bancroft Way and Telegraph Avenue between the concrete posts and the indented copper plaques."[1] We were being evicted!

We knew instantly that this would significantly cripple our work. While there were a few places on campus where we could pass out leaflets or put up posters announcing meetings, there was no place where we could set up tables, collect money, or sell stuff to pay for the pamphlets and printing. And few of these eight "Hyde Park" areas, as they were known, were on well-trodden student routes. How could we function if we couldn't collect money at Bancroft and Telegraph or reach students where the crowds were the heaviest? We had to rent space at Stiles Hall just to hold regular business meetings, since they weren't permitted on university property. The primary function of some groups, such as University Friends of SNCC, was to raise money for civil rights work in the South. The student party clubs—the UYDs, the California College Republicans (CCR), and the University Young Republicans (UYR)—existed to recruit people to work in campaigns, clearly "off-campus political action." The new prohibitions would hamstring our efforts to oppose Proposition 14 in November or campaign for President Johnson or Senator Goldwater and the other candidates in the fall elections or even to advertise our off-campus meetings and distribute our regular publications. "No recruiting" meant we couldn't even solicit for members on campus, though a requirement of recognition as an off-campus group was a membership limited to persons affiliated with the university.

Jackie Goldberg, head of Campus Women for Peace, and her brother Art, outgoing chairman of SLATE, called an evening meeting of all the student political organizations to figure out what to do. When the UYD executive board met that afternoon, I offered to represent the UYDs. Its new president, Jerry Fishkin, didn't have time to go to endless meetings and knew I'd keep him informed. I remained the UYD representative until the very end. Initially I also represented the University Civil Liberties Committee (UCLC), a group Allan Solomonow and I had formed the previous spring to sponsor the Nazi speaker if SLATE had shied from the task. We didn't need it for that, but my friends and I decided to continue UCLC to provide an independent voice for civil liberties on campus, and accordingly I had registered the names of ten student members with the dean's office, with myself as president. Vicky Blickman soon took over representing UCLC. While in New York I had visited the head-quarters of civil liberties groups and ordered literature for UCLC to put out. Boxes of pamphlets were already arriving; without the tables at Bancroft and Telegraph, what were we going to do with it and how were we going to pay for it?

We met in Art and Sandor's apartment. Sandor Fuchs was the new chairman of SLATE; he and Art were best friends and housemates. At this meeting were representatives of the entire spectrum of student political groups, from Cal Students for Goldwater to several on the far left and some nonpolitical groups as well. We talked long and hard, trying to make sense of the new situation. The new prohibition seemed so arbitrary and unfair. We weren't doing anything different than we had been doing for years. Why now? One obvious answer was the fall campaigns. Both Prop 14 and the LBJ/Goldwater race were going to be hot; perhaps the administration was engaging in preemptive insulation from charges of political favoritism. It claimed that the university was nonpolitical, but we all knew it wasn't; the Regents, who ran the university from on high, represented conservative business interests and Cal was decidedly liberal. Or perhaps it was continued picketing by the Ad Hoc Committee to End Discrimination. The administration was widely criticized in the spring when so many Cal students were arrested. However the Ad Hoc Committee was now picketing the *Oakland Tribune,* owned by conservative Republican and former senator William Knowland. A university bond issue (Proposition 2) would also be on the November ballot; perhaps the administration wanted to preclude unfavorable news coverage of its students or negative editorials.

Representatives from eighteen student groups went to see Dean Towle on September 17th. At Art's suggestion, what we called the United Front designated Jackie as our spokesperson. She radiated respectability, was a sorority sister (Delta Phi Epsilon), and had a good relationship with Dean Towle. Jackie was a senior. Art had graduated in June as a history major, but, not quite ready to leave the womb, he had enrolled as a graduate student in the School of Education. They were devoted to each other, but their personalities were so different it was hard to believe they had grown up in the same Los Angeles home and gone to the same high school. Native Californians, they were the only children of a housewares salesman and a schoolteacher who voted Democratic. Art had become interested in radical politics while at Morningside High School in Inglewood, where he also played football and won three varsity letters. He was vice president of his senior class. Jackie had been active only in her

Temple. Art went to UCLA; Jackie went to Berkeley. She told Art that Berkeley was the place to do radical politics, a conclusion he had already reached after watching *Operation Abolition,* so he transferred in 1963. While he liked to call himself a revolutionary socialist and his rhetoric was sometimes wild, Art had a pragmatic streak. Jackie leaned left, but at Berkeley she was very much a centrist.

We thought it was particularly important that *all* the student political groups be represented in the United Front. As chair of our meetings, Art worked hard to keep the three conservative groups with us; all decisions were made by consensus, so they had an effective veto over our approach. We knew the administration didn't like SLATE or the more activist groups, but we hoped that as a broad united coalition the administration would recognize the importance of our concerns and find a way for us to continue to function normally.

We were wrong. The administration had no interest in our continued operation. Dean Towle said the problem was traffic congestion and litter, but when we asked for a traffic study, she commented that continued use of our space was "almost out of the question." Later that afternoon, Jackie and Sandor took alternative proposed rules to her. Our seven points required that we police ourselves and see that all student groups act responsibly but also specified that we could collect donations and advocate action "on current issues with the understanding that the student organizations do not represent the University of California."[2] Another meeting was scheduled for 10:30 on Monday morning, the first day of classes and the day our tables were supposed to disappear.

Several groups had set up tables during registration week, and after a lengthy meeting Sunday night, we decided to keep them up. Business as usual seemed like the right response. But we also recognized that we would be in violation of the new rules and thus committing civil disobedience. The consensus of the meeting was that each group would make its own decision as to whether and which rules to violate, but none would denounce any other for making a different decision. This accommodated the conservative groups, which did not put up tables; the UYDs, which put them up at Bancroft but no place else; and the more radical groups, which soon moved their tables to previously forbidden space in front of Sather Gate. We all agreed that no one would get a permit from the City of Berkeley to use the ten feet of public sidewalk. That meant the Republicans couldn't put up tables at all. We were a United Front.

When we met with Dean Towle on Monday morning we learned

that the top campus administrators had met with Kerr on September 18th and modified some of the restrictions, but not by much. We could set up a few tables at Bancroft and Telegraph with organizational posters attached and distribute "informative" but not "advocative" literature. We couldn't collect donations or sell bumper stickers or buttons, and our literature could not "urge a specific vote, call for direct social or political action, or . . . seek to recruit individuals for such action." They did make one concession; on an experimental basis (i.e., it could be withdrawn) the base of the Sproul Hall steps was designated a "Hyde Park" area, suitable for spontaneous speaking, as long as we didn't block traffic or use sound amplifiers.[3] Having taken our cookies they gave us back a few crumbs.

We held our first press conference at 11:30, and the tables went up at noon. Nothing happened. That night we held an all-night vigil on Sproul Hall steps. Many students who would later become deeply involved in the actions of that fall took their first steps toward political participation at that vigil, where a couple hundred students sat and talked all night. We repeated our vigil on Wednesday; our numbers more than doubled. It was slowly becoming evident that support for our demands was broader than the usual cohort of student activists. Those at the vigil were deeply offended that the administration should so capriciously wipe away the political activity at Bancroft and Telegraph. They felt that the opportunity to pick up literature, learn about meetings, buy buttons, and argue with those sitting at tables was part of their education; the political bazaar was one of the things they liked about Cal. At some point Art led a group to picket a meeting of the Regents at University House, only to discover that they had left.

During the week, our support grew. The *Daily Cal* editorialized that the administration had made a mistake. By a vote of 11 to 5 the ASUC senate petitioned Kerr and the Board of Regents to let students collect money and distribute literature "advocating student participation in political and social action" and urging support of candidates or issues. At a press conference on Friday, Kerr said no, declaring that such "actions—collecting money and picketing—aren't high intellectual activity."[4] We wondered if he thought "high intellectual activity" took place at the university without money ever changing hands.

That night the United Front held a long meeting to decide what to do. There was going to be a university meeting to welcome new students and faculty at 11:00 A.M. on Monday, September 28th, in the Student Union Plaza below Sproul Plaza, at which Chancellor Strong would give the main speech. We had been trying to get an appointment with him all week but couldn't get past Dean Towle, so we decided to communicate with our bodies, adorned with appropriate signs. Monday morning we leafleted, calling for students to meet at 10:30 at the rally tree in Dwinelle Plaza. Since the rules only permitted rallies at noon and we didn't give the required 24-hour notice, we were in violation. Several people spoke to rev up the crowd, including Art Goldberg and Sandor Fuchs of SLATE, Danny Rosenthal of Cal Students for Goldwater, and Mario Savio of Friends of SNCC. Soon after the university meeting began, about 1,000 students marched from the rally tree, across Strawberry Creek, through Sproul Plaza, and down the steps, where we quietly circled the convocation. There were way too many seats for the 200 people who had come to hear Strong. The rows of mostly empty chairs were divided by three aisles. Someone broke off a group of picketers and marched down one aisle; I took another group down the middle, and someone else went down the third. Soon we were facing the speaker's stand, holding up our signs so Strong could see our message demanding free speech and no bans on political activity.

Our picketing appeared to work almost instantaneously. Strong announced two major concessions: we could now support or oppose specific candidates and issues, and we could distribute (but not sell) campaign items such as bumper stickers and buttons. He specifically rejected what we thought was the crux of the matter: recruiting people for off-campus political action and raising money. Initially we were elated. But we soon discovered that the university had included in its invitations to Family Day a request that parents support Proposition 2, the university bond issue. It wasn't *us* the administration was responding to, but anticipated charges of a double standard.[5]

That night we decided to set up tables again. Since all spots were off limits for "advocacy" and money collection, the question arose about where to set them up. Some wanted to stick to the Bancroft strip because its return was our primary demand. Others argued that we might as well move on campus, since one violation was as good (or bad) as another. The administration had claimed that the Bancroft strip was university property, so what difference did it make where we set up? Besides, Towle had said that too many tables created congestion at the campus entrance. Why not solve this problem by putting some at Sather Gate, which had been the tabling spot before the campus entrance was moved several years before? By the time we left, the agenda had changed for more than a few of the students at that meeting. We wanted to liberate the entire campus for political advocacy, not just Bancroft and Telegraph.

Nothing much happened on Tuesday. A few groups put up tables at Bancroft and Telegraph. SLATE, YSA, Campus CORE, and Friends of SNCC put them up at Sather Gate. Dean of Men Arleigh Williams and a university police officer asked those students sitting behind the Sather Gate tables for identification and told them that what they were doing was illegal; no one from the administration approached the tables at Bancroft, even though, under the new rules, they were equally illegal.

On Wednesday, our tables went up again. I was sitting at the UYD table at Bancroft when I heard that Brian Turner had been cited for refusing to move the Friends of SNCC table and ordered to report to Dean Williams at 3:00 P.M. Someone was circulating a "statement of complicity" that we were all equally guilty. I found a temporary replacement for the UYD table so I could go sign it. We didn't want Brian to hang alone; we'd go together. Four more students were cited before the deans left: Donald Hatch and Mark Bravo, who replaced Brian at the SNCC table; Beth Gardner Stapleton at the YSA table; and David Goines for selling the *SLATE Supplement*. They were told to report to Dean Williams that afternoon. While all this was going on, Mario Savio mounted a chair and spoke to the growing crowd. Quite a few others did the same.

By 3:00, between three and four hundred people had signed on; even more of us reported to the dean's office in Sproul Hall. Dean Williams didn't want to see us; he only wanted to see the five who had been cited. We sat down to wait. We filled the hallways and overflowed into the stairwell. After a few hours several students went for food, which women turned into sandwiches for the crowd. We were there most of the night. The Young Republicans organized a vigil on the outside steps while those inside debated what we were doing and why we were there. But there was only one person from the administration to debate with: Thomas Barnes, an associate professor of history and part-time assistant dean. At some point radio station KPFA showed up and began taping the discussion; its reporters taped all our public events for the rest of the fall. Shortly before midnight, a different dean read a statement from Chancellor Strong that he had indefinitely suspended *eight* students from the university. Art, Sandor, and Mario were added because of their leadership at the illegal rally on Monday. Of course, they weren't the only ones who spoke that day, but they were the best known.[6]

A wave of anger swept through the crowd. We had expected something to happen, but the effective expulsion of eight students without a hearing was not it. Mario got up and made the best speech I had heard in a long time. He brought it all together: administrative hypocrisy, civil

rights, the real political interests of the Regents who were major economic powers in California, and the arbitrariness of the restrictions on
political activity. The debate inside Sproul Hall continued for another
hour, while the United Front reps met in a stairwell to decide what to do.
About 1:30 A.M., Art announced our plans: all would go home and come
back tomorrow, when we would set up *large* tables, with several people
behind them, in front of Sproul Hall, and solicit donations to help the
eight. We would force the administration to cite as many students as possible. After some discussion, Mario proposed that we also have a massive
rally at Sproul Hall at noon, and the crowd yelled in affirmation. After
eleven hours of occupation, we left Sproul Hall.

30 | *Who Done It?*

THROUGHOUT THE WEEK there was growing suspicion that the origin
of our troubles was the *Oakland Tribune*. That night our fears were
confirmed. When someone asked Chancellor Strong at a reception for
Regents scholars why the sudden change, he referred to a phone call
from the *Oakland Tribune*. Dean Towle had made a similar statement to
Jackie. While no one could remember Strong or Towle's exact words, by
the time we sat in Sproul Hall the crucial call had come from the *Tribune*'s
owner, former senator Knowland, and the only question was whether it
had gone to Kerr or Strong.[1] We just assumed that Knowland was retali-
ating for the picketing by the Ad Hoc Committee. Inserted into some of
the *SLATE Supplements* had been a leaflet announcing a demonstration
at the *Tribune*. The previous spring, the *Tribune* had called for the suspension of students who had been arrested at the civil rights demonstrations. Administration rhetoric in response to the United Front repeatedly

referred to "political and social action" or to the recruiting of students for illegal off-campus demonstrations. And now eight students had been suspended for organizing protests of rules that restricted political activity by recognized off-campus student political groups—the very ones who had or might call for more civil rights demonstrations.

It all made sense. The fact that there was a university bond issue on the ballot in November reinforced our belief because it explained why the university acted now when it hadn't done so last spring. We believed for the rest of the year that Kerr's capitulation to Knowland was behind the removal of our political space and that it was done to stifle our support for civil rights. We put it in our publications and told it to everyone. We believed it long after the principals denied any such thing and independent researchers found no smoke, let alone a fire. Many believe it to this day.[2]

It was not true.

There was a phone call from the *Oakland Tribune*, but not from Bill Knowland. And it hadn't gone to Strong or Kerr. During the Republican convention, the *Tribune*, which supported Barry Goldwater, heard that students were being recruited on university property to support one of his more liberal opponents, William Scranton. Reporter Carl Irving asked Cal's public affairs officer, Richard Hafner, if this were true. There were two YR clubs on campus, reflecting the split in the Republican Party between conservatives and liberals. One was recruiting students to demonstrate for Scranton at the Republican convention from a table at Bancroft and Telegraph.[3]

Hafner hadn't known that the bricks between the pillars and the plaques belonged to the university and not the City of Berkeley, but once he did, he brought it to the attention of Vice-Chancellor Alex Sherriffs. The *Tribune* never ran a story, but Sherriffs ran with the information. He was unhappy about the mess at Bancroft. He didn't like the political groups, especially SLATE. He abhorred the *SLATE Supplement*, which had reviewed poorly the one psychology course he still taught. And now, he learned, we were violating university regulations on a regular basis and had been doing so for years.[4]

A meeting with the deans was already scheduled for July 22nd to discuss bicycles, bongo drums, and litter. "Item 3"—misuse of the "area outside the posts at Bancroft and Telegraph" was added to the agenda. Dean Towle was not at this meeting, though Dean Williams was. She was at two subsequent meetings held before a new policy was agreed on and her September 14th letter was written. Neither she nor Williams thought eviction was a good idea and knew that the students wouldn't either, but Sherriffs overruled them. When Williams asked Sherriffs why this "had to be," Sherriffs replied, "Because God said so." The deans assumed that "God" was Clark Kerr and reluctantly did his bidding. Only after the crisis was breaking did they discover that "God" was not Clark Kerr. "God" was Alex Sherriffs.[5]

31 | *Capturing the Car*

ON THURSDAY, AFTER my first class ended at 11:00, I went to the Political Science Department office in the newly opened Barrows Hall to talk to the chairman, Robert Scalapino. The United Front had decided that we needed faculty support to make the administration pay attention to us, so we assigned ourselves the task of talking to the faculty in our own departments. Scalapino made it clear that he was too busy with departmental matters and his work as chairman of California Professors for Johnson-Humphrey to concern himself with our complaints. His group had just printed 1,000 buttons. I told him that if his were a student group like the UYDs, it could not sell them on campus or raise money at Bancroft and Telegraph to pay for them, but he didn't see the connection. Besides, he was busy. He did suggest a few other professors I could talk to. From Barrows, I walked to Sproul Plaza where I saw several thousand people sitting around a police car parked in the middle. My jaw dropped open and my blood raced.

Over the next couple hours I pieced together the story of what had happened. Some student groups put their tables up at Sather Gate; Cam-

pus CORE brought a long door with legs and put it up at the base of
Sproul Hall steps. Several CORE members gathered behind the literature
display, determined that no one would identify themselves in order to
prevent any from being singled out. As experienced civil rights demonstrators, they were raising the ante. The administration took the bait,
better than we could ever have hoped. When two members of Dean Williams's staff walked up to the table and asked the young man sitting behind it to identify himself, he refused.

His name was Jack Weinberg.

Jack was an alumnus, unemployed, working as a full-time CORE
volunteer. Born and raised in Buffalo, New York, he lived with his parents until he quit school after two years of college. Restless and unsure
of what he wanted to do with his life, he hitchhiked to Mexico, returned
to marry his girlfriend, went to the Bay Area, worked for a while, split
up with his wife, and enrolled in Berkeley. After getting his degree in
math in January 1963, he started grad school but didn't last a year. He
had found his calling, and it wasn't math. Until he came to Berkeley, Jack
had had no political involvement, nor had his parents. But Berkeley's
highly charged political atmosphere ignited his passions; the Civil Rights
Movement's call for justice claimed his allegiance. Jack was one of hundreds who joined northern CORE chapters when the Birmingham civil
rights demonstrations captured national headlines in the spring of 1963.

Over the next year he became a fully involved, committed activist,
working in South Carolina CORE projects in the summer and becoming
head of Campus CORE when it was founded in October. Jack had been
arrested in three Bay Area civil rights demonstrations by the time the
deanlets asked for his registration card. He was comfortable with confrontation and unfazed by the possibility of arrest. The deanlets brought
Lieutenant Chandler of the campus police to tell Jack he was under arrest. The lieutenant quickly realized he needed more help and left to
get it.

While he was gone, Jack spoke to the gathering crowd, pretty much
repeating what Mario had said in Sproul Hall the night before. When the
lieutenant returned with three more officers, Jack went limp, in good
civil rights fashion, forcing the police to grab his limbs. Another officer
drove a cop car onto the plaza, perhaps thinking they would take Jack
directly to the Berkeley City jail. As they pulled him from his chair, the
growing mass of students jeered, sang, and then sat down between Jack
and the car. While the police slowly carried Jack toward the car, students

spontaneously sat down around it to keep it from moving. By the time Jack was in the car it already had one flat tire. David Goines soon let the air out of the other three and someone else crammed a potato into the exhaust pipe.

"We shall not, we shall not be moved," sang the students, followed by the "Star Spangled Banner" and "We Shall Overcome." Mario took off his shoes and climbed on top of the car. While Jack looked out languidly from the back window, the crowd clapped and chanted: "Let him go! Let him go!" Eventually it quieted enough for us to hear Mario thank the administration for bringing them to the noon rally we had planned. He then made our "simple and reasonable demands." 1) Revoke the suspensions; 2) Negotiate with the student political organizations for "reasonable regulations governing freedom of speech on this campus, [with] no arbitrary restrictions"; 3) "No disciplinary action . . . against anyone setting up tables or speaking here until . . . that meeting is held!" Otherwise, he said, there will be "continuous direct action."[1]

By the time Mario stood up on the police car he had been accepted as the most articulate of the student speakers of the week and was rapidly becoming our de facto leader. But who was he? He seemed to come from nowhere. He did not head a student group. He hadn't been at the early meetings of the United Front. Those of us who had been working in the trenches for years barely knew him. I vaguely remembered Mario as one of several students who had passed out leaflets advertising the Nazi speaker the spring before, though I was unaware of him at SLATE meetings. The reason I remembered him at all was because he stuttered so badly. Yet when he stood before a crowd in September he had a silver throat. Who was this tall, slender boy with close-cropped curly hair who combined arrogance with humility and incoherence with oratorical brilliance and who insisted on being heard?

Mario Robert Savio was an altar boy from Queens. His devout Catholic parents—a machinist and a housewife—raised him to become a priest, but his teachers saw a future scientist. He was valedictorian of his class at Martin van Buren High School. After a year at a Catholic college in the Bronx, he lost his faith in the Church, or more accurately, he transferred it to a more abstract sense of social justice. He spent the next year at Queens College, a campus of the City University of New York, and in the summer of 1963 went to Mexico as one member of a work project arranged by the Newman Club. In Mexico, he saw abject poverty and banged his head against the barriers government officials raised against efforts to build a public facility for people to wash their clothes. While Mario was in Mexico, his parents moved to southern California. In the fall of 1963, he entered Cal as a junior majoring in philosophy—Chancellor Strong's department. He still loved physics, but felt he needed to connect to the human and ethical issues raised by what he had seen. Later that fall he began going to meetings of Friends of SNCC, a group founded by former SLATE chairman Mike Miller.

In California he began a transformation, but one foreordained by his deep religious conviction that it was his Christian duty to resist evil. He dropped his childhood moniker, Bob, and told everyone to call him Mario. He was slowly pulled into the Civil Rights Movement; picketing at Mel's and tutoring junior high school students. On March 6th, he was arrested at the Sheraton-Palace after learning about the demonstration from a leaflet given him at Bancroft and Telegraph. While in jail he heard about the forthcoming Freedom Summer project and resolved to go. Mario spent half the summer doing voter registration in Holmes County and the rest at a Freedom School in McComb, Mississippi. When he returned he was no longer a cautious, inquisitive do-gooder with a stutter but a man driven to do right.[2]

Mario's genius as the orator of our ideals was that he combined the two dominant themes of the protest and made them seem one and the same. For the political groups, the issue was civil rights. We wanted the right to continue functioning as we had been, to be able to speak and distribute literature advocating any position on any issue, and to raise the money necessary for organizational survival. We also wanted to support the Civil Rights Movement with money and warm bodies at demonstrations. Eviction from our political space gutted our ability to do these things. While students were sympathetic to these aims, most weren't motivated by them enough to make major personal sacrifices. But students had their own grievances, and Mario effectively appealed to those while linking them to the issues of the political groups.

Mario's words captured student concerns. He described the university as a "knowledge factory" in which kids "go in one side, as kind of rough-cut adolescents, and . . . come out the other . . . pretty smooth." But sometimes "the machine doesn't work," and then "you throw the parts out."[3] The students who applauded his speeches felt processed, like products on an assembly line. Their needs were not met and their voices were not heard. School wasn't just education and enlightenment but was also restrictions and rules, whose only purpose seemed to be to snip and

cut away the rough edges of their individuality. The images of mechani-
zation and dehumanization that flowed from Mario's mouth rang true
for them. They saw in the university a microcosm of the ills of society.
Mario's call to action allowed them to protest their alienation through
pursuit of a noble cause: free speech to work for civil rights. He chan-
neled their discontent.[4]

Mario did not claim originality for this description of the university. He attributed it to Clark Kerr. In 1963, Kerr gave three lectures
at Harvard, which were published as *The Uses of the University*. Kerr
said the traditional university was being transformed into a modern
"multiversity"—a pluralistic institution serving many needs—by the
growth of the "knowledge industry." As in any transformation, there
were winners and losers. Among the latter were undergraduates, especially those in large, prestigious research institutions growing larger
through federal grants which freed faculty from teaching responsibilities.

> The undergraduate students are restless. Recent changes in the
> American university have done them little good—lower teaching
> loads for the faculty, larger classes, the use of substitute teachers for
> the regular faculty, the choice of faculty members based on research
> accomplishments rather than instructional capacity, the fragmenta-
> tion of knowledge into endless subdivisions. . . . The students find
> themselves under a blanket of impersonal rules for admissions, for
> scholarships, for examinations, for degrees. . . . The students also
> want to be treated as distinct individuals.[5]

By the time Kerr's observations were articulated by Mario and other
protest leaders they had been transformed. What Kerr meant as description, Mario saw as prescription. He attributed to Kerr phrases he did not
use, such as "knowledge factory," and read into his words far more omi-
nous implications than were meant. His rendition of Kerr came not from
reading his book but from a lecture on that book given by Hal Draper
at Stiles Hall on September 29th. It was attended by many students involved in the protests, including Mario, Brian Turner, and Jack Weinberg. Draper was a 50-year-old clerk in the university library with a long
history in various socialist groups and factions. An editor and writer of
socialist publications, he founded the Independent Socialist Club (ISC) at
Berkeley to promote his own views. A few days later, the ISC published
his talk as a pamphlet on "The Mind of Clark Kerr: His View of the
University Factory and the 'New Slavery.'" Draper confused the messen-
ger with the message. To him, the "multiversity" was Kerr's vision of the

future, not his critique of the present. Draper found it horrifying. The many students who heard Draper, Mario, and other protest leaders speak shared that view. Clark Kerr was held up as the personification of what was wrong at Berkeley, and even with the world.

32 | *Strongwalled*

THE SIT-IN AROUND the police car occurred exactly two weeks after we first met with Dean Towle. From representatives of eighteen student groups begging for our lives, we had gone to 3,000 determined people occupying Sproul Plaza. None of us anticipated this. The more experienced among the political activists expected nothing to happen. SLATE had jousted with the administration for years over petty rules and restrictions. What changed and when seemed almost arbitrary, without regard to our needs or concerns. Since our numbers were small and we all left Cal sooner or later, there wasn't time to create a body of knowledge about how to move the mountain. We just chipped away wherever we could. In the last year, the Bay Area Civil Rights Movement had educated thousands of students on how to respond when authorities acted oppressively. Now, thanks to the spontaneous action of people previously uninvolved in politics, a window of opportunity had opened. Would the administration listen?

Initially the answer was no. Jackie took two people to University Hall and tried to see Kerr, but he wasn't available. When she returned, ASUC president Charlie Powell addressed the crowd from the car, offering to act as their negotiator. Although his offer was vociferously rejected, he and Mario went to see Chancellor Strong and Vice-Chancellor Sherriffs, who had previously refused to meet with the United Front representatives. Strong maintained that no rules had been changed; they had merely been clarified to apply to all university property. In fact, he said, they had been liberalized. He took the position that nothing could be discussed while students were defying legitimate university authority.[1]

From the top of the car, the debate continued all afternoon and into the night. The argument wasn't about whether to change the rules and return to the status quo ante; there was consensus that that was the minimum that should happen. The debate was about whether holding a police car hostage was the way to do it and how much more we should demand. Since most of the audience was already committing civil disobedience by their very presence, opposition speakers didn't get much applause. Ron Anastasi, a psychology major who had just transferred from Massachusetts that fall, rented loudspeakers, a microphone, and an amplifier so everyone could hear. A very long electrical cord brought power from the Student Union building. Some people who would become major players that fall debuted from the top of that car. Mario became the recognized leader, though Jackie was still nominally our spokesperson. Charlie Powell's star rose and fell quickly. Bettina Aptheker overcame stage fright to make her maiden speech. Dusty Miller, a former Greek who still looked like one, emerged as MC, introducing the speakers and the singers and jollying the crowd.

Seeking to ratchet up the pressure, Mario took several hundred people back into Sproul Hall to talk to the deans. Students lined the hallway rather than blocking it, but when Jackie tried to make an appointment, the police guarding the deans' door threatened to arrest her. This made her angry. "If you're not going to let us in," she said, "we're not going to let you out!" She turned to the throng and asked them to block the doorway. They did. Several deans and their staff escaped by climbing out a window onto a back roof that adjoined their offices, walking across it to the northern wing, and entering from a window into former president Sproul's office. From there they went down the stairs and out of the building.

In the meantime, some faculty had finally realized that there was a crack in the ivory tower. A few wandered out to talk to the students in Sproul Plaza. A few others tried to serve as mediators. Sociology professors Nathan Glazer, William Petersen, and Seymour Martin Lipset told us they were trying to contact the administration and asked the students to leave Sproul Hall as a "gesture of good faith." At 6:00 P.M., while they met with Strong, the police tried to close the doors of the building, which normally stayed open until 7:00. In the ensuing struggle one officer was felled, his boots were removed, and Mario bit his leg. Strong could not be moved, but at 9:00 P.M. the students voted to leave Sproul Hall. Our numbers were dwindling; we needed more bodies around the police car.

The United Front reps met in the stairwell of the Student Union about 10:00 P.M. to figure out what to do next. We decided to repeat the day: keep the car, set up tables, hold a noon rally, and invade Sproul Hall. I went home to sleep, missing a midnight confrontation between the demonstrators and the fraternities. Jackie, through her Greek connections, had heard that they would pay us a visit that night—one reason she wanted the students out of Sproul and around the car. The frats marched in just before midnight, lining the steps of Sproul Hall, taunting those sitting around the car, throwing eggs and lighted cigarettes into the sitting students. Mario, and even Jack Weinberg, spoke from the car, trying to keep our crowd calm and perhaps cool out the frats. UFOs flew threw the air. Every speaker was booed: demonstrators, deans, ASUC officers, even a frat-rat who told his brothers to go home. After two hours of escalating hostility, Father Fisher of Newman Hall climbed onto the car and pleaded for peace. Everyone fell silent. Slowly the frats drifted away.

33 | *The October 2nd Pact*

EARLY THE NEXT MORNING, Jackie took me aside and said that things were getting dicey. Saturday was Family Day. She knew the administration would not permit all those parents coming on campus to see a student occupation of Sproul Plaza. Heads would be bloodied first, most likely those of the kids holding the car. The administration would not talk to the demonstrators, and the faculty weren't getting through either.

"Can you use your contacts in the Democratic Party to get Kerr to negotiate?" she said. "No one else can get through to him."

I phoned Jerry Fishkin and we put together a list of major Democrats for each of us to call. Then I phoned Joe Close, my former boss at the Cranston campaign, who lived nearby. He was very concerned and happy to help. He said that only Governor Brown could compel Kerr to meet with us. He would phone everyone in the state legislature that he knew, but the best person to convince Brown that he knew personally was Oakland assemblyman Nick Petris. Don Mulford, whose 16th Assembly District included Berkeley, was a troglodyte. Since Joe could not reach me, we agreed that I would call him hourly to learn of any progress. I returned to Sproul Plaza.

The United Front met frequently in the Student Union stairwell, though our numbers varied considerably. I shared only with Jackie the reports from Joe Close to avoid raising false hopes. We still thought that the faculty could penetrate the wall of administration intransigence. At some point, we chose a six-person negotiating committee: myself, Mario, Paul Cahill of UYRs, Tom Miller of CORE and ISC, Eric Levine of SDS, and Bob Wolfson of CORE. And we drew up a list of demands:

> We, the political and non-partisan groups of the University of California, will call off our demonstration, put up no tables, and refrain from all political activity for *one* week on the condition that:
> 1. The person now under arrest be released, and charges be dropped by the University.
> 2. That the students under suspension shall be reinstated.
> 3. That President Kerr enter into negotiations with the six-member negotiating committee . . . on the following demands regarding free speech:
>   1. The students shall have the right to hear any person speak in any open area on campus at any time on any subject except when it would cause a traffic problem or interfere with classes.
>   2. Persons shall have the right to participate in political activity on campus by advocating political action beyond voting, by joining organizations, and by giving donations. Both students and non-students shall have the right to set up tables and pass out political literature. The only reasonable and acceptable basis for permits is traffic control.
>   3. The unreasonable and arbitrary restrictions of 72-hour notice, student paid-for protection, and faculty moderators, required for speakers using University buildings, must be reformed.

While we were keeping the crowd content, the administration was arranging a major police assault. To aid the Berkeley city police, reinforcements were coming from the Alameda County sheriff's office, the Oakland police and the state highway patrol. Sproul Hall was closed except for one tightly guarded entrance. Inside, several police chiefs planned our removal. Kerr wanted arrests at 4:00 A.M. when the car would be thinly guarded, but the law enforcement agencies vetoed this as incompatible with their own personnel needs. Six P.M. was their designated hour. If the students didn't relinquish the car by then, they would be forcibly removed.[1]

Other meetings were going on all over campus. In Barrows Hall, several professors in the social science departments appointed themselves as mediators and sought out Chancellor Strong. Strong was not warm to their four-point proposal, arguing that most were outside his power and required approval from Kerr or the Regents. He emphasized the importance of maintaining law and order on campus and said he would not negotiate with the students as long as they held a gun to his head. Strong discouraged the faculty from approaching Kerr directly, but after he left the meeting, Henry Rosovsky of Economics phoned Kerr and read the proposals to him and his secretary.[2] They were:

1) The student demonstrators promise to abide by legal processes in their protest of University regulations.
2) A committee representing students (including leaders of the demonstration), faculty, and administration, will immediately be set up to conduct discussions and a hearing into all aspects of political behavior on campus and its control, and to make recommendations to the administration.
3) The arrested man will be booked, released on his own recognizance, and the University (complainant) will not press charges.
4) The duration of the suspension of the suspended students will be decided by the Student Conduct Committee of the Academic Senate.

We knew nothing about this meeting; these faculty members hadn't met with us as a group, though some of them had talked with some of us individually. As far as we knew, the administration paid less attention to the faculty than it did to the students. And while we wanted to negotiate, we weren't all that sure that the demonstrators would leave if we asked them to. This was not an organized protest called by leaders like the civil rights sit-ins of the spring before. This was spontaneous combustion.

Through regular phone calls to Joe Close I gave him our proposals and followed the progress of our request to meet with Clark Kerr. Nick Petris readily agreed to call Brown, but the governor was in Los Angeles and it took a while to reach him. Then Brown couldn't find Kerr, who was the luncheon speaker at the American Council on Education meeting at the Sheraton-Palace Hotel in San Francisco. There he told the press that he would not compromise with the demonstrators. Only after Kerr returned to his office in the early afternoon did the governor speak to him. Brown ordered Kerr to step in. "I don't want another Alabama or Mississippi," he said.[3]

When I phoned Joe at 3:30, he was relieved to hear my voice. "Take your negotiating team to University Hall at 5:00," he said, "and bring your proposals. Kerr will be there ready to talk." I gave him the names of our negotiators to pass on to Kerr's secretary, then returned to the meeting Tom Miller and I were having with several faculty members in Professor Sellers's office in Dwinelle Hall. They had described to us their futile efforts to reach Kerr. When I announced the meeting time they were dumbfounded. How did a mere student get through to the president of the university when his office wasn't returning their calls?

Tom and I searched for the other four members of our team, but we couldn't find Mario or Bob Wolfson. We spread the word, but Mario didn't catch up to us until 5:00, so we didn't have a meeting among ourselves to plan strategy. When I saw Jackie I asked her to come along; we were short a person or two and she had more experience with administrators than any of us. She brought in Sandor, believing that SLATE should be represented but that brother Art was best left with the crowd around the car. David Jessup (UYD and YPSL) asked if he could come as a runner to keep us in touch with Sproul Plaza. We parked one person on a phone in the Student Union and gave the number to David so he could set up a communications line. If the police acted while we were talking, we wanted to know about it. Bob Wolfson appeared, and so did Danny Rosenthal, who made a big stink about the conservative groups being underrepresented. By the time we reached University Hall, we were ten.

As we walked across campus, police from all over poured onto it, filling the streets and walkways between the buildings that surrounded Sproul Plaza. Word spread among the students that a major confrontation was mounting, and they too came in droves. By the time we got to University Hall there were several hundred cops ready for action and several thousand students ready to greet them. Spectators climbed onto balconies and roofs. Although the protestors were told that negotiations were in progress, they were also instructed in nonviolent resistance and legal rights. When eight cops waded through the crowd toward the car, students packed themselves into a solid block around it.

We were met at the entrance to University Hall and taken up an elevator to the seventh floor—the presidential floor—where we were left waiting for fifteen minutes before being taken into the conference room. Kerr was surrounded by several other people, including ASUC president Charlie Powell, *Daily Cal* editor Sue Johnson, a few faculty, and a minister. They stood around the walls while we sat at a long table: Jackie, Mario, and Tom on one side; Eric, Paul, and I on the other. Kerr stood at the head and immediately took control of the meeting. This was the first time I had been in the same room with Kerr. Indeed, I had only seen Kerr once before, at the 1962 Charter Day ceremony when President Kennedy was the guest speaker. There he was just a distant figure on the stage in the stadium; here, he was our adversary, whose ideas and attitudes we knew only as filtered by others. Strong made a brief statement and then disappeared into another room.[4] Kerr told him to make sure that the cops did nothing on their own. Our first demand was that the police not act while we talked. We found a phone for David to call the Student Union so we could learn if they did.

We expected to negotiate around the words we had written, but Kerr ignored our proposals in favor of those submitted by the Barrows Hall faculty. We didn't like them, but we also knew that we would probably accept them rather than risk a bloodbath. Well, most of us would accept them. Mario balked immediately at point 1. "Student demonstrators promise to abide by legal processes in their protest." What legal processes? For two weeks we had been trying to find some legal process through which to pursue our grievances, and all we found was deans with no power to do anything but tell us to obey the rules. The university was not a democracy. There were no courts or legislature, no public officials accountable to voters, only an administration appointed by the Regents, remote figures whose names we did not know and whom none of us had ever seen. If anything, the university followed the military model of social organization: rules were made at the top and the duty of those at the bottom was to obey. "Abide by legal processes" sounds nice, but we knew it was a formula for failure.

When we met in a closed caucus to decide what to do, Jackie and Mario almost came to blows. Jackie had no faith in the administration to act fairly and reasonably, but she wanted us to live to fight another day. Get what we could and get out was her view. In the back of Mario's head was how would he explain any agreement to the thousands of students who had listened to and trusted him for two days. He had to have something to take back that he thought the protestors would not view as a sell-out. The bottom line was that we wouldn't give up the possibility that we would return to the streets—our only leverage if future meetings were as futile as past ones had been—but we would stop the sit-in that was going on that night. We proposed that "the student demonstrators shall cease from all forms of their illegal protest against University regulations." Kerr would not accept the word "cease." After some give-and-take, Jackie said, "Why don't we use the word 'desist'?" Kerr paused, then said, "OK, I'll do it."

Points 2 and 3 of the faculty proposal we accepted almost as written, after some discussion about what the words really meant. Point 4 presented some problems. Kerr objected to the Student Conduct Committee *deciding* the duration of the suspension for the students. All committees are advisory to the administration, he said, but the chancellor accepts their recommendations. We did not want the suspended students to wait forever before learning their fate. Consequently, "decided by" was changed to "submitted within one week to" in point 4. We completely missed the real problem: the Academic Senate did not have a Student Conduct Committee. Such committees were appointed by the administration.

Just in case the administration might try to do something else to us, we added

> 5) Activity may be continued by student organizations in accordance with existing University regulations.

We were hamstrung, but we weren't going to go out of business.

Charlie Powell suggested that the ASUC buy the space at Bancroft and Telegraph and restore it to its original use. Kerr had already said that it should be given to the city of Berkeley. So we added

> 6) The President of the University has already declared his willingness to support deeding certain University property at the end of Telegraph Avenue to the City of Berkeley or to the ASUC.

The tension in the room grew tighter with each passing moment. Kerr had spent many years as a labor negotiator and he showed us some of his skill. Several times while we debated and discussed language,

Kerr's secretary went up to him and whispered loudly that the police wouldn't hold off any longer. Kerr had promised us that nothing would happen while we were talking, but now he said that he couldn't control the cops. We didn't really believe this, but when David lost the phone connection to the Student Union we did wonder if it was accidental. The faculty said sign, sign, sign. More than pressure, our open disagreement and internal bickering undermined our cohesion and resolve. If only some of us signed, what would happen? Would our nascent movement split and kids' heads get bloodied to boot? We were not greenhorns to confrontation politics—two-thirds of us had been arrested at the Sheraton-Palace or Auto Row—but we weren't organized, either. In the end, we all signed.

Except Danny Rosenthal. He had a reputation as something of a loose cannon, and he convinced us that it was well deserved. He denounced Kerr for discriminating against the conservative groups because the lefties could violate the rules with impunity and without punishment while the conservative groups were restricted by their commitment to play by the rules! Paul Cahill, the very conservative representative of the UYRs, took him on. Danny represents only Danny, he said. The UYRs and the other conservative groups are with the United Front.

The typewritten agreement, with handwritten changes to point 1, was placed in front of Clark Kerr. He signed it in a small, cramped hand on the far right. Jackie signed next, then Eric, Mario, and Tom Miller. When it came to me there was no space left on the right, so I signed my name in bold strokes at the top of the left-hand column. Paul, Sandor, and Bob signed after me. David was called in to sign as well. Danny did not sign.[5]

We were given copies, descended in the elevator, jumped into two cars waiting for us on the street, and drove madly to Bancroft and Telegraph. But we couldn't get there; the street was blocked by the cops. "We've got the agreement," we told them. "Let us get by, let us get by." They told us to move out of the way. "No, we've got to get through," we said. A cop pulled out his ticket book. We leaped out of our car and ran up the street, waving the agreement in the air and leaving our hapless driver to get a ticket.

We got to the captured car about 7:30. Art was speaking from the top, preparing the crowd for what might happen. He said that any who couldn't afford to be arrested should move out of the way. We hadn't discussed what we would say to the students, but Mario insisted that

1. The student demonstrators ~~promise to abide by legal processes in their protest of~~ University regulations. *shall desist from all forms of illegal protest against then*

2. A committee representing students (including leaders of the demonstration), faculty, and administration will immediately be set up to conduct discussions and hearing into all aspects of political behavior on campus and its control, and to make recommendations to the administration.

3. The arrested man will be booked, released on his own recognisance, and the University (complainant) will not press charges.

4. The duration of the suspension of the suspended students will be submitted within one week to the Student Conduct Committee of the Academic Senate.

5. Activity may be continued by student organizations in accordance with existing University regulations.

6. The President of the University has already ~~declared~~ declared his willingness to support deeding certain University property at the end of Telegraph Avenue to the City of Berkeley or to the ASUC.

Jo Freeman
Paul C. Cahill
Sandor Fuchs
Robert Wolfson
David Jessup

Clark Kerr
Jackie Goldberg
Eric Levine
Mario Savio
Thomas Miller

The Pact of October 2nd ended the sit-in around the police car in Sproul Plaza. It was signed by President Clark Kerr and nine students.

"*I'm* going to make the statement." Despite the excitement and his occasional tendency to get flustered, Mario read the signed agreement solemnly. There were some groans from the crowd and some jeers from the spectators. He asked for silence and spent ten minutes explaining what it all meant. Then he called for a rally at noon on Monday and asked everyone to go home.

As the crowd dispersed, Jack Weinberg got out of the car and walked with a couple officers into the Sproul Hall station, where he was booked. They wanted to take him to the Berkeley Police station but he refused, so they let him go. When he emerged from Sproul Hall most of the crowd was gone. Although glad to be released, he felt the agreement which freed him was a defeat; the students had given up everything for nothing.

Strong and Kerr watched the reading of the agreement from the steps of Sproul Hall (they probably got there before we did). The chancellor later said:

> STRONG: It was not a glorious moment for the University. I had a sense of ignominy visited upon the University when I saw Savio on top of that police car. Kitty Malloy . . . [his administrative assistant] was in tears. Alex Sherriffs was looking very grim. I was approached by a reporter asking me what I thought of the agreement. I said that this was an agreement that the President had made with the FSM and that he should speak to the President as to its significance.

> Kerr, then, did not address the group?

> STRONG: He didn't say a word.[6]

But Kerr did hold a press conference on the steps while the students cleaned up the debris. He put a positive spin on the agreement, saying, "Law and order have been restored without the use of force."

Not too far away, I could hear a low rumble. It grew louder and louder until it filled the air.

Varooom. VAROOOOOOOM. *VAROOOOOOOOOOOOOMMMMM.* Hundreds of cops gunned their cycles and roared off into the night.

34 | *The FSM Is Born*

WE ALL KNEW that this was not the end. At best it was a beginning. All we had done was postpone the conflict until after Family Day. Whether it would continue with deliberation and debate or erupt into another physical face-off remained to be seen. No one felt victorious. Mario phoned me at 5:00 A.M. to say that Syd Stapleton and Brian Turner thought we'd sold out and were mobilizing people in opposition. This turned out to be untrue; another sign that rumors more than reason would shape our perceptions for the next few months.

The next morning, Saturday, I cut through campus on my way to a meeting at Art's apartment. The car was gone and parents were happily walking around with their children as though nothing had happened. At Bancroft and Telegraph someone was passing out black armbands; I put one on. Several students asked me if I thought what we did was good or bad. "Neither," I said. "It was necessary."

At noon we gathered to get organized. There, the United Front dissolved and the Free Speech Movement was born. Jack Weinberg, recovered from his thirty-two hours in the police car, suggested the name. Though we considered alternatives, "Free Speech" had appeared in the *Daily Cal* and on some leaflets, so it was in common use, and "FSM" had a nice ring to it.

Much harder than a name was to agree on a structure and leadership to guide us during the next stage. After extensive debate on who should be represented and how, we created an Executive Committee (Ex Com) as our main decision-making body and a nine-person Steering Committee to make rapid decisions. Each campus group that so chose could send two voting representatives to the Ex Com. In addition, the Interfaith Council was allowed to send reps, and independent students—those who weren't members of political groups—were told to organize and send reps. On October 9th, roughly one hundred grad students from twenty-five departments met to form the Graduate Coordinating Committee (GCC), which chose five reps and two alternates. Even the nonstudents (most of whom were ex-students) were allowed representation; they chose Brad Cleaveland to speak for them. The eight cited students were given votes in their own right. This created a very cumbersome body and a shift in the distribution of power from that of the United Front.

Mario and Jack urged that the Ex Com elect to the Steering Committee those who had shown leadership capacity and not to be concerned with balanced representation. This shifted the center further left. Art and Jackie Goldberg, who had called the original meeting and were the most experienced of the student political leaders, were barely elected and effectively excluded. I put my name up but didn't even come close. These first battles were interpreted as a split between the CORE and SLATE people, though the fact that many of the CORE people were also in the ISC was noted.

David Goines later wrote:

> The CORE and SNCC activists, such as Jack Weinberg, Mario Savio and Suzanne Goldberg, believed that change was best accomplished by confrontation and direct action. They eschewed cooperation with those whom they perceived as their "class enemy." In the instance of student rights, the administration represented the ruling class, the faculty the middle class and the students the working class. The activists in the power structure of the FSM outnumbered the moderates, and took control of the Movement almost immediately, ousting their ideological enemies and relentlessly pursuing this bitter internal conflict throughout the FSM's existence.[1]

One of those ideological enemies was Jackie Goldberg, who was soon purged from the leadership. When she was nominated for the Steering Committee, Mario denounced her for "ingratiating herself with the administration" during the October 2nd negotiations. He said she was a sell-out and couldn't be trusted. Jackie told Mario that they had a difference in style, not politics, but he and Jack wanted her off of the Steering Committee. They were the most influential people in the FSM and simply refused to work with her. Jackie knew that Art would always support her and that if she insisted on staying the resulting fracas could split the FSM. This would not be good, so she went quietly, so quietly that most people did not even know that she was no longer in the leadership. She remained on the Ex Com as a rep for Campus Women for Peace and carved out a role for herself speaking at the different living groups about the FSM and the student demands. Art was removed once for a few days in November, but when Mario spoke at a SLATE meeting afterward he was grilled so harshly that Art was put back on. However, Art was treated like a pesky fly.[2]

My sin was being a Democrat, though my years in SLATE didn't help. The CORE and SNCC reps, heavily influenced by ISC's ideology, were convinced that the Democratic Party was their enemy, and nothing else, even my hard-earned stripes as a civil rights demonstrator, mattered. Nor did they care that most of the leaflets passed out by the United Front had been mimeographed at 7th C.D. Democratic Party headquarters on Ashby Avenue. Very few knew that the meeting with Kerr had been arranged through Democratic Party channels; in their eyes, that tarred me even more. Jack Weinberg particularly hated the Democratic Party, which he felt had betrayed the MFDP in Atlantic City. When the radicals realized that they needed to appear (but not actually be) more representative, they invited onto the Steering Committee those whom they thought wouldn't give them any trouble. Pam Horner (CCR) was on briefly, and so was Dick Roman, a grad student in sociology. Jerry Fishkin spoke to Mario about the absence of the UYDs—and was denounced for it at the next Ex Com meeting—so Mario decided that Dick would be the UYD rep. Roman was a member of the UYDs, but he represented YPSL on the Ex Com. I was the official UYD rep to the FSM Ex Com. Horner and Roman soon realized that they were just tokens and dropped off the Steering Committee. A month later, Mona Hutchin, vice president of the University Society of Individualists (USI) was brought on for balance. A junior in political science, she had graduated from a San Mateo high school after living in several states. Her father was an engineer in the aerospace industry and her mother was a housewife. Neither parent paid much attention to politics. In the eyes of that Steering Committee, Mona was the ideal Republican representative: she never said a word and often went to sleep.

From a public-relations perspective, the most controversial people elected to the Steering Committee were Bettina Aptheker and Syd Stapleton because their presence would bring red-baiting to the FSM. Both juniors, they had traveled different routes. Syd was a native Californian, son of a Republican farmer with little interest in politics. His mother died when he was 15. He entered Cal in 1962, at age 16, on a full scholarship for future engineers, having headed his high school class as a brilliant science student. Inspired by the 1959 Cuban revolution, he thought YSA was the one organization actively supporting its ideals. He joined YSA in the spring and soon became its most active member. When he returned home after his first year at Cal carrying the *Selected Works of Lenin*, his father was shocked. Syd found politics more compelling than science. By 1964, he had left engineering for pre-med and married Beth—also a rural Californian who entered Berkeley at an early age—after recruiting her into YSA.

Bettina came from New York City, ready to leave the Big Apple and see the country. Cal came to her attention with the 1960 anti-HUAC demonstrations; both she and her father were impressed with its academic rigor. A graduate of Brooklyn's Erasmus High, she followed her father by majoring in American history. She also inherited his political gene, picketing for civil rights when she was 15. At Berkeley she quickly became an active member of the DuBois Club and freely conceded that she had "a last name that's dynamite." On the left, her name also opened doors, even among those who did not like the CP. She did not publicly admit membership in the Party—and would not until November 1965— but her father was such a prominent member that most of us assumed that she was as well. During the fall, Bettina met regularly with the campus CP chapter (which wasn't an officially recognized off-campus student group) to discuss the FSM. Those discussions shaped her views about what the FSM should do.[3]

I had only spoken to Bettina once before the FSM. On election day in November 1963 we were assigned to the same precinct in San Francisco to pull voters for Democrat John Shelley. I had talked with Syd many times, as we were both regular tablers at Bancroft and Telegraph. As an open leader of the YSA, Syd was used to being red-baited, even though he was a Trotskyist and certainly not in the CP. Syd was not prone to public speeches; he did his best work behind the scenes. Bettina was outspoken and influential on the Steering Committee. She was a moderating influence on Mario and Jack, who respected her in part because of her CP connection and her father's name. I often thought that if the Steering Committee had more Bettinas and fewer radicals it would be more effective.

Only one other woman was in the leadership. Suzanne Goldberg first appeared as a GCC alternate and the secretary who took notes at Steering Committee meetings. Born in Brooklyn, she was raised in various New York City suburbs before graduating from a Connecticut high school. After getting her B.A. from Cornell and an M.A. from the City University of New York, she entered UC in the fall of 1963 as a grad student in philosophy. Suzanne did not carry the political gene; her prior involvement in political groups and demonstrations was minimal. But she was outraged by the administrative fiats of that fall and impressed by Mario's speeches. Suzanne went out with Jack a few times, but soon switched her affections to Mario, with whom she worked closely writing leaflets. She was not a moderating influence. Her suggestions were often picked up by Mario and Jack, who treated them as their own.

At the time, most of us saw the packing of the Steering Committee as a left/right split; of the thirteen who initially ran, the four who weren't elected were the reps from YPSL, UYD, CCR, and UYR. Jackie and Art were also lumped into the "right wing." I later saw it as more of a generational split between the old guard and new. I had learned in Kornhouser's political sociology course that a political generation was a cohort of similar ages who have the same experiences and similar outlooks.[4] In one sense we were all part of what came to be known as the sixties generation. But in the student world, life is so short and things change so fast that there was a new generation about every two years. What distinguished us was not our chronological age but our experiences and attitudes.

I saw three distinct waves of student activists in my four years at Berkeley; each one pushed the envelope farther than those who came before. The generation before me I thought of as the founders. These were the men—the ones we heard about were all men—who had founded SLATE and organized the HUAC protests. They included such campus legends as Mike Miller; Mike Tigar; Dave Armor; Peter Franck; Carey McWilliams, Jr.; Mike Myerson; and Ken Cloke.[5] Ken was the only one I knew personally, but the others loomed large in our immediate past. Although the founders did rally and protest, they mostly wrote and talked—and ran for ASUC office. They were trying to work within the system to move it toward their ideals.

I labeled my generation the activists. The time for mere talk was over. We had to act. We not only marched and rallied; we sat in. We deliberately disrupted institutions that would not change and were willingly arrested. But we still remained loyal to the overall political system. If we had lost our illusions about the ASUC, considering it just a sandbox, we still believed the political system worked. We assumed that our elders shared our concerns and that if they only *knew* how bad things were, they would make the necessary changes. If we were loud enough and insistent enough, if we didn't give up too soon, the authorities would realize that we were sincere, we were serious, and we were right.

Those speaking out at the FSM meetings, especially those who urged confrontation sooner rather than later, were largely newbies. Although some had political parents, only a few had been politically active at

Berkeley prior to 1963. They were far angrier than we were. They saw us as failures. We hadn't pressed hard enough. We hadn't risked enough. We had asked for change, not demanded it. In their eyes, they were the first generation of real radicals; we were just tired old liberals. They had given up on the political system, cynically believing that it only served the interests of dominant economic powers. When the administration explained that restrictions on speakers and political activity were necessary to protect the university's budget and maintain its public image as a disinterested entity, it only reinforced the radicals' negative perception of politics as usual. However, they had not given up on the legal system. Growing up in the 1950s, they had seen the federal courts order the end of racial segregation. Only the spring before, they had felt the erratic sympathy of judges and juries in the San Francisco criminal courts. A constant theme of the FSM was that only the courts should judge the legality of speech and its consequences and only the courts should punish anyone for words spoken on campus as well as off. The U.S. Constitution, especially the First Amendment, should be the only guide.

35 | *Sparring*

ALTHOUGH HE STAYED in touch with the campus, Kerr left fulfillment of the October 2nd agreement to Chancellor Strong and returned to running the university system. He assumed that the chief campus officer and his staff would follow the spirit as well as the letter of that agreement. However, once again the military model failed. Chancellor Strong had not participated in drafting the agreement, he had only a limited exposure to the discussions about its words and their meaning, he did not like it, and he did not approve of any process which displaced authority from the people in which it was officially vested. Like Mario and most of the protest leaders, he was a man of high principle. But the principles he was committed to were different ones. Despite his liberal past, he was, as many observed later, a "law and order" man. First and foremost he believed that rules should be followed and duly constituted authority should be obeyed.[1] He followed those principles in undermining the October 2nd pact.

Strong heard with dismay Mario's announcement of a noon rally for Monday, October 5th. Mario was no longer a student in good standing; what right did he have to schedule or speak at a rally on campus without appropriate sponsorship and administration approval seventy-two hours in advance? He decided to have Mario arrested, even though his faculty advisors counseled against it. Fortunately for Strong, Dean Towle decided to grant "a special waiver" for that rally only.[2] For the next two months, special waivers miraculously appeared whenever they were needed.

Indeed, many rules that Strong wanted to enforce were unofficially ignored. When we put a tub out on campus asking students to toss in money to repair the damaged cop car ($334.30)—a prohibited solicitation of funds—no one batted an eyelash. We held regular rallies from the steps of Sproul Hall—the new Hyde Park area—with prohibited amplifiers powered by car batteries, and we passed around coffee cans to collect prohibited money to support our protests against the rules limiting what we could say and do. We could now pass out leaflets on the campus proper, which we could not do before, and did so almost every day. But we couldn't sell our new white-on-blue button, which said "Free Speech F.S.M."—at least not openly on campus.

We obeyed the new rules on tabling, but their sheer lunacy only reinforced our belief that they were arbitrary and capricious. Student groups traipsed to the City of Berkeley police department to apply for one of the three weekly permits to use the ten feet of public sidewalk bordering the twenty-six feet that we had used before. The Berkeley police issued them on a first come, first served basis. This put us into competition with each other during an election year in which demand was high. It was impossible to get a permit for a sudden emergency need, even when the permit-holders for that week weren't making full use of them. The FSM used proxies to get all three permits every week that it could, which worked well for those groups which weren't in disfavor with the leadership. In the meantime, student groups that weren't selling or soliciting funds or advocating action could put tables up in the usual spots on the other side of the plaques. Private arrangements among ourselves sometimes created strange alliances. One week in October, the UYD "borrowed" a permit from CCR for a joint table with literature from the UCLC, California Professors for Johnson-Humphrey, and Students Against Proposition 14. This table sold buttons—a prohibited practice a few feet away. CCR put its own table on university property from which it "gave" out tickets to a reception. The "recipients" then "donated" the ticket price to the UYDs, which later gave it to CCR. In exchange, UYD and UCLC members sat at the CCR table when there weren't enough YRs to cover the available hours. Student groups continued to borrow tables and chairs from the ASUC and to store literature in a closet in the Student Union, conveniently located fifty feet away. We had been doing this for years without objection, and no one objected now.

Over the weekend, Strong appointed the two committees specified in the October 2nd agreement. This action was consistent with normal procedure and inconsistent with the understanding that we had with Kerr. The first problem was that there was no Student Conduct Committee of the Academic Senate. Strong asked the existing Faculty Committee on Student Conduct, appointed by him, not the Academic Senate, to hear the eight cases. He announced the formation of a Study Committee on Campus Political Activity (SCCPA), to which he appointed four faculty, four administrators, and two students, generously offering to let us choose the other two. We had expected to choose all the students and to be consulted on the faculty members. We also thought this committee would negotiate, not just study the problem, and would include in its discussions all the petty rules which hobbled our activities, not just the words we could use. Once again, we saw the administration as stacking the deck against any outcome with which they did not agree.

The FSM was shocked, shocked, at this administrative outrage and immediately charged deliberate bad faith. The Steering Committee met with Strong and then with Vice-President Earl Bolton, an aide to Kerr, but neither was willing to discuss its problems with the SCCPA. Apparently only Kerr could do this, but he was unavailable. It sent telegrams to Governor Brown and to the Regents asking to present our case to them. They said no. On the evening of October 14th, the Steering Committee met at Syd Stapleton's house to decide what to do. In the middle of the meeting, Arthur Ross, director of the Institute of Industrial Relations, phoned and asked to come over. Ross was a friend and colleague of Kerr's and offered to mediate. At the same time, Kerr was meeting with sixteen faculty and four Regents at the Davis campus, where all the Regents were to meet the next day. Between them, they worked out a deal. Kerr told Strong about it in the morning, right before announcing it to the press. The Academic Senate appointed an ad hoc committee on student discipline to hear the cases against the eight, chaired by law professor Ira Michael Heyman. Six new members were added to the Study Committee: two more from the FSM, two to be named by the Academic Senate, and two chosen by Kerr. The key change wasn't in personnel but in an understanding that each unit had a veto; a majority would not rule. Representing the FSM on the SCCPA were Mario, Bettina, Suzanne, and Syd. Peace reigned for three weeks.[3]

36 | *Energy*

As is typical of emergent social movements, the FSM released a large burst of spontaneous energy. This fueled the movement and also lit fires under people who weren't coordinated by it or even direct participants. The FSM quickly became a 24-hour operation with a large volunteer staff. Not having an office, it turned Mario's abode at 2536 College into FSM Central. During the sit-in around the car, Marilyn Noble, a grad student at Sacramento State College, had walked up to Mario and asked him "Who does your laundry?" Somewhat taken aback, he stuttered "I—I do." "Not anymore," she said. Marilyn quickly became housemother and housekeeper of Central, making sure that there was food, clean clothes, and places on the floor to sleep for everyone who needed them. Mario moved into an alcove at the front of the house. His roommates soon moved out.

Some of the eight suspended students, no longer eligible to attend classes, devoted all their time and energy to making the revolution on campus, a much more engaging prospect than classes had ever been. An informal division of labor developed among the volunteers; the women typed, cooked, and phoned, while the men wrote leaflets, drove cars, and printed. I rarely went to Central, largely because it was such a long walk from my house, but also because I was still taking classes and researching my honor's thesis on civil disobedience. When I phoned, I almost always got a busy signal. When there were meetings, Central phoned me, so I stayed loosely in touch.

When Central became too crowded, it divided and multiplied. There was Print Central, Work Central, Communications Central, and Press Central. Later would come Command Central, Strike Central, and Legal Central. And then there was Nexus, which was supposed to be the Central of all Centrals, but it didn't work. Rumor Central worked very well. The Steering Committee seemed to meet continuously, but Ex Com only got together every few days. The meetings lasted for hours; the job of the chairman was to make sure that everyone got to talk as much as he or she wanted but only one at a time. Votes were delayed until those left in the room were too exhausted to talk anymore. This almost always guaranteed that decisions would come from a consensus of those with the most time and the greatest tolerance for sleep deprivation. The FSM militants seemed to have more of both than the moderates did.

The biggest expense was for paper and ink, which was used to print materials on a small but fast machine that the FSM rented from Hal Draper. The FSM passed out a leaflet almost every day for several weeks and sold several newsletters and pamphlets. Phone bills, stamps, envelopes, posters, and rental fees for meeting halls added up. Initially the money came from collections and personal funds, but sales of buttons and records soon followed. During the entire academic year, the FSM probably raised and spent about $30,000.

Students energized by the conflict went looking for things to do. Several started a newsletter, which published five issues between October and December.[1] Another group was formed by Michael Rossman to make public the long history of conflict over rules at Cal. Rossman had been a student since he entered as a junior in 1958 and knew better than the rest of us where our protest fit into university history. He inspired and supervised about 100 students who gathered documents from personal files and university archives to produce twenty studies. Only a couple hundred copies of the complete "Rossman Report" were dittoed, but several thousand copies of a summary were printed and passed out.[2] A Fact-

FREE SPEECH MOVEMENT NEWSLETTER

FSM

Chancellor Strong   Mario Savio

(photos by s marcus)

THOUSANDS OF STUDENTS take their stand for free political expression.

WHAT HAPPENEI
day by day

On many campuses all student groups can use equally the offices, equipment, secretarial staff and other facilities provided by their student governments. At Cal these privileges are reserved for non-controversial groups such as the hiking and yachting clubs. The groups concerned with political and social questions have been relegated to a status confusingly called "off-campus." By tradition, these thoroughly student off-campus groups have used the entrances to campus, particularly the corner of Bancroft and Telegraph, to disseminate their information, obtaining a permit from the police for setting up card tables to display literature, collect signatures, donations, etc.

(Continued on page 4)

THE AGREEMENT
What it says...How it stands now

The agreement of Friday, October 3, was a first step to victory for free speech on the Berkeley campus. But the administration has begun to interpret this agreement arbitrarily and to violate both its letter and its spirit.

Below are the six points agreed to by the leaders of the student protest and the administration. Below each point is an explanation of its meaning, as agreed upon during the negotiations, and a summary of the way that the administration is keeping its part of this bargain.

1. "The student demonstrators shall desist from all forms of their illegal protest against University regulations."

This does not restrict future protests; the administration would violate

(Continued on page 4)

The first of five FSM newsletters published in the fall of 1964.

Finding Committee of Graduate Political Scientists wrote a 42 page "Preliminary Report" which compared the perspectives of students, faculty, and administration. Several people wrote songs, plays, and satires. FSM history was memorialized into music and gathered into a songbook. Dusty Miller brought together another group to write new lyrics for Christmas carols. They then produced a 45 rpm record called *Joy to UC,* which sold between twelve and fifteen thousand copies to help pay the FSM's bills.

During October I started to write long letters to my mother, Allan, and Toni, telling them the inside story of the fall events, accompanied by newspaper clippings which told the outside story. From an AP wire story that was reprinted in eastern papers, all that Toni and Allan knew was that a student mob had rioted, which certainly wasn't how we saw it. By reading multiple newspapers about events I knew well, I concluded that accuracy was inverse to distance. The *Daily Cal* had the best coverage—which was not surprising, since it was the campus newspaper. But next was *The Berkeley Gazette,* whose very conservative editor was not fond of students. *The Oakland Tribune* was in a class by itself. Third were the San Francisco papers, with little difference in their accuracy, though much in their columnists. *The Los Angeles Times,* which Helen sent me on occasion, told us things about the administration and the Regents that we did not know, but it seemed to know little about us. Bringing up the rear, with the least accurate coverage of all, was *The New York Times,* even though it had stringers on the scene.[3] Not surprisingly, my friends reacted differently than my mother. Toni and Allan were enthralled with our actions; they wished they were here. Helen tried to be supportive and agreed that taking away our political space was arbitrary and stupid, but after years as a teacher she thought that the first duty of students was to obey their elders. Her biggest concern was that I not get arrested again or get kicked out of school.

Toni's and Allan's letters were full of personal news. Allan enjoyed Antioch. Toni hated Wayne State. She desperately wanted to transfer to San Francisco State but didn't know how she would pay out-of-state tuition. She had barely started the quarter when she was knocked up by an old boyfriend and had to blow her savings on an abortion. She shelled out a couple hundred bucks to a real physician to solve what she called her "disposal problem" but still found it traumatic. I also corresponded with a new friend I had met at the Chicago Freedom House. Joyce Ley was attending Orlando (Florida) Junior College, where she was shunned after admitting to her classmates that she was an atheist. To them, she wrote me, Berkeley students were *all* Communists, and thus not to be believed.

I went to all the Ex Com meetings, which became larger in attendance and smaller in representation. Although Central only phoned members with the time and place of meetings, anyone could come, and did. Not all were FSM supporters. Robert Hull was the young campus cop assigned to report on meetings and pick up documents. He was not the only undercover agent. FSM was where it was at, and many students, some nonstudents, and even a few faculty members thought the meetings were exciting. Some were, but after a while one realized that the same people said pretty much the same things at every meeting, only they took longer and longer to say them. Stiles Hall was too small for these large meetings and we weren't allowed to meet on campus, so meetings moved among the various religious buildings catering to students (Hillel, Newman Hall, Wesley, Westminster), each of which was given votes on the Ex Com. The Ex Com voting body shrank because it was harder and harder to get group representatives who were also students to give up their studies two or three evenings a week just to listen to repetitive pontification. I would only ask another UYD to come if I thought there would be a vote and I could find someone willing to stay very late because votes were never taken early. Vicky and Mike Eisen usually represented UCLC. When one of them couldn't come, I would ask some student present as a spectator to represent UCLC. This was risky because they couldn't always be relied on to vote the organization's position rather than their own. Some of the conservative groups stopped coming (though they didn't quit the FSM) because the relentless rhetoric grated on their ears.

The Steering Committee also increased its numbers, but the working body contracted to the four on the SCCPA plus Jack Weinberg. By the end of October all decisions were made by Mario and Jack, though they listened to Bettina. This caused some unhappiness among the other members of the Steering Committee and larger portions of the Ex Com. By the end of October discontent was bubbling into the open. Betty Linsky, one of the independent reps to the Ex Com, invited me to a meeting of Ex Com members who wanted to elect a new Steering Committee which would be both more representative of student views and more accountable to the Ex Com. It was mostly independents and Graduate Coordinating Committee reps; the "right wing" wasn't there. I said that civil disobedience should always be the weapon of last resort, not first resort and that the FSM hadn't asked the help of as much of the outside world as we could. As an example of how we could do this, I told them that Jerry Fishkin had written to dozens of Democratic officeholders presenting the FSM's case and sometimes got supportive replies. Several sent him copies of letters they wrote to President Kerr and Governor Brown favoring the concept of free speech on campus. Controller Alan Cranston had phoned, and Governor Brown wrote back that "I have not supported the University's rules regarding students and student activities." Why not ask our parents and friends old enough to vote to do the same?

37 | *Escalation*

THE ENLARGED AND revised SCCPA began meeting on October 20th. Bettina and Syd were the voice of reason, while Mario often lost his cool and yelled a lot. Jack came as an observer; in between meetings he conferred with the FSM negotiators. The FSM took the position that the only rule governing political activity and speech should be the U.S. Constitution; what was okay off campus should be okay on campus. This was a brilliant tactic, but it left no room for compromise. The state legislature, the Regents, or the courts might declare this to be university policy, but the administration wouldn't. The administration delegates wanted to forbid on-campus advocacy of illegal action off campus. This seemed to shoot through the heart what the FSM wanted most to protect: the right to recruit students for civil rights demonstrations which might result in arrests. The FSM argued that students should not be disciplined by the university in addition to whatever the courts might do. At a last meeting on Saturday, November 7th, the SCCPA reached an impasse. It seemed we could have everything we wanted, including reduction of the silly rules, solicitation of funds and membership, and organizational meetings, and we could do it in Sproul Plaza and all of the Hyde Park areas, not just Bancroft and Telegraph. *But* we couldn't say anything on campus that promoted illegal off-campus activity.

The FSM had already escalated its tactics. On Wednesday, November 4th, several dozen students picketed Sproul Hall. At a Friday noon rally Mario announced that the FSM would resume direct action on Monday but didn't specify what it would be. The Steering Committee had decided to do this at a 1:00 A.M. meeting without consulting the Ex Com, which ticked a lot of people off. The loose collection of "moderates," which had been quiescent until now, began to coalesce. We felt that the militants had maneuvered the SCCPA into a deadlock to have an excuse for another sit-in. The negotiation process had not yet played itself out. It wasn't at all clear to us that we couldn't get what we needed from the SCCPA—which only made recommendations, not final rules—and we weren't convinced we needed administrative approval of unlimited advocacy to continue our support of the Civil Rights Movement. The Ex Com had never debated what our bottom line was; Mario and Jack would not let that issue come to the floor.

Just as important, popular sentiment was slipping through our fingers. After the October 2nd pact, all sorts of people had expressed their support, for our ends if not for our means. The northern California chapter of the American Civil Liberties Union, the executive committee of the Association of California State College Professors, the ASUC, numerous groups of grad students, some faculty, and even 650 Greeks passed resolutions, sent letters, circulated petitions, or otherwise blessed our noble cause. But a month of propaganda warfare, in which FSM actions outweighed FSM words, torpedoed our popularity. Students were beginning to question what the FSM was doing and *why* it was doing it. A sociology class in research methods interviewed a sample of students in November. When pressure intensified, the percentage of those who approved of both FSM goals and tactics slid from 50 percent to 22 percent.[1]

The FSM leadership got wind of the moderates' meeting and invited a select few to meet with them. They brought them back into the fold, inviting Ron Anastasi to be on the Steering Committee. Their direction became clear at the Ex Com meeting Friday afternoon (*after* Mario's announcement) that was called to discuss possible proposals to be made at the SCCPA meeting on Saturday. As chairman, Jack ruled out of order any attempt to discuss what we would do on Monday on the grounds that this meeting was solely to discuss language. We did talk about possible compromises, but when the SCCPA met the next day none of these were mentioned. The FSM negotiators insisted that the demand for free speech was absolute. Deadlock was ensured.

Ex Com resumed meeting Saturday afternoon to debate whether to accept the proposed language of the faculty delegates to the SCCPA. The moderates brought in former SLATE chairman Mike Tigar, now a law student at Boalt Hall, to argue in favor of accepting one of the faculty proposals. *Whether* to resume direct action on Monday was still out of order. The debate continued until about 10:00 P.M., when most of those who took anything other than a hard-line approach had gone home in exhaustion. Only after winning this vote did Mario and Jack call for a committee of nine to be elected to run the forthcoming confrontation. The fact that there would be a confrontation was assumed. They effectively co-opted the moderates' demand for a new Steering Committee by replacing it with one more compatible to their views. Seeing that resistance was futile, I left before the election. Wendel Brunner, another of Art's roommates, told me later that each candidate claimed to be more radical and militant than the previous one. *All* the moderates lost, including Art Goldberg, who barely qualified as one. Art's position was that we should hold off putting up tables until the administration gave us another atrocity. He wasn't for compromise, only delay.

38 | The "Right Wing" Revolt

MONDAY MORNING DAWNED gray and overcast. By the time I got to campus, the wind was cold and gusty. Half a dozen tables had sprouted like mushrooms below the Sproul Hall steps: SNCC, CORE, Women for Peace, FSM, YSA, ISC, and others all solicited donations and members.

On Sunday, Central had phoned to ask if the UYDs would man our own table or if Central should supply people. "No one will be setting up a YD table," I replied. "Certainly not FSM Central." At the spot where the police car had parked in October stood an empty chest of drawers with a chair leaning against the side, surrounded by about 200 people. A few hundred more lurked on the edge. At noon, Mario climbed on top and began to explain why the tables were there. "The university is unwilling to negotiate," he said. "Therefore we must again exercise our First Amendment rights."

The spirit of the crowd was low. They looked puzzled, not angry. From what they had read in the *Daily Cal* that morning, it was the FSM that had refused to negotiate. Of those surveyed by the sociology class on November 9th, only 14 percent supported FSM tactics. Monitors kept open a path up the stairs to the doors of Sproul Hall. About fifteen minutes after twelve, two deanlets came out and walked down the aisle. Mario greeted them warmly. Ignoring his overture, the deanlets went to the Women for Peace table and asked the girl behind it for her name. The FSM mike was passed to her, and she spoke into it. "They have just asked me for my name. It's Deborah Barlett, and I'm a junior in dramatic arts." A mumble of low voices could be heard over the loudspeaker. "Now they have asked me for my reg card. I'm telling them that my reg card says that I must show it on demand to officers of the university. Would they please prove to me that they are officers of the university," she continued. Another inaudible mumble. "They have shown me their identification, so now I will show them my reg card." Deborah continued to describe both sides of the conversation, since the deanlets wouldn't speak into the microphone.

"They are asking me if I know that I am violating a regulation of the university. What regulation? They say that I must have a permit to put up this table and that I don't have one. Someone from Women for Peace went to the dean of students' office and asked for a permit but was refused one when she wouldn't swear that she would not collect donations, solicit members, or advocate political or social action." A deanlet was heard in a low, emotionless voice saying: "Since you don't have a permit, we will have to ask you to fold up this table and leave or we might have to take disciplinary action against you." Deborah responded: "I agreed to sit at this table for this hour, I have no authority to remove the table, and I would be abrogating my responsibility if I left it sitting here." The deanlets wrote down her name and went down the line of tables, writing down the names of all those sitting behind. As soon as one name was taken, that person would rise and another would take his or her place. Some students standing behind the tables called out to the deanlets to take their names, which they dutifully did for about two hours.

While the deanlets wrote, the FSMers spoke. They damned the "so-called liberals" in the administration and redefined the struggle from one between the administration and the FSM to a clash between the students as a class and the power structure of the state of California. When they finished, the bureau/podium stood forlornly under the leaden sky. The wind whistled its hostility, but the rains did not fall. Those behind the tables pulled their coats tighter in a stubborn testimonial to their grim determination to resist anyone or anything, administration or adverse weather.

I watched all this from the sidelines, sorely troubled. I thought it was morally and tactically wrong. I wanted to speak out against the resumption of tabling, to tell the students why this was not the time for direct action. But I didn't want to give ammunition to an administration whom we did not trust; it would use any sign of internal dissent against us all. Instead, I decided to "work within the system" of the FSM itself. I knew others felt as I did. SLATE had not put up a table. Art and Sandor watched the noon rally from the terrace, not as part of the audience. But first I had to find out if the administration intended to cite the seventy-five students whose names had been taken. If they did that, it would obscure the tables as an issue. Solidarity would demand that we support the cited students and, with them, the FSM. I went to the poli sci office to talk to Scalapino. He said he had retired from the whole affair after seeing how the FSM negotiators conducted themselves, but that Professor Paul Seabury was still interested. Seabury said he'd see what he could find out; I should phone him at home at 10:00 P.M.

On the way home I ran into Kathy Whitney, who cooked dinner for Brian Turner and his roommates. I told her that some of us were very unhappy with the direction the FSM was taking and even unhappier that the militants on the Steering Committee dismissed our concerns as irrelevant. Rather than debate our differences, they wanted us to just shut up and go away. She said that Brian felt the same way. He had also been removed from the Steering Committee when it was reconstituted on Saturday. I told her that several of us wanted to do something, but we weren't sure what to do. At 8:00 P.M., Brian came over and asked me to help him organize an emergency Ex Com meeting to get the tables removed. The staff at FSM Central had said that any twelve Ex Com members could call a meeting. I had seven organizations, equal to fourteen Ex Com votes, that I could count on in the "right wing," but I knew that if we used their names we'd be dismissed as mere "right wing" restiveness. I, Brian, Art, and Sandor were one-third of those necessary. We began phoning other Ex Com members to find another eight willing to put their names on the line. At 10:30 I reached Seabury, who told me he had spoken to Lipset, who had talked to Kerr, who had assured him that the administration would not cite the students as long as there was no further escalation.

The FSM leadership quickly found out what we were doing and tried to stop it. Mario told FSM Central not to call an Ex Com meeting, no matter how many names we claimed. Jack phoned David Goines, his chief factotum and all-around gopher, and told him to remove the phone lists from the office so the staff couldn't phone the Ex Com members. Goines grabbed them and left, to the great consternation of the rest of the office staff.

Several times Mario asked the telephone operator to interrupt Brian's phone calls, claiming he had an "emergency call," so he could argue him out of calling a meeting. Brian and Mario had been close friends the year before when they lived in the same private student housing complex at 2283 Hearst Street, colloquially known as the "pink motel." They had long, involved conversations on civil rights and other ethical issues. Brian had picketed Mel's but, as a freshman still finding his academic feet, he wasn't ready to get arrested. At the beginning of the 1964 academic year, four friends from the year before rented the house on College Avenue that became FSM Central. Mario and Brian represented Friends of SNCC at the United Front meetings; Mario had encouraged Brian to sit at the SNCC table, where he was cited on September 30th. Brian felt that he was just as deeply committed to the Civil Rights Movement as Mario. He had not gone south the previous summer, but he had helped the MFDP at the Democratic Convention and driven back to California via Alabama, where he visited a friend teaching at Miles College, a Negro college near Birmingham. Mario's harsh words put Brian on the verge of tears. Nonetheless, he persevered. He finally convinced Mario to let the meeting happen; if he didn't, dissent would just fester. The FSM Ex Com needed to debate what we were doing and why. And we needed to vote, one way or the other.

Mario agreed to a meeting at 8:00 A.M. at a private house on the north side. This would not be an open meeting in a large hall; only Ex

Com members could come. We didn't know that Central's staff no longer had the phone lists to inform all the members, but we did know that we had better make sure that *our* votes were there. I stayed up all night phoning the organizations whom I knew disapproved of the resumption of direct action at that time, while Brian phoned independents and GCC reps. In the middle of the night I told each organization president to find two people to represent their group and to give each a statement signed by the president legitimating them. The only one who gave me any resistance was Al Bergman, who had replaced Jerry Fishkin when he resigned as UYD president. I needed a second UYD rep for the vote, and Bergman didn't think it was his responsibility to find one.

I recruited a friend to be the other UYD vote and to bring his car. He picked up several Republicans along with their signed statements and met me in front of the meeting house. When we entered we were a strange-looking group: a girl with long, stringy hair in a grubby green coat and torn tennis shoes leading a pack of fresh-faced young boys with short hair in suits and ties. As we stood in the hallway looking for places to sit, Mario walked by. He stopped and scrutinized my exhausted frame with dark rings underneath my eyes. "Don't let anyone ever accuse of you of being principled," he snarled, and walked on.

Brian, Sandor, Art, and I did most of the talking for our side. We wanted to delay direct action until we had truly exhausted all other possibilities. We needed faculty support. And, as Art said several times, we hadn't prepared the students for more confrontation. I stressed the need for and possibility of mobilizing outside resources. Mario and Jack countered that direct action had already started; any pullback would look like weakness or a split in the FSM. Our case was undermined by the fact that the morning newspapers proclaimed that Kerr and Strong had dissolved the SCCPA because the "FSM has abrogated the agreement of October 2." They would now seek advice from the ASUC and the Academic Senate. How could the FSM resume discussions if there was no longer anyone to talk to?

The chair, Steve Weissman, insisted on a roll call to see if everyone there was a member in good standing of the Ex Com. I expected the conservative groups to be challenged because they had been missing from the meetings. But they hadn't resigned, and their signed statements kept them on. Instead, Cal Students for Goldwater and UCLC were challenged. The case for CSG was weak. It had denounced the FSM publicly several times and the presidential election for which it was formed was over. Danny

Rosenthal threatened the FSM with another blast if CSG was removed; it wasn't. When Bob Kaufman (History Department, DuBois Club, GCC rep) moved to unseat UCLC, it caught me off guard, since Vicky Blickman and Mike Eisen had been regulars at Ex Com meetings. Unfortunately they couldn't make it to this one, and the two boys I had drafted to take their place couldn't make their case. As UCLC president I could have done so, but I opted to say nothing rather than confirm everyone's suspicion that it voted at my direction.

I watched the vote carefully. All the GCCs and independents—the very people Brian had phoned—voted to disfranchise UCLC. We had two votes each from UCLC, UYD, UYR, CCR, YPSL, DSC, SLATE, CSG, Particle (a student science journal), plus Brian Turner and Bob Jervis of SDS. By a vote of 21 to 20, UCLC was ousted from the FSM Ex Com. I knew then that we had lost. The final vote over the tables was delayed until 10:00 A.M. when more militants had arrived, Bob Jervis had left, and UCLC could no longer vote. By a vote of 17 to 29, the tables stayed up.

Not everyone was at this Ex Com meeting, but there was a clear distinction between those who were. Those voting to resume negotiations were representatives of the ongoing student groups, which would benefit most from rule liberalizations and which wanted to return to their normal political work. Voting for civil disobedience and confrontation were representatives of entities created by the FSM—the GCC and the independent students—plus a few cited students and some organizations (DuBois Club, YSA, CORE, Friends of SNCC, one from SDS). Most of these people would be politically unemployed when the movement was over.

On his way out, Mario stopped in front of me again. This time he smiled. "The difference between you and me," he said, "is that you would settle for a drab victory, while I prefer a brilliant defeat."

He was right.

39 | *The Secret Negotiations*

DEPRESSED AND DEFEATED, we walked out into a very damp day. "Even God voted no," Brian said, looking at the sky. Despondently he disappeared into the drizzle. Dick Roman suggested that the left wing of the "right wing" go for coffee. This was the two of us, Jim Burnett of YPSL, plus Sue Schwartz and Ann Kilby of the Democratic Socialist Club (DSC). We didn't see that there was much more that we could do, but we decided that Dick would talk to Lipset, for whom he was RA (research assistant), and I would talk to Seabury.

Dick later told me that Lipset listened attentively while he and Jim described the events of the last twenty-four hours. When they asked for advice, he picked up the phone and dialed. "Clark?" he said. "My RA tells me the moderates are pretty disgusted with FSM and their current actions." Lipset repeated to Kerr what they had told him, then asked Kerr to meet us at 5:15 at Lipset's home. Kerr inquired about whether Chancellor Strong should come as well, since it was his campus. Lipset turned and asked, "What about Strong?" A pained expression clouded Dick's face, while Jim slowly shook his head. "They said no," Lipset told Kerr.

Graduate students manned the illegal tables on Tuesday. Since they were much of the research and teaching staff of the university, the GCC felt the university would be cutting its own throat if they were suspended. When the deans stayed inside, the grad students sent 274 names to the dean of students demanding that they too be cited. Ten days later, Dean Towle wrote to all of them that she would consider this to be in error unless each student personally affirmed their participation.[1] She received 710 replies from grad students claiming complicity. Nothing more happened.

With representation from fifty departments, the GCC was already talking about a possible strike. Although the FSM was started and run by undergraduates, grad students were becoming a larger and more influential constituency. They had their own grievances, for which the FSM was a way to fight a proxy battle. Once the pretense of prestige was brushed aside, grad students were just an exploited low-wage labor force. TAs did work similar to that of high school teachers—teaching small classes, grading papers and exams, supervising students—but without the pay or perquisites. RAs did grub work for faculty. Being a TA or an RA was a way to finance graduate education, but only at a poverty-level lifestyle.

I had to cut half a class to get to Lipset's house in time, as it was high in the north Berkeley hills. It was dark when we arrived. Kerr was late. He was nervous as he gave us the same "You have to trust me" speech I had heard on October 2nd. We didn't trust him, and we said so. First he wanted us to cool down Mario to give him some maneuvering room. That we cannot do, we said. We have no control over Mario. Then he wanted us to precipitate an open break with the FSM so he could have a "realistic" group to deal with. Seabury had told me that Kerr was willing to give us everything we wanted—minimal rules and no restrictions on advocacy—but he would not give in to the FSM and particularly not to Mario Savio. We were willing to be that group, but only if we had a firm agreement first. And even with that, we would try to persuade the Ex Com to support it before we made a public split.

Once we got past these barriers, we had a good discussion. We parted optimistically, agreeing to meet at University Hall the following day. We would bring representatives of more groups with us and concrete language to discuss. In the meantime, we said, make sure no student gets cited. That will blow everything. When I got home, I asked Jerry and Al to come over. We massaged the language of the SCCPA faculty proposals that the FSM had opposed on Saturday to make it acceptable to all but the most hard-line members of the Ex Com. Wednesday morning the Poli Sci Department made copies for me to give to everyone who would be meeting with Kerr. We had heard that the faculty delegates to the SCCPA were preparing another version of their proposal, but we couldn't get a copy.

The eight who went to University Hall included people from the conservative groups. Vice President Bolton greeted us. Kerr was only half an hour late this time. He wouldn't even discuss our proposals. He was going with the faculty version, which we hadn't seen. All he wanted was for us to openly break with the FSM and trust him to do the right thing. We asked to meet by ourselves and everyone else exited from the room. All of us were angry, the conservatives most of all. We felt used. We left.

Several of us walked to Hillel, where the Ex Com was to meet. There we learned that Strong had cited the seventy-five students whose names had been taken on Monday; they were to report to the dean's office for disciplinary action. Kerr had promised us no citations as a precondition to our discussions; either the man who told us to trust him had lied, or he had no idea what his subordinates were doing. That was the end of the "right wing" revolt. The administration had united us at last.

Our new bitterness did not restore us to the good graces of the militants who were now firmly in control of the FSM. While we agreed not to mention the meetings with Kerr, word leaked out. We thought of ourselves as The Loyal Opposition. They saw us as The Enemy. Our talks with Kerr confirmed their worst suspicions of our perfidy. Brian Turner had been eliminated from the Steering Committee for his conciliatory views and for conferring with Arleigh Williams on the side. Now, Mario's old friend and comrade was a pariah on the Ex Com, even though as a cited student he had a permanent place and could not be removed. Art was returned to purgatory—reinstalled on the Steering Committee and ignored. I was consigned to hell, labeled a rat fink, traitor, and general sell-out. From Rumor Central came stories so outlandish that they were almost amusing (e.g., that I was making regular reports to the governor's office, that I had told Mona Hutchin to seduce Jack Weinberg). On November 18th, I phoned Central to find out why I hadn't been called for that day's Ex Com meeting. I was told that I had resigned as "free speech coordinator" for the UYDs. Puzzled, I phoned Bergman and asked if I had been removed. "No way," he said. "You're the only one keeping the YDs in the FSM. If you go, we go." I knew that if the UYDs left the FSM, all the Republican and conservative groups would as well. Bergman phoned Central and told them that my reported resignation was not true.

40 | *Changes*

I DID LIE LOW for a while, skipping Ex Com meetings to catch up on my schoolwork, but I stayed in touch. Both the Ex Com and the more important Steering Committee underwent changes in personnel as some members shifted from protest to course work and others were energized or disgusted with what was essentially a stalemate. Before our showdown over the tables, the Steering Committee was functionally reduced to five people: Mario, Jack, Syd, Bettina, and Suzanne. Within a few days, Art Goldberg, Brian Turner, and Dusty Miller had been removed, while Mona Hutchin, Ron Anastasi, and Marty Roysher were added. Syd Stapleton left Cal to go to trade school, excited about the prospect of joining the proletariat with a full-time job. Art was restored. New people came and went. Now they were "co-opted" onto the Steering Committee, needing only the approval of Mario and Jack.

Of these new people, two graduate students had more than a token presence. Steve Weissman, 24, was born and raised in Tampa, Florida. After getting an M.A. in European History at the University of Michigan the spring before, he had come to Berkeley to study Latin American history. He joined the Ex Com as a GCC rep where he demonstrated a talent for chairing the often-contentious meetings. Michael Rossman was a mathematician of many talents, from many places. Originally from Colorado, he finished high school in San Francisco and spent two years at the University of Chicago before coming to Cal in 1958. At 25, he was probably the oldest member of the Steering Committee and the only one in the leadership who had been in the 1960 HUAC demonstrations. The report he coordinated was officially presented to the SCCPA the day the tables were set up, which was also the day the SCCPA was dissolved.

Some of the militants thought these changes had co-opted the moderates, but in fact they had only silenced us. We thought they were going in the wrong direction, but we were clearly a minority on the Ex Com, and our ability to influence events was nil. To us, the FSM leadership had lost sight of the original goal. We had all long since moved beyond wanting our political space back. We now wanted to do *on* campus what we had previously done only at Bancroft and Telegraph, subject to *reasonable* rules and restrictions. By now, the faculty and many in the administration were willing to let us do this; they were also willing to let us hold large public rallies and organizational meetings on campus, which we had never been able to do. Far from hobbling the political groups, the rules proposed by the six SCCPA faculty reps would give us wheels.[1] The sticking point was on-campus advocacy of illegal off-campus action. While those of us in the "right wing" understood the *principle* involved, we thought it was nitpicking over a restriction that would have no impact on our work and would be impossible to enforce. If we were wrong, we could fight that battle when there was an actual controversy, not just a theoretical one. In our more cynical moments, we saw the stalemate as just a power struggle; instead of declaring victory, the militants had locked horns with the administration and would not budge.

From listening to Mario, Jack, Bettina, and Syd, I realized that what they wanted was a revolution on one campus. They wanted the empowerment of students and saw the FSM as the means to this goal. I thought it was a beautiful vision, but totally out of touch with reality. And after my experience with the militants on the FSM Steering Committee, I had no more confidence in the ability of students to be fair and reasonable than I did in the administration.

41 | *Mutual Misconceptions*

NEITHER THE FSM nor the administration had a realistic assessment of each other, nor did either try to see the world from the other's point of view.

The FSM leaders thought of the administration as a monolith and administrators as adversaries with very different ideas about and goals for the university than those held by faculty and students. Nor did it view administrators as role models. At best they were weak-kneed wimps, sacrificing principles to the whims of the legislature. At worst they were puppets of the major economic interests represented by the Regents, who were deliberately trying to undermine the Civil Rights Movement. Although most administrators were then or had been members of the faculty, the FSM did not put them in the same camp or give them the same deference as it did the faculty.

Yet from the very beginning there were lines of fissure. In fact, there were at least three administrations—the deans, the chancellor's office, and the president—with quite different attitudes toward the politically active students. These administrators often worked at cross-purposes.

Katherine Towle and Arleigh Williams had dealt directly with students for a long time. Towle was appointed dean of women by Chancellor Kerr in 1953 after she retired as the country's first director of the women's marines with the rank of colonel. In 1961, she became the first woman to be Cal's dean of students. Williams was appointed dean of men in 1959 after several years as director of student activities for the ASUC. He had played football as a Cal undergraduate and coached high school teams before becoming a professional administrator.

The deans were the closest to the students, the most sympathetic, and the most pragmatic. They viewed congestion and litter at Bancroft and Telegraph as minor matters not requiring major surgery and knew that there was no pressure from the *Oakland Tribune* or the politicians to put a lid on student political activity. They also knew that Thomas Cunningham, general counsel to the Regents, had written Sherriffs in September that there was no basis "either in law or university regulation" for permitting some types of political literature to be passed out on campus but not others, for forbidding either advocacy or recruitment. The Regents' chief lawyer had advised the administration that some of the restrictions the deans were ordered to enforce were not legally proper.[1]

Towle and Williams kept in touch with a few of the FSM activists throughout the fall. Towle and Jackie Goldberg spoke to each other on the phone regularly, albeit cautiously. However, both were out of the loop, so neither had any power to affect attitudes or events. The FSM militants saw the deans as mere puppets, but in their own way, they tried to maximize student freedom within the rules. They did not write the rules, but they could "interpret" them, and tried to be helpful when they could.

At the top was Clark Kerr, president of the entire university system, who was answerable only to the Regents and could, if he chose, overrule decisions by campus administrators. Regulation of student activity was not the only thing on his agenda, and he thought that once he laid out the guidelines, the campus administration should decide how to apply them. The fact that SLATE had repeatedly challenged his codifications, and, he thought, misinterpreted them as tightening rather than loosening the reins, did not predispose him to give credence to student claims. A Quaker, Kerr had spent three summers in the early 1930s as a peace caravanner for the American Friends Service Committee. He thought of himself as a peacemaker and was most comfortable in the role of mediator; leading one side of an adversarial confrontation was not where he wanted to be. He thought the students should trust him because he was their best hope to liberalize the rules and never quite understood why they didn't.

In between were Chancellor Strong and Alex Sherriffs, who appeared to be of one mind about student conduct, reinforcing each other's views. They had the least direct contact with students or Regents and the most rigid attitudes toward student conduct. Strong, a philosopher by training who joined Cal's faculty in 1932, believed in taking a principled position and sticking to it. He thought that students should obey the rules and not challenge duly constituted authority. The fact that these rules were unfair, arbitrary, and crippling was not open to debate; content or consequences were irrelevant to the issue of who was in charge. Sherriffs had come to Cal in 1944 while finishing his doctorate in psychology at Stanford and was made a vice-chancellor by Kerr in 1958. He thought our behavior was the result of bad parenting.[2]

Kerr, Strong, and Sherriffs shared many experiences. All had received some of their higher education at Stanford. All had served on Cal's faculty for many years. Kerr and Strong were at Cal in the mid-1930s (Strong as junior faculty, Kerr as a graduate student) when student strikes were Communist led. All had been involved in the loyalty-oath controversy of the early 1950s. None supported the oath, though none were willing to risk their jobs in opposition; all sought some equitable resolution. Perhaps that's why they survived long enough to become administrators. All were Democrats, though Sherriffs was the only one who dabbled in electoral politics. In 1953, he narrowly lost a race for the Berkeley school board and was involved in CDC. None were hostile to the Civil Rights Movement or thought the students shouldn't support it.

It's unlikely that any would have been receptive to a personal request from William Knowland that the university punish students who were picketing his newspaper. Indeed, Kerr and Knowland shared a mutual distaste for each other. But since all had some experience with public relations, we never knew if they really believed what they said about us, let alone what they were quoted as saying.

The newspapers readily printed administration descriptions of who we were, most of which made us laugh. The day after we signed the October 2nd pact, we learned that the United Front was mostly way-out leftists and nonstudents. Funniest were statements the press quoted Kerr as making *before* our negotiations: under the front-page headline " 'Reds on Campus'—UC's Kerr" the *San Francisco Examiner* wrote:

> University of California president Clark Kerr yesterday declared flatly that a hard core of "Castro-Mao Tse-tung line" Communists were in the crowd of demonstrators gathered in front of Sproul Hall on the Berkeley campus.
>
> Kerr told an Examiner reporter that very few university students were actually involved in the hard core leadership.
>
> "There is an extreme left wing element there," he said. "Forty-nine percent of the hard core group are followers of the Castro-Mao line."

The version on page nine in the *San Francisco Chronicle* was a little more restrained:

> "Some of them are just back from Alabama and Mississippi," he said, "and full of ideas of direct action, and that you only get somewhere by direct action."
>
> "I am also sorry to say that some elements have been impressed with the tactics of Fidel Castro and Mao Tse-tung. There are very few of these, but there are some."

Kerr added that "many, many of the demonstrators" are not university students.

We spent some time during the founding meeting of the FSM joking about who were the 49 percent. Art was the only one who claimed to be a Maoist, but he wasn't a member of any Maoist group (indeed, there weren't yet any such groups on campus). Jack was the only nonstudent we knew of, and he was an alumnus. Mario was the only one who had been to Mississippi. Bettina and Syd were the only real "reds," but neither was a Maoist, and their parties were bitter enemies.

While the administration was telling the press that we were a small, discontented radical minority, we were collecting data. Between October 24th and 27th, 618 of those who sat in around the car filled out a lengthy questionnaire drawn up by an undergraduate physics student that was made available from an FSM table. While not a random sample, it sketched an outline of the early October demonstrators. About half had never been in a demonstration before; 17 percent had been in seven or more. Only a quarter were members of "a campus political or social action group." Eight percent were Republicans, half were Democrats, a quarter were democratic socialists, and 10 percent were revolutionary socialists. What moved them to action was their feeling of a "need to take a stand on free speech" (60 percent) and disgust at the "Administration's handling of the affair" (63 percent). Over half were willing to "risk arrest and expulsion" if negotiations broke down.[3]

The accuracy of the administration's public descriptions didn't improve even though it had time to find out who we were. A few days after signing the October 2nd pact, Kerr told the San Diego Chamber of Commerce that we were "encouraged, as never before, by elements external to the University." After the October Regents meeting, Kerr once again told the press that some in the FSM "had Communist sympathies." While technically correct, it implied much more than was true. On October 20th, Strong warned that "the professional demonstrators" would strike again. He identified these as having spent the previous summer in Mississippi but added "I won't smear all the other good kids by calling it Communist-led."[4]

Kerr was mostly wrong about who we were. Strong was half right. The FSM was too anarchistic to listen to Communists; it accepted the few there were largely to defy the pervasive anti-Communist sentiments of the era. Our moral imperative was racial justice, not class conflict. Nonetheless, very few of us had gone south for Freedom Summer, and of those, only Mario was a moving force. A few more had gone to Atlantic City for the MFDP vigil. But almost all of us, at least among those investing major time and energy into social protest, were inspired by the Civil Rights Movement. While we weren't "professional demonstrators," we had learned our tactics from that movement. Our teacher had not been the southern Civil Rights Movement, but the San Francisco sit-ins of the spring before. *That* was our model for action, not Mississippi, where sitting in was far too dangerous. The source of campus protest was right at home.[5]

42 | *The Heyman Committee Report*

ON FRIDAY, NOVEMBER 13TH, the Academic Senate Ad Hoc Committee on Suspensions, otherwise known as the Heyman Committee, released its report. After thirty-five hours of hearings and deliberations, the five faculty members recommended that six of the eight suspended students be reinstated as of the date of their suspension with the words "indefinite suspension" expunged from their records. They recommended six-week suspensions for Art and Mario, as leaders of the demonstrations, beginning on September 30th and ending on November 16th. The report criticized the administration for its "unusual" procedure of indefinitely suspending students before any hearings were held. Its overall tone was sympathetic to the students.[1] The FSM was elated. The administration was not.

Chancellor Strong was furious. First, the Heyman Committee stepped on his toes when its chairman sent the report to the Academic Senate rather than to him. He saw this as a slight to his authority as chief campus officer. After an angry exchange of memos and phone calls, Heyman retreated and confessed "that our report dated November 12 should have been delivered to the administration with copies to the Academic Senate, Berkeley division." Second, Strong did not like the critical attitude of the Heyman report or what he saw as the paltry punishment of students for knowingly and deliberately violating university regulations. On November 18th he wrote President Kerr that accepting the committee's recommendations would be seen as "showing weakness . . . in the face of deliberate violations."[2] Strong was not alone in his dismay. Dean Arleigh Williams had been chief witness for the "prosecution," a role he played without enthusiasm. Williams had not favored the administrative actions which led to the suspensions, but he was the dean who wrote the reports and the one who was cross-examined by lawyers representing the cited students. Williams had favored leniency, but not this much.[3]

On the night of October 2nd, when we discussed point 4 of the proposed agreement, we were told that the recommendations of faculty committees about student discipline were advisory to the chancellor but that he always accepted their advice. Yet once the agreement was signed and the captured car released, Strong balked. Heyman initially asked that the suspended students be reinstated pending the hearing, but Strong refused to do so. He told Heyman that the Board of Regents had asked that he and Kerr confer with them before acting on any recommendations of the student conduct committee. They would report to the Regents, who would make the final decision about the academic fate of the eight. Strong repeatedly said, privately and publicly, that the Heyman Committee was only concerned with violations by students through September 30th and that for "serious misconduct since that date . . . regular disciplinary procedures will prevail." Nonetheless, most of us, and probably most of the faculty as well, thought that the Regents' meeting on November 20th would be the final word on discipline for the fall. After all, the rules were about to change. Why prosecute students under the old rules for conduct not in violation of the new?[4]

The FSM prepared for the Regents' meeting by putting up tables in still-forbidden space near Sproul Hall steps every day. The administration did nothing. Numerous groups, on and off campus, proclaimed their support of the FSM's goals, if not its methods. Mail to the Regents ran in favor of the FSM's goals. Charlie Powell, president of the ASUC, formed a five-man committee to review the recommendations of the SCCPA. It suggested several "improvements" very much like the proposals we had drafted to discuss with Kerr. Mario Savio and Michael Rossman criticized them as insufficient. The law students' association condemned the administration's restrictions on political activity. Even CDC's Board of Directors asked the Regents to protect "the constitutional liberty" of the students. Student approval of the demonstrators' goals *and* tactics rose to 47 percent.[5]

43 | *The Regents Meet*

FRIDAY WAS A brilliant day. The Regents, who rotated their monthly meetings among the campuses, fortuitously held this one at University Hall. As a welcoming party, the FSM organized a massive noon rally on Sproul Hall steps. To ensure a large turnout, it asked folksinger Joan Baez to come and sing. She had given a concert on campus in the Greek Theater on October 2nd and there announced to all assembled that she supported the students who had sat around the police car. The crowd was further swollen by the unanticipated presence of a "Big Game" rally on the other side of the Plaza. The annual football game with Stanford University was a major Greek gala, but this was not the usual location for the pre-game rally. For a while the pep rally strove to drown out our speakers. Then Steve Weissman grabbed the mike and led us in a "Beat Stanford" yell. The cheerleaders responded with a "Free Speech" yell, and after a while each group was yelling for the other. Soon our speakers could talk without further interruption.

We had been told to dress for the occasion, and some of us turned out in our Sunday best. Someone was beginning to think about public relations and how we looked in the press. Speeches stressed that the U.S. Constitution was the paramount law of the land. After Joan Baez led us in singing "The Lord's Prayer" and "We Shall Overcome," the leaders marched through Sather Gate, carrying a banner that said FREE SPEECH, followed by thousands of students. In the front line, Mona Hutchin carried the American flag. As we passed under the university's chief symbol, prominently displayed on its stationery and on the doors of police cars, dozens of photographers took what became the classic shot of earnest student protestors. With the student union building in the background, the famous gate framed the neatly dressed, short-haired sons and daughters of California taxpayers, proudly waving the American flag and demanding the most basic of all our constitutional rights. This was our finest moment.

It didn't last long.

Students rally at the western entrance to campus while the Regents meet across the street in University Hall on November 20th. *Photograph taken by the informant for the Mississippi Sovereignty Commission. The names in the margins were probably written by him. Reprinted with permission of the Mississippi Department Archives and History.*

The Regents didn't see our display of middle-class patriotism, unless they watched TV that evening. They met in closed session in the morning. The public proceedings in the afternoon were programmed and pro forma. The FSM had written an open letter to the Regents asking permission to appear before them to state its case. Permission was denied, but five people from the FSM were invited to sit in the audience with the press and observe. They were Mario Savio, Steve Weissman, Michael Rossman, Mona Hutchin, and Ron Anastasi. After parading through the campus, the rest of us vigiled on the lawn at the western entrance across the street from University Hall.

The Regents endorsed without discussion or debate all of Kerr's and Strong's recommendations on the two concerns which had caused the conflict: discipline and political activity. These were less generous than the faculty recommendations had been. All eight students were suspended from September 30th to date. Mario and Art were put on probation for the rest of the semester. Point 4 of resolution 1 warned that "new disciplinary proceedings before the Faculty Committee on Student Conduct will be instituted immediately against certain students and organizations for violations subsequent to September 30, 1964." As for the problem which started it all, that was addressed in the second paragraph of resolution 2 (which some Regents disapproved).

> 2. The Regents adopt the policy effective immediately that certain campus facilities, carefully selected and properly regulated, may be used by students and staff for planning, implementing, or raising funds or recruiting participants for lawful off-campus action, not for unlawful off campus action.

Specific regulations were left to each campus. Kerr told a news conference that those for Berkeley would be drawn up by Thomas Cunningham, general counsel to the Regents. By implication, this excluded students, faculty, and Chancellor Strong.[1]

When Mario and Michael reported to us what the Regents had decided, they were angry and disappointed. "We're not going to take this sitting down," Mario said.

44 | *The Abortive Sit-In*

SITTING DOWN, or sitting in, is precisely what the FSM decided to do. After a marathon 48-hour meeting, the exhausted Steering Committee voted early Monday morning, by 5 to 4, to hold a sit-in in Sproul Hall that afternoon.

The usual noon rally on Sproul Hall steps was very unusual. In honor of the season, it began with Christmas carols. Not the usual ones of course; the words were changed. To the tune of "Jingle Bells" we heard:

Oski Dolls, Pompon Girls, U.C. all the way!
Oh, what fun it is to have your mind reduced to clay;
Civil Rights, politics, just get in the way.
Questioning authority when you should obey!

There were many more. The tension that had built up was released with acts of creativity, ones which would proliferate for the next month. The words of the songs captured the essence of what was happening on campus. Students, alienated by what they saw as arbitrary administrative fiats, were fusing their personal concerns with the larger social issues of civil rights and free speech and rebelling against what they felt to be a common oppression.

This was only the beginning. After a few speakers had presented the case for occupying Sproul Hall, Vice-Chancellor Alan Searcy opened the door and emerged with a portable lectern and his own public-address system. He set it up and asked to read a statement by Chancellor Strong. The crowd urged him on. Strong's statement simultaneously accepted the new Regents' rules and excluded the FSM from participating in further discussion about them. He reiterated that mounting unlawful action on campus would not be tolerated and said he would consult on "specific rules and regulations" with his faculty committees and the ASUC senate. Beginning immediately, "permits for tables may be obtained from the Office of the Dean of Students" for Bancroft and Telegraph. After all that had happened, we had our original political space back, only now we had to get permits whereas we had not had to do so before. While we would probably get more political space, pending discussion with various bodies which did not include the FSM, we still had no say in the rules under which we would live. Searcy turned to leave. "Hey! Get back here!" Mario demanded. Searcy returned to his microphone but would not engage in debate. He just asked the students to wait twenty-four hours to see what the specific rules were before taking further action.

As the dust settled, Steve Weissman told the crowd that "we're going to have a discussion of whether or not to have a sit-in." Weissman had opposed the sit-in in the Steering Committee. This was a first, a public debate of Steering Committee decisions, an appeal to the students to sup-

FSMers hold a public debate on whether or not to sit-in at Sproul Hall on November 23rd. A few hundred sat in for a few hours, but then left. *Photograph taken by the informant for the Mississippi Sovereignty Commission. The names in the margins were probably written by him. Reprinted with permission of the Mississippi Department Archives and History.*

port one side or the other. The speakers generally favored sitting in, though some expressed ambivalence. Mario said he was going in as a personal statement of protest and asked others to join him. Around 2:00 P.M., clusters of students began drifting inside. No one had given a cogent statement against the action. Sitting in the Plaza, I heard two kids next to me say they opposed the sit-in but were afraid to speak out. They felt they would be shouted down if they publicly opposed the FSM leaders. Their reluctance motivated me to do something I had never done before: make a public statement before a large crowd. I could speak out in meetings, but crowds frightened me. I went up the steps, took the mike, and told the assembled students why the sit-in was wrong. Fear gripped me so hard that everything in front of my eyes went blank. I have no memory of what I said, only of the sick feeling in the pit of my stomach. There is nothing in my notes or letters, so I probably did not remember what I said right after I said it. Whatever it was, it broke the ice; others spoke out against the sit-in. I later heard that I had solidified my place on the FSM's shit list.

Of the 2,000 gathered in the Plaza, about 300 students went inside. They lined the second-floor hall where the dean's offices were located and debated why they were there and what to do next. They didn't block doors or enter offices. This wasn't really a sit-in; it was more a display of personal angst. Jack Weinberg called it an "existential cry." As the students argued inside and out, the Steering Committee met in a stairwell. After much heated discussion that alternated between dismay and despair, they voted 6 to 5 to leave at 5:00. This decision was not well received by the students inside Sproul Hall. They continued to debate, some insisting on the importance of staying and others on the need to follow the decisions of the Steering Committee. Even Weinberg, who had urged the sit-in and voted to stay, asked everyone to leave. But it was Bettina who made the bitter pill easier to swallow. "If we're gonna win," she said, "we gotta stick together!"[1]

45 | Resurrection

By THE TIME Strong announced his new rules the next day—which essentially gave us what the United Front had asked for in September but at more places than Bancroft and Telegraph—the FSM was consumed by a mood of despair. The optimists thought the movement was running out of steam. The pessimists thought it was dead. In just a few days, we had gone from our finest moment to our lowest point. Many, myself included, thought that we had done all that could be done and that it was time to return to our studies and business as usual. We would fight again another day.

From this near-death experience, the FSM was soon saved. Its savior was Chancellor Strong.

Right after Thanksgiving, Mario Savio, Art Goldberg, Jackie Goldberg, and Brian Turner received new letters from the chancellor's office charging them with violating university regulations for leading the October 1st and 2nd demonstrations. Mario was also charged with biting a police officer and Art with threatening one. All were ordered to appear before the Faculty Committee on Student Conduct, a committee appointed by Strong whose recommendations were advisory to him. This was consistent with the Regents' resolution of November 20th and with Strong's repeated but implicit threats of further discipline. However, it was contrary to the verbal promises Kerr had made to us on October 2nd that no students would be disciplined for the actions of those two days.[1]

The FSM was absolutely ecstatic. This was the atrocity they needed, the opportunity they thought would never come. Art and Mario were in southern California speaking at other campuses and visiting their parents, so the Steering Committee met at 4:00 P.M. on Sunday without them. It voted to hold a sit-in on Wednesday, followed by a general strike of students and TAs on Friday. This decision was not publicly announced. Officially the FSM demanded that the new charges be dropped, but it knew they would not be.

At the Monday noon rally, students were told of the new charges and the FSM demands. Plans for the strike were announced, but not the sit-in. We were also told that disciplinary actions had begun against Friends of SNCC, Campus CORE, YSA, Women for Peace, and the DuBois Club. The dean's office had asked the presidents of "recognized student organizations" that were violating the rules to come in for a talk. Neither UCLC nor the UYDs got one of these letters, but our tables were only at Bancroft, not Sproul Plaza, and we were careful about what we did at them. Sympathy demonstrations were held at UCLA, and the FSM said that more would be held on other campuses. As expected, Strong rejected the FSM demands. Kerr did not issue a public statement.

The Ex Com met that evening and unanimously voted to sit in on Wednesday. The members who opposed a sit-in, if any, just didn't come. I spent Monday afternoon trying to talk to people in the ASUC and the administration about how to avert a showdown but without success.

Others made similar attempts, but we all got the same response. Kerr was out of town. Vice President Bolton said that student discipline was up to each campus administration. Dean Towle opposed the new charges, but it was out of her hands. And Strong could not be moved. For that matter, he couldn't even be reached. He had placed so many layers of people between himself and the students that no one could get through. By the Ex Com meeting, I had shifted from reluctant opposition to a sit-in to full support. If no one in the administration would listen to our words, perhaps someone would listen to our bodies.

None of us understood why the administration had acted so stupidly. Didn't they know that singling out some students for punishment for actions that dozens, hundreds, and even thousands of us had engaged in was the best way to ensure that thousands would rise in protest? Perhaps Strong, the philosopher, knew nothing about group solidarity, but Kerr was a labor negotiator and Sherriffs was a professor of psychology. Did they not know that an attack on one would be seen as an attack on all?

Tuesday, December 1st, the FSM issued its ultimatum. 1) Drop all charges. 2) Acknowledge that only the courts can regulate the content of political speech. 3) No more discipline of students or organizations for political activity. Do all this by noon the following day or direct action will follow.

Consternation broke out all over Berkeley.

The ASUC senate condemned the impending sit-in, which it wrongly thought would be in Chancellor Strong's office in Dwinelle Hall (because a leaflet circulated with a map and directions to his office). The real plan was to invade Sproul Hall, and if it was closed and locked, to occupy the Student Union. To prevent a lockout, David Goines stuffed the locks in the doors of both buildings with toothpicks. Central became battle-ready, requisitioning an apartment at Bancroft right across from Sproul Hall as Command Central. Hall monitors were identified, and armbands, microphones, and numerous supplies were stored in readiness for the occupation. Four hundred grad students put the GCC on record in support of a sit-in and subsequent strike. Joan Baez was alerted that she was needed again. Students were told to come to a noon rally on Wednesday and to bring books, food, and sleeping bags.

46 | *The Real Sit-In*

Sᴘʀᴏᴜʟ Pʟᴀᴢᴀ ᴡᴀꜱ packed with people. They spread out from the steps, onto the terrace, down into the Student Union Plaza, and through Sather Gate across the bridge into Dwinelle Plaza. They filled the balconies of the Student Union and gaped through its glass windows. Gigantic speakers were set up on the southern end of Sproul Hall steps. I settled myself behind the speakers, where I could see clearly but not be blasted by the sound.

In a speech that would be quoted many times, Savio told those assembled why we were going in. Once again he denounced the university as a factory whose students were raw material that were sick of being processed. "There is a time," he said, "when the operation of the machine becomes so odious, makes you so sick at heart, that you can't take part; you can't even passively take part, and you've got to put your bodies upon the gears and upon the wheels, upon the levers, upon all the apparatus and you've to make it stop. . . . Unless you're free, the machines will be prevented from working at all."

Joan Baez had the most magnificent voice. It resonated through all the plazas; even from behind the sound system I felt enveloped by her passion. She also spoke, asking us to come inside with love, not anger. As she sang, a steady flow of students filed up the steps and into Sproul Hall. When she stopped, she too went inside and stayed with us until almost midnight.

Around 1,500 people were inside at any given time of day, though many came and went. When the doors were shut at the usual closing time of 7:00 ᴘ.ᴍ., almost 1,000 of us were prepared to stay the night. After that, the campus police let anyone leave but no one could enter, though some climbed ropes to the second-floor balcony. That is also how baskets of food were brought in. Communication Central was on the roof with walkie-talkies that reached Command Central across the street. The university offices had closed early and their personnel sent home. We watched Dean Towle leave her office at 6:00 ᴘ.ᴍ. A path opened for her as she moved down the hallway and descended the stairs. She appeared quite unperturbed by our barely organized chaos, having held her regularly scheduled meetings during the day, which had included forty-five minutes with the presidents of student organizations cited for violating the rules. The office doors were locked; we made no attempt to enter them. The public bathrooms were almost locked; we took the doors off the hinges.

Around 10:00 P.M., Mario phoned Bob Treuhaft and asked him to come to Sproul Hall. Treuhaft was a well-known left-wing lawyer in the Bay Area who had left the CP in 1958. He was a friend of Bettina's father, and Mario had asked for his advice on legal matters during the SCCPA meetings. He had turned the task over to a junior lawyer in his firm, Malcolm Burnstein, though he and other attorneys were available when needed. On December 2nd, Burnstein was with his ill father in Detroit, so Mario phoned Treuhaft. He told his wife he would be back in an hour. The university police guarding the doors recognized him; when he said he was there as our lawyer, they let him in. Treuhaft met with the Steering Committee and advised them on the likely consequences of various options they were considering.[1]

I went in and out of Sproul Hall during the day but when close-up time came, I staked out a spot on the second floor. This was the main activity floor; two movies were shown and a Hanukkah service was held for about 150 people. Folk dancing and singing were on the first floor; the third was reserved for those who wanted to study. Classes were held in the stairways, at the newly created "Free University of California," on such timely topics as civil disobedience, conflict resolution, and "The Logarithmic Spiral and the Nature of God." We were not sure whether we faced a siege or a rout, but were prepared for either.

While we were waiting, all of the people who had refused to talk to us were trying to decide what to do. Kerr met with the Regents near the San Francisco airport for three hours. They decided to postpone deciding whether or not to take action until the next day. In the meantime, other people, some close to the scene and some not, importuned Governor Brown to kick us out. Sometime around 11:00 P.M. Governor Brown, *my* governor, the man whose reelection I had sought so avidly that I almost failed a semester, ordered our removal from the building. By so doing, he joined Alex Sherriffs and Edward Strong as Patrons of the FSM. They made martyrs of us all.[2]

Soon after 2:00 A.M., word spread that the cops were coming. Anyone who did not want to be arrested or who was a juvenile or on probation was told to leave. We were given instructions for going limp and for resisting tear gas. Weissman asked that "if anyone has illegal objects, either smoke them, drink them, or eat them." On his way out of Sproul Hall, Attorney Treuhaft saw Sheriff Frank Madigan of Alameda County and Deputy District Attorney Edwin Meese III, holding a press briefing and stopped to listen. He heard Meese announce that the governor had ordered the police to clear the building. When Meese spotted Treuhaft, he told the sheriff to arrest him. Our attorney was handcuffed, removed from the building, and taken to jail. At 3:00 A.M., the Steering Committee went to greet Chancellor Strong at the office of the campus police in the basement. Ignoring our welcoming committee, Strong and Lieutenant Chandler went from floor to floor telling us to leave or be arrested. When they reached the second floor at 3:15, we greeted them with a chorus of "We Shall Not Be Moved." Police buses were lining up in the parking lot and on Barrows Lane behind Sproul Hall.

Arrests started at 3:30 A.M. on the fourth floor. Some students went upstairs to pack the floor and make it harder to remove arrestees. The cops used the elevator and the stairs to drag, pull, push, and shove students to holding cells in the basement, where they were photographed before being taken to the buses. It took several hundred cops thirteen hours to clear the building. Reporters were let in to observe; faculty were not. However, several faculty members as well as many students witnessed our departure from the outside. Soon phones were ringing all over Berkeley. By 6:00 A.M. picket lines were at all entrances into the south side of the campus.

As students came on campus, many demanded to be let inside so that they too could be arrested. These requests were refused. Several climbed up the ropes to join us. Someone yelled to Steve Weissman that he should leave so one member of the Steering Committee would be on the outside to do whatever needed to be done. He slid down the ropes. A little before 8:00 A.M., a microphone was raised to the small second-floor balcony facing the plaza; from it, different people described what was happening within to the growing crowd in Sproul Plaza. While Jack Weinberg was speaking, the police ran up the circular stairs from the first-floor foyer and pulled him back inside, trampling people in front of the window. As he was being dragged downstairs, we packed around the window to keep that from happening again. I was next to the opening, so I went outside onto the balcony, took the mike, and continued to describe events inside. Don Castleberry of the YRs, still looking immaculate in a suit and tie, stood at the other end of the balcony holding the American flag. Arrests had started on the second floor, so a couple of us took turns observing inside and describing what we saw to those outside. The police tried an-

While those in Sproul Hall were being arrested on December 3rd, students took turns describing events from a 2nd floor balcony facing Sproul Plaza. Don Castleberry of the Young Republicans holds the American flag while Jo Freeman of the Young Democrats addresses the crowd below. *Photograph taken by the informant for the Mississippi Sovereignty Commission. The words in the margins were probably written by him. Reprinted with permission of the Mississippi Department Archives and History.*

other raid, but the students were too thickly packed. We lasted until 10:30, when arrests had thinned our guards.

When the cop stuck his head out the window and told us to come in, I threw the mike to the crowd down below. We came inside without resistance, then sat down, expecting to be arrested. Two police officers grabbed my wrists and pulled me downstairs. Initially I bounced on my butt, which was rather unpleasant, so I stiffened my legs and rode down on my heels. Instead of arresting me, the police just dropped me at the bottom and left. After waiting about fifteen minutes for them to return and finish the process, I went back upstairs. My turn came at 12:30. I was sitting next to a pillar in the second-floor foyer as the cops worked their way down the hall, arresting and hauling off each student. Most were given a choice between walking and being dragged. I wasn't going to walk, but I wasn't going to resist either. I uncrossed my legs and held up my arms, expecting two or more cops to grab my outstretched limbs. Instead, one took my arm and twisted it behind my back, flipping me over onto my face. Another twisted my other arm behind me and the two cops pulled me down the hallway, face down, with my arms behind my back, and threw me into the elevator with a loud thump.

It was a long bus ride to Santa Rita, a minimal-security prison that twenty years earlier had held American citizens of Japanese descent. The large white bungalows had a desolate feeling. Girls were put into a 5 × 30–foot enclosure with heavy wire mesh that the matrons called "the cage." I counted fifty-one of us. More were elsewhere. We were both tired and exhilarated, wanting sleep and wanting to see everything. One by one we were taken to a room, searched, questioned, and fingerprinted, allowed to make our one phone call, then returned. My booking number was 64-11120. Long before anyone got out, faculty and students with cars drove to Santa Rita to bring us home. Cars were parked for two and a half miles along Highway 50. Some were still there when the last students were released Friday afternoon.[3]

47 | *Strike!*

THE HEADLINES said it all:

"801 Sit-Ins Arrested"
"Strong's Ouster Sought"
"Governor Defends His Decision"
"Friends Keep Watch Outside Jail"
"Judge Reduces the Bail"
"Kerr Calls It 'Anarchy' "[1]

The UC student sit-in and strike made headlines all over.

We were called "the 800," but we did not know exactly how many had been arrested. Some people were arrested outside Sproul Hall; some arrested inside were released without being properly booked; some were juveniles and handled separately; some names were simply garbled. We were the largest mass arrest in California history, and the python couldn't process the pig. Although most of us went to Santa Rita, two other jails and the gymnasium of the San Leandro Armory also became holding cells. Judge Rupert J. Crittenden declined to ROR (release on our own recognizance) anyone except Treuhaft, but he did reduce the bail to $55 for two charges or $110 for three. We were all charged with trespassing and unlawful assembly; those who did not walk willingly—about 75 percent —were also charged with resisting arrest. The faculty quickly raised $8,500 to pay the bail bondsman, and Jerry Barrish put up $83,710 for a blanket bail bond. Individual bonds were prepared for early arrestees, but record-keeping fell behind so no one knew exactly how many or who we all were, let alone where we were being held. Rather than contain us for the days necessary to figure it all out, Crittenden released us. By the time we appeared for formal arraignment, we were down to 768.[2]

The faculty were outraged. Whatever they thought of the FSM, a police invasion was sacrilege. At a two-hour meeting on Thursday afternoon, over 800 professors passed two resolutions essentially supporting the FSM position on rules governing political activity and the FSM demands for amnesty. When Roger Stanier of the Bacteriology Department read a telegram addressed to Governor Brown condemning the presence of the state highway patrol on campus, 361 professors quickly signed it. The executive committee of the Berkeley chapter of the American Association of University Professors (AAUP) called for "complete amnesty" for the students and for Strong's replacement. Political Science chairman Robert Scalapino announced the creation of a Council of Departmental Chairmen to provide the leadership lacking from the campus administration.

The students acted. Brown's office in Sacramento was picketed by forty students and faculty from UC Davis—the closest campus—who were not appeased when he invited them in to talk. As the GCC implemented strike plans, the *Daily Cal* reported that at least half of the TAs would not hold class. GCC surveys estimated that half were on strike and another quarter honored their picket lines. Strike Central organized a phone bank to all Berkeley students to ask them not to go to class. The TAs took over some departmental offices (with permission of their chairmen), commandeering the phones and running "STRIKE" leaflets off on departmental mimeographs. The rally tree became Picket Central, with a blackboard listing assignments, instructions for picketers, plus poster-board and marking pens for students to make their own signs. Every campus entrance and every building where undergraduates took most of their classes had a picket line. About 40 percent of all students actively supported the strike; 15 percent actively opposed it.[3]

Faculty response varied widely. Norman Jacobson, from whom I was taking American Political Theory that fall, posted a notice announcing "there will be no class today." After "witnessing the astonishing scene at Sproul Hall," he was "incapable of violating the palpable air of protest which today surrounds [the] campus." Alex Sherriffs held his Psych 33 midterm as scheduled; when strikers entered to ask students to leave, they were chased out. Most of the large undergraduate courses were can-celed or dismissed when their professors saw how few came. More than 5,000 people went to Friday's noon rally, where a disheveled Savio was greeted as a hero. A university, he told the cheering crowd, consists of faculty and students. The administration is there to serve them. His lengthy speech was followed by those of several faculty and three Bay Area assemblymen. Arrestees paraded around campus proudly wearing paper cutouts of large white V's on a black background. Other students pinned IBM cards to their clothes, which had been punched to read "STRIKE," "FSM," or "FREE SPEECH."[4]

Not everyone was sympathetic. Brown, Kerr, and Strong all issued statements condemning our actions. ASUC president Charlie Powell and the California Alumni Council were less restrained in their censure. A few students formed an anti-FSM group called University Students for Law and Order, which lasted about two weeks. Nine political science professors, previously uninvolved in faculty efforts to resolve the conflict, published a statement condemning "the illegal occupation." The Califor-nia State Chamber of Commerce, normally critical of Governor Brown, praised his decisive action, while the heads of local unions and promi-nent Bay Area Democrats criticized it. Newspaper editorial writers had a field day.[5]

Over the weekend everyone who was anyone met with someone. Kerr canceled a trip to Chicago to confer with Governor Brown, key Regents, and the Chairmen. Several of them met at the airport Hilton to approve proposals for peace. Some grad students met with Bay Area members of the legislature hoping to counter our negative portrayals in the press. They were told that if we thought the Regents were bad, the legislature was worse. Nonetheless, those legislators who seemed sympathetic were asked to speak to Brown. A faculty group sympathetic to the FSM's position hammered out their own peace plan to present to the Berkeley Division of the Academic Senate at its monthly meeting on Tuesday. This was an expansion of the resolutions passed by the informal faculty meeting on December 3rd. They invited other sympathizers among the faculty to approve it Sunday evening. Soon the newly formed Committee of Two Hundred was phoning all the Berkeley faculty to enlist their support.[6]

At a defendants' meeting Sunday night in the local junior high school auditorium, we learned that Kerr had canceled Monday morning classes so the entire university could prepare for a 11:00 A.M. university convocation. He had asked all the departmental chairmen to discuss the peace proposals of the chairmen's council in meetings with their faculty and grad students beforehand. Then everyone would hear them be formally proclaimed by Chairman Scalapino at an open meeting in the Greek Theater. At noon, the ASUC would hold a rally in the student union plaza to rouse support, and in the afternoon undergraduates could talk with faculty. The Regents would meet in Los Angeles on December 18th to make this plan official.

The FSM intelligence network relayed these plans as they evolved and even obtained advance copies of the speech Kerr was preparing. The Steering Committee met nonstop to decide what to do. At one point, they phoned Governor Brown to ask him to intervene. He declined to do so. Concluding that classes were being canceled to undermine the strike, they (and the GCC) decided to end it at midnight Monday, before the meeting of the Academic Senate. The Steering Committee wanted the proposals from the Committee of Two Hundred rather than those of the chairmen to become the official faculty position. Five thousand copies were passed out to students as they entered the campus Monday morning.

Probably the only person with an interest in the outcome who wasn't rushing from meeting to phone call to meeting was Chancellor Strong. On Saturday he was admitted to the hospital with gall bladder problems and stayed there, conveniently out of sight, for a week. He ceased to be the chief campus officer, though he wasn't officially relieved of his duties until January 2nd and his formal resignation wasn't handed in until March.[7]

At the Monday morning departmental discussions, many faculty and more graduate students, especially in sociology, history, and English, were critical of the chairmen's proposals. Forewarned, they came prepared to shoot the proposals down. Kerr had asked the chairmen to sit with him on the stage while Scalapino spoke, but after the departmental discussions, about a third of the seventy-three chairmen opted to sit in the audience. The Greek Theater was the largest arena on campus after

Memorial Stadium. From the outdoor stage at the base of a hill, seats climbed steeply in a semicircle. Large as it was, it could not hold the fifteen to eighteen thousand people who came that morning. They filled the aisles and populated the hill above. The Greek houses were asked to arrive early in order to fill the front seats with friendly faces. Picketers came later and occupied the back rows.

Last of all came the defendants. We had appeared for arraignment at 9:00 A.M. at the Berkeley Community Theater because no courtroom was large enough to hold us all. Under strict orders from our attorneys to dress neatly and act orderly, we had sat quietly while Judge Critten-den admitted that he still didn't know how many of us there were and granted a postponement. Upon leaving, "the 800" filed through the Berkeley streets to the Greek Theater, looking very respectable.

Kerr had asked about two dozen campus police to be present but kept them out of sight. He had heard that the FSM planned to disrupt his or Scalapino's presentation and wanted to be prepared. However, he thought the sight of police officers, even campus police officers, would be provocative.

Accompanied by Bettina and wearing a suit and tie, Mario went backstage to ask Scalapino for permission to address the audience at the end of the official program. This request, and another one to announce the noon rally, was turned down. After telling Scalapino that he was try-ing to usurp the authority of the Academic Senate, Mario and Bettina went to the press section near the stage. As they emerged into public view, Mario was met with rousing applause from the students. Seeing that the crowd was with him, he told reporters that he would make an announcement at the meeting's end, with or without permission.

Scalapino read the chairmen's proposals and explained how they were drafted. Kerr announced that they were "in full force and effect" pending the Regents' meeting. In five separate points, their only conces-sion was amnesty. The university "will not prosecute charges against any students for actions prior to December 2 and 3" and would accept the judgment of the courts as full discipline for those students who were ar-rested. But "the new and liberalized political action rules" would stand.[8]

As Kerr finished speaking, Mario went up the steps on the south end of the stage and waited for his chance. When Scalapino announced that the meeting was adjourned, Mario walked to the podium, his speech rolled up under his arm. As he reached for the mike, three campus cops emerged from behind a curtain draping the entrance to backstage. Two grabbed his arms and another his tie and they dragged him through that door.

All hell broke loose.

Kerr stood there, dazed and dumbfounded, watching his carefully constructed scenario fall apart. The audience rose and cried out, aghast at the drama unfolding before their eyes. Several students went to help Mario. Most were tackled by cops and pinned to the ground. Art Goldberg, the former high school football player, made it all the way backstage. Bettina stood up and led the crowd in a chant: "Let him speak. Let him speak." Alex Hoffman shouted, "Release him! I'm his lawyer." Joseph Tussman, chairman of the Philosophy Department, told Scalapino to release Mario. Robert Beloof, chairman of the Speech Department, yelled something similar at Kerr. Others argued with the police. Art emerged from backstage and went over to Kerr. He thanked him for having created the disruption and then told him that if he didn't release Mario the students would tear the place apart. Finally, Mario was released and Scalapino announced to the crowd that he would be allowed to talk. Once free to say what he wished, Mario only asked us to come to the noon rally. "Clear this disastrous scene," he said.

Ten thousand people filled Sproul Plaza. They dwarfed the few hundred at the ASUC rally in the plaza next door. Most of the speakers were faculty members. On the eve of his twenty-second birthday, Mario Savio, the philosophy undergraduate who articulated our innermost feelings so well, did not need to say more. In the war of words and the clash of symbols, the FSM had won.

48 | Victory

THE LARGEST Academic Senate meeting in anyone's memory assembled in Wheeler Auditorium at 3:00 P.M. on Tuesday, December 8th. Loudspeakers were set up outside so the thousands of students who sat on the steps and lined the slope could hear the faculty debate about what to do about us. The only item on the agenda was a resolution presented by the Committee on Academic Freedom (CAF). Based on the proposals approved by the Committee of Two Hundred, the resolution had been revised by CAF and distributed to the faculty that morning.[1] The FSM provided copies to the students. Its five points asked for complete amnesty for "activities prior to December 8"; only reasonable "time, place and manner" regulations for political activity; no restrictions on "content of speech or advocacy"; future discipline for political activity to be determined by a "committee appointed by and responsible to the Academic Senate"; and "unremitting effort" to secure adoption of these policies.

Most of the three-hour debate was over an amendment proposed by Professor Lewis Feuer of the Philosophy Department. He moved to limit unrestricted speech or advocacy to that involving "no immediate act of force or violence." He had cogent memories of European universities during the 1930s, from which Nazi students organized attacks on the outside community. There, universities were traditionally immune from the civil police, and the students had claimed immunity from university authority as well. The fact that this limitation rather than the new Regents' rule (no on-campus advocacy of illegal off-campus action) was proposed illustrated how far the debate had moved toward the FSM's position. If it were not for the events of the preceding week, most of the faculty might have agreed with Feuer. But they realized that this was a symbolic debate. Only the Regents could set policy. The real issue was whether the faculty would support the students, whose principles, if not their actions, were much like their own. The amendment was defeated by 737 to 284, and the original resolution passed by 824 to 115.

As the faculty filed out of Wheeler Hall, the crowd parted like the Red Sea, cheering and applauding. We felt vindicated. Many students thanked them. Some cried. Now it was the faculty who were the heroes.

Why did these distinguished and honored members of the intellectual elite, who had been so slow to recognize that there was a problem, so thoroughly support the FSM? A couple dozen had been fighting for civil liberties on campus and off for years. They were the core of the Committee of Two Hundred, but absent a crisis they had few followers. There was no survey of faculty opinion, and most who wrote articles about the student rebellion were angry about it so are not helpful in understanding the vast majority who voted yes. Consequently, one can identify reasons but can't assess their weight. Certainly some professors simply wanted peace and saw this as the best way to get it. Most, however, came to realize that the protestors were right. They recognized that we did what they taught us to do: think for ourselves and stand up for our beliefs. Nor was there disagreement about the substance of those beliefs. "Free speech," even advocating illegal acts, is part of the American creed. "Questioning authority" is an old and honored American tradition. The pilgrims who emigrated from Europe for the freedom to practice their own religious beliefs and the committees of correspondence who organized the American Revolution were far more radical than we were. Every graduate of a California college must pass an exam or course in American history and American institutions. In our history, the Boston Tea Party looms large; bowing low before the Crown is barely mentioned and not revered.

In the weeks between October 2nd and December 2nd, the faculty had undergone an education. While few faculty listened to undergraduates, fewer communicated with the administration. Their contacts were with graduate students, especially their TAs and RAs. As the grad students became more involved in the FSM, explanations for our unruly behavior became more readily available to their professors. The grad students were the bridge between the FSM and the faculty.

The faculty also had their own grievances and their own experiences with arbitrary administrative authority. Many still distrusted the administration twelve years after the loyalty-oath controversy, which had an eerie similarity to our eviction from the small island of political space on September 14th. Others were simply appalled at the administration's lies about that eviction (that it was due to traffic or trash problems), about us (that we were mostly nonstudents, Communists, or dupes), or conditions on campus (that we already had free speech, that the strike was ineffective). When Governor Brown ordered the highway patrol onto the campus and the police acted like thugs, it was too much even for those who wanted to stay in their ivory towers.[2]

That was not the only victory that day. Elections for the ASUC senate were held every semester; half were chosen each time for one-year terms. SLATE, which could not officially be a political party, ran a full slate of seven candidates. Two of these, Brian Turner and Dusty Miller, were well known from their work in the FSM. All won with substantial margins; no one else came close. The turnout of 5,276 voters was twice the norm. When the old student senate met the following week, it approved the Academic Senate resolution by a vote of 6 to 5.[3]

The following day, December 9th, 250 TAs and RAs formed a union, in part to prevent their being fired for participation in the strike. Federal labor law protected those involved in labor actions; nothing protected students protesting campus rules. In order to participate in the GCC, departments which did not have organizations of grad students created them. These became the nucleus of a local of the American Federation of Teachers (AFT).

These victories did not mean we could unreservedly return to our studies; there was much left to do.

What "rules" would govern student political activity were not written, and who would write them was not resolved. On December 14th, the Academic Senate elected an Emergency Executive Committee (EEC) to negotiate with the Regents. The Committee of Two Hundred ran a full slate, but only Carl Schorske of the History Department won. Arthur Ross, to whom Kerr had turned for help and advice on many occasions, became the chairman of the EEC.[4] The "moderates" on the faculty did what the "moderates" in the FSM could not do: mobilize a majority of the voting members to elect those who were well known through their years of experience on faculty committees. The new EEC had "a frank discussion" with twelve Regents and Governor Brown the day before the December 18th meeting but could not convince them to adopt the Berkeley Division's proposals. Instead, the Regents approved a statement with recommendations for action proposed by President Kerr. Kerr's proposals came from the Academic Council—the steering committee of the statewide Academic Senate—which met on December 16th to find ways to "be helpful to the president" and "buy time" for the Regents. The Regents' resolution expressed "devotion to the 1st and 14th Amendments to the Constitution" but demanded preservation of "law and order" and left student discipline to the administration. In effect, the Regents conceded our right to advocate on campus but not amnesty or faculty overview of student discipline in political cases. Both the EEC and the Regents declared victory. The FSM was shocked.[5]

For those who had been arrested, there would be a trial. We knew from the spring civil rights demonstrations that it was the district attorney, not the "injured party," who decided whether or not to prosecute, and we knew that the Alameda County DA would not be lenient. Fortunately there were many movement lawyers willing to defend us pro bono, but a good deal of money still had to be raised to cover costs and many days still had to be spent in court appearances. As we went home for the holidays we were told to raise whatever we could. I asked my mother to invite her friends and fellow teachers to her home so I could tell them about the FSM. Her doubts eased by the faculty vote, she readily did so, and they listened avidly to my stories and explanations. But when I tried to pass the hat, Helen put her foot down. She had invited them to her home for their edification, not to make donations. I returned to Berkeley empty-handed. Other students did better. Mario's parents told the press they were proud of him. His father showed them the book he thought had most influenced his son. It was the Bible.

Mario, Bettina, Steve, and Suzanne went east on a speaking tour of college campuses. The ABC television network paid their fare to New York City so that they could appear on a TV show, and they used the opportunity to talk about the FSM at several campuses. The press generally reported this trip as a flop because only hundreds, not thousands, of students came to hear them speak. But for hundreds to turn out for anything political on most campuses was a lot, especially the last week of classes before the Christmas break, which was also exam week for some. They left the evening of December 9th and spoke at Michigan, Wisconsin, Brandeis, Columbia, and of course Queens College, where Mario had once been a student. All but Steve were from New York.

As students returned for final exams in January, they were greeted by a new Acting Chancellor. Martin Meyerson, who had been lured from Harvard to become dean of the College of Environmental Design only eighteen months before, had replaced Strong, who was granted a leave of absence, at full salary, to recuperate from his illness. In fact, Strong was not ill; he'd started writing regulations. His removal was the one thing on which Regents, faculty, and students all agreed; the Regents had authorized the search for his replacement at their December 18th meeting.[6]

Meyerson held meetings with everyone and then issued his own temporary regulations. Sproul Hall steps would continue as an open discussion area with the university providing the loudspeaker systems. Tables could be put up in several places to distribute literature, recruit members, solicit donations, and sell items. The petty rules that had made sponsoring off-campus speakers so onerous were reduced to one requiring forty-eight hours' advance notice, and the dean of students could waive that when called for. On January 4th, the FSM held its first legal rally from the steps of Sproul Hall. It denounced the new rules and announced an "investigation of the Board of Regents."

49 | *Intermission*

As 1965 BEGAN, some things changed and some stayed the same. A few people left my house and I found new housemates. One of them was Steve Weissman. His wife had kicked him out and he needed a room, fast. My housemates thought it would be cool to have Steve in the house, but he was never there. However, he gave out the house phone number to all and sundry, so we became Steve Weissman's answering service. Some of the guys took to answering the phone that way, sarcastically, because 95 percent of the calls were for him. When he left in February to go on a speaking tour of southern schools, everyone was glad to get the phone back.

I almost became a nonstudent, but not for violating any rules. One day Shelly Morgan, a friend who worked in the political science office as a secretary, frantically phoned me with the news that I was on the graduation list for February. She saw my name as she was typing the list of political science majors soon to be leaving. Did I know I was to graduate? No, I didn't, and what's more, I didn't want to do so before June. I wanted to finish my honors thesis so I could graduate with honors in political science. Besides, I couldn't leave Berkeley as long as the trial was pending. If I became a nonstudent I wouldn't be able to continue as a member, let alone an officer, of any "recognized off-campus student organizations," check books out of the library, or do most of the things I normally did.

Initially we thought someone was doing this deliberately to get rid of me, but it turned out to be the usual application of bureaucratic rules about which none of us knew. All who fulfilled the requirements for a degree, including those of their major, were automatically graduated. The state of California wasn't going to pay for anyone's education longer than it had to. As soon as I took final exams I would have sufficient units and would have met all the qualifications. I asked the department for a reprieve but was turned down. Rules were rules, I was told. Shelly found the solution. Two semesters of economics were required to major in political science. I had taken Econ 1A in the spring of 1963 but hadn't gotten around to Econ 1B until summer of 1964, when I had to take an incomplete. I didn't have enough money to buy the required books for the three courses I took that summer, and as luck would have it, Econ 1B was taught by a visiting professor who did not use the text I had bought for Econ 1A. His text was so new it wasn't even in the library. Without a textbook, and having missed one-third of the class meetings for my Auto Row trial, I couldn't take the exam. I had signed up for the Econ 1B exam for the fall course, which used the text I already had. Shelly canceled the test and rescheduled it for the spring. I was removed from the graduation list.

As soon as the *SLATE Supplement* for the spring semester went on sale, another political science secretary phoned to tell me that Scalapino wanted to see me. He had been prominently misquoted on the front cover of the spring *Supplement* and, since I was listed as one of the editorial staff, I must know something about it. At the bottom of the bright red cover, bold white letters proclaimed, "No one wants this university to become an arena for controversy and debate." In smaller letters off to the side appeared "Robt. A. Scalapino, Chairman, Dept. of Poli. Sci. at Berk." I was grilled, but I honestly knew nothing; I had only written course reviews. I soon found out that the misquote came from the *New York Times* report of Scalapino's December 7th speech at the Greek Theater. It was the *Times*'s error, but since many thousands had heard his actual words, a little skepticism was called for. A flurry of angry letters soon appeared in the *Daily Cal*. The *Supplement*'s new editor had used the quote because it "represented the crux of the problem that faced the campus last semester—people who are afraid of controversy are very likely to want to stop free political debate on this campus."[1]

The error was discovered only after 8,000 copies had been printed. The *SLATE Supplement* retracted and reprinted the cover, but not before distributing half of them with Scalapino's name removed and a "correction" inside. The new covers said: "No one wants this university to stop being an arena for controversy and debate." Off to the side, in small type, appeared "R. A. Scalapino." This incident reflected how much suspicion and distrust remained between those on different sides of the events of the fall, and how willing they were to believe the worst about each other.

In January, Delmer Brown (History) and Seymour Martin Lipset

(Sociology) formed the Faculty Forum to support Kerr. Only a few of those who joined this group had been actively involved in the fall; they were afraid that the leftist faculty represented by the Committee of Two Hundred would take over the Berkeley Division of the Academic Senate.[2]

The moderate students were just as despised by the FSM stalwarts as the moderate faculty, even though many who opposed the militants in November had been arrested in December. While I was studying for finals, Hal Draper asked if we could talk about the secret negotiations with Clark Kerr the previous November. He was writing a book on the FSM and wanted to get his facts straight. Dick Roman had told him to talk to me. I knew Draper was the éminence grise of the FSM, but not being part of the in crowd, I had never spoken to him and did not know how much he disliked liberal Democrats and democratic socialists. On the contrary, I was imbued with the importance of creating an accurate record. Scholarship, I thought, was impartial. Not wanting to shift mental gears from finals to the FSM, I invited Draper to come to my house to read a letter I had written describing who did what and when. I told him he couldn't take notes and he couldn't quote me because it was a personal letter, with a personal interpretation, and that I had stopped writing at a high point, so it was also misleading. While I sat on my bed reading my econ text (for the exam that was soon to be postponed), Draper sat at my desk and read my lengthy letter. As far as I could see, he wrote nothing down, and he didn't ask me any questions.

Two days later Jim Burnett asked me why I was circulating a letter discussing the details of our meetings with Kerr. He showed me a mimeographed sheet entitled "Excerpts from a personal letter on the meetings with Kerr and some of the ExCom members by Jo Freeman." There was no other attribution; certainly none to Hal Draper. The sheet contained actual quotes interspersed with paraphrased passages and named five of us. If my unfinished letter was misleading, this was more so. It made us look like a bunch of finks, selling out for our own glory.

Pissed, I phoned Draper later that night; actually, I phoned him at 2:00 A.M. He said he hadn't mimeographed the leaflet, but he had written up a page of "notes" for interested parties. His agreement not to quote me only applied to his book, he said, not for any other purpose. I railed at him so long and so loudly that he finally hung up on me. The leaflet continued to circulate. A restrained version, sans quotes, paraphrases, and attribution, showed up on the back cover of the third issue of *Spider,* a biweekly magazine that began publishing in March. This page was devoted to an "atrocity of the month," featuring leaflets from the White Citizens Council or groups promoting lynching. My debut in this role was titled "Moderation Über Alles."

Spider was just one of many new seeds that blossomed that spring. On February 1st, the graduate student union was formally chartered as Local 1570 of the American Federation of Teachers. Student groups multiplied and expanded. Some days there were more noon rallies than steps on which to hold them. New people showed up on campus and off, hawking ideas and selling their wares. I added between sixty and seventy buttons to my collection and replenished my bank account from selling buttons I bought from organizations in New York. UCLC printed and sold its own buttons, giving it liquid assets for the first time. The youth culture was becoming politicized. It was also becoming more sectarian, more purist, and more dogmatic. SLATE and the FSM had been fairly inclusive. Now groups with a more rigid party line, such as the Progressive Labor Party (PL) and its front the May 2nd Movement (M2M, named for a 1964 NYC demonstration) were attracting more adherents. The three activist cohorts of prior years were being supplanted by a fourth: heavy radicals who wanted to smash the state. Almost in response, an apolitical or semipolitical cohort emerged which was more into feeling good than doing good. These kids heralded the counter-culture.

The SLATE senators on the ASUC were also breaking new ground. Brian Turner sent letters to fifty campus health services on ASUC stationery asking advice on setting up a program to provide birth control information to students. This was illegal in many states; the Supreme Court wouldn't release its controversial decision declaring legal restrictions on contraceptives for *married* couples to be unconstitutional until June. Only three years earlier, the SLATE membership had defeated a motion to add a proposal for a student birth control clinic to its candidates' platform because it was felt to be too controversial. Turner implied that the campus health service was involved in this plan, and when its director found this out, he denounced Turner's letter as "unethical, irresponsible and immature." Charlie Powell said Turner made UC "a national joke." Although few acknowledged it, sleeping around was becoming a popular pastime in the student world; it was even called "FSM-ing." But the consequences were still seen as a personal problem, or, more accurately, a woman's personal problem. Birth-control devices were not readily available to unmarried women in California, and abortion was illegal. At one meeting I attended, a young man asked if anyone there knew how to arrange an abortion for an unnamed young woman; the interruption was deemed inappropriate as we quickly returned to our important business.[3]

Ideas were fermenting among the faculty as well, especially about education. On March 1st, Chancellor Meyerson asked the Academic Senate to examine the state of education at Cal. A year later, the Select Committee on Education presented its report and recommendations, prompting UCLA to create a similar commission. Several professors led by Joseph Tussman proposed the creation of an experimental college in which five faculty would lead 150 freshman in two years of intensive study of four crucial periods in western history. It opened in the fall.[4]

Rule-breaking can become habit-forming. On Tuesday, February 2nd, Mona Hutchin, the Republican member of the FSM Steering Committee, mounted the running board on the outside of a San Francisco cable car with a male companion. This was verboten. Only men were allowed to ride on the running boards; women had to sit inside. The gripman refused to move the car until she did, and she refused to move. "This is an outmoded, asinine law," she said. On being told that it was for her own safety, she countered that "the law should apply to men as well as women." After forty-five minutes, six cars were backed up at the Market Street turntable of the Powell Street line. Still wearing a button that read, "I Am a Right Wing Extremist," she was taken to the Hall of Justice by three policemen who tried to find something to charge her with. They were convinced that it was against the law for women to ride on the outside but could find nothing in the statutes. So they lectured her and let her go. The next day, Mona's "Cable Car Battle" was on the front page of the *San Francisco Chronicle*.[5]

UCLC decided this would be a great time for a Freedom Ride. We planned it for Sunday afternoon, wrote leaflets "to protest the refusal of full civil liberties to women," and called the press. I lined up ten of us to go to the city and ride the running boards, leafleting as we did so, but as the day came closer, one by one they backed out. When we were down to three, I called the press and called it off. I wrote the *Chronicle*, explaining that we had just postponed our demonstration because we had learned that only the *Chronicle* had Sunday staff to cover it. In reality, we were ahead of our time. There was little interest in wrongs to women.

By April the Municipal Railway had decided that this "tradition" was not worth keeping. There was no existing law or ordinance that applied, and the city attorney's office didn't want to write one. The Muni superintendent issued an order that women be allowed to ride on the boards. That should have ended it, but cultural biases were stronger than administrative fiats. The head of the Transit Union "advised" his members "to protect the safety of their vehicle by requesting—insisting—that women ride inside the cars." Women, he said, "aren't capable of riding out there. They'll be falling off a dozen to a block and it'll be the conductor or gripman who'll be at fault." Women "should get off the steps. They don't belong there." Even though he demanded that a law be written "in essence of safety," there was no outcry in opposition. Protests over sex discrimination would have to wait for another year and a better issue.[6]

Most students returned to the political work that had brought them into the FSM in the first place. When the Ad Hoc Committee dissolved after failing to dint the intransigence of the *Oakland Tribune,* CORE took over civil rights work in the Bay Area. Campus CORE used campus rallies to recruit several hundred picketers to protest job discrimination by Oakland businesses, leading to a few arrests but no mass civil disobedience. By the time this activity fizzled later that spring, the sticking point of the fall—on-campus advocacy of illegal off-campus action—had become irrelevant. Cal Students for Goldwater recast itself into Cal Conservatives for Political Action (CCPA). Still run by Danny Rosenthal, it made full use of the greater opportunities for political outreach brought by the FSM, tabling regularly at Bancroft and Telegraph. CCPA recruited students to counterprotest the picketing of the *Oakland Tribune.*

The southern Civil Rights Movement was back in the national news, overshadowing our local actions. In order to push Congress to pass the Voting Rights Act, SCLC began a campaign in Alabama to illuminate the need for federal intervention. Selma was chosen for demonstrations because Sheriff Jim Clark was notorious for his racist views and violent responses. Throughout January, there were daily marches to the Dallas County Courthouse. In February, hundreds of demonstrators were arrested, including Dr. King and many schoolchildren. A young civil rights worker was killed in a neighboring county. On Sunday, March 7th, several hundred protestors began a walk from Selma to Montgomery. In full view of the TV cameras, Clark's troopers attacked them. After a false start, another death from police beatings, a federal injunction, and a major speech by President Johnson, the marchers completed the fifty-four miles to Montgomery on March 25th.

Along with the rest of the country, our attention was riveted on Alabama. Mario and a few dozen others from the Bay Area went to Alabama to join in the demonstrations. Throughout March, we held regular support rallies on the steps of Sproul Hall. These reminded us both of why we had fought for political freedom and that the conflicts on the Berkeley campus that spring were pretty trivial in comparison.

50 | *FUCK*

On March 3rd, a young man recently arrived from New York City borrowed a piece of lined notebook paper from Danny Rosenthal, who was sitting at the CCPA table at Bancroft even though he was no longer a registered student. He folded the sheet, wrote the word "FUCK" on it with a red marking pen, sat down on the edge of the planter near the Student Union, and held up his sign. John Thompson wasn't too sure why he was doing this. Mostly he was bored. A street poet and unpublished writer, he had come to Berkeley to find himself, or at least something to write about. He did a little work for PL and M2M, but he wasn't a serious politico. By his own admission, he thought that "maybe if I got put in jail overnight, or for a few days, I'd have a story."[1]

Just as he was ready to give up and go home, a passing Greek caught sight of his sign, lectured him on displaying dirty words, grabbed the paper, crumpled it, and threw it at him. A couple guys at the *Spider* table gave him more paper and he made another sign. It read "FUCK (verb)." The guys made faces at each other and generally made fun of the sign to pass the time. After what seemed hours, the Greek returned with a plain-clothes cop, who arrested Thompson and took him into the police station in Sproul Hall. He was taken to the Berkeley house of detention, booked, and released an hour later.

That night he went to a party at Art Goldberg's apartment. Art was one of the very few campus activists who thought Thompson had done a great thing. Most, myself included, were more prudish than libertine, and virtually none wanted to take "free speech" into uncharted territory, especially *this* uncharted territory. In those days, comedian Lenny Bruce could be convicted of obscenity for saying "fuck" on stage. Art was a complex mixture of practical politician and way-out revolutionary. During the fall his practical side had governed; in the spring, the rebel took hold. What moved Art to action on behalf of Thompson was the recent Ugly Man contest, which was annually held by fraternities to raise money for Cal charities. The winner was "Miss Pussy Galore" (named for a character in a James Bond novel) who ran a campaign that bordered on the obscene and was certainly in bad taste. "I Like Pussy" buttons proliferated. "Put your money where your mouth is," was Miss Galore's campaign slogan. Lenny Bruce, whose routines made vulgar sound respectable, would have loved it. The administration looked the other way, as it usually did when "boys were only boys." Art was angered by the double standard.

A rally for Thompson on the Student Union steps (Sproul steps were taken) attracted about 150 people. What they heard could have been a Lenny Bruce routine, complete with arrests. Thompson may have been the only speaker who didn't say "fuck," though he said everything else: fornicating, fooling around, flowering, figging. Art fucked everything. Danny announced that CCPA would soon offer "FUCK Communism," posters from its table. Nicholas Zvegintzov, a grad student in business administration, led a cheer: "Gimme an F." . . . "What does it spell? FUCK!" At a nearby table, freshman David Bills collected money for the "Fuck Defense Fund." While four people were being booked in the basement of Sproul Hall, English graduate student Michael Klein read passages from *Lady Chatterley's Lover,* which had once been banned for its foul language. After another rally the next day there were more arrests. Within a few days, nine people, but only three students, were charged with various combinations of uttering an obscene word, displaying obscene material in public, and disturbing the peace. Thompson and Goldberg were arrested twice. Five of the nine had been arrested in the December sit-in.[2]

Once the novelty was gone, student interest dropped very quickly. Thousands of students rallied around Selma, but barely a handful went to the third "fuck" rally. The FSM Executive Committee met for the first time since December. We were angry at Art and the others for making us look like irresponsible juveniles, but it was hard to condemn anyone for public speech, so we voted to stay out of this one. However, the press knew a good story even when there wasn't one. Bay Area newspapers wrote front-page reports about "bad" words on campus after each rally, grossly exaggerating the number in attendance. The *Daily Cal* editorialized on March 5th that "there is absolutely no need for a Filthy Speech Movement." Much ado about nothing, or so we thought.[3]

On March 10th, the newspapers greeted us with banner headlines blaring "Kerr Quits UC." Kerr had told the press the night before that he and Meyerson would submit their resignations at the March 25th Regents meeting. While Kerr gave no explicit reason, Meyerson traced it to "the four-letter word signs and utterances." The president confirmed the following day that "the 'filthy speech movement', as the *Daily Californian* has called it," had started an avalanche. He said that Edward W. Carter, chairman of the Board of Regents, phoned him repeatedly to demand that the students involved be immediately expelled. Angry at this interference in campus administration, Kerr insisted that due process must prevail. However, the existing faculty committees disclaimed jurisdiction, which made prompt due process problematical. The administration threatened to resign because some Regents wanted action that the faculty wanted to avoid.[4]

The cascade of consequences was best captured in a satirical column by *San Francisco Chronicle* humorist Art Hoppe. "In the Beginning Was the Word," he wrote on March 12th. And then . . .

> The president and the chancellor of the biggest, greatest, grandest university in the whole wide world immediately resigned. The regents demanded 10,000 students be expelled. The alumni stopped their checks. Every newspaper decried and deplored. The Legislature launched a thorough investigation. And the prospects of the Governor for re-election were seriously dimmed.

The response was all that Kerr could have wanted. A special session of the Berkeley Division of the Academic Senate asked Kerr and Meyerson to withdraw their resignations by a vote of 891 to 23. Similar support came from the faculty on other campuses. Everyone from Governor Brown to the ASUC asked them to stay. There were some exceptions. Several legislators, a few Regents, and the Steering Committee of the FSM did not join in the chorus, though they did agree that the speakers of the previous week had been irresponsible. The SLATE members on the ASUC senate voted to support Meyerson but abstained from the resolution in support of Kerr. In the legislature, 44 of the 80 members of the assembly signed a petition to expel all students involved in the obscenity rallies.[5]

A special Regents' meeting was held on the afternoon of Saturday,

March 13th, to resolve the crisis. Kerr apologized for holding a press conference without first consulting with the Regents and gave his version of events. Chairman Carter was angry. He denied demanding the students' expulsion without due process. He said that Governor Brown had phoned him and Kerr demanding action; as chairman of the board he had merely counseled that the situation be dealt with firmly to "get the campus under control." Carter wanted the Regents to accept both resignations as of June 30th. Regent McLaughlin demurred. Agreeing that what had happened on campus was "shocking," he still thought that the proffered resignations should be declined. Assembly Speaker Jesse Unruh, in his capacity as an ex officio Regent, said they were all "paying the price" for "indecision last year" and that Kerr and Meyerson should be instructed to "expel the student leaders of the so-called filthy speech activity." In the end, the motions and the resignations were withdrawn. While nothing official was done, there were some heated exchanges. One Regent, sitting directly across from Kerr, pounded the table and screamed, "You know what that word was? Do you know what that word was, President Kerr?" That word was fuck, Fuck, FUCK!!! Kerr thought that was more obscene than anything said in Sproul Plaza.[6]

There was one casualty of the week: Chancellor Strong wrote his formal resignation. He may have been the only one who thought that with a little patience he might get his job back, but after the *Oakland Tribune* published a front-page story on March 12th headlined "Appeasement Wrecked Discipline, Strong Says," even the chancellor knew he was out. It was written by Carl Irving, the reporter whose phone call to UC's public information office the previous July had started the ball rolling which led to our eviction and formation of the FSM. Attributed to "several reliable sources," it was obviously based on confidential reports prepared by Strong for the Regents that were not meant for public consumption. In these, Strong accused Kerr of capitulating to us. Even though Knowland's paper agreed with Strong's assessment of what went wrong, its exposé was the final blow. Strong's wife took his handwritten resignation to the Regents' meeting and personally handed it to Regent Donald H. McLaughlin.[7]

Meyerson appointed an Ad Hoc Faculty Committee on Obscenity to hear the cases of four students (the leader of the FUCK cheer wasn't arrested) despite protestations of the FSM Steering Committee that they should only be tried in the courts. Not wanting anything to happen at a faculty hearing that might affect the criminal trial, lawyers for the students asked the court for a restraining order but only obtained a temporary delay. The faculty committee submitted its conclusions the day before the obscenity trial began on April 20th. The next day Meyerson announced that Art was expelled, grad students Michael Klein and Nicholas Zvegintzov were suspended until the fall, and freshman David Bills was suspended for the spring "for their roles in the March obscenity incidents." This decision mobilized the FSM Steering Committee—all four had been arrested in Sproul Hall—despite its disapproval of their actions. At a quickly called rally of well over 1,000, Mario, now a non-student himself, announced the end of the truce. Double jeopardy was not acceptable. That night the Ex Com voted to send a telegram to the Regents demanding a new faculty committee after the court trial. "FSM Leaders Threaten New Revolt at UC" roared the *Chronicle* the next day. The *New York Times* told the world that the "four letter vulgarisms . . . printed on signs is an effort to maintain the impetus of last fall's free speech drive."[8]

The local newspapers had almost as much fun reporting the obscenity trial as Art Hoppe did satirizing its origins. They told us that Assistant District Attorney Carl Anderson had said "fuck" twenty-nine times in his opening statement. We learned that this word was "very offensive to women and police," even though only civilian males filed official charges and the eight women sitting in court appeared unaffected by this assault on their sensibilities. When called to testify, campus police lieutenant Chandler used the word "fuck" twenty times. He said grad student Michael Klein had "shocked" the police when he read pages from *Lady Chatterley's Lover* at the Sproul Hall police station. Just to show how shocking it was, Klein read it again for the court when he took the stand. The defendants had waived a jury trial; on May 11th, the court found them all guilty of disturbing the peace; it found five guilty of speaking obscene words and three of distributing obscene materials. On June 8th, Judge Floyd Talbott sentenced them to jail. Art got sixty days; Thompson got thirty. Only David Bills, the freshman behind the FDF table, got off easy: ten days suspended and one year's probation. The other six got from ten to twenty days, none of which were suspended. All appeals were denied a few months later.[9]

When the dust settled, the administration had regained some of the authority it had lost in the fall. It successfully disciplined students for conduct for which they were also tried in court. The FSM lost its wind when the faculty EEC said there was "no merit" in a new disciplinary committee. "Handling of the obscenity cases has been in accordance with due process and with the spirit of the December 8 Resolutions," it said. Leaders of the Committee of Two Hundred, who had been our strongest advocates in the fall, said publicly and privately that this was not an issue worth fighting.[10] Although there was some grumbling among the students about excess punishment, especially when compared with the treatment of fraternity boys, none of us were moved to do much about it. The right to use dirty words was not something students were willing to die for, or even to be slightly wounded for. Most of us thought the whole thing was silly, not political.

The administration did retreat in one skirmish that spring, but not because it feared a sit-in. On March 15th, the second issue of *Spider* went on sale. The eight people who put it out were current and former SLATE members, including Art's sister Jackie and his roommate Sandor. Issue No. 2 featured a poem by John Thompson and statements by him, Art, and two others under the heading "To Kill a Fuckingword." In between admitting that they hadn't committed civil disobedience and wouldn't have said what they said if they had known they would be arrested, they all (except Thompson) used "fuck." Thompson put "Motherfucker" into his poem. A few days later Chancellor Meyerson banned *Spider*'s sale or distribution on campus as "conduct unbecoming a student." He also banned a satirical play written by political science undergraduate Richard Schmorleitz and sold as a pamphlet from the tables. It was titled

For
Unlawful
Carnal
Knowledge

The ban put *Spider* on the map. The magazine made the headlines. It made *Esquire*. It sold 10,000 copies. Its ban created dissent within the administration. Even the *Daily Cal* said "banning 'Spider' represents censorship."[11] Students and nonstudents could and did sell it just off campus and on other campuses in the Bay Area. Words in a booklet that one must pay to see are not as offensive as words uttered loudly to an unwilling ear. No one was arrested for selling *Spider* on the city's sidewalk at Bancroft and Telegraph. It was quickly pointed out that the ASUC bookstore, right in the Student Union, sold novels and commentary with the offending word in them and girlie magazines with much worse. Even the campus humor magazine, the *Pelican,* sometimes said "fuck." Indeed, the chief symbols of the campus were Sather Tower and Sather Gate, "donated by and dedicated to the happy marriage of Jean and Pader

Sather." These adorned everything from the doors of university cars to its stationery.

Meyerson shifted ground. First he offered to let the magazine be sold in the ASUC bookstore; finally he decided that it could be sold from tables on campus by a recognized off-campus student group. SLATE stepped in and became *Spider*'s sponsor. On April 1st, it was back on sale. The play, whose title was on the cover, stayed banned. Dean Williams told the author that if he persisted in selling it, he wouldn't graduate in June.[12]

In the meantime, the anarchistic element in the student body took bad taste to a level that rivaled that of the fraternities. Buttons appeared reading:

> Freedom
> Under
> Clark
> Kerr

The initial buttons were hand drawn on paper that was pasted onto leftovers from the fall elections. After a couple weeks, someone found a printer willing to risk arrest and began selling real buttons, white letters on blue background. I heard that there were bumper stickers as well. No one was brought up on charges for wearing or selling them, even though the buttons were displayed for public view.

Crueler was a cartoon which was circulated privately. Someone brought back from Mississippi a drawing of two men holding a woman in a supine position. The woman was Justice, blindfolded. The man at her head, holding up her arms, was dressed in a Ku Klux Klan robe. At her other end, naked from the ankles up, was a hefty good ole boy with the Confederate battle flag on his shoulder. He was fucking Justice. In the campus version, the men were redrawn. The one at her head was wearing an academic cap and gown. At the other end was Clark Kerr. An academic year that began with an act of petty revenge by the vice-chancellor ended on the same note.

The lasting legacy of the spring confrontations was that in the popular mind the Free Speech Movement became the progenitor of the Filthy Speech Movement. In reality, there was no filthy speech movement; just a few boys acting like boys, for which they paid dearly. But over time, FSM became another acronym for Filthy Speech Movement and the two merged into one in historical memory. Sixteen years later, I was peacefully taking notes in my constitutional law class at New York University School of Law when my distinguished professor told us how the Free Speech Movement became the Filthy Speech Movement. It was all I could do to keep my mouth closed until class was over and I could set him straight. The lesson of the spring was how words became reality.

51 | *The Trial*

TRIAL OF "the 800" began on April 1st, an appropriate day, in the Veterans Memorial Building near the courthouse before Judge Rupert Crittenden after four months of legal maneuvers. It lasted forty-one days, spread out over ten weeks. When we were finally arraigned in February, the courts and the prosecutors had settled on our numbers: all 773 of us were charged with trespassing and unlawful assembly; 614 were charged with resisting arrest. Of these, 657 pled not guilty, 101 pled nolo contendere, 8 were handled as juveniles, the charges against 6 were dismissed, and one died before trial.[1]

Initially the district attorney filed eighty complaints, and it was expected that there would be eighty trials of roughly ten people each, as there had been in San Francisco the year before. But we didn't have enough attorneys for eighty trials and knew we would never get key witnesses to appear eighty times. We also knew the judicial system would choke on the number of courtrooms, judges, prosecutors, and other personnel required for that many criminal trials. Both sides bargained over what kind of trial to have. Our lawyers wanted one trial, either of us all or of a representative number with the rest stipulating to facts of our individual arrests (i.e., that we were in the building, were told to leave, and walked or went limp). The prosecution wanted a trial by the court—

a judge without a jury—because it feared that a jury might acquit us. They could not deny us our constitutional right to a jury trial but could refuse a single trial and did so until we agreed to waive our right to a jury trial. After weeks of motions in which Judge Crittenden denied our every request, our lawyers agreed to one court trial of 155 representatives, with the rest of us stipulating to relevant facts, and our acceptance of the verdict on them as the verdict on ourselves. Following individual meetings with lawyers, all of us accepted this except for Howard Jeter, a longtime activist who was not a student. He and Attorney Robert Treuhaft insisted on jury trials.

Being political people, we mobilized community support. On January 20th, 139 faculty members led by Jacobus ten Broek (himself a lawyer) asked the court to dismiss the charges against us "in furtherance of justice." Appearing as friends of the court, ten Broek (Speech and Political Science), Albert Bendich (Speech), Howard Schachman (Biochemistry), Norman Jacobson, and Sheldon Wolin (both Political Science) submitted a 55-page brief, including a seven-page analysis of the constitutional issues prepared by Boalt Hall law professors and sent to the Academic Senate a week before. It essentially argued that those arrested in a nonviolent sit-in to protest rules which were unconstitutional should be treated leniently. Another 105 faculty members soon signed on. On February 1st, fifteen representatives of religious organizations ministering to the Berkeley community made a similar request by letter. The day before, CDC's Board of Directors had asked the Regents to intervene on our behalf and authorized an amicus brief seeking dismissal. The Regents had already voted in January that it would be "improper" for them to influence the courts. Crittenden turned down all requests for dismissal, but no one expected otherwise. They were made to provide balance to what everyone knew was intense political pressure to hang us by our thumbs.

Our lawyers worked pro bono, as they had in the San Francisco sit-in trials, at great cost to themselves from time for their normal practices. Malcolm Burnstein was the lead attorney. Around forty lawyers contributed some time to our defense, but the burden was borne by only a few.[2] Attorney-client conferences were difficult; mass meetings and mimeographed mailings were not very confidential; just finding a place to meet was a problem. A truly honest discussion of our options was not possible. Nonetheless, we were told, and accepted, the fact that we would most likely be convicted of trespassing and we would appeal. There were some legal and constitutional issues that could be raised on appeal which wouldn't work at trial. We might be acquitted of resisting arrest, since such a charge for merely going limp was unprecedented. We were also told that the quick way out was to plead nolo, and the penalty for doing so would be less than for a conviction. But a trial would give us an opportunity to publicly air our grievances, and for most of us that was what we wanted. That and a sense of group solidarity persuaded us to agree to one representative trial before Judge Crittenden.

Legal Central opened an office at 2214 Grove Street. Kathie Simon Frank and David Stein were each paid $125 a month to manage the cumbersome and complex logistics. They helped the lawyers, mailed memos, raised money, ran the phone bank, and kept track of us all. David also got a mattress on the floor of Attorney Alex Hoffman's apartment. Several others volunteered part time. We were assigned to groups to be represented by a Council of Twenty, which did not function very well. Several people wrote five issues of a *Free Speech Trial Newsletter,* which summarized court events and trial testimony for those who were not there and exhorted us to "COME TO COURT" and to "SUBMIT A LIST OF POTENTIAL CONTRIBUTORS WITHIN THE NEXT WEEK." Even without attorney fees, trials are not cheap.[3]

The judge insisted that we each appear before him and personally state on the record that we were waiving our right to a jury trial. On March 1st, we lined up and one by one went through the routine. On March 3rd, Crittenden broke the boredom by asking Mario Savio if he knew "that throughout history, people had held that trial by jury is the greatest protection against oppression and tyranny." Mario replied, "I fully understand the shameless hypocrisy this court has been reduced to." The judge promptly found him in contempt and sentenced him to two days in Santa Rita, to begin the following day. Mario missed the start of the dirty-word dispute because he was in jail.

The 155 selected to represent us included leaders and spokespersons but also ordinary students who either volunteered or had stories to tell about how they were treated by police. We were asked to submit statements describing our arrest experience, and a little over 400 did so. I was not asked, and I did not volunteer, to be part of the trial. Having sat through two trials the year before, my main objective was to finish my thesis and graduate. As in the San Francisco sit-in trials, ours was conducted only four hours a day, but unlike them, no one was forced to be in court for the entire proceeding. The 155 could excuse themselves for work and classes. They soon discovered that sitting in an auditorium listening to attorneys haggle over the rules of evidence was much more bor-

The Defender
Free Speech Trial Newsletter

May 30, 1965

TO ALL DEFENDANTS:

1) Beginning Tuesday June 1, COURT WILL COME TO ORDER AT 9 A.M.
instead of at 10 a.m. This change is permanent. The schedule will otherwise
remain the same, with the morning session ending at 12 and the afternoon
session running from 2-4 p.m.

2) NO ONE MAY LEAVE THE AREA THIS SUMMER WITHOUT EXPRESS
PERMISSION. Anyone wishing to do so must make a written request to Mal
Burnstein to present to the Court. This request, which should be submitted
at the Lawyers' office as soon as possible, must contain your name, your
prospective destination and address, and your planned dates of departure and
return.

3) The attendance problem will be aggravated by finals. IF YOU ARE ONE OF
THE 155 CURRENTLY ON TRIAL, be sure you are in attendance at all court
sessions except those during which you are taking an exam or working. In
order to be excused for exams, you must submit your final schedule to the
lawyers. OTHERWISE YOU WILL NOT BE EXCUSED. If you are not
currently on trial, come to Court to help maintain the attendance during this
difficult period. YOUR MINIMAL OBLIGATION IS TO ATTEND ONCE A WEEK.

4) We are still in desperate need of funds. PLEASE MAKE AN EFFORT TO
SUBMIT A LIST OF POTENTIAL CONTRIBUTORS WITHIN THE NEXT WEEK
to Albert Litewka, Lawyers' Committee, 2214 Grove Street, Berkeley 4.

The past week in court

The defense called 11 witnesses, including University of California President
Clark Kerr, to the stand this week. Beginning with Professor Reginald
Zelnick, whose testimony carried over from May 20, and ending with defendant
Herbert Henryson II, whose testimony will be continued on Tuesday, May 31,
it further developed the states of mind of the defendants prior to and up until
the time of their arrests. Additionally, it attempted to demonstrate the
reasonableness of those states of mind and also to corroborate the testimony
of earlier witnesses, particularly that given by defendants Goldberg, Aptheker,
and Savio. Finally, it sought, to the extent allowed by the Court, to explore its
theory that President Kerr, the person ultimately responsible for the University,
had opposed the December 2 arrests but had been overruled by Governor Brown.

TO ALL DEFENDANTS: SEE PAGE NINE

One of five newsletters published by and about the trial of "the 800"
during the spring of 1965.

ing than almost anything else. When attendance lagged to fifty and Judge Crittenden threatened to issue bench warrants, David Stein borrowed a seatless microbus and spent mornings hunting enough warm bodies to keep the judge happy. This often required some detective work. Since not everybody slept in their own beds each night, David became the reigning expert on who was sleeping with whom. All of us were asked to come when we could. By virtue of their prominence, leaders had to be in court virtually every day. When Mario missed two days because his draft board ordered him to take a physical, it made the papers.[4]

Alameda County district attorney Frank Coakley's opening statement for the prosecution attacked Mario personally. He implied that Mario was a glory hound who had led otherwise naïve students to perdition. He characterized the FSM as a "small group of seasoned demonstrators" (seasoned, yes; small, no) and a "motley array of students and non-students" (motley, yes; nonstudents, few). It was too much even for Judge Crittenden, who twice told Coakley to "temper your remarks." Former Chancellor Strong testified that he had asked us to leave but denied that he was inaccessible to students who did not like his regulations. He gave no hint that the student rebellion had led to his resignation. Associate Dean Peter van Houton described how he protected the dean of student's office from being entered by protesting students—during office hours. Most of the other prosecution witnesses were police who testified about individual arrests or lower-level administrators who testified that we disrupted the ordinary course of business. They told the court that all female employees were ordered to leave soon after we arrived and that two male deanlets spent the night with us, barricaded inside their offices.[5]

After making the front pages as opening attorney, Coakley turned the rest of the trial over to Lowell Jensen and two other deputies.[6] The prosecution rested on April 27th, and the defense opened on May 3rd. In between, our lawyers subpoenaed Governor Brown and President Kerr, hoping they would tell the court when and why the decision was made to arrest us. Our expectation was that Kerr would testify that he did not intend to arrest us but to do what the University of Chicago had done earlier and just let us sit. The plan was to place responsibility on Brown's shoulders and then argue that the governor had interfered against the wishes of the president of the university. Both men sent their lawyers to ask the court to quash the subpoenas; Brown was successful, Kerr was not. However, Brown did publicly state that police officials had "called on me for help and I gave it to them. I'll take full responsibility for it." He also opined that taking over a building was an illegal trespass. This prompted a motion for a mistrial, which Judge Crittenden denied, saying he did not read press coverage of the trial.[7]

Kerr didn't testify until May 25th, and when he did he was not allowed to speak about the substance of conversations leading up to our arrests or what he would have done had not the governor intervened. All we learned was that he had spoken to Brown twice around 11:00 P.M. and had sent Vice President Bolton to campus to talk to Chancellor Strong. "Objection; sustained" was heard so often it was almost a chant. Bolton had testified that around 6:30 P.M., he, Kerr, and Regents Meyer, McLaughlin, and Carter had met at the airport Hilton, but he wasn't allowed to disclose the content of their conversations. The defense even called Edwin Meese, one of our prosecutors, to the stand. He testified that he spoke to Governor Brown around 10:50 on December 2nd but was not allowed to tell the court what he said, let alone what the governor said to him. Our best administration witness was Dean Towle, who was allowed to describe all of her meetings with students over the rules.

Of the defendants, our star witnesses were Jackie Goldberg, Bettina Aptheker, and Mario Savio. Jackie testified for two days on events leading up to and including the October 2nd pact, emphasizing the futile efforts of the United Front to find someone to negotiate with. Her task was to establish the real and reasonable nature of our grievances and the lack of channels through which to pursue them. Bettina took up the story with the formation of the FSM, relating repeated examples of what we thought was bad faith by the administration. The only thing that moved the administration to talk to the FSM was rule violations or threats of violations; otherwise, it was ignored. She was on the stand for three and a half days. Mario's testimony took almost a week. He was cross-examined by the prosecution far more ferociously than the others. Lowell Jensen made him testify about the two incompletes he had taken in the Spring 1964 semester, but not that he did so due to the time he spent on trial for Sheraton II.[8] The defense did not rest until the second week in June, after twenty-seven witnesses, including nineteen defendants, had been examined, cross-examined, and reexamined.

On June 28th, Judge Crittenden began reading the verdicts. He found us all guilty as charged of trespassing and resisting arrest and not guilty of unlawful assembly. Mona Hutchin was acquitted of resisting arrest because the evidence on whether she walked or went limp was inadequate. Our lawyers had admonished us to stay in Berkeley to be present when this happened, but I had left to do voter registration in Newberry, South Carolina. I knew we would appeal and didn't think I had to be in court to be told I was guilty. A couple weeks after I started work, Legal Central frantically phoned to tell me that I was one of sixty-three defendants referred by the court to a probation officer for a pre-sentence investigation. I had to return by July 14th, even though my date with the judge was not until 2:00 P.M. on July 26th. I spent a major chunk of my small nest egg on round-trip bus fare to go back to Berkeley and saved money by not eating on the way.

My probation officer was Jacqueline Lesmeister, a young woman quite sympathetic to our cause. We became good friends and corresponded for several years. I did not follow our lawyer's advice to solicit letters "from parents, teachers (including high school teachers and principals), ministers and other respected persons in your community . . . [on] your character and reputation." But I did write the letter the judge requested on why I had participated in the FSM. I called my 18-page essay exploring the conflict between one's civic obligation to obey the law and one's moral duty to follow one's conscience "A Time for Choosing."[9] It was probably the best paper I had ever written; certainly the most eloquent. Instead of a grade, I was ordered to pay $250 (plus $26 in court costs) or serve 28 days in jail.

It was the standard sentence for those convicted on two counts who didn't plead nolo and who didn't accept probation. The standard sentence for trespass only was $100 or ten days in jail. Most convicts were offered probation, which carried with it the burden of avoiding arrest; for those who took it, the standard sentence was roughly half. A few defendants campaigned to persuade the rest to refuse probation, but most opted for the lower sentence. I did not, largely because I expected to spend at least a year as a civil rights worker in the South and avoiding arrests was not a realistic promise for me to make. As predicted, those who pled nolo (only three of whom rejected probation) were also rewarded with a sentence roughly half that of those who insisted on trial (and accepted probation). There was no difference in the standard sentence of the 155 and those who did not commit themselves to be in court every day.

Not everyone got standard sentences. A dozen people identified as leaders got straight time that was not an alternative to a fine, with or without probation. Mario, Art, and Jack got 120 days; Michael Rossman got 90; Brian Turner was sentenced to 60 days even though he accepted probation; Suzanne and Bettina got 45 and others from 30 to 60 days. Jackie accepted two years' probation but still had to choose between a $400 fine or 40 days in jail. Even lesser leaders generally got higher sentences than the others, and nonstudents were hit harder than students. Howard Jeter was tried separately by a jury, which hung, and his case was not retried. The charges against Treuhaft were dismissed.[10]

Some people chose to serve their sentences immediately; 572 of us filed an appeal. Judge Crittenden declined to continue our bail and set new bail at $220 for those convicted on one count and $550 for those convicted on two. In November of 1965, my mother received a letter from Mal Burnstein requesting funds and sent $55 to cover my bail bond. Our appeal was rejected at every step. On June 12, 1967, exactly two years after the close of trial, the Supreme Court of the United States declined to review our case. We were told to pay our debt to society, or at least to the people of the state of California.[11]

52 | On Regents and Rules

ONE OF THE FEW things on which administration, faculty, and students all agreed was that the Regents should confine themselves to policy and not make specific rules. Many Regents thought otherwise and interpreted the administration's inability to discipline disruptive students as an open door to more direct control. They were encouraged by a plethora of letters from the public urging them to crack down on students who did not obey the rules. The Regents began by telling us that the grad students could not rejoin the ASUC, even though both graduates and undergrads voted to do so by comfortable majorities of larger-than-normal turnouts. Voting rights for grad students was SLATE's strategy for control of the ASUC senate, a fact well known to Kerr and the Regents. In this the GCC concurred, seeing itself as the group which would provide leadership. On

February 24th, grad students voted by 1,876 to 1,193 to join the student government. On March 1–2, the undergraduates amended the ASUC constitution by 3,345 to 1,293 to include them. Another vote was set for later in March to confirm specific language and elect grad reps to the ASUC, but before it could be held the Regents declared that these votes were invalid.[1]

Digging way into the past and citing elections on other campuses, President Kerr said that in votes which would result in raising ASUC fees, at least half of the affected students must vote and must approve the decision by a two-thirds majority. Joining the ASUC would increase the incidental fee paid by grad students by $2.25 per semester, and only 20 percent of them had voted to do this. Even though the institutional memory of students is short, they do spend a lot of time in libraries and soon discovered that this "established policy" had not been consistently followed in the past. Articles in the *Daily Cal* and *Spider* pointed out the many elections, polls, and registration-line surveys whose various results had been interpreted differently depending on the outcome desired. Rarely, if ever, did a majority of students vote on anything, and the "fee Rule has been applied only occasionally and capriciously over the last eleven years."[2]

The Regents' rejection electrified the normally compliant ASUC senate, which voted by 13 to 2 to hold the elections anyway. Regent McLaughlin threatened to abolish the ASUC if it did so, and Chancellor Meyerson canceled the election. The GCC sponsored a "Freedom Ballot" in early April, like those held in Mississippi. Over 8,000 students voted to bring the grad students into the student government by a vote of 7 to 1. While this election did not change anything, it did throw the ASUC senate into a state of crisis. In April, it voted to allow grad students to join voluntarily, but by the May 3rd ASUC elections, only eleven had paid the necessary $3.25 to do so. In the fall, students were told to work within the system; in the spring we tried to do this. What we learned from this attempt was that if the powers that be don't like the results, they will change the rules.[3]

In other ways the administration at Berkeley and other campuses had already reminded students that their government was of, by, and for the administration. In March, the ASUC senate and its equivalent at Riverside passed resolutions asking President Johnson to intervene in Selma. The Riverside chancellor told its student council that this was illegal and to withdraw it or be dissolved. They did so, but the student body president and five council members resigned in protest. Chancellor Meyerson threatened to make the ASUC senate "voluntary," but nothing further happened.[4]

At their December 18th meeting, the Regents created two committees: the Meyer Committee to review "policies on use of University facilities, privileges of student organizations and student conduct" and the Forbes Committee "to investigate the basic causes of recent disturbances." With a $10,000 special allocation, Regent Theodore Meyer began his work by writing to 500 student organizations on all campuses requesting written comments on what university policies should be. The committee members met with top administrators, faculty representatives, alumni, the leaders of the student governments, and editors of the campus newspapers. The Regents gave $25,000 to the Forbes Committee, which was increased to $64,300 when it hired Beverly Hills attorney Jerome C. Byrne early in February. For three months, he and six professional staff members interviewed hundreds of students, faculty, Regents, and administrators and also consulted with university presidents in several states. On February 10th, Byrne held a sparsely attended open meeting in the Student Union to listen to Cal student opinions. There, Mario expressed skepticism that any conclusion he came to that didn't condemn the FSM would be buried by the Regents. By then the Regents, who for years had only been distant shadows, were looming like storm clouds, with flashes of lightning and rumbles of thunder. The victory given us by the faculty would be hollow unless confirmed by the Regents, and now we knew that this they would not do.[5]

At the April meeting of the Regents, the Meyer Committee proposed "University-wide Regulations Relating to Student Conduct, Student Organizations and Use of University Facilities" to replace the Kerr Directives. While they confirmed that "students have the right of free expression and advocacy" these proposals were quite different from the spirit and language of the faculty's December 8th resolutions. In many ways they were a reaction to the events of the spring semester more than the fall. Student governments would be creatures of the chancellors, who could determine their members, duties, and responsibilities. Such governments could take positions only on university-related issues, and chancellors would dictate what those were. Chancellors would impose student discipline short of expulsion and could impose penalties for any violation of university regulations, on or off campus, regardless of whether the student was also being prosecuted in the courts. The issue of the fall—on-campus advocacy of illegal off-campus action—was dropped as impracticable. In its place was a requirement for students "to observe generally accepted standards of conduct."

Campus organizations would be limited to current students and staff; others could not post or distribute anything on university property. Student organizations could raise money on campus, hold meetings, and sponsor speakers, but some activities would require administrative approval.

Regent Laurence Kennedy dissented, writing that what was needed was better administration, not more rules. He said "we should not keep repeating the mistake of appeasing the faculty and FSM, who, I expect, will accuse us of meddling and call the new rules worse than the old." That is exactly what happened. The FSM even quoted Kennedy in its leaflets denouncing the Meyer Committee's recommendations. Faculty from the Committee of Two Hundred wrote detailed critiques which were published widely. Even the Faculty Forum was critical of many of the proposals. The Berkeley Division of the Academic Senate voiced its disapproval by 192 to 24, and faculty organizations on the other UC campuses did likewise. The statewide Academic Freedom Committee called the Meyer proposals "negative and repressive in tone." Letters from students and faculty flooded the Regents' office in University Hall; an analysis of these by Regent Kennedy found that 92 percent were critical. Only the Alumni Council unanimously approved.[6]

In light of these reactions, the Meyer recommendations were substantially revised before being presented to the Regents at their May meeting, but the new ones were not made public. Instead they were given to Kerr to incorporate into proposals he would make for the Regents' June meeting. After some discussion and a few modifications, the new policies were released on July 1, 1965. In keeping with Kerr's desire for decentralization, much was delegated to the chancellors to write regulations specific to each campus. They could not only regulate "time, place and manner" of all speech outside the classroom but could veto outside speakers "incompatible with the educational objectives of the University." But clearly stated was the primary goal of the FSM that "students have the right of free expression and advocacy." Gone was the distinction between different types of speech, different types of meetings, and different types of student organizations. A properly registered group could use university facilities as long as all members were affiliated with the campus and it did not use the name of the university. Such organizations could do all the things we had wanted to do: hold meetings, raise money, recruit participants, distribute literature, and take positions. Not all was golden. Students could still be disciplined for "conduct . . . affect[ing] his suitability as a student." What was and was not an "off-campus" issue would continue to plague student governments. And the fact that chancellors wrote the rules that student groups had to follow did not end the debate over what they could do. But it was a workable framework.[7]

Even as the Meyer Committee was investigating the rules, the FSM was investigating the Regents, as it said it would do. Marvin Garson, an alumnus and student spouse, met with the Regents' treasurer on January 4th to request documents on their financial interests and how these might affect decisions. He was given a few public documents. Using these and other public material he wrote a 22-page pamphlet, *The Regents,* to show that "taken as a group, the Regents are representatives of only one thing—corporate wealth" who conducted all important business in secret. Indeed, the sixteen appointed Regents did reflect the major economic interests in the state, including heads of banks, stores, transportation, mining and oil companies, and agriculture. Even two of the three women belonged to newspaper dynasties (the *Los Angeles Times* and *The San Francisco Examiner*). There were also Regents whose professional lives were spent working for unions, the alumni, and the Democratic and Republican Parties. William Forbes, for example, was an advertising executive and former president of the UCLA alumni association. Theodore Meyer was a partner in one of the state's top law firms; as president of the Mechanics' Institute, his seat was ex officio. Edwin Pauley was CEO of Pauley Petroleum. Chairman Edward Carter was president of the largest department store chain in the West. All sat on the boards of major corporations. Having policies for the University of California made by the power elite of the state had its virtues—it was certainly conducive to major capital contributions—but it didn't produce people likely to understand student protest. In their eyes, we were ungrateful wretches who bit the hand that fed us.

Thus, the Regents were not happy with the Byrne report, which did not tell them what they wanted to hear. The 40,000-word document concluded that the "crisis at Berkeley last fall . . . was . . . caused by the failure of the President and Regents to develop a governmental structure at once acceptable to the governed and suited to the vastly increased complexity of the University." As an example of "governmental problems," Byrne described the voiding of the vote to bring grad students into the ASUC *after* students had worked through the system to achieve this goal. The report correctly identified our motivating force as the Civil Rights Movement, our model for action as the Bay Area sit-ins, and our defiance

of established authority as an American tradition. Byrne exonerated the
FSM from the charge of Communist influence or control. He noted that
nonstudents "were not a crucial element" and that those who were involved were virtually all alumni, recent dropouts, relatives of students, or
university employees. There was no "nefarious outside influence." While
faulting all sides in the conflict, the report left the impression that the
adults had acted less responsibly than the students. Finally, Byrne recommended that the Regents stick to broad policy and let each campus govern itself. The president of the university should be the chairman of the
Board of Regents rather than its employee.[8]

As Mario had predicted, the Forbes Committee didn't want to release the report. Meeting on May 7th, the committee voted to not make
it public, or even give it to another Regent, at least not before extensive
discussion, study, and (it hoped) revision. However, Byrne had already
sent it to Governor Brown, who insisted that it become public immediately. Reluctantly, Regents Carter and Forbes, accompanied by President
Kerr and Byrne, held a press conference in Los Angeles on May 11th to
announce completion of Byrne's investigation. While the Byrne report
got a lot of press attention—a full page in *The San Francisco Chronicle*
and almost a full section in the *Los Angeles Times*—it was not well received by the Regents; Regent Carter found it "disappointing." But Governor Brown praised it and FSM leaders were "jubilant." Because the
Daily Cal editor didn't like it, the student newspaper editorial was written by the managing editor, who called it "a masterpiece . . . [which] explains the situation better than any to date." Riverside students picketed
the Regents' May meeting, with signs praising the Byrne report and criticizing the Meyer recommendations. Most of the Regents were distressed
by Byrne's investigation, his conclusions, and with the report's direct distribution to the public. They referred it to Kerr as "source material," not
policy proposals. He incorporated the ideas he agreed with—mostly on
decentralization—into his own reform proposals. Mimeographed copies
of the Byrne report circulated and the alumni association printed an
abridged version in its monthly magazine, but only the successor to the
FSM published it for the general public. Students cut and pasted columns
of the text printed in the *Los Angeles Times* into a 20-page pamphlet and
sold copies for ten cents each.[9]

53 | *The State Legislature*

THE BERKELEY UPRISING provided many opportunities for the 120 members of the state legislature to strut their stuff. They didn't have to guess about which bandwagon to jump on. The respected California Poll surveyed public opinion in mid-January and found that 74 percent disapproved of the "student protest movement." Four percent approved strongly, and 14 percent with reservations. Knowing little about what we did and why besides what was in the press, most people thought we were "mobs" who had engaged in "riots" or "strikes," and many thought we were Communist influenced. Among those who had been to college or were themselves young, a few more expressed approval, but not many more. Another survey in April asked the public how it felt about the goals and/or tactics of the students, the faculty, the Regents, and President Kerr. Over 64 percent disapproved of the students' goals *and* tactics, 9 percent approved of both, and 14 percent approved of the goals but not the tactics. Public opinion on the other parties was more diverse. Kerr scored the highest with 40 percent approving both goals and tactics and 14 percent disapproving of both. The Regents' highest rating was "no opinion."[1]

The first week in January our elected representatives began introducing measures to signify their disapproval or to punish us in some way. Nine bills, three constitutional amendments, and four concurrent resolutions were dropped into the hopper. Several of these would require in-state students to pay tuition. The only one that passed was sponsored by Berkeley's assemblyman, Don Mulford, and originated with the Regents. In their October 1964 meeting, they had asked their counsel to draft a bill specifically criminalizing the unwanted presence of nonstudents. On June 1, 1965, Governor Brown signed into law Assembly Bill 1920, which made it a misdemeanor for a person not a student, officer, or employee of the university to refuse to leave a campus if asked to do so "if it appears that person is committing any act likely to interfere with the peaceful conduct of the activities of such campus." Since the trespassing statute covered that and more, it effectively added little but words to the Penal Code.[2]

More damaging was a line in the university appropriations bill to cut an amount equal to the salaries of 264 TAs. This was precisely the number who had joined the American Federation of Teachers local created in the aftermath of the strike. Our legislators also raised the tuition charged to out-of-state students, who were, according to the legislative debate, more "revolting" than the innocent in-staters, and reduced tuition waivers for nonresident TAs. Assembly Speaker Jesse Unruh and Senate President Pro Tempore Hugh M. Burns requested $150,000 to investigate student protests at Berkeley, but Governor Brown shifted it to a joint legislative study of the needs of higher education.[3]

Of course, this did not prevent the Honorable Mr. Burns from submitting on June 18, 1965, the *Thirteenth Report* of his Senate Fact-Finding Subcommittee on Un-American Activities in California, highlighting what happened at Berkeley. Bound in a bright red cover, the *Thirteenth Report* introduced many students who had not previously been aware of its existence to the Burns Committee. What we read did not inspire confidence in the investigative skills of our legislators or the ability of our elected representatives and their staff to assess and evaluate a situation of which we had first-hand knowledge. What we did not know, being young with little legislative experience, was that the committee was run by its counsel, Richard E. Combs, who was paid $16,200 a year to maintain voluminous files in his home in Tulare County, from which he prepared the biennial reports. He had been collecting information on California "subversives" for twenty-five years. In 1940, after a decade of practicing law and local Democratic Party politics, Combs became counsel to the Yorty Committee on recommendation of his good friend and neighbor, the assembly speaker. He stayed when it became the Tenney Committee in 1941 and the Burns Committee in 1949. The only reporter to profile him wrote in 1967 that he "commands its elaborate espionage system, directs its pursuit of subversives, compiles its dossiers (by the thousands, he claims) and fashions its reports." Although employed by a subcommittee of the California senate, Combs operated independently, exercising power through press releases rather than with hearings or threats of legislation.[4]

Those of us who did know what had happened that fall thought the *Thirteenth Report* was the funniest fiction we had read all year. Even its chronology belied its claim to have thoroughly investigated "the most recent troubles." According to the Burns report, the problem started with congestion at Sather Gate. After Weinberg was arrested on October 1st, "150 to 200 students entered Sproul Hall to take Dean Towle a hostage." Contrary to 15,000 eyewitnesses, we learned that at the December 7th Greek Theater meeting, "Savio, flanked by several of his supporters, shouldered his way to the microphone, shoved the speaker aside, and was dragged away by police." I discovered that Brad Cleaveland was an elder statesman of SLATE, the brains behind the *Cal Reporter* and the *SLATE Supplement,* and that I was on the staff of *Spider.* Five pages were devoted to the "Filthy Speech Movement" where President Kerr was raked over the coals for shirking his responsibility to discipline errant students.[5]

> It is painfully clear that at this point the university campus at Berkeley was operating without any discipline or restriction whatever, compendia of filth were being distributed on and off the campus, and in support of this nauseating campaign were some of the most prominent leaders of the Free Speech Movement whose dedication to Communism they had disdained to conceal.[6]

The Burns Committee had its own agenda, and impartial investigation was not on it. Right after its chronology of the FSM were sections on the "History of Communism at Berkeley," and "Red Chinese Propaganda." Throughout were detailed descriptions of meetings and conventions all over the country of allegedly Communist groups in order to explain "why the Berkeley Campus was selected as a target for the mass demonstrations that started in September 1964." It was heavily seeded with names of people I had never heard of, let alone seen at an FSM meeting, and asserted that "the two student organizations that played the dominant roles in the Berkeley rebellion are SLATE and the DuBois Clubs." CORE and Friends of SNCC were mentioned only in passing. These leftist organizations, it said, used the classic Communist tactic of forming a United Front controlled by Communists. It was this "minority of Communist leaders [that] managed to bring this great educational institution to its knees." The one person over 30 whose opinions were attended to by the FSM militants—Hal Draper—was mentioned only in the bibliography.[7]

If the FSM was controlled by Communists, President Kerr was a dupe. While not a Communist himself, "we do make clear," the report said in a section called "The Role of Clark Kerr," that many of Kerr's most intimate colleagues during these years were at the same time teaching at the Communist school and participating in a wide variety of pro-Communist activities. Some of them came to work at the Berkeley campus after Kerr became its Chancellor, and some found places with the Institute of Industrial Relations, which he headed.

Kerr was soft on communism, it implied, and that was why he was so easily taken advantage of by the Communist led FSM. Kerr held a press conference the day the Burns report was released to defend himself and his staff, past and present. Governor Brown denounced the report, and even the *San Francisco Examiner* criticized it. One of the three senators on Burns's committee refused to sign, saying it was "just drivel." The Regents were divided. At their monthly meeting that day, Edwin Pauley passed out copies of the report when Kerr was not present and urged his dismissal. Governor Brown deftly deflected this move into a pat on Kerr's back and approval for his proposed university reorganization, which Kerr had prepared in response to the Byrne report.[8]

Battle having been joined, Kerr and Burns continued to spar, with each jab making headlines in the California newspapers. In October, Kerr released his own 42-page "Analysis of the Thirteenth Report" documenting its inaccuracies and distortions. He challenged Burns to waive the legislative immunity which protected him from libel suits. The following May, the Burns Committee issued a *Supplement* to the *Thirteenth Report,* attacking Kerr even more vehemently than it had the year before (and stating that statutory immunity was not subject to waiver). Expanded to five senators, all of whom signed, the committee report's acerbic tone remained the same. Again Kerr prepared a lengthy analysis, but it was not released. Instead, the Regents appointed their own committee to decide how best to respond. Its chairman, Jesse Tapp, met with Burns, who agreed that there should be no public hearings on the charges, particularly since gubernatorial candidate Ronald Reagan had demanded them. On August 5th, after several committee meetings, the Regents issued a polite one-page repudiation carefully worded to avoid further confrontations. Although this ended it for the Burns Committee, by then the university had become an election issue. Charges and countercharges continued in the press.[9]

Unknown to the students, Burns had long wanted to discredit Kerr because Burns "was unimpressed with his diligence in ferreting out subversive activities on the campus." Soon after Kerr was inaugurated as president, Combs had held a secret meeting in his home with the heads of various Bay Area Police Department red squads. Combs had compiled a dossier on Kerr and wanted help from those present in getting even more information that could be used to undermine and possibly remove him. The men he brought together were part of the intelligence network that President Sproul had linked into in the 1930s when he sought information on student radicals. Now that same network of subversive specialists in law enforcement was being used against his successor, President Kerr.[10]

Combs saw Kerr as a barrier to enforcement of his antisubversive policies and a possible subversive himself. In 1952, as the loyalty-oath controversy was winding down, Burns met with presidents of the California colleges and asked them to appoint liaisons with his committee. These would provide to Combs the names of faculty and staff who were candidates for hiring or promotion to be checked against his list of known subversives. Combs would also screen "organizations seeking to meet on the campuses or to establish branches." In its 1953 report, the Burns Committee reported that "during the 10 months that this cooperative plan has been in existence, more than a hundred persons with documentable records of Communist activities and affiliations have been removed from the educational institutions of California."[11]

But not from Berkeley. President Sproul asked the new chancellor to be the official "contact man" for the Berkeley campus. Kerr agreed, but did nothing. Unknown to Kerr, the actual liaison was William Wadman, a graduate of the FBI academy and chief of the campus police. At Burns's request, Sproul had already appointed Wadman to be the university-wide security officer. As such he reported to Vice President Corley, not Chancellor Kerr, even though he kept his office in Room 39 of the Administration Building. On March 1, 1952, Corley wrote the San Francisco FBI office that Wadman was his "representative on police matters for the University . . . [and] is to engage in highly confidential investigations." From his dingy basement office, Wadman furnished the FBI as well as Combs "information contained in personnel files of students and employees as well as information relating to subversive activities on the campus." He also sent reports to individual Regents. Since Kerr disapproved, Corley kept Wadman's work secret from the chancellor. After Kerr became president, Wadman "was assigned to work on insurance matters." Although he kept his title of security officer, his office was moved to the business office in University Hall—one floor below President Kerr's.[12]

Senator Burns was dismayed at Kerr's refusal to cooperate with his committee and "his aversion to loyalty investigations in general." On September 14, 1961, and again on January 17, 1962, Combs and Burns met with Kerr and select Regents to urge the discharge of two Berkeley faculty members they thought were subversives. They also protested Wadman's being assigned "so much insurance work that his counter-subversive operation was smothered." When Kerr did nothing, Burns tried to get the Regents to remove him by revealing a "rumor" that Kerr had been observed by the Central Intelligence Agency to engage in "undesirable contact and associations during a South American trip." The attack on Kerr in the 1965 *Thirteenth Report* and its 1966 *Supplement* was just the latest in a long-term effort to rid the university of the man who would not cooperate with Burns and Combs in their efforts to remove campus subversives.[13]

The Burns report was merely a curiosity to the students, but in hostile hands it could do real damage. After my sentencing, I returned to the South, where I spent over a year doing voter registration in Alabama and Mississippi. The Burns report followed me. The four paragraphs with my name in them were clipped and pasted onto a single page with other excerpts on "Communists in the Rebellion." Titled "MISS JO FREEMAN, WHITE FEMALE PROFESSIONAL COMMUNIST AGITATOR," it was circulated in some of the small towns in which I worked. On August 18, 1966, the *Jackson Daily News,* which called itself "Mississippi's Greatest Newspaper," exposed me in an editorial headlined "Professional Agitator Hits All Major Trouble Spots." It cited the Burns report as its major source of information, even for things it did not say, such as that I was "a sparkplug in the Filthy Speech Movement recently in California." The editorial was accompanied by five photographs, including one taken on December 3rd of me speaking from the second-floor balcony of Sproul Hall.

Neither the Alabama leaflet nor the Mississippi newspaper mentioned the extensive criticism of the Burns report. On the contrary, they both distorted what it said and invented things it did not say. My four mentions in the 1965 Burns report are trivial, and three were true. I'm listed as a signatory of the October 2nd agreement, as an arrestee, and as a member of the editorial staff of the *SLATE Supplement* and *Spider.* But in the flyer and the editorial, the Burns Committee report was used as evidence that I was either a Communist or almost one. For myself, and probably for others, the Burns report had greater consequences than the Byrne report. It was fuel for those who claimed that civil rights workers were just Communists out to destroy America.

54 | *Graduation*

On Monday, April 26th, Mario Savio told the noon rally at Sproul Hall that he was leaving. After a speech denouncing the Meyer recommendations, he surprised us all by saying that the time had come for the movement to continue on its own. Wishing us "good luck and goodbye," he walked down the steps, leaving us all to wonder what had happened. The following day he explained in a letter that "if the student rights movement at Berkeley must inevitably fail without my leadership, then it were best that it fail."[1] A changing of the guard had been happening for some time. The FSM notables were preoccupied with the trial; those that weren't still in school were also involved in civil rights and other causes. At the final Ex Com meeting that dissolved the FSM, I was the only one there who had been part of the United Front in September and one of a few who had been FSMers in October. A new cohort of activists was emerging.

On Wednesday, Bettina Aptheker and Jack Weinberg announced that the FSM would be replaced by the Free Student Union (FSU), which would be a trade union for students. Mario was not present; he stayed away from the remaining rallies other than as an observer. The FSU had been in the works for some time, but it wasn't quite ready to go public. A week later a deanlet told it to remove its table from Sproul Plaza because it hadn't registered as a student organization with the dean of students. Bettina protested that it couldn't register because it had no constitution, by-laws, or officers, only about 3,000 members who had paid a quarter to join. ASUC president Charlie Powell averted a confrontation by registering the "Friends of the FSU" to sponsor the table. At the organizing meeting held in Harmon gym the next day, 350 students completed the formalities. They were organized into locals based on time, department, and interest, but no one went to meetings. Eventually the FSU just faded away, to be replaced by organizations focused on specific issues.[2]

The political students were less concerned with student rights than with national problems, and in the spring a new issue emerged which would eventually swamp everything else—the war in Viet Nam. As early as 1963, students had protested U.S. support of the unpopular government in South Viet Nam headed by Ngo Dinh Diem. That fall, when his sister-in-law Mme Ngo Dinh Nhu toured the United States to drum up support, Berkeley was one of several places to picket "the Dragon Lady." Even as we demonstrated, our government was secretly encouraging a military coup. On November 1st, Diem and his brother were assassinated, two days after Mme Nhu spoke on campus. We didn't picket UN Secretary U Thant when he spoke at the Spring 1964 Charter Day ceremonies but we did hold up signs asking him to "Help Stop the War in Viet Nam." These attitudes reflected an awareness of the war in Southeast Asia that had not been present only a year earlier.

Not until spring 1965 did opposition to the war in Viet Nam become a mass student movement. After President Johnson committed large numbers of U.S. troops to what he had said during the fall campaign was an Asian war to be fought by Asian boys, mathematics professor Stephen Smale and ex-student Jerry Rubin started the Vietnam Day Committee (VDC). It sponsored a marathon teach-in in the Student Union Plaza on May 21–22, one of several nationwide. For thirty-three hours, the lower Student Union plaza and an adjacent athletic field became a fairgrounds, with speakers, booths, and entertainers. An estimated 30,000 people came at some point, with the crowd peaking at 12,000. Although advertised as a debate, speakers who supported U.S. policy withdrew, claiming that the event was too biased for their views to get a fair hearing. Consequently, the steady denunciations of U.S. actions in Viet Nam took on the flavor of a religious revival. "Teach-ins" became the rage at dozens of campuses as the war in Viet Nam became the top issue on the student agenda. The VDC registered with the dean of students as a permanent campus organization.[3]

I was there most of those thirty-three hours, even though I hadn't quite made up my mind on Viet Nam and did not find one-sided debates to be persuasive. I had an ulterior motive, which was to sell enough buttons to keep myself solvent for a few months. I had been selling buttons all spring at Bancroft and Telegraph, but I would soon leave and needed a financial cushion. Although everyone now knew that the campus began with the plaques and not the pillars, commercial sales were overlooked at Bancroft that would have attracted attention elsewhere on campus. UCLC put its table up at Sather Gate, but when I sold my own buttons I did so at Bancroft, even though I stood on university bricks. *Spider* had been ignored when sold at Bancroft; only when its table moved to Ludwig's Fountain did the deanlets come out from Sproul Hall to tell them to pack up. At least one other student, or ex-student, sold buttons for his personal profit at Bancroft. Ed Rosenfeld and I recognized each other as fellow entrepreneurs, even competitors, though we didn't blare it to the world. Nor did we apply for the peddlers' license the city would have required if we had asked for permits to use the city sidewalk. Thus, I felt uncomfortable when I sold for myself at the teach-in, as I had to cross that invisible boundary that demarcated the campus as a special place in my mind. But I needed the money, so I followed the customers.

My button-collecting brought me an invitation to a small 42nd-birthday party for Paul Seabury, organized by his wife. Seabury was also a collector of political buttons, as were all the guests. My present to him was a small green-and-white Stevenson/Kennedy/1960 button, which was considered quite a prize because only a thousand had been printed. Allan had headed Students for Stevenson in 1960 and kept a few, which he passed on to me when he left for Antioch.

My leftover buttons went to Jerry Fishkin, both my collection and my selling and trading stock. It was his idea to store them for me and trade for both of us. In exchange, he asked for inheritance rights if I should be killed in the South. I decided my buttons were safer with Jerry than with Helen, who did not appreciate their value. When I graduated from high school, she gave me a trunk and told me to put in it anything I wanted to keep. Whatever did not fit she would feel free to keep or dispose of as she saw fit. She was going to give me another trunk for my college souvenirs, and my buttons would take up too much space. Jerry took care of my buttons for the next twenty years.

As the end of the semester approached, most of us were moving on. Jerry was graduating, as were Jackie Goldberg and many other political activists. Allan was leaving the Antioch Graduate School of Education with an M.A.T. to become program director of the Foundation for Integrative Education in New York City. Toni had returned to the Bay Area after finishing two quarters at Wayne State. She had hooked up with another old boyfriend who had been drafted and sent to the army language school in Monterey to learn Vietnamese. On May 29th, they got married so she could live with him. I don't know which of us was more surprised; Toni wasn't the type to tie herself down to one man (the marriage only lasted three years). I missed her wedding to finish my honors thesis because the deadline to get the "with honors" designation on my diploma was the following week. There was no quick way to get to Monterey and back, and I couldn't afford two days off from writing. So I baked her a cake, plain but tasty, and sent it down with her friends on a poster that said "STOP WAR." I still barely finished the thesis in time. To my ever-lasting gratitude, Professor Townsend let me turn in the draft with its inserts, emendations, corrections, and typos. It was very long and would have taken me three days to retype. I didn't have three days.

I had long since decided to go south after graduation, naïvely assuming that there would be another Freedom Summer. However, the main civil rights organizations, of which I knew very little, were at odds with each other. SNCC, CORE, and SCLC all planned separate summer projects in different states, smaller and less publicized than in 1964. I applied to all three but favored CORE since that was the group I had worked with in the Bay Area. Strong in the North, CORE was the only one that had a local screening committee. One of my interviewers was Barbara Garson, who had been an editor of the FSM newsletter. I knew this did not bode well. The issue of *Spider* with my perfidy publicized on the back cover had just come out to remind FSM stalwarts that I was a sell-out/ratfink/traitor. Thus, I was more amused than surprised when CORE wrote in May that due to "the extreme conditions one will have to work under in Louisiana, we feel that it would be too dangerous to send a person with your limited civil rights experience into the state." Fortunately, both SNCC and SCLC were happy to have me. For SNCC, I was interviewed by a Cal professor whom I did not know, and SCLC accepted me based on my paper application. I was torn between the two; SNCC had more cachet but SCLC had a better-organized summer project. Called SCOPE, it would send 400 northern students into six southern states. Vicky's boyfriend, Ted Jacqueney, had returned to the Bay Area after working for SCLC for many months and persuaded me that it would be the better choice. Given SNCC's subsequent history, it was.

All three organizations required a parent's signature for applicants under 21 and a release of liability. This pissed me off. While I was only 19, I was about to graduate from college, had been supporting myself for over a year, and had been tried three times as an adult by the state of California. Why should I need my mother's permission to do anything? She was not thrilled by my plans, though how much was fear for my safety and how much was fear of what her siblings would say I could not tell. I soon discovered another fear: that I would skip the graduation ceremony in order to go south in time for orientation. We agreed that she would sign my applications and I would stay in Berkeley long enough to graduate.

Helen drove to Berkeley before graduation to help me pack and clean up. I had to leave the house clean to get my deposit back, and I knew that if she found that the house needed serious work there would be hell to pay. I nudged my housemates out so I could clean before she arrived. Then Max Heirich phoned and asked to interview me for his sociology dissertation on the FSM. I'd seen him around and knew a lot of people were being interviewed for the many studies going on, but he was the only one to ask me. Torn between my desire to do the interview and fear of my mother, I told Max that he could come over and interview me while I cleaned the kitchen. I had started on the stove when he arrived and he found it difficult to get good audio while I was working. He sat me down at the kitchen table and told me talk into the tape recorder while he cleaned my stove.[4]

June 12th was one of those bright beautiful days that make the Golden State so appealing. Over 20,000 people came to Memorial Stadium to watch 7,827 degrees and professional certificates be awarded; 4,337 to my graduating class. President Kerr gave the commencement address. The trial of "the 800" had ended the day before. So many commentators had forecast the end of this great university because of what my generation of students had done that he thought our parents, friends, and alumni should know how common this was. To provide a "perspective on the prophets of doom" he quoted from the *Los Angeles Times* of 1902:

> It is to be hoped that there will be no whitewashing and no halting of justice in the punishment of the Berkeley students who may be found guilty of criminal acts in connection with the recent riotous demonstrations.

To this he added gloomy predictions from other newspapers after other demonstrations and the glum opinion of professional educators after the loyalty-oath controversy. Cal had withstood all these disasters, he said, and had gone on to be even better and more prestigious than before. He urged us all to learn from the experience, to "rise to even greater heights."[5]

After the speeches were over, graduates marched by schools and colleges to receive a cardboard tube. Inside was a piece of paper commemorating our attendance at the 102nd Commencement of the University of California. Our diplomas would be mailed after the university determined that we had met all our degree requirements. When the College of Letters and Science was called, two-thirds of the audience stood up. We were divided into ten lines, each to receive our tube from a different administrator. As luck would have it, Clark Kerr was at the head of my line. As I drew near, I wondered if he would remember me and the negotiations we had engaged in so long ago. He did. "What are you going to do next year," he said, "besides stirring up trouble?" I smiled and replied, "I guess I'll be stirring up a little trouble in Alabama and Mississippi. And you?"

"We'll continue improving the university as always, depending, of course, on the directions of the Regents." He shook my hand, handed me a tube, and wished me luck.

Thus ended my education at Berkeley.

55 | *The FBI Files*

In June of 1975, when I returned from my three-day interview for the White House Fellows competition, I made an FOIA (Freedom of Information Act) request for my FBI file. I'd long suspected I had one, but until the commissioners who selected the fellows let on that this was what had eliminated me from serious consideration, I had not been curious about its contents. This file was not available to the regional committee that selected me as one of its three finalists, but it had been given to the full commission. A few months later, I paid for and received 129 pages. Most of these contained my own words, reported in complaints to the FBI while I was a civil rights worker in the South, plus bad paper copies of mug shots and clippings from newspapers followed by a sheet of people identified at demonstrations with every name except mine whited out. There were a few interesting tidbits from my days at Berkeley.

In 1993, as I contemplated writing this book, I asked the FBI for more. I had heard that the regional offices kept files with more in them than headquarters did. I requested from headquarters and the regional offices files on myself, the FSM, SLATE, and student protests at Berkeley. In the intervening years, the FBI had become quite sophisticated in avoiding the Freedom of Information Act. It took seven years, about two inches worth of correspondence and several letters from members of Congress before I got more, and I didn't get much that I didn't already know from purely public sources. In 1994, I learned that there were 3,450 pages of files on the FSM in the San Francisco field office, but my requests for these were repeatedly denied or stalled. The FBI claimed it needed time for processing, but I learned later that everything I asked for had already been processed. In 1977, the *Daily Cal* asked the FBI for its records on political activity at Berkeley. By 1982 it had received 9,217 pages, including all the files I requested. In 1996, the FBI phoned to tell me that Seth Rosenfeld, a reporter for the *San Francisco Examiner,* had obtained the FSM files after fifteen years of requests and a federal court order and that I should get a copy from him. I tried, but he didn't answer my letters or phone calls. In fact, he had obtained most of what he asked for years before I made my first request, and most of that had been cleared in 1988. Not until Spring 2000 did the FBI send me 2,592 pages from its files on the FSM—much less than it gave to Rosenfeld. In August, the FBI sent 1,090 pages on "U of C/Berkeley"; another 2,603 pages arrived in October. In March of 2001, after I'd finished the book, 2,890 pages on SLATE landed at my door. Most of the items from the FBI were documents and newsclippings, which would have been of more value at the beginning of my research than at the end. There were also numerous highly repetitive blacked-out lists and multiple copies of FBI reports on various "subversive" organizations, especially the DuBois Club and the SWP. Equally revealing was what was not in their files—or at least not released to me. Nonetheless, what I got tells a lot about our government's attitude toward those who challenge the status quo.

As best I can tell, the FBI opened a file on me in 1964 after I was arrested for the second time in a civil rights demonstration. An agent obtained my records from the office of the dean of students, and upon discovering I had a few credits transferred from Valley State College and the University of Arizona (the summer in Guadalajara) sent agents to see if those institutions had any negative information on me. My mother told me about a visit from an FBI agent in October, made to inform her that I had visited Nazi headquarters the preceding August. No report of that visit was released to me, perhaps because the agent learned I had gone there as a *Daily Cal* reporter, or maybe because he didn't like my mother's response. "I just got her snapshots back from the drug store," she told me she said. "Would you like to come in and see them?"

My file had a copy of the *Jackson Daily News* editorial and photos, but nothing from the Burns report. This gave the false impression that there really had been a Filthy Speech Movement and that I had been involved in it as well as the knowledge that I had "worked with Bettina Aptheker who has admitted in interviews she is a member of the Communist Party." The San Francisco FBI office supplied headquarters with synopses of news stories from the October 1964 demonstrations and a copy of the October 2nd agreement with Kerr. It reported I was an officer of SLATE in a document titled "Communist Infiltration of SLATE" but also said that "no subversive activity is known." Of course my arrests were there, as well as the fact that I had signed a petition in 1962 in opposition to the McCarran Act. I was surprised that I even knew what the McCarran Act was at the age of 16 because I've long since forgotten.

There was nothing in this file on how a photo of me speaking from the Sproul Hall balcony got into the Mississippi newspaper. I only found that out when a 1994 court order opened the files of the Mississippi Sovereignty Commission (MSC) in 1997–1998. Formed in 1956 to gather information on persons active in the Civil Rights Movement and closed only in 1973, I had not even known the MSC existed when I worked in Mississippi from June to August 1966. But I learned from the pages I received that the state of Mississippi had its own informant on the Berkeley campus. On December 1, 1964, Edgar Downing of Long Beach, California, phoned Erle Johnston, Jr., director of the MSC, and offered him "valuable information concerning communist activity in Mississippi." Since several Berkeley students had participated in Freedom Summer, the MSC was interested. For over two years, Downing supplied reports and photos to the MSC, which paid his "expenses." The fact that Mario Savio was in the national news after working in Mississippi enhanced the MSC's interest, but it paid for information on us all, including a list of everyone arrested in Sproul Hall. Downing gave the MSC several photos of me and even the address and phone number of my mother. A native of McComb, Mississippi, Downing regularly returned home, and in August of 1966 he took photos of the demonstrations SCLC was leading in Grenada, including a couple of me. He sold these to the MSC.[1]

Johnston was a professional publicist who knew just was to do with

Downing's information. He gave Jimmy Ward, editor of the *Jackson Daily News,* the photos, pages from the Burns report, and a draft of the editorial that eventually appeared on August 18th as an example of "professional agitators who are now working in Mississippi and have been on the scene in other riots throughout the nation." The newspaper published it as true, even though HUAC's chairman responded to a query from a Mississippi congressman that there was no record of my having an "association with officially cited Communist or Communist-front organizations."

The Jackson office of the FBI clipped the page from the newspaper and sent it to headquarters. This began a feedback loop. Reports from the Jackson FBI office state that (name blacked out) contacted them, and identified JO FREEMAN as a demonstrator in Grenada, Mississippi. "[Name deleted] who has furnished reliable information in the past, advised that FREEMAN is . . . also listed by the Un-American Activities Committee of California as a subversive." Statements that California thought I was a subversive show up on several pages, even though the San Francisco FBI office repeatedly says I am not and the Burns Committee didn't say I was. I realize that to the state of Mississippi all civil rights workers were subversives, but it is California that is credited with my designation as such. Mere mention in the Burns Committee report was enough.

Out of curiosity, I also asked the FBI if it had a file on my mother, which one can do once a person has died. It replied that she had no personal file but that her name did appear in some reports. Most of these were on me; the FBI repeatedly phoned her to find out where I was, claiming to be an old college friend seeking to resume contact. A 1966 document reported that in 1962 she was elected to the Executive Council of Local 1021 of the American Federation of Teachers. From a 1964 document, I learned that she had participated in a July 1963 demonstration at the Board of Education, whose pickets carried signs reading "Stop De Facto Segregation" and "Teach Negro History." At least the state of California didn't find her to be a subversive for having made one of me!

After Mario Savio died in 1996, I requested his file and got 1,296 pages three years later. Most pages were either blacked out or were multiple bad copies of newspaper clippings (which by then told me little that I did not know). The FBI did background checks on everyone involved in Freedom Summer. On July 7, 1964, an agent reviewed Mario's application to Cal and other records in the office of the dean of students. When he emerged as chief spokesman for the FSM, the FBI collected everything it could find on him, including the records from his New York schools (and all of his numerous high school awards). Although it found nothing more subversive than his close working relationship with Bettina, this was enough for FBI agents "to intensify their coverage of all the activities of Savio." It continued to keep him under surveillance for many years, even though agents said he was not a "subversive." Deeply offended by his "contemptuous attitude," the FBI used the same technique that it used to keep track of me—phoning his parents under the pretext of being an old friend—and talking to neighbors who might know him. The FBI regularly sent information on his whereabouts to the Secret Service, checking box 3 for "potentially dangerous." In 1968, it identified him as one of three "Key Activists" of the New Left in San Francisco and thus subject to the "new Bureau counterintelligence program." The last page that was released is dated January 17, 1975, and is completely blacked out. Eleven years after Mario became a public figure and at least five after he tried to fade from public view, he was still being tracked by the FBI.

SLATE came to the FBI's attention when university security officer William Wadman gave the FBI documents from SLATE's founding convention and a list of eighty-five members. He assessed the group as "weak," "ineffective and impotent." No doubt it also got information from the red squad of the Berkeley Police; Officer Ed Skeels was a familiar figure on campus, always standing off to the side in plainclothes as he observed rallies and demonstrations at Sather Gate. The San Francisco FBI office placed the "case" in "a closed status." Its attention was revived in December of 1960, when headquarters listened to *Sounds of Protest,* the record SLATE produced about the May 1960 anti-HUAC demonstrations. If SLATE's public critique of HUAC put it back under the FBI's microscope, SLATE's sponsorship of Frank Wilkinson's campus talk in March 1961 sharpened its focus. Assemblyman Mulford phoned the FBI as part of his campaign to get Kerr to cancel Wilkinson's talk, telling them that "now is the time to force the University of California to get rid of SLATE."[2] However, the FBI had little or no idea what SLATE was, as reflected in the captions of its spring 1961 memos: "COMMUNIST INFILTRATION OF STUDENT LEAGUE ALLOWED TO EXIST (SLATE)." In its subsequent reports, the FBI appended lengthy descriptions of numerous other organizations that were on its subversive list, some of which weren't even in Berkeley.

In the spring of 1961, the FBI obtained a current membership list from Alex Sherriffs. A headquarters memo of June 31, 1961, says:

SLATE is currently under investigation with the San Francisco Office as office of origin to determine the extent of Communist Party (CP) infiltration, domination, and control. Of the approximate 110, eleven members, including SLATE chairman, Michael Myerson, have attended instruction classes being conducted by northern California CP leaders. Two members are on the Security Index and five others are past or present members of the CP, Labor Youth League (LYL), the Socialist Workers Party (SWP), or the SWP youth group Young Socialist Alliance. . . .

In addition the California State Un-American Activities Committee in its report released 6-13-61 termed SLATE a "transmission belt" for communist propaganda.

The FBI sent "informants" from Los Angeles to SLATE's 1961 summer conference, reporting that it "attracted 208 registered delegates from forty colleges." It subsequently collected SLATE newsletters and programs and even the *SLATE Supplement*. Every semester a special agent wrote a report on SLATE's newest officers and most active members, including any "reported to have been involved in left-wing activity." Added to this were newspaper clippings, leaflets, and a summary of general activities. Alex Sherriffs regularly supplied information from his office, as did the campus police. Occasionally informants were recruited to report on membership meetings; some called up the FBI office to volunteer. Special agents wrote up major events, such as the speeches of Mickie Lima and Malcolm X. The final FBI report, dated January 31, 1967, summarizes the *Daily Cal* on SLATE's dissolution.

The FBI opened an internal security file on the FSM in October, after our sit-in around the car, in order to ascertain the influence of "groups whose goals are to achieve political or social change through activities that involve force or violence, or who advocate anarchy, or are under control or direction of hostile foreign powers." The FBI had its own network of informants in the left-wing groups (identified only by code numbers, if at all). It regularly sent special agents to observe our demonstrations and to confer with Vice-Chancellor Alex Sherriffs throughout the fall. William Wadman, still on the university payroll as a security officer, was just one of its many sources. The FBI did not share information with Senator Burns or his committee counsel Richard Combs or Wadman, preferring to keep them at arm's length. Although the bureau initially thought that the FSM "was heavily influenced, if not at times controlled, by individuals who were members of or affiliated with subversive organizations," eventually it realized that there were barely a "handful" involved. Among the identified leaders it named only Bettina and Art as "subversives" and admitted that Art was not a member of a "subversive" organization. Mario, Suzanne, and Steve Weissman were "not participants in subversive groups." The FBI barely noticed Syd Stapleton, even though the SWP was on its list of subversive organizations. In January, the San Francisco office sent a "comprehensive memorandum" on "subversive influence" in the Berkeley demonstrations with profiles of people and groups. Although claiming that "CP leaders were pleased with the campus incidents," the FBI concluded that the Party was not behind them and they would have happened with or without a left-wing presence. It sent copies to federal agencies and to Regent Edwin Pauley at the request of his "close personal friend" John A. McCone, UC alumnus and director of the Central Intelligence Agency. Pauley also received profiles of nineteen students and faculty members with "subversive" backgrounds. President Kerr neither requested nor received information from the FBI on the FSM and its activities.[3]

I learned more about FBI activities from reading two federal court decisions, which decided a lawsuit Seth Rosenfeld filed on February 22, 1985, after the FBI stalled on his FOIA requests. By the time the district court wrote its decision in 1991 and the ninth circuit wrote its decision in 1995, Rosenfeld had obtained most of what he requested (and, unlike me, had his fees waived on the grounds that his requests were in the public interest) and his pro bono lawyers were arguing over redactions and missing documents.[4]

The circuit court generally concurred with the district court's findings, adding interesting items from the FBI's files on Clark Kerr in its decision. Rosenfeld had Kerr's written permission to obtain his files (needed because Kerr was still living) and from them concluded "that the FBI waged a concerted effort in the late 1950s and 1960s to have Kerr fired from the presidency of UC Berkeley." The FBI identified the Regents most opposed to Kerr and fed them information to undermine their confidence in his administration. The court found that the campaign to fire Kerr began in 1958, after which "the statements of dislike for Kerr in the record are egregious." Even FBI director J. Edgar Hoover stuck in his two cents, noting "on the margin of one report that he knew 'Kerr is no good.'" While I did not see Kerr's personal files, a January 28, 1965, memo on "Background of Incident" illuminates the FBI's distaste. It investigated him in 1947, 1952, 1958, and 1964 as a possible candidate for appointment to various federal bodies. Although the FBI did not find him to be disloyal, he was clearly too liberal and too lenient toward Communists, sympathizers, and other "subversives" for its taste. Nor did the bureau believe he was sufficiently respectful of it and its mission. It is ironic that the FBI, the Burns Committee, Regent Pauley, and the FSM all had the same opinion of President Kerr: none of them liked him and all were glad to see him go.[5]

I did learn a few things from the few thousand pages I finally received from the FBI, though I knew from reading my own files to treat them skeptically. The FBI is a vacuum cleaner; it sucks up information without regard to accuracy. It does not subject it to the evidentiary standards of scholars or even lawyers. But when Director J. Edgar Hoover testified before the House Appropriations Subcommittee on March 14, 1965, he discussed the FSM as though his information was solid rather than speculative. He said that there were forty-three persons with "subversive backgrounds" in the FSM, including five faculty members. Hoover did admit that the FSM was not started or controlled by Communists, though he thought it was exploited by them. He did not say whether the FBI had tried to influence the FSM, though its agents actively sought to manage many groups and shape their actions. Prior to the December Regents' meeting, the FBI gave information on us to Governor Brown, at his request, and to some of the Regents. One memo said the purpose was so the Regents could "curtail, harass and at times eliminate Communists and ultra liberal members on the faculty." The FBI normally exchanges information with law enforcement agencies and did so with our prosecutors. It may have provided background information on some defendants to Judge Crittenden prior to sentencing. It gives background information to friendly news reporters on condition that they not reveal the source, and its agents pose as reporters to get information or ask provocative questions at press conferences. All these things were done to the FSM, though we did not know it at the time.[6]

56 | *Aftermath, Afterword, and Afterthoughts*

THE DOCUMENTS I got from the FBI and the Mississippi Sovereignty Commission, plus the Burns reports, gave me a perspective on the Free Speech Movement's place in history that I did not have at the time. We saw ourselves as part of the Civil Rights Movement and assumed that our opponents were trying to stifle our civil rights activity. This is only a partial truth. We were motivated by the Civil Rights Movement and a desire for racial justice, but to move from that to the assumption that the university administration was opposed to these things is as credible as the innuendoes and allegations in the *Jackson Daily News* editorial. The administration wasn't opposed to the Civil Rights Movement, or even to our participation in it. They were trying to protect the university from the state legislature, some of whose members saw Communist influence behind every disruption. In doing so they lost sight of an underlying principle of our democracy: free speech is crucial even when the speech or the speaker is provocative or unpopular.

The crisis that consumed the Berkeley campus in 1964 was a not a battle in the Civil Rights Movement but a skirmish in the Cold War. That war was fought at home as well as abroad and damaged many people and institutions. The rules and policies devised by the university to distance itself from any hint of Communist contamination eroded basic American rights and contravened basic American values. The faculty, or some of them (including Kerr and Strong), fought this erosion when they protested the loyalty oath. The students also scuffled over this retrenchment for years, primarily through SLATE, demanding the right to do on campus what they could do as citizens off campus. But it was the FSM that reclaimed the territory lost in the Cold War that enabled Berkeley students, staff, and faculty to exercise their constitutional rights on campus.

This skirmish caused many casualties, most of which will never become public. To start with persons better known, Governor Brown was defeated by Ronald Reagan when he ran for re-election in 1966. The charges in the Burns reports that the Berkeley campus was a haven for Communists, dupes, and sympathizers was one of Reagan's weapons; the university budget and the lack of tuition was one of his campaign issues. On May 12, 1966, Reagan told thousands of people in a major speech just outside San Francisco that the "leadership and morality gap in Sacramento" had let "a small minority of beatniks, radicals and filthy speech advocates" bring "shame to a great University." He relied on the official report of the California senate subcommittee to back up his charges, even though he hadn't read it.[1] Brown wrote in 1970 that

> The Berkeley issue was one of the main factors in my defeat. . . . I was caught in the same political vise that has squeezed many moderate or liberal incumbents out of office. The growing number of indignant conservatives in the state were against me because I had not appeared to be tough enough in cracking down on student disorder during the Free Speech Movement. The ultraliberals and more militant allies of the students were against me because I had called out extra police to end the sit-ins.[2]

Clark Kerr was fired on January 20, 1967, at the first Regents' meeting over which Ronald Reagan presided. As the new board chairman Theodore Meyer explained later, "His relations with the Regents were adversely affected by his handling of the Berkeley campus disorders in the fall of 1964." Governor Brown derailed an attempt to remove him made by Regents Pauley and Canaday at the June 1965 meeting, but Governor Reagan asked Kerr to resign after his election in November 1966. While Kerr did not publicly take sides during the campaign, he opposed Reagan's proposal to cut the university budget by 10 percent and to charge tuition to all students, including state residents. Some Regents had been after Kerr's hide for years, believing him "the captive of leftwing professors at Berkeley," but only with Reagan's election did the balance of power shift. When some who had previously supported him spoke to Kerr about resigning so Reagan could choose his own university president, Kerr refused, stating that such a move would make his position into a political office.[3]

In December of 1966, Cal experienced a week-long strike after a sit-in at the Student Union to protest a naval recruiting table. History appeared to be repeating itself, though this time the arrests were limited to three students and six nonstudents. After weeks of speculation and rumors about Kerr's fate and the election of a conservative governor by a large majority of the California voters, Kerr had run out of political capital. During a break in the January Regents' meeting, he told Chairman

Meyer that they should act one way or the other to stop the speculation and uncertainty. Meyer asked him to absent himself; after two hours of acrimonious debate the Regents announced to the press that they had voted 14 to 8 for Kerr's immediate dismissal. On the lawn across from University Hall 2,000 students vigiled in opposition to tuition, oblivious to the drama within.[4]

Kerr's removal was not unanticipated, but it was premature. The Regents had no one else in mind for the position; it was not until September that they selected Charles J. Hitch, university vice-president for finance and former assistant secretary in the Department of Defense, as the thirteenth president of the university. While Kerr would never again have the power or influence he had had as a university president, he kept his tenured position on the faculty and remained in the Bay Area, becoming head of the Carnegie Commission on Higher Education and holding a variety of other prestigious jobs. He still lives in El Cerrito, not far from the campus where he spent most of his professional life.[5]

Clark Kerr was blindsided by history. Ascending to the presidency at the advent of UC's most dramatic expansion, Kerr expected to remain at the helm long enough to be a major architect of an even greater University of California. In a different era, that might well have happened. Although the FSM militants held up Kerr's book on *The Uses of the University* as an example of what they opposed, it was quite prescient. Kerr and the FSMers held similar values; both were concerned about the quality of undergraduate education, both thought that public service was a proper goal for educated citizens, and both wanted to remove most of the burdens and restrictions on student activity imposed during Sproul's tenure. Both resisted the incursions of the Cold War into basic American civil liberties, and both supported civil rights. Student activists had demanded the removal of racial discrimination in the Greek houses, the end of compulsory ROTC, and abolition of the speaker ban, but it was Kerr (and Brown) who engineered these policy changes through the Regents. Students made demands, but if Kerr hadn't agreed, these changes would not have happened. As with all social movements, demands often escalate faster than institutions can cope. Sherriffs' sudden removal of student political space (the safety valve, as Dean Towle aptly called it) triggered an explosion on campus that politicians and public opinion were not ready for. Kerr was toppled for trying to straddle two tectonic plates rapidly shifting in opposite directions as students demanded immediate change while the Regents, politicians, and taxpayers insisted on peace, stability, and gratitude.

Edward Strong was felled by his own intransigence, though he maintained to the end that he consulted with Kerr before every move and received his approval for everything he did. He too did not favor tight restrictions on student political activity, but his stubborn belief that nothing mattered more than "respect for duly constituted authority" blinded him to the seismic activity which brought him down. He also got a soft landing. He was appointed Mills Professor of Intellectual and Moral Philosophy and Civil Policy, a nice sinecure with no responsibilities. He retired in 1967 and died in 1990. His chief administrative assistant, Kitty Malloy, who took notes at meetings, drafted documents, kept his files, and egged him on, was simply fired and died an early death. After Strong resigned, most assumed Meyerson would become the permanent chancellor, but the Regents conducted a nationwide search and did not seriously consider keeping him, supposedly because he was "too lenient in disciplinary matters." Meyerson's appointment as acting chancellor ended on July 31st; he soon became president of the State University of New York at Buffalo and then of the University of Pennsylvania. Roger W. Heyns, the vice president for academic affairs at the University of Michigan, became Berkeley's fourth chancellor on August 13th and served for six years. He added to his staff as special assistants the most pro-FSM faculty member and a member of the campus police force.[6]

Of all the participants, Alex Sherriffs was probably the only one who personally benefited from the FSM, which is ironic in light of his singular role in creating the crisis. He kept his title of vice-chancellor throughout the spring, though Meyerson appointed sociologist Neil Smelser, author of a major work, *Theory of Collective Behavior* (1964), as his special assistant to deal with the student political groups. When Heyns chose his own vice-chancellors and staff, Sherriffs took a one-year sabbatical, keeping his job as a professor in the Psychology Department. For the next two years he spoke all over the state on the problems of modern society. This brought him to the attention of Governor Reagan's staff; late in 1967 the governor asked him to become his education advisor. As such he represented Reagan and/or advised him at meetings of the Regents. Sherriffs stayed until the end of Reagan's term as governor and then became second in command of the state university system.[7]

At least two of our prosecutors also rode on Ronald Reagan's coattails. Edwin Meese became legal advisor to Governor Reagan, and later counselor to President Reagan and then Attorney General of the United States. He resigned a few months before the end of Reagan's first term after a 14-month investigation by an independent counsel suggested that he had violated tax and ethics laws. Reincarnated as a senior fellow at the Heritage Foundation, he continues to comment on public affairs. Lowell Jensen was elected district attorney of Alameda County in 1969. Reagan brought him to Washington in 1981 as head of the Criminal Division of the Justice Department and returned him to California as a federal district judge in 1986.

Our legal defenders continued to fight the good fight, but not in as prestigious positions as our prosecutors. Malcolm Burnstein still practices law in Berkeley. Stanley Golde was appointed judge of the superior court in Alameda County by Governor Reagan in 1973 on the recommendation of Meese. He retired in 1996 and died in 1998. A few months after our trial ended, Legal Central was closed and the files moved to Kathie Frank's apartment on Shattuck Avenue. She fielded late-night phone calls from anxious defendants and early morning demands from lawyers until May of 1967, when she moved to England with her husband. She later worked for the University of Minnesota as an undergraduate advisor until she retired at the end of 2000. David Stein returned to Cal for a master's degree in city planning. He moved around, planning and consulting for a variety of government agencies, most recently in North Carolina.

Katherine Towle retired in 1965 and died in 1986. Arleigh Williams succeeded her as dean of students and in 1970 became vice-chancellor for student affairs. Although Williams held his posts during some of Cal's most tumultuous years, he always managed to keep the respect of the students. He retired in 1976 and died in 1991.

The fate of the faculty was less uncertain, since most of the ones who spoke out had tenure. While personal relations in some departments were strained and existing factions sharpened, no one lost his job. The Berkeley Division of the Academic Senate divided into political groupings, with the Committee of Two Hundred leading from the left and the Faculty Forum restraining from the right. Some professors departed, but Cal was not gutted of its fine faculty. In an era in which professors were in demand, it was easy for those who wanted out to find quieter quarters; those who stayed did so willingly, even when they felt like a beleaguered minority on campus. Seymour Martin Lipset moved to Stanford and Henry Rosovsky went to Harvard. Carl Schorske left in 1969 for Princeton. Robert Scalapino continued in the Political Science Department until he retired. Paul Seabury also stayed, though he became bitter toward students and anyone else who threatened the status quo. In 1975 I went to visit him in Barrows Hall after attending the annual meeting of the

American Political Science Association in San Francisco. My newly published dissertation had won an APSA prize and I wanted to give him a copy of the book. He opened his door on my knock, looked at me long and hard, and shut the door in my face.[8]

Just as the FSM was born from the Civil Rights Movement, it in turn produced its own progeny. In the spring, students protested at a dozen campuses from Yale to New Mexico over a wide range of issues. For the rest of the decade, student unrest spread and grew until it consumed the academic world. This changed higher education from an ivory tower removed from reality to a place where the social conflicts of the sixties were played out on the streets. Some faculty at Cal thought teaching became more "invigorating" because "students seemed to be constantly raising questions about social issues." Some took advantage of the turmoil to engage in educational experimentation. Some became interested in student protest and the problems of higher education as a topic for scholarly inquiry. And some faculty simply withdrew and tried to insulate themselves from the chaos around them.[9]

Civil rights was eclipsed by Viet Nam as the top issue on the activist agenda. CORE and Friends of SNCC focused more on raising money for work in the South than raising hell at home. Those who wanted to work locally shifted to the Student Committee for Agricultural Labor and support of the Delano farmworkers' strike. SLATE was a casualty of increased student activism. When it was the main game on campus, political students who found the more sectarian organizations unappealing, and some from those organizations, joined. As the universe of political activists expanded, so did the number of organizations through which they could be active. The Vietnam Day Committee (VDC) and SDS siphoned off a lot of students who would have joined SLATE before the FSM. This left to SLATE the task for which it had originally been founded—turning the student government into a meaningful institution, something more than a mere administrator of student activities.

SLATE went from almost capturing the student government to dissolution in a little over a year. In the spring 1965 elections, fearing that SLATE would finally get a majority on the senate, the Greek houses marched their members to the polls. Although former chairman Sandor Fuchs was defeated for ASUC president by a vote of 3,970 to 2,078, two SLATE candidates won. This left SLATE just shy of a voting majority. But SLATE lost ground in the fall, leaving it with only one-third of the senate votes. Nonetheless, it had persuaded the student body to hold a convention to revise the ASUC constitution, and it elected twenty-six of sixty delegates. Since its ally, the GCC, elected another twenty-three, the two organizations controlled the convention. During the spring 1966 semester, SLATE activists did little but work on the proposed constitution. When students rejected it in an April referendum, SLATE skidded to a halt. At its May 2nd general meeting, SLATE concluded that working through the ASUC was hopeless; it would no longer run candidates for office. Left with little to do, SLATE officially dissolved on October 10th. It had outlived its usefulness, the *Daily Cal* declared. Perhaps as a sign of its success, its final meetings were held on the campus from which it had been unceremoniously expelled only five years before.[10]

The *Supplement* continued for a few more years, subsidized by the ASUC. It came to be known as *Slate*. The ASUC provided an office and about 10 percent of the necessary funds, but the magazine operated as a collective; anybody who showed up and worked counted as a member. Lack of volunteer labor and constant criticism led to its being taken over by a small faction of radicals who insisted that *Slate* reflect their views in its pages. It sputtered out of existence in 1974. Concurrently, the ASUC obtained money for a new course evaluator from money budgeted by the legislature to improve undergraduate education. *Primer* appeared as *Slate* disappeared, but it too was constantly criticized and insufficiently staffed and eventually died.[11]

The fate of the major student activists also varied. Those who came to the 20th- and 30th-anniversary reunions of the FSM all agreed that the FSM was a pivotal experience that had shaped their lives. It encouraged me to make the study of social movements one of my scholarly fields. But the burdens and benefits were not evenly spread or in proportion to participation.

Mario Savio was perhaps the greatest casualty of all. The Free Speech Movement made him famous and it ruined his life. Mario dropped out for the spring semester, while we were on trial, intending to return in the fall. But he didn't want to be a campus celebrity. After marrying in May, he and Suzanne went to England, where he enrolled as a student at Oxford University and she birthed the first of their two sons. They returned to the Bay Area the following May.[12] I had learned a lot about charisma from watching Mario in 1964, and I learned the perils of celebrity from seeing what it did to him. When you become a public figure, you become public property. Other people, even total strangers, think they can tell you what to think, to say, and to be. No one wants to hire you because you come with so much baggage. Even your friends and colleagues want to keep you in the box created by your public persona, removing all opportunities to explore and grow. Celebrity should not be visited upon the young and can be a burden even for those who are settled in life.

Mario tried to return to Cal, but the administration found reason after reason to not readmit him, even though he had never been expelled and was academically eligible to return. Regent Canaday made a personal project of keeping Mario from becoming a UC student. For a few years, Mario's actions as a nonstudent reinforced fears about what he might do as a student. He protested against the Viet Nam War while working as a bartender and clerking in a bookstore. On November 30, 1966, he was arrested at the Student Union during a sit-in around the naval recruiting table, along with Jerry Rubin and seven others. Sentenced to 80 days after conviction by a jury, he served his time for this and the FSM in 1967 but was released early because he was such a model prisoner. He made friends with the other inmates by writing letters for them.

While there were many like him in the penumbra of people around the campus, Mario could not fade into the crowd. He rejected the role of "elder statesman." While he did give speeches occasionally and ran for the state senate on the Peace and Freedom Party ticket in 1968 (against incumbent Nick Petris, who had moved from the assembly in 1966), he mostly wanted to make his contribution to bettering the world and be left in peace. Another application for readmission, for January 1967, was denied on the grounds that he had violated a rule prohibiting nonstudents from distributing literature on campus. He was finally readmitted for the winter 1971 quarter as a physics major, telling the press that he was going to stick to his studies. But he found himself unable to concentrate and did not finish the year. He and Suzanne moved to Los Angeles, where Mario's parents still lived. Their second son was born in 1970, and they separated in late 1971. Not until 1984 did Mario graduate—from San Francisco State University with a B.S. in physics. He received an M.A. in 1989. His SFSU professors, as had his high school teachers in Queens, thought he was a brilliant scientist, but it was too late for a professional career in physics. Mario finally found a niche teaching remedial math at Sonoma State University. He married Lynne Hollander, another FSM vet, with whom he had another son, and died from heart failure on November 6, 1996, at the age of 53.

Suzanne Goldberg dropped out of the Philosophy Department and for the next few years raised her sons and occasionally taught junior college classes. She reentered Cal in 1973 in a special program to train mental health professionals. In 1978, she received her doctorate and moved to Washington, D.C., where she is a practicing psychologist and a serious artist.

Jack Weinberg found his life's work as a political activist. He shifted from civil rights to anti-war, organizing many Bay Area demonstrations in the next couple years. His last tie to student life ended when he was turned down for admission to UC summer school in 1966. "I was told," he said, "that I would not make a responsible member of the academic community." Instead, he devoted the next few years to organizing in Berkeley and Los Angeles. Although considered one of the more pragmatic movement workers, he was ever hostile to the Democratic Party; his one concession to electoral politics was to run the Peace and Freedom Party's California voter campaign. As the sixties ended and the movement splintered into ideological factions, Jack decided that the revolution he longed for lay in the working class. After moving around for several years, he became a steel worker in Gary, Indiana. When that industry declined, he moved to Chicago; in 1989, he joined the Greenpeace Chicago office as an organizer on environmental issues.[13]

Although David Goines had slavishly followed Jack throughout the FSM, they went in different directions when it was over. David quit school to become a professional printer. He stayed in Berkeley but dropped out of politics, instead becoming the printer of choice for protestors. He produced the posters and leaflets passed out at demonstrations for the next few decades.

Syd Stapleton, who had worked with Goines printing the FSM newsletter, also quit school that fall, never to return. He too became a printer for a while, but stayed active in politics, first in the VDC and then for the SWP. He left California in 1966 to work in Seattle and New York City and ran for mayor of Cleveland as the SWP candidate in 1969. Syd was the chief administrator (permits, platform, transportation, Porta-Potties, collections, marshals, etc.) for several big anti-war marches on Washington, D.C., between 1971 and 1973. He and Beth split; both remarried and had children a few years later. Beth died in the 1970s. Syd retired in the 1980s, becoming a tool-and-die designer and eventually owning his own business in Washington state.

Bettina Aptheker lost a year of academic work because of the FSM but didn't leave, even for a semester. She became a student leader, carefully walking a fine line between radicalism and respectability. She was one of five students elected to an Advisory Campus Rules Committee created by Chancellor Heyns. Believing that "because of my role on campus people have a right to know," on November 9, 1965, she publicly announced what most already knew, that she had been a member of the CP since she entered Cal in 1962. Three months later, she was charged with violating Heyns's rules at a VDC rally and put on disciplinary probation. When she graduated in 1967, she was pregnant with her first child, having married Jack Kurzweil, another CP member, a couple years earlier. The end of the FSM appeal sent Bettina almost immediately to jail to serve her 45 days. She spent the next few years organizing against the war, writing, and raising her children. During the 1970s, Bettina traded in Marxism for feminism, left the CP, and became a professor at UC Santa Cruz in women's studies, a field that did not exist when that campus opened to undergraduates in 1965.[14]

Mona Hutchin was a feminist long before the other women at Berkeley. Graduating in 1966, she went off to see the world, alternating travel with office work. In 1970, she put down roots in Wales in order to marry, raise a daughter, and become a science teacher in an inner-city London secondary school. She continued to be a practicing feminist, but not a political one.

Steve Weissman spent the spring of 1965 speaking and organizing on campuses, mostly in the South, to build participation for an SDS antiwar march in Washington in April. He came back to the Bay Area in time for the teach-in. After working in an SDS community-organizing project in West Oakland and for the Vietnam Day Committee he returned to the study of Latin American history—at Stanford. In 1968, he left academia to write for *Ramparts* magazine and become a freelance writer, film producer, and researcher. Steve returned to his native Florida in 1983, where he remarried, founded the Swamp Dog Press, and continued to write.

Jackie Goldberg was one of the most successful FSM alumni, but she too bore its burdens. Graduating in 1965, she paid her $400 fine and went to the University of Chicago to get an M.A. in education, where she was accused of fomenting a sit-in that she did not even participate in. She taught in the Los Angeles City school system for many years before being elected to the school board and then to the Los Angeles City Council in 1993. She and David Stein sometimes worked together professionally on planning problems in southern California. In 2000, she was elected to the California state assembly.

Art Goldberg left Cal without getting a single credit for his year in the School of Education. He went to Howard Law School but found it too bourgeois for his taste. Howard found him too disruptive and expelled him after two years, but with full credit for his time. Narrowly admitted into Rutgers Law School, he graduated and passed the California bar exam. By then he had served between eight and nine months in jail for his numerous arrests, largely during semester breaks and summer vacations. However, it took two and a half years of denials, hearings, reviews, and appeals before he was admitted to the California bar.

Sandor Fuchs spent thee years as a graduate student in economics before deciding to study for the bar exam, which he passed even though he had not attended law school. His half-dozen arrests and 30 days in jail also delayed his admission to the bar, but only for six months. He and Art founded the Working People's Law Center in Los Angeles, where both still live and practice law.

After graduating from Berkeley in 1967, Brian Turner went to jail, along with the other FSMers sentenced to straight time. They served their time in Santa Rita, where their days were spent working in the fields. Brian was particularly appalled at how the prisoners segregated themselves racially into gangs, replicating all the worst aspects of the larger society he was trying to change. He organized an integrated touch football game after dinner each day which brought some prisoners together, at least for an hour. In the fall he went to Kings College at Cambridge University in England to study social anthropology on a UC fellowship and had an opportunity to debate Kerr on "liberalism" when he visited the campus. In 1978, he got a Ph.D. in social anthropology from Columbia University. Eventually he followed his father and grandfather into the trade union movement. He spent most of the next few decades working in various departments of the AFL-CIO's Industrial Union Department or doing research and consulting on employment and union issues.

Brad Cleaveland, the man whose rant in the *SLATE Supplement* put Alex Sherriffs on red alert, became a good friend and admirer of Clark Kerr. Brad went into construction, probably one of the most useful things he could do with his M.A. in political science (though he completed coursework toward his Ph.D.). While working on a project in Saudi Arabia in 1976, he went to hear Kerr lecture at a university seventy miles away. Recognizing him, Kerr invited him to his lodging after his speech. He wanted to know why Brad had attacked him back in 1964. They soon discovered their common interest in improving undergraduate education and talked for two and a half hours. When he returned to the Bay Area, Brad called on Kerr and they've been friends ever since.

The university as an institution went through many changes; some would have happened without the FSM, but some would not. There was a conspicuous ripple effect. The student protests and subsequent reactions to them focused attention on the problems of university governance. Assembly Concurrent Resolution 156, passed by the legislature in June of 1965, created the Joint Committee on Higher Education. In 1971 it morphed into the Joint Committee on the Master Plan in Higher Education. One recommendation was to reconstitute the Board of Regents. The California constitution was amended in 1974 to create a board of twenty-six members. The governor appoints eighteen Regents to 12-year terms. Seven more are ex officio members—the governor, lieutenant governor, speaker of the assembly, superintendent of public instruction, president and vice president of the alumni association of UC, and the UC president. These can appoint a student to be Regent for one year. In addition, two faculty members—the chair and vice chair of the Academic Council—sit on the board as nonvoting members.[15]

The right of students to engage in political advocacy on campus became an accepted fact of life. In the spring of 1965, even as the Regents discussed what their overall policy should be, Dean Towle issued new rules and a map showing where tables could be put up near Sproul steps, Sather Gate, and Ludwig's Fountain, as well as at Bancroft and Telegraph. They are still there. However, the administration made some concessions it deeply regretted. The biggest of these was sound amplification in Sproul Plaza. The one thing the administration (and the staff in Sproul Hall) wanted most was to move the loudspeakers to some other place. But this was the one gain which students wanted most to keep; forty years later, the microphones are still at Sproul Plaza. In 1997, slightly over a year after Mario died, the steps from which so many speeches were made were officially renamed the Mario Savio steps.[16]

The FSM became ensconced in campus history. Two reunions, in 1984 and 1994, were held on campus under university auspices. In 1998, alumnus Stephen M. Silberstein donated 3.5 million dollars to the university to honor Mario Savio. Most of this was used to build a cafe next to a new undergraduate library with photographic exhibits of the FSM, and most of the rest supports a library archive on the FSM. In Sproul Hall, another photographic exhibit of great moments in university history displays an FSM photo. There are no monuments to Edward Strong, Alex Sherriffs, or even Governor Brown, but a nearby campus is named for Clark Kerr. A few former students run tours of campus hot spots of the sixties.

The ripple spread throughout the country and even the world. Just as the 1963 civil rights demonstrations in Birmingham, Alabama, inspired civil rights supporters to become active in the North, the FSM inspired students everywhere. It portended more than an era of heightened political activity by students. In 1984, Franklin Murphy, who was UCLA chancellor from 1960 to 1968, told a reporter that "the FSM and its resolution signaled the end of a major epoch in American higher education defined by the phrase *in loco parentis*. . . . Universities stopped serving as the surrogate parents of college students in terms of behavior. When that happened all kinds of things happened in terms of mores and lifestyles."[17]

The university continues to be buffeted by California politics, despite Article IX, § 9 of the state constitution. Ronald Reagan, governor from 1967 through 1974, was no friend of the university or its students. While the idea of tuition was dropped for a while, student fees were increased, as was out-of-state tuition. An "educational fee" for all students was added for the 1969–1970 academic year. Small at first, this tuition substitute took a great leap upward in the 1990s. Tuition might have come anyway, but its roots are in the legislative reaction to students who bit the hand that fed them in the 1960s.

The reapportionment of the state senate ordered by the California courts in 1964 happened in time for the 1966 elections. It brought into the senate many people who had represented urban areas in the assembly, significantly altering the balance of power. When Senator James Mills (D-San Diego) became president pro tempore of the senate in 1971, he discovered himself and "more than a score" of legislators listed on the 5" × 8" cards in the 20,000-name index Richard Combs had compiled over thirty years. He promptly abolished the Subcommittee on Un-American Activities, sealed its 500 cubic feet of material, and consigned it to permanent storage in the state archives. Both Burns and Combs retired from the legislature; their fifteenth and final report was released in 1969.[18]

The Sproul Hall sit-ins generated many studies asking who did what, when, and why. Because it occurred on a campus well endowed with social scientists, the FSM may be the most intensively studied single protest of our time. Max Heirich's dissertation and book is by far the most thorough and the best, but there were other analyses which asked different questions.

In 1969, Dean of Students Arleigh Williams profiled the 735 students who had been arrested on December 3rd after his staff looked up information from student files. He found out that 688 were registered in the fall of 1964. Women were 43 percent of the 547 undergraduates and 23 percent of the 141 grad students—roughly equal to their proportions in the student body. The median age was 21; both freshmen and grad students were underrepresented. While they had sixty different majors, one-third were in the social sciences and the rest were more likely to be in the humanities than in the hard sciences or professional schools. Majors in history, political science, and psychology were significantly over-represented. Student grade point averages were similar to those of the student body as a whole, despite the disruption to studies caused by the arrests. But the curve was a little lower for graduates and a little flatter for undergraduates; the arrestees did both better and worse than average. Only 10 percent lived in university-approved housing, compared to 40 percent for the student body. This was a significant distinction; we were GDIs (God-Damned Independents). So was the fact that 30 percent came from southern California and 10 percent from New York, compared to 23 and 3.5 percent respectively of the student body. The rest of the East Coast provided twice the number of arrestees (6.7 percent) as students (3.4 percent). Since out-of-state students were even more numerous on the FSM Steering Committee, the obvious conclusion is that outside influence was important in the FSM, but it came from New York, not Moscow.[19]

In the spring of 1965, Kathleen Gales, a visiting professor of sociology from London, analyzed student attitudes toward the FSM from data collected by her students. Of 528 Berkeley students chosen at random, 439 were successfully interviewed in April for half an hour. Since Somers's survey the previous November, agreement with FSM goals had increased from 63 to 83 percent and agreement with tactics had gone from 34 to 49 percent. This illuminated the vast gulf between student and public opinion (two-thirds of the public disapproved). Of those interviewed, 9 percent had been in Sproul Hall in December, though most left before the arrests, and 11 percent had sat around the car in October. The FSM had a solid base of support among the student body. But which students? Approval of the FSM "was highest among those with high grade-point averages, majoring in the social sciences or humanities, living in apartments, and either of no religion or the Jewish faith." Despite the fact that 78 percent thought "the University sometimes seems to operate as a factory," 92 percent said it "is a good place to go to school." There was only a mild relationship between approval of the FSM and dissatisfaction with the university. FSM rhetoric to the contrary, alienation did not seem to be a driving force. But support for civil liberties was. The strongest support for the FSM came from students with libertarian attitudes, who did not support HUAC and thought civil disobedience was sometimes justified. Party preference was also important. A little over half of the sample were Democrats and 20 percent were Republicans; 73 percent of the former compared to 37 percent of the latter approved of the FSM. Independents and socialists, though small in numbers, approved of the FSM at an even higher rate. In short, the Berkeley students were liberal and libertarian; the Free Speech Movement reflected their views and its participants acted out their beliefs.[20]

This social base of liberal and libertarian students was present long before the FSM, indeed well before the 1960 anti-HUAC demonstrations. A study done in December of 1957 revealed that Berkeley students were far more sympathetic to civil rights and civil liberties than the average American and became more so during their years at Berkeley. The patterns were the same in 1957 as they were in 1965. The largest number of opponents to HUAC and supporters of the Bill of Rights were in the social sciences, especially among the better students. Support for civil liberties among those majoring in the sciences, engineering, and business administration trailed that of humanities majors. Protestants were more libertarian than Catholics but less so than Jews (or those who claimed no religion). Democrats were more supportive of civil liberties than Republicans but less so than independents. The gap between apartment-dwellers and Greeks was also large, with those living in dorms or co-ops in between. In short, even before Berkeley became known as Red Square West and the HUAC film *Operation Abolition* brought radicals to where the action was, the campus was a cauldron of civil libertarians.[21]

This data does not answer the question that most consumed the administration: Could anything have been done to avoid the turmoil of the fall of 1964? Was the Free Speech Movement inevitable? Having thought about this while writing this book, I will pose an answer, but it is more from a participant's perspective than that of a social scientist. There was a period of about one week after we got the September 14th letter during which all we wanted was to return to our usual activities—setting up tables and selling buttons and passing out literature at Bancroft and Telegraph. If President Kerr had overruled the campus administration and reversed our eviction when he returned from his summer abroad, he may have faced some repercussions from administrators, but not from us.[22]

That window of opportunity quickly closed; we adopted the view of the administration that Bancroft and Telegraph was part of the campus and should be subject to the same rules. But here we differed: we wanted to extend the freedom of the public street to the rest of the campus, and the administration wanted to apply the campus rules to Bancroft and Telegraph. After that week was up, confrontation would have continued in one form or another for a long time. However, it could have been more like low-level guerilla warfare rather than sit-ins and strikes. The political class was still not very large; mass student sentiment was mobilized only when the administration cited some students for things many had done or had thought it was okay to do. Amnesty would have bought the administration a lot of peace, if not the status quo ante. The administration's determination to punish students for defying authority guaranteed a major face-off at some point.

Neither Strong's nor Sherriffs' oral histories explain why it was so important to pursue this path despite growing evidence that it was a road to disaster. They seem to have carried a lot of historical baggage. Some of this came from their own observations of student movements in the 1930s; some came from their experience with SLATE. In the previous seven years, SLATE had sallied forth several times to do battle over the rules on political action and advocacy, usually to retreat bloodied but unbowed. The administration was used to winning. It had never faced mass mobilization and did not recognize the sea change brought about by the Civil Rights Movement, which was the morally compelling issue of the day.

Administration views of student actions were shaped by past events. The student interpretation of administration actions was shaped by current events. Students viewed everything through the lens of civil rights, which provided their motivation and strategy. They interpreted adverse actions by the administration as opposition to civil rights, and this in turn reinforced their determination to resist. The administration had little understanding of this moral compulsion to right racial wrongs because they were just as opposed to racial discrimination, in California and in the South, as the students were. Even our bête noire, Bill Knowland, supported civil rights legislation.[23] Thus, they could not comprehend why the students saw them as opponents of civil rights. The experience which shaped their perceptions was that of the Cold War, which saw Communist influence everywhere. Even though the administration did not believe that Communists were behind our protests, they believed that others did. HUAC and its California cousin had been hunting for reds on campus for over two decades. Public outrage could easily be triggered by raising the red flag. The Burns Committee had attacked the university in its biannual reports and stood ready to do so again. It wasn't the *Oakland Tribune* the administration was worried about; it was worried about glaring headlines in newspapers all over the state of California. These would generate letters from the public and parents, which would cause problems with the legislature when it debated the university budget. The future would find this fear to be well founded.

The future was coming, with or without the FSM. If the campus hadn't erupted in 1964–1965, it would have done so soon, as the Viet Nam War supplanted the Civil Rights Movement as the source of student protest. What Arleigh Williams came to call the six-year war might have been only a five-year war. Berkeley was hardly unique; the FSM was a harbinger. The generation that came of age in the sixties was far too idealistic to put up with blatant injustice or silly rules, even if we did sometimes confuse the two. We were our parents' children, and our parents had won World War II. Many had fought in it; all sacrificed to serve their country and the ideals it represented. They taught us that personal sacrifice for the larger social good was our calling. President Kennedy's call to "ask what you can do for your country" resonated with our souls.

We found much to do and fully expected to do it all.

World War II only interrupted the anti-Communism crusades that had begun after World War I and the Russian Revolution. These were the domestic front of the Cold War, on which a battle waged until dissidence of any type became suspect. At the same time, Cold War rhetoric extolled American ideals of freedom, justice, and equality in order to contrast them with the Communist ogre. We grew up hearing that America was the greatest country on earth and that America was great because America was good. This rhetoric shaped our perceptions and our values like a sculptor molds clay. When the Civil Rights Movement was greeted with violence in the South and resistance in the North it revealed a very different reality. And when we saw the war in Viet Nam on the nightly news, we were the Nazis, committing atrocious acts to conquer another country. It didn't take Communist influence or outside agitators for us to see that these things were wrong. We were our parents' children.

There is always a political class, carriers of the political gene which compels one to public action if not always to public service. But it is only occasionally in American history that an entire generation is consumed by the need to correct social injustice, let alone in ways that significantly disrupt the political system. In the early sixties, Berkeley saw political concerns expand beyond the political class as the numbers of people soared who thought their personal participation could make a major difference. They were prodded by the twin prongs of Cold War and cold truth. It was in the growing gap between rhetoric and reality that the radicalism of the sixties was born.

By the end of the sixties, radicalism had become an end in itself and had ceased to be self-critical; idealism was corrupted into nihilism and the need for action into an urge for destruction. By the end of the seventies, cynicism was the residue. But by then, the sixties generation had transformed American politics and American culture. While the Cold War was not yet over, dissidents were commanding attention and forcing changes. The political space that had contracted so severely in the 1940s and 1950s was expanding once again. While not all the changes were for the best and not all were permanent, one legacy will always remain: the 1960s showed that ordinary people, working together, can make a difference.

Notes

1. The Train to Berkeley

1. The "Master Plan for Higher Education in California," as codified in the Donahoe Act of 1960, organized one of the world's largest systems of public higher education into three tiers. The University of California grew from five undergraduate campuses in 1961 to eight in 1965, plus separate medical and law schools in San Francisco. The middle tier of state colleges, open to the top third of California high school graduates, numbered eighteen in 1961 and nineteen in 1965 (and twenty-one in 1990). In 1972 some of the colleges became universities, and in 1982 the system was renamed The California State University. The third tier of 73 public junior (community) colleges was open to any high school graduate. Thus, any Californian with a high school diploma could get a publicly financed higher education. Those who did well in junior college could transfer to a four-year school for their bachelor's degree.

2. Fees could be charged only for services not related to teaching; Coons 1968, 129. Student fees were 4 percent of university income in 1960; 28 percent came from the state legislature and over half from the federal government; Otten 1970, 128. Free higher education for California residents was mandated by the university's 1868 charter; Douglass 1999, 395.

3. This was a liberalization of Stanford's quota on women. In 1899, alarmed by the number of girls in the student body, founder Jane Lathrop Stanford specified that no more than 500 women could ever attend Leland Stanford Junior University at one time. This quota was enlarged in 1933, but it took a 1972 act of Congress and a 1973 court order to remove it; Jensen and Lothrop 1987, 51.

2. Cal

1. *Education at Berkeley* describes the varieties of students as of fall 1965; 1966, 13, 16–17, and 218–221.

2. Stadtman 1970, 394–398. Harry R. Wellman's 1976 oral history describes the various ways in which Kerr decentralized administration (126–137) and the 1952 reorganization which created the chancellorship (75). Taylor (2000) devotes chapter 5 of *Speaking Freely* to "Clark Kerr's University"; Rowland 1978, 46. Otten 1970, 160, describes the different style Kerr brought to the office of president, supported by cites to Kerr's 1963 book. He observed that the university had been moving "away from personalized paternalism toward an impersonal, rational, bureaucratic pattern of control" for some time (131). Sproul was not an academic; he moved into the presidency after serving as the university's comptroller. Kerr was a faculty member.

3. Politics and the University

1. Stadtman 1970, chapter 6 on the 1870s. Article IX, § 9 of the California constitution of 1879 was intended to protect the university from becoming a creature of the legislature.

2. Heirich 1971, 68. The ex officio Regents were the governor, lieutenant governor, speaker of the assembly, state superintendent of public instruction, president of the state board of agriculture, president of the mechanics institute, president of the alumni association, and the president of the university. In the early 1960s, three of the appointed Regents were women, all wives of important men. Dorothy Chandler and Catherine Hearst married into newspaper dynasties. Elinor Heller was a Democratic Party activist appointed to replace her husband as Regent when he died in 1961.

3. Heirich and Kaplan 1965, 12–18; Cohen 1993, xiv–xvi, 93–94, 100–101, first quote on 124; Stadtman 1970, 293–297, second quote on 297; "Police Chief Was Music Major, Now Calls Legal Tune for Students," *Daily Californian,* January 8, 1952.

4. Otten 1970, 129, 139–144, quote on 139; Hugh M. Burns oral history, 1981, 48. Rowland 1978, chapter 1, describes how the 1940 Yorty Committee evolved into the Tenney Committee. Both men were left-wing Democrats who became anti-communists after the CP organized against them. Tenney, a professional piano player and officer in the musicians' union, was elected to the assembly in 1936. After defeat for reelection as union president in 1939 he began his investigative career, taking his committee with him when elected to the state senate, representing Los Angeles County, in 1942. He also switched parties, running for vice president on the Christian Nationalist ticket in 1952 while serving in the senate as a Republican. The Los Angeles County Republican Central Committee refused to endorse him when he ran for reelection in 1954; he was defeated in the primary by Mildred Younger; Mildred Younger oral history, 1983. Healey and Isserman 1990, 70; Gardner 1967, 9. Barrett 1951, 4–6, 11–14, 17. "Yorty allegedly turned against the Communist party when they refused to support him for mayor in the 1938 recall election in Los Angeles"; Rowland 1978, 5. He was eventually elected mayor in 1961 and served until defeated in 1973. After leaving office he became a Republican and supported Ronald Reagan when he ran for governor in 1976.

5. Kingman oral history, 1973, IV.

6. Barrett 1951, 306–310. Oath controversy in Stewart 1950; Gardner 1967; Stadtman 1970, 321–339, quote on 322; Strong oral history, 1992, section VII; and Taylor 1998, 15–35. James H. Corley was university comptroller from 1939 to 1948 and vice president for business affairs from 1948 to 1958; Corley oral history, 1969, xix; Corley obituaries in the *San Francisco Chronicle,* December 27, 1974; *Berkeley Gazette,* December 26, 1974; and *California Monthly,* January/February 1975. As the person responsible for getting the university budget through the legislature, he thought an oath would keep Tenney happy and prevent passage of a more onerous constitutional amendment. Neither Tenney nor his bills had much support in the legislature, but on October 3, 1950, the Levering Act, requiring an oath from all public employees, was signed. *Tolman v. Underhill,* 39 Cal.2d 708, 249 P.2d 280 (1952) held that this preempted the field and the Regents did not have the authority to demand more. When he met faculty resistance, Sproul changed course, but by then Regent John Francis Neylan had made the oath a personal priority. On the faculty tradition of self-government, see *The University of California Centennial* 1968: "In 1919 and

1920 the Berkeley campus lived through the 'Great Faculty Revolt,' a rejection of the principle of presidential fiat that won for the Academic Senate the right to set its own rules, select its own members, and appoint its own committees." There was an earlier loyalty-oath crisis in 1918; see Sevilla 1967, 471. The Regents declared in 1940 that "membership in the Communist Party is not compatible with membership in the faculty of a state university"; minutes of meeting of October 11, 1940. "Twenty percent" in Gardner 1967, 291n6. "Salary pool" in Stampp oral history, 1998, 146. For the views of a conservative faculty member who eventually signed, see October 1949 letter to Sproul explaining initial refusal; in Constance oral history, 1987, 103–105. "Loyalty Oath or No Job, Cal Professors Are Told," *San Francisco Chronicle,* February 25, 1950, 1. The faculty who did not sign were reinstated but were denied back pay until they sued; "Reinstated Professors Plan Suit for Back Pay," *Los Angeles Times,* January 31, 1954, 25:1.

7. Among the accused was Elinor Heller, Democratic National Committeewoman and future Regent (1961–1976). All thirteen of Tenney's bills were defeated; Carey McWilliams, "Mr. Tenney's Horrible Awakening," *The Nation,* July 23, 1949, 81. Born in Arizona and raised in Fresno, Burns became interested in politics during the Depression. He formed a YD club and won an open seat to the assembly in 1936. Although a small businessman with interests in a funeral home, an insurance company, and savings and loans, he enjoyed strong union support, even when he joined Yorty and Tenney in opposing Governor Olson in 1940. Rowland 1978, 20–21 (quote on 31; Burns oral history, 1981, on Burns 2–3, 6; on Corley 57). Burns was elected to the Senate in 1942.

4. SLATE

1. Computed from figures in *Education at Berkeley* 1966, 26, 218. Williams's oral history says the Greeks housed 14 percent of undergraduates; 1990, Appendix 7.
2. Kerr 1956.
3. Cloke 1994, 22–23; Myerson 1970, 38; Horowitz 1962, 19. Interview with Mike Miller, 1984, in Cohen 1994, 9. The idea for a student political party came from a course Thygeson took from Professor Jensen at San Diego State College. Most of those who would join TASC met in William Kornhauser's course on social movements. The state's Organic Act of 1868 required all male students to take military training. The federal Morrill Land Grant Act of 1862 required colleges receiving federal lands to offer military training but did not make it compulsory. Student objections to compulsory ROTC erupted regularly until 1962, when the Regents made it voluntary; Heirich and Kaplan in Lipset and Wolin 1965, 13–23; Cloke 1994, 19–22; Cohen 1993, 203–204. For the history of ROTC struggle, see "Regents End Rule On Required ROTC," *Daily Cal,* June 29, 1962, 1.
4. Quote from *SLATE,* an eight-page mimeographed pamphlet, n.d. (1958). SLATE's early history is in its pamphlets, the *Cal Reporter* (copies in Bancroft Library); Cloke's 1980 UCLA dissertation; and 1984 interviews with Mike Miller and Brad Cleaveland in Cohen 1994. SLATE's history is summarized in Stadtman 1961, 10, 54; Stadtman reports that 2,962 students voted in the spring 1957 elections and 4,688 voted in the fall. Founding convention described in the *Daily Cal,* February 10, 1958, 1; April 11, 1958, 1.
5. Sevilla 1967, 414–420; Cloke 1994, 32; quotes in Seaborg 1994, 161–162.
6. Heirich 1971, 71–74; Room 1984. Membership estimates from Room 1984; Cloke 1994, 78, 93n1, 94n11; and from SLATE newsletters for 1963–1965. The two

female SLATE chairmen were Cindy Lembcke, spring 1959, and Susan Kaiser (soon to be Currier), fall 1962. These were the only women to head SLATE in its nine-year existence.

7. Efforts to modify Regulation 17 began in 1956 by Hank DiSuvero, Peter Franck, and Pat Denton, all of whom would later join TASC. These were boosted by an Academic Senate resolution in 1957. The new Regulation 17 took effect on April 1; Otten 1970, 148–149; first quote from *about SLATE,* 15-page pamphlet, 1962, 7; Cloke 1994, 32; Stone's quote on 33. For the rally and the controversy surrounding it, *Daily Cal,* March 10–13, 1959.

8. Seaborg (1994, 163–166) has a slightly different version of this conflict (ACLU quote on 165); *Daily Cal* editorial of April 10, 1959, quoted on 166.

9. Heirich 1971, 76–77; Cloke 1994, 34–37; Myerson 1970, 41. Kerr reported with satisfaction at the Regents' meeting of May 19, 1960, that SLATE had "failed to elect a single member of its group in the recent student body elections."

10. Seaborg 1994, 153, 167, quote on 534, sample songs on 536–538. One song particularly poked fun at Alex Sherriffs. Sternberg was one of the graduate reps who was no longer permitted to participate in the ASUC.

11. "Kerr Gives Directives for All UC Campuses," *Daily Cal,* October 23, 1959, 1. Stadtman 1970, 436; Seaborg 1994, 423–425, 441–444; Letter to Chancellor Seaborg, July 28, 1960, in Towle oral history, 1970, Appendix. Alex Sherriffs was on this committee.

12. Unger 1975, 43. Description of the 1960 conference by Bob Gill, quoted in Goines 1993, 72.

13. Morgan 1991, 93; Sale 1973, 28–29. Sevilla identifies the campus parties in 1967, 417; *about SLATE* records half a dozen, 11. Cloke 1994, 32–33, lists ten student political parties, including ones at Michigan, Oklahoma, Illinois, and Columbia. Myerson says many of these came "after a dozen visits by some of us to other campuses" in 1970, 43. Mimi Sternberg organized PLATFORM after visiting Berkeley; interview of May 13, 2000. VOICE was modeled on SLATE but became an SDS chapter; Hayden 1988, 33, 43.

14. Report in *SLATE newsletter,* May 5, 1962, 6–7. SLATE founder Carey McWilliams, Jr., was then a professor at Oberlin.

5. Exploring the Political Bazaar

1. Not until 1969 was evidence of nuclear fallout's lethality made public, and only after the Atomic Energy Commission was abolished in 1974 did its role in suppressing this and more damning evidence become known; Miller 1986, 369–389. From 1945 through 1992, the United States conducted 1,030 nuclear tests (215 atmospheric, 815 underground) both in the States and the South Pacific. The Soviet Union held 715 tests (219 atmospheric, 436 underground). Great Britain, France, and China conducted 45, 210, and 45 tests respectively.

2. Room 1962, 6. Towle memo of October 27, 1961, and SLATE press release in personal files of Ken Cloke, Southern California Library for Social Studies and Research. "Slate Awaits Ruling for 24 Hour Vigil," *Daily Cal,* October 27, 1961, 1; Towle quotes in "Slate Withdraws; Vigil Still Planned," *Daily Cal,* October 30, 1961, 1. Towle became acting dean in July of 1961 and the regular dean in January of 1962. She had been dean of women for eight years and was president of the National Association of Women Deans and Counselors in 1957–1959.

3. In the summer of 1963, the United States, the USSR, and Great Britain ne-

gotiated a treaty to ban tests in the atmosphere, under water, and in outer space. The Limited Test Ban Treaty was signed on August 5, 1963, and ratified by the Senate on October 7, 1963. Miller 1986, 336–340. All U.S. tests were put on hold after September 23, 1992. On September 24, 1996, all five nuclear powers signed a comprehensive test ban treaty adopted by the UN General Assembly. The Senate did not ratify this treaty.

4. Isserman 1987, membership figures and history on 185, SPU described on 194–197.

5. Isserman 1987, 185; and Berkeley YSA papers in author's files.

6. Kayo Hallinan quote from Civil Rights Documentation Project interview, July 24, 1969, 32. Hallinan was also a founder of SLATE, which had a core of red diaper babies among its early members.

7. Seaborg 1994, 172–173.

8. Ibid., 174–179. Kerr told an interviewer in 1967 that "two powerful Regents" blocked the transfer, but he didn't name them; Hall 1967, 31.

6. The Young Democrats

1. Quote from Halberstam 1993, 236. See Snyder oral history (1977, 79–80, 83) for a first-person account of Stevenson's magnetism.

2. Carney 1958 and Wilson 1966 analyzed the Democratic Party reform movement. CDC was less welcome in southern California because there was more political organization there; official party leaders and organized labor viewed the new clubs as competitors for influence; Wilson 1966, 122–123, 273–274.

3. In 1952, an initiative proposal to abolish cross-filing was narrowly defeated by the voters, in part because the legislature had put a competing proposal on the ballot to require that party affiliation appear on the primary ballot. This was approved. Once the voters knew who were the Republicans running in the Democratic Party primary, the number of Democrats elected increased significantly. By 1959, there were enough Democrats in the state legislature to abolish cross-filing. Carney 1958, 5–6. Wilson 1966, 96, 103. Registration figures from Lee 1963, 28–29. Hyink, Brown, and Thacker 1975, 70, 97–98; quote from Wilson 1966, 298.

4. Quote from Wilson 1966, 110; see also 296, 301, 147, 186. Knowland got 40 percent of the vote, and Knight lost to Claire Engle with 43 percent. Knowland had been appointed by Governor Warren to replace Senator Hiram Johnson when he died in 1945. Knight was Warren's lieutenant governor and rival.

5. Democrats Cranston and Unruh were political rivals. As a founder and president of CDC, Alan Cranston was well known throughout the state prior to his election as state controller in 1958. Unruh was first elected to the assembly in 1954 from a Los Angeles district and became speaker in 1961. He sought to undermine CDC by passing a bill prohibiting pre-primary endorsements. Although it passed the legislature, Cranston persuaded Governor Brown to veto it. Fowle 1980, 147, 186; and Hyink, Brown, and Thacker 1975, 70, 97–98.

6. These positions are from the CFYD 1962 "Platform," the 1963 "Platform and Resolutions," both mimeographed, and the 1964 "Platform." Quotes are from the 1963 and 1964 platforms. Picketing and abortion mentioned in *California Young Democrat* newsletter 15, no. 1, March 1963. East Bay activities mentioned in *16th Assembly District Democratic News* 1, no. 1 (June 1963). See also the Associated Press story on the 1963 meeting of YDs from thirteen western states, which passed resolutions advocating diplomatic relations with Cuba, troop withdrawal from south

Viet Nam, compulsory arbitration of labor disputes, and abolition of HUAC, the McCarran Internal Security Act, and the death penalty; "Democrats Urge Ties with Cuba," *The Evening Star* (Washington, D.C.), August 19, 1963.

7. "Liberals Lead Young Demos Again," *San Francisco Chronicle*, May 7, 1963, 1; "Young State Demos Pick a Liberal," *San Francisco Examiner*, May 7, 1963, 1; "YD's Elect President," *Daily Cal*, May 7, 1963, 9.

8. The sole woman legislator was Pauline L. Davis, of Portola. More women had served in the assembly in prior years, but the first woman wasn't elected to the state senate until 1977; Wyman oral history, 1979, esp. 52, 82. The first woman on the Los Angeles City Council was journalist Estelle Lawton Lindsey, elected in 1915; *New York Times*, June 3, 1915, 20:2. The "very bitter election campaign" is discussed in Snyder oral history, 1977, 102–112. Snyder's view is supported by letters written by former Democratic National Committee Women's Division head India Edwards to Katie Louchheim, director of the Office of Women's Activities, July 21, 1953, and August 7, 1954; "India Edwards" file in Box 3 of the Katie Louchheim Papers, Library of Congress.

7. Student

1. In 1964, only 10 percent of the single student population lived at home. University of California Housing Services, "Survey of Residence" reports issued yearly; cited in Heirich 1971, 448n19. "Seventy percent" figure from September 1965 survey conducted by the Select Committee on Education of the Berkeley Division of the Academic Senate, *Education at Berkeley* 1966, 13.

2. Quotes from Sherriffs oral history, 1980, 16. He added, "The males did some very dangerous and ugly things." Sherriffs implies but does not say that the administration wanted integration in the belief that women would civilize the men.

3. Cloud 1952, 76–77. California Constitution of 1879, Article IX, § 9; reprinted in Cloud 1952, 261. Douglass 1999, 395; Stadtman 1970, 83. On early UC women, see Clifford 1995, 21. Quote and 1958 survey in Seaborg 1994, 382. California held a referendum on woman suffrage in 1896. While it lost, the campaign no doubt enlightened many and may explain the timing of these events.

4. Between 1961/1962 and 1964/1965, women increased from 40 to 42 percent of undergraduates and from 25 to 27 percent of grad students; Stadtman 1967, 224. For statistics on gender at UC, Douglass 1997, 15, charts "Enrollment by Gender: 1869–1995." There is no indication that UC thought there was a "sex balance problem," as did the trustees of the state colleges, where girls predominated. In 1964–1965, the trustees altered the admissions standards in order to reduce those eligible from the top 40 percent to the top third of high school graduates, as mandated by the California Master Plan of Education. They wanted to divert three to four thousand new students to junior colleges each year, "most of them girls." The trustees debated but rejected using different admissions standards for boys and girls in favor of changing the standards for both. Under the old standards, only grades in academic courses counted because these were the best predictor of success in college. Since girls got better high school grades than boys and fewer went to the more prestigious university, girls outnumbered boys in the state colleges. In order "to make it relatively easier for boys than girls to get into a State College" the trustees increased the courses whose grades counted to all but physical education and military training and added test scores on one of two standardized academic tests to the admissions requirements. Boys did better than girls on these tests, especially the sections on mathematical aptitude.

"Sex as Factor in College Admissions," November 5, 1964, 7:5; "Colleges Shun Hot Potato," November 6, 1964, 2:5; "State Faculty Plan on Admissions," December 2, 1964, 1:4, 22:4; "Tough College Admission Plan," December 4, 1964, 30:1–4; "College Trustees Adopt New Admission Plan," December 5, 1964, 2:6; all in *San Francisco Chronicle*.

5. Seaborg (1994, 388–391) quotes an article on UC written by Joan Didion in the January 1960 issue of *Mademoiselle*, which quotes an undergraduate saying, "A lot of us don't admit it, but what we came here for was to meet a husband." True or false, it reflects the attitude about coeds. Didion was honored as Alumna of the Year in 1980. The report of the Select Committee on Education also observed the "different orientations of men and women" but added that "we must question a social and educational system that does not encourage more women to develop profitably their intellectual potential"; *Education at Berkeley* 1966, 18.

6. UC required a year of composition and three semesters of a foreign language to graduate. Entering students were tested on basic writing skills and those who failed had to take a noncredit remedial course, known as Subject A. Those who passed took a year of English, speech, or comparative literature. I didn't have to take Subject A. With three years of high school Spanish, I placed into second-semester college Spanish, so I had to take one more year.

7. Years later I read my high school term papers and decided that I had some natural talent as a writer despite my memories of frustration and failure. However, my talent was for clear and concise expression, not the ruffles and flourishes which the high school teachers seemed to want. I couldn't write essays; I could write analysis.

8. Seaborg 1994, 385, reports a 1960 survey showing that 4.7 percent of the faculty were women; in 1970, 5 percent of the faculty were women.

8. Protest

1. For the Chessman sit-in, see Horowitz 1962, 36–41; and Rossman 1971, 33–45. For the southern sit-ins, see Carson 1981, 10–11; and Lewis 1964, 85–87.

2. Quote from Roosevelt's extended remarks in *Congressional Record*, April 25, 1960, 86th Cong., 106, pt. 7: 8653. Excerpts were reprinted widely and distributed as fliers as opposition to HUAC's arrival mounted. See Horowitz 1962, 65.

3. "Subpoenaed Student Tells 'Why,'" May 4, 1960; editorial on "The Committee," May 5, 1960; both in *Daily Cal*. Kenneth Kitch told the *Daily Cal* that "the idea . . . originated with three people—Aryay Lenske, Gene Savin, and Richard Chesney, all past presidents of the Student Civil Liberties Union, none of whom are Communists"; March 22, 1961, 3. Michael Myerson, Marvin Sternberg, and Herb Mills of SLATE were also key organizers. "City Hall in Angry Protest of Red Probe" and "1000 at Union Square for Protest," *San Francisco Chronicle*, May 13, 1960, 1:5, 5:1. Burnstein 1960; Werthman 1960. See Rossman's eyewitness description (1971, 47–71). Horowitz relies on newspaper coverage and a transcript of a KPFA report (1962, 67–81, quote on 69).

4. Horowitz 1962, 67–81, 130–143; Heirich 1971, 82–83; Myerson 1970, 69–70; Seaborg 1994, 449–474. Special front page: "100 COPS BATTLE MOB AT CITY HALL," May 14, 1960, with full-page photo of city hall steps, followed by regular front page: "Police, Crowd Battle Outside Red Hearing: 5000 Gather at City Hall for Red Hearing Protest," May 15, 1960, 1; all in *San Francisco Chronicle*. HUAC was finally abolished on January 3, 1975, after fourteen years of lobbying by people whose lives had been harmed by its investigations.

5. U.S. House, Report No. 2228, 1960 (Washington Video Productions mentioned, 6); and Supplement to Report No. 2228, 1961. Horowitz 1962, 81–92; Seaborg 1994, 473–488, Kragen quote on 477; Jacobs 1960, 41. Students came from many Bay Area schools, though Berkeley provided leadership. The film is described by Barlow and Shapiro (1971, 39). "Overflow Crowds View HUAC Movie," *Daily Cal,* October 1, 1960, 1. Searle (1971, 190–191) writes that in 1960 he was prevented by the administration from participating in a campus showing of the film by a law-school club on the grounds that it was "too controversial." The event was moved to a frat house. He doesn't give the date. International House was not a university building.

6. Quote from *San Francisco News-Call Bulletin,* January 26, 1961. See Herb Caen's column in the *San Francisco Chronicle,* November 20, 1960, excerpted in Horowitz 1962, 81–82; California Legislature 1961, 77; U.S. House 1961, 1. Second quote from Goines 1993, 73n; Goines names Lee Felsenstein and Frank Bardacke as recruits. Others were interviewed in Mark Kitchell's film *Berkeley in the Sixties.* Charles Leinenweber of Indiana and Art Goldberg of Los Angeles, activists in 1963–1965, also came to Berkeley because of the film; see Leinenweber's oral history, 1986, 56–57. Other Bay Area colleges were similarly affected. Student groups modeled on SLATE were formed at San Francisco State and San Jose State in response to the HUAC hearings.

7. Compare Rossman's description of Doug Wachter as someone who "had been very active in CORE and the picketing of Kress/Woolworth stores in Berkeley to support the sit-in strikes down South," with that of HUAC's report that he was a member of the CP and a delegate, along with his father Saul, to the Seventeenth National Convention of the CPUSA in December 1959; Rossman 1971, 51–52; U.S. House 1961, 9. See "Demos Blast S.F. Riot Film—'Flagrant Distortions,'" *San Francisco Chronicle,* February 17, 1961, 8, reporting a survey by the Santa Clara County Democratic Central Committee.

8. "Foreign Student Visas Denied After HUAC 'Riots,'" September 26, 1960; "Student Loses Position after 'Riot' Involvement," October 6, 1960; both in *Daily Cal.* Quote from Myerson (1970, 71), who blamed the administration rather than Immigration. Seaborg (1994, 468–472) describes administration efforts to intervene with Immigration over a third grad student, who was finally saved from losing his visa through adverse press publicity.

9. Sherriffs' memos of May 5, 1959, to Kerr in Seaborg 1994, 167–169. Cloke 1994, 55–56; Heirich 1965, 24–25. "'Sounds of Protest' Disc Explained to Empty Auditorium on Campus," *Daily Cal,* March 22, 1961, 3. Quote from Dean of Students William F. Shepard in "UC OUSTS LIBERAL CLUB—As Freedom Is Defended" (front-page headline), *San Francisco News-Call Bulletin,* June 10, 1961. "University Revokes Slate's Recognition," and editorial, "SLATE's Freedom Untouched," June 20, 1961, 1, 14; both in *Daily Cal.* Office of the President, "A Chronology of University Policy Regarding use of University Facilities by Student Groups," says "problems . . . [were created by] certain groups [which used] the name of the University not only for the quite appropriate *discussion* of political and social issues, but also for political and social *action* as well"; July 20, 1961, 4. "Political Action Here Ruled Off-Campus," *Daily Cal,* August 1, 1961, 1. For the letter of August 23, 1961, to Clark Kerr from eight faculty members regarding SLATE, see Schorske oral history, 2000, 27, 151–153.

10. Speech provided by Clark Kerr from his files. The *News-Call Bulletin* says Kerr was working on this speech when a reporter phoned for comment on SLATE's suspension, but he refused to come to the phone. Other speeches at that commence-

ment, including that of Governor Pat Brown, also proclaimed the importance of open debate with a diversity of opinions. Newspaper coverage of these speeches and SLATE's removal appeared on the same day, often in the same story, highlighting the contrast between talk and action; "Backstage Battle at Cal Commencement," *San Francisco Examiner,* June 11, 1961.

11. "Alarming Red Drive in College Described," *Los Angeles Times,* June 12, 1961, 1; "U.C. Under Fire in State Senate's Subversive Study," *San Francisco Chronicle,* June 13, 1961, 1; "Probers Rap Red Inroads at U.C.," *Oakland Tribune,* June 13, 1961, 1; "Senator Feels SLATE Faces Campus Ban," *Daily Cal,* March 22, 1961, 1. Cloke (1994, 56–57) quotes statements made by Burns (D) and Assemblyman Mulford (R) to argue the causal connection. The chancellor's office surely knew that SLATE's removal had been on its agenda for some time but could hardly issue a press release admitting that. When Burns became leader of the senate, and with it chairman of the important Rules Committee, the two parties each had twenty seats; the Democratic sweep of the 1958 elections solidified Burns's place for a decade.

12. California Legislature 1963, 190.

13. "Reps Relate Apathy to Kerr Directives," October 26, 1961, 1; Column on "One Man's Opinion," November 13, 1961, 6; "Text of Kerr's Letter," "Ex Com Backs 'Directives,'" "'Kerr Directives Misrepresented,'" all in November 15, 1961, 1; "'The Big Lie,'" November 15, 1961, 8; "Open Letter to Clark Kerr," "President's Letter Under Heavy Attack," "Reps Explain Action on Kerr Directives," and "Slate, SCLU Give Views on Rules Row," all in November 16, 1961, 1; editorial, "Slate's Tactics," November 17, 1961, 1; all in *Daily Cal.* History of Kerr's directives summarized in "Kerr Directives Old Controversy for ASUC," *Daily Cal,* October 11, 1962, 3; Cloke 1994, 80–83.

14. Commencement speech by Governor Edmund G. Brown at the University of Santa Clara (a private Jesuit college) on June 3, 1961; reprinted in SLATE pamphlet "The BIG Myth?" undated, probably December 1961 or early 1962. This widely read pamphlet also contained statements from former UC president Benjamin Ide Wheeler (1908) and the presidents of Antioch College (May 1961) and Harvard College (November 1953). Brown does not quote this speech in his 1970 memoir.

15. First quote in Horowitz 1962, 125; second quote in Heirich and Kaplan, 1965, 28. See also "Kerr Calls for Idea Freedom," *Daily Cal,* March 22, 1961, 1.

16. Quote in *Blue and Gold 1962,* Vol. 89, 1962, 23, in author's possession.

17. "University of California Policies Relating to Students and Student Organizations," September 1961; "Information for Student Organizations, 1962–1963," Office of the Dean of Students, University of California, Berkeley Campus. The "prior notice" for outside speakers had just been reduced from one week to three days.

9. Summer Vacation in Washington, D.C.

1. *Boynton v. Virginia,* 364 U.S. 454 (1960).
2. Meier and Rudwick 1973, 135–143. For freedom riders, see Peck 1962, chapters 8, 9, 10; and Schlesinger 1978, 294–300.

10. Crossing the Line

1. Henretta, Brownlee, Brody, and Ware 1987, 905.
2. Ibid.

11. The Speaker Ban

1. Otten 1970, 120–125.
2. On Wallace, see Isserman 1987, 58; and Otten 1970, 139. The professors' debate was sponsored by the Graduate Student Association, and the provost limited attendance to faculty and graduate students. This caused the undergraduates to demand liberalization of the speaker rules; Gardner 1967, 14–21. On Laski, see Stadtman 1970, quote on 324. Stevenson speech in *Daily Cal,* May 9, 1956, 1; Heirich 1971, 70. On Brown, see Wellman oral history, 1976, 119.
3. Henretta, Brownlee, Brody, and Ware 1987, 866–869. Executive Order 9835 was revoked and superseded by Executive Order 10450, which Eisenhower signed on April 27, 1953. According to historian Howard Zinn (1973, 157), "By 1954, . . . [the list] included, besides the Communist Party, the Socialist Youth League, the Ku Klux Klan, the Chopin Cultural Center, the Cervantes Fraternal Society, the Committee for the Negro in the Arts, the Committee for the Protection of the Bill of Rights, the League of American Writers, the Nature Friends of America, People's Drama, Inc., the Washington Bookshop Association, and the Yugoslav Seaman's Club." Otten 1970, 145.
4. "Balanced" meant that opposing candidates could speak serially rather than on the same panel, a requirement which had kept all candidates off campus; Otten 1970, 147–150, 175. Rabbi Alvin Fine and Rev. Roy Nichols had also spoken on campus after May 1958; Heirich and Kaplan 1965, 24.
5. "Rule 5 Keeps Aptheker Off Campus," *Daily Cal,* February 19, 1963, 1. Schorske oral history, 2000, 28–31, 156–158. Herbert Aptheker received his Ph.D. in history from Columbia University in 1944, writing a dissertation on "American Negro Slave Revolts." More scholar than activist, he pioneered in a field that was not a popular subject for historians aspiring to tenure. According to CP Southern California chairman Dorothy Healey: "Aptheker was widely known as the Party's 'theoretician', but inside the Party everyone knew that his opinions didn't count for much in determining policy"; Healey and Isserman 1990, 224. Also: "Later [Nemmy Sparks] returned to New York and acted as the clandestine editor of *Political Affairs* while Herbert Aptheker was its 'open' editor"; ibid., 104.
6. Stadtman 1970, quote on 437–438. Wilkinson, a former housing administrator in the Los Angeles city government, never said whether he had ever been a member of the CP. The Burns Committee's *Eleventh Report* claimed that "at one time [he] directed the security apparatus of the Communist Party of Los Angeles County" but "was exposed before this Committee in an executive hearing, and discharged from his position in 1952." It listed his campus talk as one more "capitulation" to the "radical Left" by "the administration of President Clark Kerr"; California Legislature 1961, 25, 95. HUAC claimed that Wilkinson was a known Communist, but Healey's autobiography of her four decades in the Los Angeles CP does not mention him in any capacity; Healey and Isserman 1990. To provide "balance," Vice-Chancellor Adrian Kragen invited the FBI to campus to talk about communism, but the offer was refused, in part because Director J. Edgar Hoover saw it as a ploy; FBI memo of March 20, 1961, Mohr to DeLoach, handwritten note from "H" on bottom of page 2. "Cancel Wilkinson's UC Talk—Mulford," *San Francisco Examiner,* March 21, 1961. "Wilkinson Controversy Rages; Delegation Protests to State Leaders," March 22, 1961, 1; "Wilkinson Talks at UC," March 23, 1961, 1; both in *Daily Cal.*

7. These events are summarized in Heirich and Kaplan 1965, 28–29; and in Cloke 1994, 69–67. "AAUP Speaker Ban Statement," December 5, 1962, 9; "Strong Criticizes Speaker Ban, Tuition," April 29, 1963, 1; "ACLU to Drop Red Ban Suit," May 15, 1963, 1; "SLATE Institutes Speaker Ban Test Case," May 16, 1963, 1; all in *Daily Cal*. "UC's Stand—Better Read than Said," *San Francisco Chronicle*, May 17, 1963, 2. Lima headed the Northern California CP from the late 1950s until he retired in 1985.

8. "Nixon Stand on Campus Talks," *San Francisco Chronicle*, September 23, 1962, 10:1; the language of his expanded ban was a response to Wilkinson's 1961 speech. Regental change was "anticipated" in the press; Ronald Moskowitz, "Communists on Campus—Opinions Have Changed," *San Francisco Examiner*, June 2, 1963, II:3:C. Moskowitz later became Governor Brown's education aide. Six Regents were not present. Regent Jerd F. Sullivan, Jr., wrote a long letter strongly opposing allowing Communists to speak on campus because it would "tarnish" the "good name" of the university. His term ended in 1964 and he was not reappointed. The Regents continued to receive many letters opposing Communist speakers on campus.

9. The quotes are from letters to my mother, October 11 and October 19, 1963.

10. "Students Mob Cops at UC"; "Student's View of Madame Nhu"; both in *San Francisco Examiner*, October 30, 1963, 14. "The Dragon Lady at Harmon"; "Hisses vs. Applause—A Polite Reception"; "Near Riot As Mme. Nhu Exits—1 Jailed"; all in *Daily Cal*, October 30, 1963, 1.

11. The *Daily Cal* later reported that Forbes failed to show for the USC speech and the UCLA one was canceled; May 13, 1964.

12. "Slate Calls Off a Rally," *Daily Cal*, October 11, 1963, 1.

13. Forbes event reported in *Daily Cal*, May 11, 13, 19, 20, 21, 22, 1964. Van Dusen Kennedy was one of the faculty's civil libertarians but was unknown to us.

12. The *SLATE Supplement*

1. *Cal Reporter*, 4, no. 1, May 13, 1963. The other five editors were Brad Cleaveland, Mike Schwartz, Sandor Fuchs, Ken Cloke, and Steve DeCanio. "Cal Reporter Condemns UC—But 'No Constructive Solutions,'" *Daily Cal*, May 15, 1963, 1.

2. In addition to those already identified, the first full *Supplement* (Spring 1964) listed as editorial staff Wendy Bearge, Jon Petrie, Steve Plagemann, Ron Rohman, Joan Roos, and Madge Strong. Production managers were Sue Currier, Mike Schwartz, and Mike Travis. Jerry Miller was the managing editor, and Sandor Fuchs was the business manager. Additional names which appeared in the *Supplement* for fall 1964 and spring 1965 were Rosemary Feitis (who replaced Phil Roos as editor in the spring), Kathy Buss, Claire Davison, Barry Silverman, Marston Schultz, David Goines, Marvin Garson, Wendy Dannet, Deward Hastings, Art Goldberg, Lorie White, Kathy Kahn, Pete Sessions, Al Solomonow, Carl Blumstein, Terry Stauduhar, and Jon King.

3. Quote by Irving Putter, professor of French, Letter to Editor, "Slate Supplement: Dangerous Inaccuracies," *Daily Cal*, May 21, 1964, 8.

13. Fair Housing

1. U.S. Bureau of the Census, *U.S. Census of Population: 1960. General Population Characteristics, California. Final Report PC(1)-6B* (Washington, D.C.: Govern-

ment Printing Office, 1961), Table 15. The category "nonwhite" includes Negro and other minorities in this table.

2. The California constitution of 1879 authorized cities to remove Chinese or segregate them within their borders; Article XIX, § 4. *In re Lee Sing,* 43 Fed. 259 (1890) found that this violated the Fourteenth Amendment to the U.S. Constitution.

3. These federal programs are described in Miller 1964; and McEntire 1960. This ended when President Kennedy signed Executive Order 11603 on November 20, 1962; 27 *Fed. Reg.* 11527.

4. Larson, Halvonix, and Crilly n.d. [1961].

5. Rorabaugh 1989, 51, 54.

6. Bernice Hubbard May oral history, 1976, 259, 262.

7. Committee on Discrimination in Housing n.d. [1961], 1.

8. The private residence, Hanson House, didn't allow Jews either; "University Condones Race Bias," *Cal Reporter,* November 7, 1958, 1.

9. Seaborg 1994, 369–374; Seaborg says that Brown's opinion was prompted by a complaint made by "fifteen minority rights organizations" on October 10, 1958.

10. Rorabaugh 1989, 55–57; Casstevens 1965.

11. Casstevens 1967; see Appendix A for text of Rumford bill. It is codified at Cal. Health & Safety Code §35700–35744. Meier and Rudwick 1973, 242. Burns was one of two Democrats who voted consistently against fair housing in what was a strongly partisan division; Casstevens 1967, 37–38.

12. Casstevens 1967; see Appendix B for text of Proposition 14.

13. Ibid., 81–84; *Reitman v. Mulkey,* 64 Cal. 2d 529, 413 P.2d 825, 50 Cal. Rptr. 881 (1966); *Reitman v. Mulkey,* 387 U.S. 369 (1967); Hyink, Brown, and Thacker 1975, 74.

15. The House on Parker Street

1. "Beer Busted—It's Milk," *Daily Cal,* March 15, 1963, 1; "Two Slate Members Charged with Illegal Beer Sale Sentenced," *Daily Cal,* March 20, 1963, 1; *SLATE Newsletter,* March 17, 1963. The alcohol law dated from 1947 and was aimed at fraternities, which ran bars in their houses; Sevilla 1967, 470.

16. The Assassination of JFK

1. *Daily Cal,* November 23, 1963, 1.

17. The Bay Area Civil Rights Movement

1. Rossman 1971, 86–87; Meier and Rudwick 1973, 109, 121, 199. *SLATE Newsletter* of April 21, 1963, mentions the previous summer conference.

2. Murray 1967, 52.

3. Len Holt's description of the "Birmingham Demonstration, 1963" is in Grant 1968, 344–349.

4. "Overflow Crowd Hears Baldwin on Race Issues," May 8, 1963, 1; "CORE Head Sees Victory for Negro," September 17, 1963, 1; September 18, 1963, 1; all in *Daily Cal;* Heirich 1971, 85–86. Rossman 1971, 88.

5. Quotes from Meier and Rudwick 1973, 4, 13. See also Farmer 1965, 53–57; Sitkoff 1981, 46.

6. Farmer 1965, 58–64, 74, 88. Farmer claims membership reached 80,000 but admits that that figure includes financial contributors. According to Meier and Rudwick, "CORE at its height remained a remarkably small organization, with an estimated 3,000 to 5,000 members," citing an August 20, 1963, letter (1973, 227). Both agree on the rapid rate of expansion in 1963. "Between June and October, twenty-six affiliates were added, making a total of ninety-four, or about a 40 percent increase since Birmingham"; ibid., 225.

7. Meier and Rudwick 1973, 94, 96, 121, first quote on 187, 225–227, second quote on 234; Weinberg 1964, 23–24.

8. Rossman 1971, 88; Heirich and Kaplan 1965, 30–31. "Bigotry and the Beauties: Jaycees Snub UC Negro: To 'Protect' College Queens," September 23, 1963, 1; "Apology from Jaycees: 'No More Racial Bias,'" September 24, 1963, 1; all in *Daily Cal.* "Berkeley's JC's Apologize in Race Incident During Football Festival," *Berkeley Daily Gazette,* September 24, 1963. The men escorted the candidates for queen in a promenade before a football game. The wife of the JayCee chairman asked Sims to withdraw without consulting anyone. When asked later by reporters, the girl Sims was to escort, who came from a Pennsylvania school, said she had no objection to his doing so.

9. U.S. Civil Rights Commission, *Hearings before the U.S. Commission on Civil Rights,* San Francisco, January 27–28, 1960, 610, excerpting the progress report, November 1958, of the Berkeley Study Committee on Equal Employment Opportunities, "Employment Opportunities for Members of Minority Groups in Berkeley."

10. Heirich and Kaplan 1965, 31; Heirich 1971, 86.

11. Heirich and Kaplan 1965, 31; Heirich 1971, 86; Barlow and Shapiro 1971, 44; Meier and Rudwick 1973, 251, 254, 308; Myerson 1970, 111–113.

12. Weinberg 1964, 24.

13. "Mass S.F. Sit-In Arrests—Dobbs, Shelley Argue," *San Francisco Chronicle,* November 4, 1963, 1; "Sit-In Pickets—114 Are Arrested," *San Francisco Examiner,* November 4, 1963, 1. "Behind the Mel's Sit-Ins" November 5, 1963, 1; editorial, November 5, 1963, 6; November 8, 1963, 1; November 11, 1963, 1; all in *Daily Cal.* The press noted that the home of his co-owner, Mel Weiss, was not picketed. His opponent, John Shelley, won.

14. Myerson wrote in 1970 (111–112) that "When I returned to the Bay Area from Europe early in 1963, I found that Marxist discussion groups calling themselves W. E. B. DuBois Clubs had been set up in Berkeley and San Francisco, on the initiative of young Communists. . . . We decided to have a go at the racist hiring practices of a number of business concerns. Mel's Drive-In Restaurants . . . was selected as the first target. . . . Arraignment day was also election day, and Harold Dobbs lost heavily. In the winning Democratic headquarters, unofficial word was a begrudging admission that the sit-ins were the deciding factor. For the first time in a generation, a Marxist movement was a major factor in the political life of an important American city"; arraignment was in fact the day before election day. In a January 14, 1997, interview he told me that members of the DuBois Clubs rented three adjoining houses in the Fillmore District of San Francisco, where kids and black activists hung out and partied. Among them were Will Usury and Bill Bradley of CORE and Attorneys Willie Brown and Terry François of the NAACP. They collectively decided to go after Mel's because it had eateries in San Francisco, Oakland, and Berkeley and the kids spent their pocket money there. Myerson denied that Mel's was chosen because its co-owner

was running for mayor. Au contraire, he said, they were discouraged by adult advisors from picketing Mel's at that time on the grounds that it might create sympathy for Dobbs, but since the DuBois Club didn't support Shelley, they didn't care.

Barlow and Shapiro (1971, 44) say: "Art Sheridan, the twenty-one-year-old black student [at San Francisco State College] started an organization of his own, the Direct Action Group (DAG). . . . In the fall . . . [it] began investigating the hiring practices of Mel's Drive-In. . . . By this time DAG had been joined on the picket lines by other student organizations, including Youth for Jobs and several chapters of the DuBois Club. Together, they formed an umbrella organization called the 'Ad Hoc Committee to End Discrimination'; within [this] . . . Sheridan's leadership was effectively supplanted by the better organized and more politically sophisticated DuBois Club people."

François claimed responsibility in his Nov. 11, 1968, interview for the Civil Rights Documentation Project.

In March 1964, the *People's World,* the West Coast paper of the CP, said the Ad Hoc Committee "was made up of the Direct Action Group, the W. E. B. DuBois Clubs of Berkeley and San Francisco, Youth for Jobs of Oakland and San Francisco, SLATE . . . and the Citizens Committee for Nuclear Disarmament"; 2. Jack Kurzweil told Heirich that the Ad Hoc Committee "was formed to conduct the campaign against Mel's Drive-in Restaurant"; Heirich 1971, 450n58. Kurzweil was a founder of the DuBois Clubs and a member of the CP. Although Myerson doesn't identify the DuBois Clubs as an arm of the CP, Dorothy Healey does and confirms that Myerson was a CP member; Healey and Isserman 1990, 185–186, 207, 214, 232, 239. Myerson said that some, but not all, DuBois Club members were in the CP and that he didn't join the CP until he left the Bay Area in 1966.

18. On Civil Disobedience

1. King 1963, 86.

2. Quotes are from Plato's *Apology,* which is about the trial of Socrates, as translated by F. J. Church.

19. The Sheraton-Palace

1. Heirich and Kaplan 1965, 31; Goines 1993, 85; Meier and Rudwick 1973, 59, 235–236, 255; Rorabaugh 1989, 128–129. " 'Milestone' Agreement Ends CORE, Lucky Shop-In Strike," *Daily Cal,* March 2, 1964, 1.

2. Myerson 1970, 113–114. The *San Francisco Chronicle* reported that "A Palace Hotel spokesman later reiterated its claim . . . that 25 percent of its employees are of minority groups. They are, the spokesman said, Negroes and Chinese." *San Francisco Chronicle,* March 7, 1964, 7:3. Myerson told me that it was the SLATE-sponsored demonstration against Mme Nhu when she spoke at the Palace in September which persuaded the Ad Hoc Committee to target this hotel for its anti-discrimination action a few months later. He knew that the layout and the location were good for a picket.

3. "The Facts Behind the Palace Dispute," 5-page pamphlet. Mike Myerson interview, April 11, 1997; Myerson 1970, 114–115; Heirich and Kaplan 1965, 31–32.

4. Taken from a term paper written for my political science junior honors seminar, spring 1964. See also "Mass Arrest of Pickets at Palace Hotel," *San Francisco*

Chronicle, March 2, 1964, 1; "Police Break Up Palace Picket Line," *San Francisco Examiner,* March 2, 1964, 1; "81 Pickets Arrested in SF," *Daily Cal,* March 2, 1964, 1.

5. "The Law vs. the Pickets" and "A Thousand Students Test A Court Order," *Daily Cal,* March 6, 1964, 1. "1200 Pickets at the Palace Hotel," *San Francisco Chronicle,* March 7, 1964, 7:5–6. "The Facts Behind the Palace Dispute" pamphlet.

6. "Visiting Africans Puzzled," *San Francisco News Call-Bulletin,* March 7, 1964, 3:1.

7. Term paper written for my political science junior honors seminar. For descriptions of the sit-in, see "Chanting Pickets at Palace Hotel," March 7, 1964, 1; "Peace at Palace" and "Shelley Wins Agreement After Biggest S.F. Arrest," March 8, 1964, 1A; "On to Jail—for Freedom," March 8, 1964, 1B; all in *San Francisco Chronicle.* "1,000 Picket Hotel," March 7, 1964, 1; "Pact Ends Siege at Palace," March 8, 1964, 1; both in *San Francisco Examiner.* "Hotel Picket Bedlam: 200 Jailed, Hundreds Jam Lobby," *San Francisco News Call-Bulletin,* March 7, 1964, 1; "30 Pickets Jailed in S.F. Palace Hotel Mass 'Sit-In,'" *Berkeley Daily Gazette,* March 7, 1964, 1; "Demonstrators-1, Sheraton Palace-0," *Daily Californian,* March 9, 1964, 1; "Mass Picket: 150 Jailed," *Golden Gater,* March 9, 1964, 1. Willie Brown and Terry François were the lawyers for the Ad Hoc Committee. Both urged us to "sleep in" rather than go to jail. Later that year François was appointed by Shelley to fill a vacancy on the San Francisco Board of Supervisors; he was reelected in November 1964. Brown was elected mayor of San Francisco in 1995 after serving for many years as speaker of the California assembly.

8. I never knew who paid Barrish his bond fee. The *San Francisco News Call-Bulletin* reported that $5,000 came from the NAACP, March 7, 1964, 1:8. The *San Francisco Chronicle* said leftist attorney Vincent Hallinan bailed out sixty-seven after his three sons said they wouldn't leave without their friends; "Hallinan Gets Bail for 67," March 8, 1964, 1C:4.

9. "Hotel Hiring Agreement" and "End of the Siege," *San Francisco Chronicle,* March 8, 1964, 1, 1C. Disturbing the Peace is § 415 of the California Penal Code. Myerson credits Dick Lyden, head of ILWU Local 6, for bringing about the final agreement and for drafting its language. He said that the children of union leaders were active in the DuBois Clubs, creating a network of familiarity among the mayor, the unions, and the protestors; Mike Myerson interview of April 11, 1997. "The Cost —$10,105.81 Cash, Plus," *San Francisco News Call-Bulletin,* March 10, 1964, 1:8.

10. Appendix A of my term paper. Also *San Francisco Chronicle,* March 8, 1964, 1A; "List of Those Arrested," March 8, 1964, 18. "78 Berkeleyans Jailed at Palace Hotel 'Sit-In,'" *Berkeley Daily Gazette,* March 9, 1:4. This list missed me, so was clearly incomplete. On March 9th, in an article on repercussions from the demonstrations, the *Chronicle* said that fewer than 20 percent of the demonstrators were Negroes; "Palace Pact: [Former Mayor] Lapham Blasts Shelley," 18. On March 10th, the *Chronicle* revised its figures to 171 arrested, including six juveniles, "Only Four Negroes among the Adults"; 14:2. I know there were two Negro women arrested, because we were jailed together, and I was told there were ten Negroes among the men. I estimated that "there were four times as many Negroes in the demonstration than among those arrested." From the names, I also recognized that "the non-student categories includes at least four CORE employees. About half of the rest of the non-student categories I know to be former students who have graduated or dropped out."

11. "At 18, a Civil Rights Veteran," *San Francisco Chronicle,* March 8, 1964, 1A; "Spark Behind Hotel Pickets," *San Francisco Examiner,* March 8, 1964, 3:4. Paul Richards, who was chairman of the Berkeley DuBois Club at the time, reported that

"when it came time to serve our sentences, Mike left the state and never came back. Tracy took a big fall; after serving time in jail I never saw her again. Jail took it out of her. The fact that Myerson wasn't there to help her when the shit came down didn't help"; interview in Goines 1993, 89. Myerson says he was arrested in Sheraton I, not Sheraton II, and that the charges were dropped. The sentence he didn't serve was for an unintended arrest at the *Oakland Tribune* several months later. He had encouraged Sims to take a leadership role because she was young and dynamic and, since he was white, he could not be a public spokesperson; Mike Myerson interview of January 14, 1997. Although Tracy was the public persona of the demonstration, the chief negotiator was Attorney Terry François.

20. Auto Row

1. "Pickets Violated Law: Brown Rips Hotel Sit-In," *San Francisco News Call-Bulletin,* March 10, 1964, 1; "Brown Hits the Sit-In at Palace," *San Francisco Chronicle,* March 11, 1964, 1; "Brown and Pickets," *San Francisco Examiner,* March 11, 1964, 1. Shelley quote in "An Appeal by Shelley to City's Negro Leaders," *San Francisco Chronicle,* March 12, 1964, 8:2. "A Battle of The Headlines," *San Francisco Examiner,* March 10, 1964, 17:5; "Churchmen Rap Pickets," *San Francisco Examiner,* March 13, 1964, 7:5; "Top Clergymen Join Criticism of Palace Sit-In," *San Francisco Chronicle,* March 13, 1964, 1; Columnist Charles Denton, "A Little Child Leads Them, But Where?" *San Francisco Examiner,* March 16, 1964; Ed Montgomery, "Who Is Running the Rights Sit-Ins: How Many Are Radicals? A Look at the Records," *San Francisco Examiner,* March 16, 1964, 8; and the subsequent editorial: "The Marxist Influence." Montgomery wrote, "By actual count, 91 of 167 persons arrested already were known to intelligence agents as party members or party adherents and sympathetic to party causes." Montgomery was a regular outlet for the FBI. Editorials for March 10, 1964, in *Daily Cal* ("The Aftermath"); *San Francisco Examiner* ("Aftermath of a Lawless Weekend"); and March 12, 1964, in *San Francisco Chronicle* ("The Wrong Way to Civil Rights"). There were some supporters in the establishment: "9 Pastors Defend Pickets," *San Francisco Examiner,* March 17, 1964, 16:5; and Arthur Hoppe, "Protest Is A Bum Deal," *San Francisco Chronicle,* March 8, 1964.

2. "A Short History of the Cadillac Negotiations," 2-page pamphlet; "The Picketed Cadillac," *San Francisco Examiner,* March 10, 1964, 17; "Pickets Move on to Cadillac Agency," *San Francisco Chronicle,* March 10, 1964, 14:1. A month later, the Cadillac agency said that "based on a visual count on March 23, [there were] 23 non-whites among a total of 255 employees"; *San Francisco Examiner,* April 14, 1964, 12:1. The *San Francisco Chronicle* reported that "recent State surveys show that about 2,600 people work in the city's 54 car dealerships"; April 21, 1964. "Cadillac 'Pickets' Arrested," *Daily Cal,* March 16, 1964, 1:5.

3. "B. of A. Warns the Picketers," *San Francisco Chronicle,* March 13, 1964, 1:8 and 10:2, 3.

4. "Auto Pickets Go Wild," *San Francisco News Call-Bulletin,* April 11, 1964, 1. See also "What's Behind the Sit-Ins: When Mediation Broke Down," *San Francisco Examiner,* April 12, 1964, B:6.

5. Quotes from "Sharp Warning to S.F. Auto Dealers," *San Francisco Examiner,* April 6, 1964, 1, 9.

6. "Auto Pickets Go Wild," *San Francisco News Call-Bulletin,* April 11, 1964,

1; "226 Sit-In Arrests," *San Francisco Chronicle,* April 12, 1964, 1; "226 Auto Pickets Jailed," *San Francisco Examiner,* April 12, 1964, 1.

7. "Sit-In on Auto Row Jails 226," *San Francisco Examiner,* April 12, 1964, B:4.

8. California Penal Code Sections 415, Disturbing the Peace; 602(j), Trespassing; 407, Unlawful Assembly; and 409, Remaining Present at Place of Riot.

9. Data come from newspaper listings of arrestees; calculations from Appendix B of my term paper. The *San Francisco Examiner* reported that "of the more than 600 demonstrators, police estimated that no more than 10 percent of the total were from minority groups"; April 12, 1964, B:5. This is inconsistent with other information but does reflect the strategy of delegitimating the protests as lacking support from the Negro community.

10. "S.F. Judge Calls Sit-Ins 'Criminal,'" *San Francisco Chronicle,* June 2, 1964, 1; "Bishop Pike Condemns S.F. Sit-Ins," *San Francisco Examiner,* April 14, 1964; "Auto Sit-Ins to Continue Across U.S.," *San Francisco Chronicle,* April 13, 1964; "Auto Row Picketing On Again," *San Francisco Examiner,* April 13, 1964; "Pact Is 'Near' in Auto Row Dispute: Picketing Threatened Today," *San Francisco Chronicle,* April 18, 1964, 1:8; "2,000 May Join Auto Sit-In Today: Mediation Fails," *San Francisco Examiner,* April 18, 1964, 1:7; "Auto Row Pact Called Landmark," *San Francisco Chronicle,* April 21, 1964.

11. "CORE Will Picket Bank Tomorrow," *San Francisco Chronicle,* May 21, 1964, 1, 16. Meier and Rudwick 1973, 238. Writing in September 1964, Jack Weinberg said that CORE demonstrations in Berkeley had "several hundred participants," and that "B of A has hired over 450 minority persons in California in one month"; "Campus CORE Summer Activities," *Campus CORE-lator,* September 1964, 35. I don't remember any big demonstrations in Berkeley, but I wasn't there all summer. "CORE Asks City, State to Mediate," *San Francisco Examiner,* May 21, 1964, 1, 16; "Bank Signs FEPC Pact: New Tactics by Pickets," *San Francisco Chronicle,* June 2, 1964, 1:5, 8.

12. *S.F. CORE-lator,* n.d. but postmarked April 1964, 5.

21. Clogging the Courts

1. Under attack from his own members, Burbridge resigned the presidency of the San Francisco NAACP three months before his term ended and dropped out of political activity; Thomas N. Burbridge interview, Civil Rights Documentation Project, July 18, 1969.

2. Kayo Hallinan later said, "Those trials just took the heart out of everybody. The Movement just collapsed after that"; Kayo Hallinan interview, Civil Rights Documentation Project, July 24, 1969, 18; Myerson 1970, 121; Barlow and Shapiro 1971, 47. "SF Police to Press Charges," *Daily Cal,* March 11, 1964, 1; "Cahill Won't Drop Charges," *San Francisco Chronicle,* March 11, 1964, 1; "We'll Prosecute the Pickets —DA," *San Francisco Examiner,* March 10, 1964, 1, 17. Cahill was the police chief, Thomas C. Lynch was the DA.

3. There are fifty-six names (including three women) on the "Trial List of Lawyers" in Axelrod's files, dated July 1, 1964. However, the attorney who handled my second trial is not on it, so the list is incomplete.

4. Ginger 1965; quote from "Pickets Ask 500 Jury Trials," *San Francisco Examiner,* March 17, 1964, 1. It reported that "if each trial lasted just one day, the extra cost to the City would be $17,500, according to estimates prepared by court officials." For 500 trials, this would be $8,750,000. "Trials Set for First 30 Palace Hotel

Picketers," April 1, 1964, 2:1; "Jury Trials for S.F. Sit-Ins Start," April 6, 1964, 1, 9; "Squabbles Slow S.F. Rights Trials," April 17, 1964, 1, 14; all in *San Francisco Chronicle*. "Picket Trial 'Track Meet,'" April 6, 1964, 1, 12; "New Judicial Row on Sit-Ins' Trials," April 11, 1964, 1, 10; both in *San Francisco Examiner*.

5. One disgruntled convict told the *San Francisco Examiner* he had been duped. "We were told that anyone that went counter to the majority was a fink and if we pleaded nolo we were defeating the entire civil rights movement," "Split Over Sit-In Trial Tactics," June 8, 1964, 1, 22. The same story said, "As of Friday, 20 out of the 517 defendants arrested in the Sheraton-Palace Hotel and Automotive Row demonstrations had pleaded nolo contendere." In the end eighty-eight pled nolo, so not all felt pressured to go to trial.

6. Thoreau did not coin the term "civil disobedience." It was added later by a publisher as the title of his tract.

22. On Trial

1. "Jury Bias Charge at Sit-In Trials," April 17, 1964; "Hallinan Tries to Try Cops," April 18, 1964, 1, 7; "Shelley—Silent Witness," April 21, 1964, 1, 14; all in *San Francisco Examiner*. In thirty-four of our trials, 204 Negroes were called for jury duty, but only ten served; Ginger 1965, 12–13. "S.F.'s Lively Civil Rights Front: Court Is Crowded, Judges Are Feuding," April 14, 1964, 1, 16; editorial, "Bail Juggling by Municipal Judges," April 16, 1964; both in *San Francisco Chronicle*. The bail dispute was between Judges Clayton Horn and Fitz-Gerald Ames, who were running against each other for a vacant seat in Superior Court; Ames lost the June election. Judge Leo Friedman doubled Kayo's bail for missing the morning session and sent him to jail when he didn't pay the extra amount. "New Wrangling at Sit-In Trials," *San Francisco Chronicle*, April 18, 1964, 1, 6. Ten defendants went to jail for missing trial days; Ginger 1965, 13. "Sit-In Trial—Shelley Subpoenaed," April 21, 1964, 1, 12; "Feud Among Judges at Sit-In Trials," April 24, 1964, 1, 13; "Rights Jury Uproar," May 21, 1964, 1, 16; all in *San Francisco Chronicle*. Kayo, UC Berkeley '59, had spent the summer of 1963 in the Mississippi delta and returned to his hometown "to find the same conditions prevailing in San Francisco that had prevailed in Mississippi"; Kayo Hallinan interview, Civil Rights Documentation Project, July 24, 1969, 9. In 1995, he was elected San Francisco's district attorney, the job which launched Governor Pat Brown's political career; he was re-elected in 1999.

2. Edmund Burke's speech of March 7, 1771: "I like a clamor where there is an abuse. The fire-bell at midnight disturbs your sleep but it keeps you from being burned in your bed."

3. *Civil Liberties Docket*, November 1964, 16. Thomas N. Burbridge interview, Civil Rights Documentation Project, July 18, 1969. Burbridge was disappointed that Brown did not completely pardon him.

4. "Tracy Sims Guilty"; and editorial, "The Singling Out of Tracy Sims," May 1, 1964, 1, 10; "Palace Sit-Ins Guilty," April 22, 1964, 1, 13; all in *San Francisco Examiner*. "Tracy Sims Convicted," May 1, 1964, 1, 15; "S.F. Pickets Guilty," April 22, 1964, 1, 17; both in *San Francisco Chronicle*.

5. Art remembered a hung jury, but the *San Francisco Chronicle* says he was acquitted.

6. "Sit-In Arrests—Student Expulsion?" April 23, 1964, 1; "Mulford: Action Against Sit-Ins," April 30, 1964, 1; both in *Daily Cal*. Mulford letter to Governor Brown and press release, 6; Kerr Charter Day speech, 7–11; both in *California*

Monthly, July/August 1964. Memos, press releases and arrest list in "Public Relations: Student Demonstrations and Sit-Ins, General," 1964–Sept. 1965, CU-5, series 5, Box 55:20, Records of the Office of the President, University of California, Bancroft Library. The list is dated April 1st, which may explain why the 226 persons arrested in Auto Row on April 11th were not included. I counted only 411 names, of whom 106 were identified as current Berkeley students. I recognized many others I knew as Berkeley students, but they may not have been registered at that time.

   7. *Democracy in America*, chapter XV, section on "Power Exercised by the Majority in America Upon Opinion." Pages vary with edition.

23. Freedom Summer

   1. It was a close and vicious race. Senator Engle died in July. Governor Brown appointed Salinger to fill the remainder of the term, but he lost in November to actor George Murphy. In 1966, Cranston was defeated for reelection as state controller in the Republican landslide which made Ronald Reagan governor. However, in 1968 Cranston won the senate seat held by Thomas Kuchel, who was defeated in the Republican primary by right-winger Max Rafferty. He served for twenty years. Fowle 1980.

   2. Schlesinger 1978, 300–305; voter registration figures from Lewis 1964, 151; and Silver 1966, 86–87. Chapter 8 in Lewis gives a description of how Negroes were kept from voting in the South. Pat Watters and Reese Cleghorn describe the early registration efforts (1967, chapter 3). The Voter Education Project was created so that financial contributions from the Taconic and Field Foundations and the Stern Family Fund would be tax exempt.

   3. Rothschild 1982, 6–9; Carson 1981, 19–20.

   4. Silver 1966, 105ff, has two copies of Mississippi voter application forms that were admitted as evidence in a Fifth Circuit case and a description of the experiences of one Negro and one white applicant from the court records.

   5. Stoper 1977, 13–28.

   6. Carson 1981, 96–99; Rothschild 1982, 19–22; McAdam 1988, 37. "SNCC Chairman Here; Says Negroes May March," *Daily Cal*, December 9, 1963, 1.

   7. Schlesinger 1978, 640; Henretta, Brownlee, Brody, and Ware 1987, 494, 730; Silver 1966, 326–329.

   8. Huie 1965; McAdam 1988, 70-71, 155–156; and Silver 1966, 263–264, quote a portion of Cheney's autopsy; the pathologist concluded that "I have never witnessed bones so severely shattered except in tremendously high speed accidents such as aeroplane crashes." Summer statistics from Rothschild 1982, 58. Michael Anker and David Friedman, "Sit-In at Cecil Poole's Office," *Campus CORE-lator*, September 1964, 3–6. The authors, who were white, described U.S. Attorney Poole as someone who "used to be a Negro."

24. Summer Session

   1. James Townsend was denied tenure at Berkeley but granted it by the University of Washington in Seattle. I expressed my gratitude to him for his kindness on the dedication page of my third book when it was published in 1983.

   2. Carson 1981, 108–109; Rothschild 1981, 23–24, 66–68; McAdam 1988, 77–78.

   3. Mills 1993, 105–133.

4. Carson 1981, 109, 124.

5. *San Francisco Chronicle,* July 15, 16, 1964.

6. *New York Times,* January 28, 1964, 1:2, speech excerpts 17:4. Margaret Chase Smith's nomination in *New York Times,* July 16, 1964, 16:2.

7. The Pacifica Foundation was founded by a group of pacifists who had been imprisoned during World War II. In 1946, it started radio station KPFA in San Francisco, which became an important part of the limited alternative culture of the fifties. One of the first to use the FM bandwidth, it played jazz and folk music and featured offbeat commentary and radical analyses of contemporary events. In 1961, KPFA was broadcasting from Berkeley and had affiliate stations KFPK in Los Angeles and WBAI in New York City. Unknown to me at the time, Congress had held hearings on KPFA in 1963. U.S. Senate, Committee on the Judiciary 1963.

26. The Democratic Convention

1. "Challenge of the Mississippi Freedom Democratic Party" and "Mississippi Faces Challenge," MFDP pamphlets, Atlantic City, 1964, in author's possession. Civil rights organizations regularly quoted from University of Mississippi professor James W. Silver's *Mississippi: The Closed Society,* which was first published in 1963. The *Brief Submitted by the Mississippi Freedom Democratic Party for the Consideration of the Credentials Committee of the Democratic National Convention,* August 1964, is in Box 86 of the Joseph L. Rauh Papers, Library of Congress.

2. Mills 1993, 111–123; Gitlin 1987, 153.

3. Mills 1993, 124–127; Gitlin 1987, 155–158, quote on 158.

4. Gitlin 1987, quote on 156, vote on 160; Mills 1993, 128–131; Belfrage 1965, 242.

27. New York City

1. Meier and Rudwick 1973, 252–253; *New York Times,* April 23, 1964, 1.

2. Shapiro and Sullivan 1964.

28. First Week of the Fall Semester

1. Sherriffs' quotes from memo of September 15, 1964, sent to President Kerr; Strong oral history, 1992, 297. See also Appendix III, which traces "disruption" to Cleaveland's letter but not by name. The letter is reprinted in Lipset and Wolin 1965, 66–81, and excerpted in Heirich 1971, 99–101. It called upon readers to consider demanding the resignation of Clark Kerr and the reconstitution of the Board of Regents. Sherriffs wrote that it "represented . . . activity by the Progressive Labor Movement . . . the youth movement of the Chinese Communist persuasion." He pointedly said it came out as a Supplement to SLATE's "so-called faculty evaluations"; Strong oral history 1992, 297. The PLM had not yet become active on the Berkeley campus; neither Cleaveland nor SLATE was involved with it.

2. Quotes from the inside cover of Volume I, Number IV. Roos added: "The SLATE SUPPLEMENT's devotion to controversy about education is, to our knowledge, unique among college publications. No manuscript is turned down out of hand."

29. Eviction!

1. Towle letter of September 14, 1964; reprinted in Heirich 1971, 102–103; and Lipset and Wolin 1965, 100–101.

2. Student Proposals reprinted in Heirich 1971, 106; Lipset and Wolin 1965, 103; and Towle oral history, 1970, Appendix. Towle quote in "Demonstration Leaders, Kerr Reach Agreement: Police Were Poised," *Daily Cal,* October 3, 1964, 1; and Heirich 1971, 105.

3. Confidential memo, Chancellor Strong's files, of meeting of September 18, 1964, of Kerr, Strong, Sherriffs, Towle, and Richard P. Hafner (Hafner was the campus public affairs officer); Towle oral history, 1970, Appendix; and Heirich 1971, 109–110. Most of the memos in the chancellor's files were prepared by his administrative assistant, Kitty Malloy. As Heirich points out, Kerr, Strong, and Towle all have different versions of their meeting, each placing primary responsibility on someone else, but only Strong memorialized his version. Towle meeting with United Front reported in *Daily Cal,* September 22, 1964, 1.

4. September 22, 1964, 8; September 23, 1964, 1; both in *Daily Cal;* Heirich 1971, 113, petition reprinted 455n12; Lipset and Wolin 1965, excerpted 105. Kerr statement of September 25 in *Daily Cal,* September 28, 1964, 1; Heirich 1971, 116; and Lipset and Wolin 1965, 106.

5. "Strong Yields to Political Groups," *Daily Cal,* September 29, 1. Strong speech reprinted in Lipset and Wolin 1965, 239–241; excerpted in Heirich 1971, 118. Strong's oral history, 1992, section XIV, reports from the minutes of the Regents meeting of September 24, 1964: "With respect to the latter, it is permissible to distribute materials presenting points of view for or against a proposition, a candidate, or with respect to a social or political issue. It is not permissible to recruit for social or political action."

6. The "case" against each of the eight is in Williams's "Memo to Chancellor E. W. Strong regarding student violations, October 1, 1964," Williams oral history, 1990, Appendix I. The only ones cited were those Williams or one of his assistants personally said were in violation of the regulations. More details are in the "Report of the Ad Hoc Committee on Student Conduct," which evaluated the students' actions; Lipset and Wolin 1965, 560–574. The dean who read the citation was Sanford Elberg, eminent historian and dean of the Graduate Division.

30. Who Done It?

1. Towle statement to Goldberg in Max Heirich 1971, 106–107. Michael Rossman (1971, 90–91) wrote that "it was the common supposition, supported by uncautious statements by the Chancellor, that pressure from the Oakland Tribune had caused the crackdown." I was personally told the story of the Knowland phone call by Jeremy Bruin at the time, based on his memory of what Strong said. The FSM Archives have written statements by Mike Rodenbush and Bill Miller that at the chancellor's reception for Regents Scholars on September 21st, they heard Strong say that the *Oakland Tribune* had called to ask him if he knew about picketing being organized on university property. Strong said that he didn't know it was university property but would investigate. To his surprise, it was. FSM Archives, Folder 1.5, Bancroft Library.

2. This charge was repeated frequently in FSM leaflets and newsletters and to reporters; see Jack Weinberg in Lipset and Wolin 1965, 221; Raskin 1965, 80; Trillin

1965, 264. Most students believed that "outside pressures" caused the crackdown; see Somers in Lipset and Wolin 1965, 537. Those that I've spoken to since then still believe that Knowland was the originator. See also the interview with Malcolm Burnstein, who says that Nolan [*sic*] phoned Strong: "Speaking Out for the Free Speech Movement," *The Recorder,* April 8, 1998, 1; Jon Carroll column on the opening of the FSM archives, *San Francisco Chronicle,* April 17, 2001, C:12; and Roysher 2002, 141–142. Knowland denied exerting any pressure to ban campus political activity. "I have never personally talked to President Kerr, Chancellor Strong, or the Regents on this issue," he told the *Daily Cal,* "Knowland Interview: Never Talked to Kerr," December 4, 1964, 5:1. Kerr confirmed this at an Associated Press banquet in January of 1966, with Knowland, class of '29, in his audience; "Berkeley Administration to Blame for FSM, Kerr Says," *California Monthly,* March 1966, 44.

3. *Tribune* city editor Roy Grimm had heard that the Scranton recruiters were members of the Dubois Club; when they turned out to be YRs, Grimm concluded there was no story; Heirich 1971, 92–98. Hafner told Heirich that the picketing by the Ad Hoc Committee did not come up in conversation and that it never occurred to him that that was a motivation. He said the same to the press, when asked: "Kerr to Remain at California," *New York Times,* March 14, 1965, 46:6.

4. The spring 1964 issue said: "Psych 33: Any resemblance between 33 and academic psychology at Cal is minimal and accidental," though several positive quotes from students were included; 47–48. The fall 1964 issue said it was "general, superficial, fun . . . not terribly challenging, and not at all profound"; 38. Sherriffs' low opinion of SLATE, known to us at the time, is repeated in his oral history, 1980, 17, 22, and is clear from his memos reprinted in Seaborg's book. Sherriffs claims he was unaware that students were putting up tables on university property prior to 1964; oral history, 1980, 24. Towle says she knew the strip was university property but "really didn't think about it"; Towle oral history, 1970.

5. Quotes in Williams's oral history; 1990, 91, 95. Law professor Adrian Kragen's oral history, 1991, 170–171, says: "It was Alex Sherriffs. Everybody knows it. Alex is . . . devious . . . , second-guessed the dean of students . . . [and] did a lot of things that were bad judgment"; see also Taylor 2000, 150. William J. Rorabaugh's independent investigation, 1989, 18, concluded that it was Sherriffs and not Knowland, Strong, or Kerr who took the initiative. Kerr was out of the country from the middle of July to the middle of September. Strong was in Hawaii from July 8th to August 9th. Sherriffs says it was "the university president's office" which initially alerted him to the problem and that he was "stunned . . . to learn that this student political activity had been going on for several months"; Sherriffs' oral history, 1980, 23, 24. In fact, this "activity" had been going on for several years—ever since the campus boundary was moved from Sather Gate. During the three years I had been a student, no one told us not to set up tables or to move to the ten feet of city-owned sidewalk on the other side of the plaques.

31. Capturing the Car

1. Quotes from Savio's speech in Heirich 1971, 156–157, as recorded by KPFA.

2. Freeman 1997 (abridged version in Cohen and Zelnik 2002, 73–82); Gatti 1997. Interview with Tom Savio, April 5, 1997. Several newspapers published background stories on Mario, not all of which are accurate. They include: "Mario's Father Approves," *San Francisco Examiner,* December 9, 1964, 75; "Close-up of Mario

Savio," *San Francisco Examiner,* December 9, 1964, 1; and "A Rebel on Campus: Mario Savio," *New York Times,* December 9, 1964.

3. Quotes from Savio's speech of September 30, 1964, to the sit-in at Sproul Hall, as recorded by KPFA and reprinted in Goines 1993, 151–153. See also Savio 1964 to see how he blended fighting for civil rights and against "depersonalized, unresponsive bureaucracy" into "a struggle against the same enemy."

4. Jack Weinberg made the same point about the rhetorical themes of the FSM in "The Free Speech Movement and Civil Rights," *Campus CORE-lator,* January 1965. Mario was not the only one who fused these themes, but he did it best.

5. Kerr 1963, 77–78.

32. Strongwalled

1. Strong did not describe this meeting in his oral history, but Vice-Chancellor Constance did; Constance oral history 1987, 255: "I wanted to reach across the table and smack Savio right in the face because he was insolent and brash, and frankly I thought he was off his rocker. He was just sprouting. And Strong reacted to that; I did too."

33. The October 2nd Pact

1. Strong oral history, 1992, section XIV; Stadtman 1970, 450, citing September 26, 1967, interview with Kerr; *Berkeley Daily Gazette,* October 3, 1964.

2. They were William Kornhauser, William Peterson, Neil Smelser, David Matza, and Nathan Glazer of Sociology; Paul Seabury, Robert Scalapino, and Ernst B. Haas of Political Science; Roy Radner and Henry Rosovsky of Economics; Joseph Tussman of Philosophy; Carl Schorske from History; Constance oral history, 1987, 266, and Strong oral history, 1992, section XIV.

3. Brown quote in Kerr and Meyer oral history, 1995, 52. Kerr press statement in "Kerr Ruled Out Compromise," *San Francisco Chronicle,* October 3, 1964, 9:1.

4. Strong oral history, 1992, section XIV. When interviewed that evening, Kerr told KPFA that "Strong was in on most of the discussion"; interview reproduced in Goines 1993, 234. Strong testified at trial that he was present only briefly and did not see the agreement until after it was signed; Transcript of Trial, April 2, 1965, 182. Kerr testified that "both Chancellor Strong and I were in and out of the room a fair amount. . . . Chancellor Strong was in on the discussions of the points as I was, . . . and when it was signed and I took a copy to him"; Transcript of Trial, May 25, 1965, 97. Strong's testimony on this matter is more accurate than Kerr's. Kerr later said that the Alameda County sheriff threatened him with political repercussions if he didn't allow the students to be arrested; Kerr and Meyer oral history, 1995, 53.

5. Final agreement in Heirich 1971, 185–186; and Lipset and Wolin 1965, 578. Copy of original and earlier draft in author's files.

6. Strong oral history, 1992, section XIV.

34. The FSM Is Born

1. Goines 1993, 91. Suzanne had not been active in CORE or the civil rights demonstrations of the prior year and didn't join the Steering Committee until later. Goines was a sophomore on academic probation who had no prior political involve-

ment and did not know who had done what earlier. Recruited to design the cover for the *SLATE Supplement,* he was cited at a table while selling it. Once involved, he became Jack Weinberg's right hand.

2. Jackie remembers these as Mario's exact words. Goines remembers Mario's attitude, if not the words (1993, 228–229, 244).

3. Aptheker letter of March 10, 1969, in Heirich 1971, 462n3. W. E. B. DuBois was a good friend of Bettina's father; their families visited in each other's homes and he was named by DuBois to be his literary executor. She was profiled in "Girl Revolutionary: Leader of UC Rebels Calls Self 'Marxist,'" *Los Angeles Times,* May 2, 1965.

4. Heberle 1951, chapter 4.

5. What I thought was one preceding political generation was actually two. Four of these men had left campus by the end of 1958. Armor, Myerson, and Cloke were leaders between the founding generation and my own.

35. Sparring

1. "Upon my resignation as Chancellor I [made] two public speeches. . . . I pointed out that the issue was not one of freedom of speech but of challenged University authority"; Strong oral history, 1992, section XV. He repeated this theme many times during and after the FSM.

2. Strong oral history, 1992, section XIV. Lipset and Wolin 1965, 121. Heirich 1971, 217–219. Towle decided to grant the waiver on her own initiative.

3. Strong initially appointed to the SCCPA Robley Williams as chairman (Virology), Joseph Garabino (Business Administration), Theodore Vermeulen (Chemical Engineering), Henry Rosovsky (Economics), Katherine Towle (Dean of Students), Milton Chernin (Dean of the School of Social Welfare), William Fretter (Dean of the College of Letters and Science), Alan Searcy (Vice-Chancellor for Academic Affairs), Charles Powell (ASUC President), and Marsha Bratten. Added were Earl F. Cheit (Business Administration), Sanford H. Kadish (Law), Robert B. Brode (Academic Assistant to the President; Physics) and Frank L. Kidner (Dean of Educational Relations, Economics). Zelnik in Cohen and Zelnik 2002, 280; and Strong oral history, 1992, section XIV.

36. Energy

1. Started by Barbara Garson, Stephen Gillers, and Deward Hastings, it quickly added Truman Price, Mickey Rowntree, Marston Schultz, Linda Sussman, and Luis Hernandez to the staff.

2. The summary says that in addition to Rossman, "Lynne Hollander has been responsible for editorial coordination, and Marston Schultz and Tom Irwin for technical co-ordination." The individual reports were hastily compiled and their contents have a lot of flaws. For example, the unsigned report on the UYDs says that the UYDs had never had a table at Bancroft and Telegraph before the summer of 1964. This is not true.

3. News stories reviewed in C. Miller in Miller and Gilmore 1965. Schorske thought the *Los Angeles Times* wrote "first-class crisis journalism" about the FSM, largely due to the skill of its education reporter, while the *New York Times* used "a really poor journalist"; Schorske oral history, 2000, 91–92.

37. Escalation

1. The class interviewed a carefully drawn sample of 285 students on their attitudes toward the issues and the parties involved; Somers in Lipset and Wolin 1965. Max Heirich, 1971, 241, reanalyzed the interviews by date. While it was not available to us at the time, the data substantiates what I was hearing from students.

39. The Secret Negotiations

1. An administration analysis of the names submitted revealed that 74 were TAs, 23 were RAs, 89 were grad students without such positions, 28 were readers, 5 were post-doctoral fellows, and 41 names were illegible. There were 1,306 TAs that semester.

40. Changes

1. Recommendations and introductory statement by Kerr in *California Monthly,* February 1965, 81–82; Lipset and Wolin 1965, 574–578.

41. Mutual Misconceptions

1. Quote from memo of September 21, 1964, from Thomas J. Cunningham, Vice President and General Counsel to the Regents, to Vice-Chancellor Alex C. Sherriffs, cc: President Kerr, Dean Towle; Towle oral history, 1970, Appendix I. On September 24th, Cunningham told Towle that "any regulation which denied political advocacy on campus was very suspect from a legal point of view." He had written a 1961 memo to Sherriffs which said that one could make a distinction between types of religious literature that could be passed out on campus but one could not do so for political literature; memo to Vice Chancellor Sherriffs, May 3, 1961, cc: President Kerr, Chief Campus Officers; ibid. Cunningham also told the Regents that restriction of political speech and advocacy on campus was not legal, but he was not listened to; Heller oral history, 1984, 543, 578.

2. Sherriffs oral history, 1980, 6–12, 31–32. Strong's views are clearly stated in his December 16, 1964, memo on "Student Demonstrations at Berkeley," which was prepared for the December 18th Regents' meeting; Strong oral history, 1992, Appendix III. See evaluation of him by one vice-chancellor; Constance oral history, 1987, 253–256. Constance says that he and Kerr thought that Sherriffs, Strong, and Strong's administrative assistant, Kathlyn Malloy, formed "a small, beleaguered, nuclear group"; Constance oral history, 1987, 273. The students were unaware of Malloy's role, though we did know something about Sherriffs'.

3. Lyonns in Lipset and Wolin 1965.

4. All quotes from the *California Monthly,* February 1965, 48–49; reprinted in Lipset and Wolin 1965, 125–132. On December 1, 1964, the *Daily Cal* published a letter to the editor from Kerr with his "actual quotations":

1. At a press conference held in conjunction with a speech before Town Hall in Los Angeles on Oct. 6 and in response to a reporter's question, I said:

"Experienced on-the-spot observers estimated that the hard core group of demonstrators—those who continued as part of the demonstrations through the night of Oct. 1—contained at times as much as 40 percent off-campus elements. And, within that off-campus group, there were persons identified as being sympathetic with the Communist Party and Communist causes."
2. On October 2 at a press conference in San Francisco following a meeting of the American Council on Education, I said:
"I am sorry to say that some elements active in the demonstrations have been impressed with the tactics of Fidel Castro and Mao Tse-Tung. There are very few of these, but there are some." (Reprinted in Lipset and Wolin 1965, 59)

5. Strong told Heirich that he never believed the FSM was a communist front. After years of teaching in New York and observing CP members, "the only person who never surprised him" was Bettina Aptheker; Heirich 1971, 461–462n3. Those who interviewed FSM leaders in the spring of 1965 all concluded that they were too free-spirited to accept CP discipline; see Goodman 1965; Trillin 1965; and Raskin 1965. By comparing lists of Freedom Summer volunteers with those involved in the FSM, I found that only Mario and Malcolm Zaretsky, a grad student in biophysics, were in both. However, some other FSMers had experience in the Southern Civil Rights Movement. Ken Cloke and Brian Shannon, both Boalt Hall law students, went south with the Law Students Civil Rights Research Council (LSCRRC) in the summer of 1964 and worked with the FSM in the fall. Cloke worked in Alabama and Albany, Georgia; Shannon in Montgomery, Alabama, and Albany, Georgia. Cloke had been active in SLATE and Shannon in YSA at Cal for many years. They would have been involved in the FSM regardless of what they did in the summer of 1964. Robert Hurwitt spent summer 1964 in Louisiana between graduating from New York University and entering Cal as a graduate student in English. Richard Schmorleitz took his "junior year abroad" at the University of Alabama, where he joined SCLC demonstrations in Tuscaloosa during the spring of 1964.

42. The Heyman Committee Report

1. The 14-page report is reproduced in *California Monthly*, February 1965, 82–87; and Lipset and Wolin 1965, 560–574. The members were Chairman Ira Michael Heyman (Law), Robert A. Gordon (Economics), Mason Haire (Psychology), Richard E. Powell (Chemistry), and Lloyd Ulman (Economics and Industrial Relations). The transcript alone cost $1,300, which was more than the fall registration fees of the eight students; Heyman 1966, 77. The students were represented by attorneys with the northern California chapter of the ACLU, specifically Peter Franck, a founder of SLATE; Ernest Besig, who had previously represented SLATE in its disputes with the administration; and Wayne M. Collins.
2. Strong views from his 1992 oral history, quote in section XIV. Second quote from his memo to the Regents, "Student Demonstrations at Berkeley," December 16, 1964; oral history, Appendix III. See also *California Monthly*, February 1965, 56.
3. Williams oral history, 1990, Appendix 4, has his memo to Chancellor Edward Strong about the Heyman Committee. It recommends probation for everyone for the 1964–1965 academic year and censure for Mario and Art.
4. Quote from Strong statement of November 13, 1964, reprinted in *California Monthly*, February 1965, 54; Goines 1993, 333–334.

5. Reports, proposals, and statements in *California Monthly,* February 1965, 54–56. Mail to Regents identified in minutes of November 20, 1964, Item 11. Approval ratings from Somers 1965, who only reports the amount of "unreserved approval"; Heirich 1971, 250.

43. The Regents Meet

1. *California Monthly,* February 1965, 57; Heirich 1971, 255–257; Lipset and Wolin 1965, 155. There were three separate votes, as some Regents wanted to go on record in opposition to item 2 of resolution 2. We did not know about Cunningham's earlier memos to Sherriffs with copies to Kerr, or we would have realized that they had shaped the Regents' resolutions and Kerr's decision to exclude Strong from writing specific campus regulations.

44. The Abortive Sit-In

1. Weinberg's explanation was given to the Plaza crowd; quote in Draper 1965, 92, and Goines 1993, 343. Aptheker quote in Heirich 1971, 262. Bob Starobin reports in Goines (1993, 346) that voting to leave were himself, "Bettina, Roysher, Weissman, Mona and Art" (voting in absentia). Voting to stay were "Mario, Jack, Suzanne, Rossman and Anastasi." I did not go inside, so this is based on others' reports. Bettina later said that an initial vote in the Steering Committee opposed a sit-in by 7 to 4, but Mario kept arguing until two left and Anastasi shifted. Weissman and Weinberg then agreed to have a debate at the rally over whether to have a sit-in. The five who initially voted for the sit-in were probably the five who voted to stay.

45. Resurrection

1. Art and Mario's letters, dated November 25th, arrived on Saturday, and excerpts were published in Monday's *Daily Cal;* see also *California Monthly,* February 1965, 58; Heirich 1971, 265–266; and Lipset and Wolin 1965, 159–160. The letters to Jackie and Brian did not arrive until the following week and weren't published. FSM leaflets and a letter Mario and Suzanne sent to Kerr on December 1 on behalf of the Steering Committee omit Brian's name from demands that all charges be dropped. Strong and Kerr had discussed a month earlier charging some leaders with further violations but held off until the Heyman Committee completed its report; Heirich 1971, 238–239. An official investigation found that the citations were "with the full concurrence of the President"; *California Monthly,* July/August 1965, 50. Kerr named Art and Mario; Strong and Cunningham added Brian and Jackie because there was "clear documentary evidence of violations"; Heirich 1971, 265. Kerr shared this information with John Dunlop, a friend and colleague in the Institute of Industrial Relations. Dunlop phoned Brian's father, whom he knew from his years as a labor negotiator, who told Brian. Thus, Brian was the first FSMer to know about the letters, but since he was persona non grata to the Steering Committee, they didn't find out from him.

46. The Real Sit-In

1. Treuhaft oral history, 1990, VI.
2. Max Heirich says Brown ordered the building cleared, but not the arrests (1971, 274–275). The report of Berkeley chief of police A. H. Fording to the city

manager says that at 10:50 P.M. Brown phoned the campus police and ordered "local law enforcement agencies to take whatever police action was necessary to restore order on the Campus"; December 21, 1964. Alameda County district attorney J. Frank Coakley told two newspapers that assistant prosecutor Edwin Meese III, made the key phone call to Brown in Los Angeles at 10:30 P.M.; "Gov. Brown Blocks 'Anarchy,'" *Oakland Tribune,* December 3, 1964, 1:8; "UC's Day of Turmoil—801 Rebels Jailed," *San Francisco Examiner,* December 4, 1964, 23:4. In fact, Brown was phoned by an unidentified person from the campus police office in Sproul basement and then asked to speak to whomever represented the DA's office; Dallek 2000, 86. Asked by Davis students if he acted on his own initiative or at the request of the university, Brown said he took "full responsibility in every shape, form and manner" after consultation with the Berkeley police, the Alameda County sheriff's office, and the highway patrol; AP release printed in several papers on December 4, 1964. In the spring of 1965, Ron Moskowitz, Brown's education aide who was often on campus, told me that he had persuaded Brown to wait no more. This is confirmed by Sherriffs' oral history (1980, 37, 48–49), where he says he phoned Moskowitz to tell him that freelance photographer Peter Whitney had been roughed up, prompting Moskowitz to phone Brown. Whoever tipped the balance, it was the governor's decision; he did exactly what the FSM wanted him to do.

3. According to a report by A. H. Fording, Chief of Police, to John D. Phillips, City Manager, December 21, 1964, "approximately 830 police officers participated in the 27-hour ordeal." They carried "something in excess of 50 tons of dead weight." Between October 2nd and December 2nd, the various police departments had drawn up plans for coordinating mass arrests and trained arrest squads in handling limp protestors.

47. Strike!

1. These are from the *San Francisco Chronicle,* December 4, 1964, 1, 2, 4, 18.

2. Bail was originally set at $150 for two charges (P.C. §602(o) [Trespassing] and §409 [Unlawful Assembly]) and $250 for three (plus P.C. §148 [Resisting Arrest]). English professor Henry Nash Smith organized the bail fund. The police raised the number arrested to 814, then lowered it to 761. The DA filed complaints against 776. The administration claimed 814, stating that there were 590 students, 135 nonstudents, and 89 staff, including TAs. (The larger number allowed them to lump the garbled names and unidentifiable people with nonstudents.) The GCC estimated that 20 percent were grad students. Some people were moved between jails and booked at each one, and some names were in the newspapers as arrestees who weren't on the prosecutor's list and never came to court. Names from all sources totaled 825. There were two arrest teams using different sequences of numbers. Since the last person arrested in Sproul Hall was assigned #795, that plus the five people arrested outside Sproul Hall and Treuhaft probably accounts for the 801 initially claimed.

3. Strike estimates from Gales's spring 1965 survey, reported in Heirich 1971, 287. This survey was of the entire student body, including the professional schools and the sciences that were hostile to or uninterested in the conflict. The FSM checked class attendance and claimed the strike 70 percent effective; the figure is probably accurate among undergraduates in the humanities and the social sciences.

4. The assemblymen were Democrats Willie Brown and John Burton of San

Francisco and William Stanton of San Jose. Rally statements in "Savio Takes on the State," *San Francisco Chronicle,* December 5, 1964, 8:1.

5. Statements in the *California Monthly,* February 1965, 64–65. The nine professors were Charles Aiken; Eric Bellquist; Thomas C. Blaisdell, Jr.; Joseph P. Harris; George Lenczowski; Albert Lepawsky; Frederick C. Mosher; Julian Towster; and Dwight Waldo. Union opposition came from the locals of the American Federation of Teachers and the Building Service Employees, which represented employees of the university. In addition to the three assemblymen who spoke at the rally, public statements in support of the FSM and in opposition to the arrests were released by Josiah Beeman, president of the CFYD, and Joe Close and Michael Schneider, directors of the CDC chapters of the 6th and 7th congressional districts. "Comments Fly in Wake of Sit-In," *Berkeley Daily Gazette,* December 4, 1964, 1:6–7. The assemblymen and three San Francisco supervisors were six of fifty-four Bay Area educators and civic leaders to sign a statement criticizing the university; "Big Names Back the UC Rebels," *San Francisco Examiner,* December 8, 1964, 17:1–6.

6. Key professors in this group included Charles Sellers, Carl Schorske, and Kenneth Stampp (History); Leo Lowenthal, William Kornhauser, and Phillip Selznick (Sociology); Jacobus ten Broek (formerly Speech, then Political Science); Herbert McClosky, John Schaar, and Sheldon Wolin (Political Science); Charles Muscatine and Henry Nash Smith (English); Howard Schachman (Biochemistry); and John Searle (Philosophy). Its emergence over the previous two months from the group of faculty who met with us in Professor Sellers's office on October 2nd is recounted by Zelnik in Cohen and Zelnik 2002.

7. Strong was involved in the meetings of Kerr and the departmental chairmen prior to his hospitalization Saturday evening. He consistently counseled firmness and opposed any amnesty. Kerr agreed with him on Friday but by Saturday had changed his mind. When Scalapino and several chairmen visited Strong in the hospital to tell him about meeting with the Regents, he expressed disapproval of their plan, but his opinion no longer mattered; Strong oral history, 1992, section XIV.

8. Full text in *California Monthly,* February 1965, 67; Lipset and Wolin 1965, 76–77; and Heirich 1971, 294–295.

48. Victory

1. Members of the committee were Joseph Garbarino (Business Administration), Everett Dempster (Genetics), Carl Helmholz (Physics), Kenneth Stampp (History), and Jacobus ten Broek (Political Science). Garbarino had sat on the SCCPA; Stampp and ten Broek were part of the Committee of Two Hundred.

2. For faculty views, see Searle in Miller and Gilmore 1965; and Zelnik in Cohen and Zelnik 2002. For long-term distrust due to the oath, see Constance oral history, 1987, 113. Searle, one of our strongest supporters, combined many of these factors. He had been angry at the administration since it forbade him, a faculty member, from speaking on campus about the 1960 HUAC demonstrations and *Operation Abolition.* Suzanne Goldberg was his TA and Mario was one of his best students.

3. The other SLATE Senators were Tom Meyer, Bob Nakamura, Gary Feller, Shirley Arimoto, Marston Schultz, and Stephen Cornet. UYD President Al Bergman also ran, but without SLATE backing he lost. Nakamura, who introduced the support motion, was also a UYD. There were five abstentions.

4. EEC members discussed in Heirich 1971, 318; and Schorske oral history,

2000, 39–41. The other professors elected to the EEC were Raymond C. Bressler (Agricultural Economics), Earl F. Cheit (Business Administration), Arthur M. Ross (Chairman of Business Administration), and Robley C. Williams (Molecular Biology), with Richard W. Jennings (Law), ex-officio as chairman of the Berkeley Division. Williams had chaired and Cheit had been a member of the disbanded SCCPA; Ross and Cheit were friends of Kerr's.

5. "UC Regents 'Clarification' Talks," December 18, 1964, 1:2; "Regents Stand By Free Speech Rule," December 19, 1:1; both in *Los Angeles Times.* Full text of statements in *California Monthly,* February 1965, 73; and Lipset and Wolin 1965, 194–197. Quotes from the Academic Council in Taylor 1998, 64–66; and Taylor 2000, 178–185. When the FSM leadership later invited Schorske, the most liberal of the EEC members, to a meeting where he was grilled and laughed at, they probably did not know that the institutional faculty leadership had undermined the new leaders chosen by the Berkeley Division; Schorske oral history, 2000, 95–96.

6. Strong says in his oral history, 1992, section XIV: "At 2 P.M., January 2, 1965, a special meeting of the Regents was held at the airport in San Francisco. I was presented with three alternatives by Regent Carter, the Chairman of the Board: resign office; be fired from office; or take a leave of absence awaiting a final decision. . . . I took the leave of absence option." He was charged with insubordination for writing regulations which he claims embodied what the Regents and the faculty had authorized. His fate was sealed on December 16th, when he gave his opinion of what happened and why to an informal meeting of sixteen Regents and the chancellors and drew "a battle-line between him and Kerr"; Taylor 2000, 182.

49. Intermission

1. "Slate Criticized," February 5, 1961, 12; quote from editor Rosemary Feitis's letter "To the Defense," February 5, 1961, 12; "Scalapino Supplement Statement," February 12, 1965, 12; all in *Daily Cal.*

2. Others in the Faculty Forum were Albert Fishlow (Economics), Paul Seabury (Political Science), Charles Zemach (Physics), Martin Malia (History), Henry May (History), Dale Jorgenson (Economics), and Hans Mark (Nuclear Engineering). May says there were two groups; Henry F. May oral history, 1999, 129–131. Brown says there were three and that his was the moderate middle; Brown oral history, 1998, 143–147. Seabury and May had been active in the fall.

3. "Slate Platform Excludes Birth Control Clinic," November 30, 1961, 8; February 16, 1965, 1; both in *Daily Cal.* Quotes from "A New UC Hassle—Birth Control," *San Francisco Chronicle,* February 17, 1965, 2:4. *Griswold v. Connecticut,* 381 U.S. 479 was released on June 7, 1965.

4. *Education at Berkeley* 1966. The committee members were Charles Muscatine (Chairman, English), Richard Herr (History), David Krech (Psychology), Leo Lowenthal (Sociology), Roderic Park (Botany), George C. Pimentel (Chemistry), Samuel Schaaf (Mechanical Engineering), Peter Scott (Speech), and Theodore Vermeulen (Chemical Engineering). Stadtman 1970 ("The Muscatine Report," 476–479; "The Kneller Report," 479); Tussman college at 475–476.

5. "Cable Car Battle," *San Francisco Chronicle,* February 3, 1965, 1:1–4, 14:6.

6. "Sure, Hang On, Lady," April 27, 1965, 3:1–4; "A Woman's Place in the Cable Cars," May 1, 1965, 1:2; both in *San Francisco Chronicle.* Leaflets and letter in author's files.

50. FUCK

1. Quote in Goines 1993, 486. Goines interviewed and corresponded with Thompson in 1990 and turned his responses into a soliloquy for his book.

2. The three currently registered students were Art Goldberg, David Bills, and Michael Kline. Charles Artman and Edward Rosenfeld had been Cal students at one time. In addition to Thompson, Danny Rosenthal, Jim Prickett (a San Francisco State student), and Stephen Argent (a former Cal student then enrolled at Oakland City College) were also arrested.

3. "For the Courts Only," *Daily Cal* editorial of March 5, 12:1; Justin Roberts was the editor during the spring semester.

4. This was the *San Francisco Examiner*'s headline. Other newspapers wrote similar ones. Kerr statements in "Kerr, Meyerson Announce, Withdraw Resignations; Strong Resigns," *California Monthly*, April 1965, 14. See the following articles in the *San Francisco Examiner:* "History of Free Speech Crisis Behind UC Resignations," March 10, 1965, 19:1; "Kerr States His Case," March 11, 1965; "Blames Students, Profs, Regents," March 11, 1965, 1:1; and "Full Text of Kerr's Statement," March 11, 1965, 21:6. Meyerson statement in "Meyerson Resignation," *Daily Cal*, March 10, 1965, 8:2; "Resignation—Complete Text," *San Francisco Examiner*, March 10, 19:5, excerpted in *California Monthly*, June 1965, 53. Kerr 1967 interview with Stadtman in Stadtman 1970, 470.

5. *California Monthly*, June 1965, 54; "Faculty Backs Kerr," *San Francisco Examiner*, March 10, 1965, 1:8, 19:5; "The Lawmakers Are Angry," *San Francisco Examiner*, March 11, 1965, 22:1; "EXTRA! Pressure Developing to Keep Kerr and Meyerson" and "Brown to Ask Two Leaders to Reconsider," *Berkeley Daily Gazette*, March 10, 1965, 1:7, 4:1; "FSM Blasts Kerr in Rally," *Berkeley Daily Gazette*, March 11, 1965, 1:1 4:1; "Reactions to the UC Resignations," *San Francisco Chronicle*, March 10, 1965, 10:8; "How the Campus Views It" and "The Role of the Hero and the Goat," March 11, 1965, 13:5; "Big UC Vote for Kerr: 'Mandate' From Faculty, Brown," March 13, 1965, 10:3; "FSM Praises Meyerson But Neglects Kerr," March 14, 1965, 1A:7; "Hard Line on UC in the Assembly," March 17, 1965, 1:4, 12:1; all in *San Francisco Chronicle*.

6. Quotes from minutes of Regents' meeting, special session, March 13, 1965. Last quote in Kerr and Meyer oral history, 1996, 31, and also in interview with Russell Schoch for "California Q and A: Interview with Clark Kerr," *California Monthly*, March/April 1982, 11. Kerr did not use the F-word. He said, "and then at the top of his voice, he shouted it three times, with three women Regents in the room. I found that obscene."

7. *Oakland Tribune*, "EXCLUSIVE: The Inside Story of U.C. Revolt And Resignations: Appeasement Wrecked Discipline, Strong Says," March 12, 1965, banner headline. Strong oral history, 1992, section XV; one of these documents is in Appendix III.

8. *San Francisco Chronicle*, April 23, 1965, 1:7, 10:1; April 24, 1965, 12:7. Quote in *New York Times*, April 23, 1965, 71:3. "4 Students Punished by UC Threaten Court Suit," *Los Angeles Times*, April 23, 1965, 3:6. Other actions in "Students Protest: Dirty Word Advocates Fail: Berkeley Ouster to Rouse Crowd," *California Monthly*, June 1965, 55–56; and Heirich 1971, 372–373.

9. "UC's Dirty Word Echoes Through the Courtroom," April 21, 1965, 2:1;

"Nine Guilty in Dirty Word Case in UC," May 12, 1965, 1:5; "Jail Sentences for 8 of UC's Dirty Worders," June 9, 1965, 2:1; all in *San Francisco Chronicle.* Art remembers a sentence of 90 days, but the newspaper says 60.

10. Quotes in "UC Faculty Rejects New FSM Demand," *San Francisco Chronicle,* April 26, 1965, 4:1; and *California Monthly,* June 1965, 56. See also Andrew L. Pierovich, "FREEDOM and Campus Unity," *California Monthly,* May 1965. The professors who publicly criticized the "uncouth actions" included Charles Muscatine (English), Thomas Parkinson (English), and Charles Sellers (History).

11. "Why?" *Daily Cal,* March 19, 1965, 12:1; "Chancellor Forbids 'Spider' Sales at UC," *Berkeley Daily Gazette,* March 19, 1965, 1:3.

12. Meyerson's statement explaining his reasoning is in the *Daily Cal,* April 1, 1965, headlined: "New and Additional: Meyerson's Interim Rules." See also *California Monthly,* June 1965, 55; and "Guidelines for UC Conduct," April 1, 1965, 1:1, 10:2; "SLATE Picks Up Spider," April 2, 1965, 10:6; both in *San Francisco Chronicle.*

51. The Trial

1. Appellants' Opening Brief 1966, 3. Charges against those arrested outside Sproul Hall were dismissed.

2. They were Burnstein, Richard M. Buxbaum, Henry M. Elson, Stanley P. Golde, Douglas J. Hill, and Norman S. Leonard. Their names appear on most of the legal papers. Appearing on early legal papers were Milton Nason, Howard Jewel, John J. Dunn, and Joseph Landisman. Buxbaum was a professor at Boalt Hall. Golde was a former law partner of Crittenden, specializing in criminal defense. The others were also in private practice. The appeals brief was written by Siegfried Hesse, who couldn't sign because of his "day job." Burnstein and Leonard had also represented the civil rights demonstrators in the San Francisco trials the year before.

3. *The Defender* was written and produced by Dana Shapiro, Kathie Frank, Bettina Aptheker, and Albert Litewka. Major volunteers included Alice Haberman, Lee Goldblatt, Adrienne Thon, Myrna Wosk, and Jack Radey. David Stein left in May of 1965. Sue Strommen succeeded Kathie as staff in May of 1967.

4. "Mario Skips Court—for Draft Board," April 16, 1965, 3:7; "Gaps in Ranks of UC Defendants," April 21, 1965, 2:5; "Judge Angry—Sit-Ins Not Sitting In," May 11, 1965, 3:1; all in *San Francisco Chronicle.* When asked on his induction exam for a character reference, Mario wrote "Clark Kerr."

5. "Fiery Start of Trial for UC Sit-Ins," *San Francisco Chronicle,* April 2, 1965, 1:4. There were daily reports about the trial in the press. Five issues of *The Defender* summarized testimony almost weekly. The trial transcript is available on microfilm. Quote from transcript of April 1, 40, 41.

6. They were Edwin Meese III, who falsely claimed credit for persuading Brown to arrest us, and David C. Dutton. Most of the counsel on both sides had law degrees from Cal.

7. Draper 1965, 100–102; Stadtman 1970, 458; Heirich 1971, 274; and Goines 1993, 367. "Brown at Issue in UC Sit-In Trial," *San Francisco Chronicle,* May 4, 1965, 5:6. The *Chronicle* reported that Kerr said about the students sitting around the car: "This is a nationwide thing. I have just talked to Chancellor George Beadle of the University of Chicago; he recently had a nine-day sit-down in his own office"; "Kerr Ruled Out Compromise," October 3, 1964, 9:2. The defendants made an offer of proof to the court that at a meeting on December 2nd of Chairman of the Regents Carter and President Kerr, "it was decided to allow the protest to die a natural death,"

but the court would not permit this; Appellants' Opening Brief, 1966, 218. The defense hadn't interviewed Kerr but did have information that he intended to let us sit in until we got tired; "Declarations of Malcolm Burnstein in Opposition to Motions to Quash . . . " Katherine Towle and Alex Sherriffs were also subpoenaed; Strong testified for the prosecution.

8. "Incomplete" testimony; Transcript of May 17 at 58.

9. Posted at <http://www.jofreeman.com/sixtiesprotest/sixties.htm>.

10. Appellates' Brief, 1966, sentences at 287–326, charts at 327–328. Treuhaft sued Meese for false arrest and dropped this suit in exchange for the dismissal; Treuhaft oral history, 1990, VI.

11. *Savio vs. California* (cert denied) 388 U.S. 460, 87 S.Ct. 2115, 18 L.Ed.2d 1320 (1967). There was no written decision by a California court for our case, but the appeal of four juveniles is *In re: Bacon,* 240 Cal.App.2d 34, 29 Cal.Rptr. 322 (1st Dept. 1966). Judge Crittenden died on May 8, 1966.

52. On Regents and Rules

1. Regent Heller describes the letters and says many were the result of an organized patriotic letter-writing campaign; Heller oral history, 1984, 580–581. *California Monthly,* June 1965, 52–53; Heirich 1971, 358, 368. "Two Rebuffs From UC Regents," March 26, 1965, 1:5, 6:3; "Regents Reject Grad Students—FSM Will Fight," March 27, 1965, 1:1; both in *San Francisco Chronicle.* The Regents voted in accordance with President Kerr's recommendations; minutes of March 26, 1965, Item 11-K.

2. Quote from Phil Roos, "The Issue Is Law and Order," *Spider* 1, no. 3, April 15, 1965, 3–4. The *Daily Cal* printed many stories, editorials, and op-ed pieces on this issue.

3. "Meyerson's Statement," *Daily Cal,* April 1, 1965; "UC Grad Students New Vote," *San Francisco Chronicle,* April 9, 1965, 4:1. The votes were gathered over three days, increasing the opportunities to vote over the usual one- or two-day election. Those voting included 3,000 grad students, about 31 percent of those eligible, and 5,000 undergrads, or roughly one-third of the electorate. The constitutional amendment won by 7,184 to 868; the GCC candidates were all elected by roughly 4 to 1. Heirich 1971, 370, citing the *Daily Cal.* None of this is in the *California Monthly*'s otherwise comprehensive chronology. However, it does say that in April the Regents rescinded their invalidation of the March undergraduate vote, but not the February graduate vote; June 1965, 56; reports on the elections, July/August 1965, 38–39. "New UC Poll and New Results," May 4, 1965, 5:4; "UC Election Aftermath," May 6, 1965, 3:1; both in *San Francisco Chronicle.*

4. Stadtman 1970, 481. See also the editorial in the *UCLA Daily Bruin,* April 5, 1965, 4, arguing that the Kerr Directives should be changed to allow student governments to take positions on outside issues.

5. First quote from February 3, 1965, letter from Theodore Meyer to the heads of student organizations; second from minutes of the Regents, December 18, 1964, item 14. "Regents Set Full-Scale UC Inquiry," *Los Angeles Times,* February 5, 1965, I:1. The Meyer Committee came from a recommendation to the Regents by Kerr; the Forbes Committee was an attempt to forestall a legislative investigation threatened by Jesse Unruh. Byrne meeting described in Trillin 1965; and Goodman 1965. Forbes Committee members were William Forbes, Dorothy Chandler, Edwin Pauley, Jesse Tapp, Philip Boyd, and Norton Simon. Meyer Committee members were Theodore R. Meyer; Donald H. McLaughlin; Samuel B. Mosher; Catherine Hearst; Laurence J.

Kennedy, Jr.; John E. Canaday; and Elinor Heller. President Kerr and Chairman Edward Carter participated in both committees as ex officio members.

6. Committee of Two Hundred comments appeared in the *Daily Cal* on May 4 and 5. They were signed by William Kornhauser (Sociology), Leo Lowenthal (Sociology), Charles Muscatine (English), Howard Schachman (Molecular Biology), John Searle (Philosophy), Charles Sellers (History), Philip Selznick (Sociology), Jacobus ten Broek (Political Science), Sheldon Wolin (Political Science), and Reginald Zelnik (History). SLATE and the FSM issued separate leaflets. Heirich 1971, 376–377. "Student Code Urged in Calif," *New York Times,* April 24, 13:2. "Stringent UC Rules Proposed," April 24, 1965, 1:3; "12 Profs Appeal to UC Regents," May 5, 1965, 3:6; "UC Rules Debate Open," May 7, 1965, 3:5; "Cal Faculty Votes for Less Stringent Rules," May 11, 1965, 2:5; all in *San Francisco Chronicle.* "UC Faculty Takes Strong Stand Against Report on Student Rules," May 11, 1965, 3:1; "2-Day Meeting of UC Regents Starts Today," May 20, 1965, 3:2, 34:1; both in *Los Angeles Times.* A copy of Kennedy's analysis is attached to his letter of May 18th, which was incorporated into the minutes of the Regents' meeting of May 19th. Almost 75 percent of the 918 letters were written by faculty, and 97 percent of these were critical. Almost 98 percent of 171 letters from students were critical. The nine letters from legislators and twelve from administrators were favorable. Taylor (2000, 195) emphasizes that these proposals were significantly softer than the committee's initial positions.

7. "2-Day Meeting of UC Regents Starts Today," May 20, 1965, 3:2, 34:1; "UC Regents to Examine Byrne Study," May 22, 1965, 1:1; "Kerr Offers New UC Conduct Code," June 18, 1965, 3:1; all in *Los Angeles Times.* On August 15, 1994, new policies were issued which retreated from the liberalized rules won by the FSM in 1964, declaring, among other things, that "University properties . . . shall not be used for the purpose of organizing or carrying out unlawful activity" and that members of the University may be subject to "disciplinary action" as well as "legal penalties."

8. Last quote from Byrne oral history, June 8, 1993. Byrne later said that he made a special effort to find out from contacts in both the FBI and the CP if there was any Communist influence in the FSM. Dorothy Healey told one of his investigators, "No, we didn't have anything to do with it, but we damn well wish we had." This was confirmed by the FBI.

9. "A Good Evaluation," editorial signed by Peggy Krause (editor Justin Roberts was a conservative), *Daily Cal,* May 12, 1965, 8:1. "Drastic Change in UC System Urged: Plan for A 'New UC,'" May 12, 1965, 1:6; "The Regents 'Cool' Reaction to Report," May 12, 1965, 8:1; "Top Level UC Talks on the Report," May 13, 1965, 1:8; editorial, "New Concepts for the Regents," May 13, 1965, 46:1; all in *San Francisco Chronicle.* "Sweeping UC Changes Urged in Byrne Report," May 12, 1965, 1:5, 3:24; "FSM Leaders Jubilant Over Byrne Report," May 12, 1965, 3:1; "Byrne Report Disappoints Regent Head," May 12, 1965, 3:1; full text of report, May 12, 1965, IV:1–8; all in *Los Angeles Times.* The background in "Byrne Findings Ran Tortuous Pathway," *Los Angeles Times,* May 12, 1965, IV:8:1, did not come from public meetings, and education reporter William Trombley did not cite sources. However, Regent Dorothy Chandler was vice president of the Times-Mirror Company, which published the *Los Angeles Times,* and a member of the Forbes Committee, so the information in this story is probably reliable. It included the tidbit that "Byrne, 39, is a Democrat," and also described the members of Byrne's staff and the members of the Forbes Committee. The staff were: Stephen R. Powers, Jr.; Christopher Jencks; Bruce C. Busching; Stephen Chitwood; Richard Kite; and Myron Rothbart. On June 13th, Trombley reported that the "*Times* has discovered more than adequate substantiation for the ma-

jor conclusions reached in the Byrne Report," *Los Angeles Times*, June 13, 1965, B:3, 24:1. The next day he disclosed that a few Regents did agree with Byrne on the necessity of a "drastic shake-up" but that most only wanted "minor adjustments." *Los Angeles Times*, June 14, 1954, 3:7, 16:1. "Student Union Group to Attend Regents Parley," May 19, 1965, 27:1; "UC Regents to Examine Byrne Study," May 22, 1965, 1:1, 15:1; "Regents Accept Kerr's UC Reform Proposals," June 19, 1965, 8:1; "Regents Defer Action on Loss of Authority," July 17, 1965, 1:4; all in *Los Angeles Times*. Kerr proposals in "President Kerr's Proposals for the Reorganization of the University of California Presented to the Board of Regents," *California Monthly*, May 21, 1965.

53. The State Legislature

1. Mervin D. Field (California Poll), "The UC Student Protests," *San Francisco Chronicle*, February 2, 1965, 33:1, reprinted in Lipset and Wolin 1965, 199–200; and "Public Against UC Student Protestors," April 13, 1965, 13:1. The most supportive group in the January survey were those between the ages of 30 to 39, not those under 30, and the least disapproving in the April poll were those under 30 (52 percent).

2. The California assembly had eighty members, which were elected from districts based on population. The state senate had forty members, which were elected from counties regardless of population. In 1964 the Supreme Court wrote several decisions requiring all state legislative bodies to be based on population. The 1965 California legislature was still based on the old system. The implications of the new Penal Code § 602.7 are discussed in "Comment: The University and the Public—The Right of Access by Nonstudents to University Property," *California Law Review* 54:1 (March 1966); other measures introduced are listed at 134n9. The Mulford bill was the only one supported by Governor Brown; "Tough Talk for Strikers at UC," *San Francisco Chronicle*, May 5, 1965, 2:1. It was clearly aimed at future Jack Weinbergs, but since California law already precluded convicting someone under more than one statute for the same act, it was little more than symbolic.

3. Heirich 1971, 380–381; "University Knew Highlights of Developments," *California Monthly*, October 1965, 25. Unruh had threatened a legislative investigation at the December 18th Regents' meeting if law and order were not maintained; "Regents Stand by Free Speech Rules," *Los Angeles Times*, December 19, 1964, 1:1. Despite occasional statements that there would be no outside inquiry, Unruh persisted: "Sweeping Legislative Probe of UC Indicated," May 13, 1965, 3:2; "State Senate Joins Assembly UC Probe," June 19, 1965, 9:1; "State Senators Named for UC Inquiry Board, July 15, 1965, 8:1; all in *Los Angeles Times*. "Bill for UC Investigation Hits Snag in Senate," *San Francisco Chronicle*, June 14, 1965, 6:6. Only the Regents could raise tuition, but their decisions were influenced by negotiations with the legislature over the budget. The *Los Angeles Times* says the Regents raised out-of-state tuition from $600 to $800; May 21, 1965, 30:5. See Mar 1966 (13–14) for an explanation of how the legislature affects specific budgetary items. The department chairmen found money to pay TA salaries from other funds. The state senate tried to cut them from the budget again in 1966, but after a confrontation with the assembly in conference, TA salaries were restored.

4. Burns oral history, 1981, 74–76. When asked at a June 30th press conference if Combs had written the report, Burns only said "we have a staff of five that work off and on"; Kerr October 1965, 26. But Burns told Rowland that "I read very thoroughly and very carefully all the reports and made corrections on them. . . .

Everything that was published was with my approbation"; Burns oral history, 1981, 62. Identifying Combs as the author, Rowland (1978, 65, 68) said the total cost of producing the *Thirteenth Report* of the Burns Committee was about $80,000. Barrett (1951, 352) has several pages on Combs, who ran the hearings but did not write the reports of the Tenney Committee. As it changed chairmen, Barrett observed that "Senator Burns does not appear to have the fanaticism or personal ambition of Tenney. Committee counsel Combs, a man of integrity, ability, and moderation, has been given greater control of the planning and conduct of the committee hearings." Burns made it a subcommittee of the General Research Committee in 1959 so that its budget would be hidden from public view; Burns oral history, 1981, 59, 77. Combs profile and quote in Leary 1967. Committee member Senator Stephen Teale (D-West Point) told Leary that "we don't ever see any of the underground stuff. We take it all on Combs' authority" (497).

5. California Legislature 1965, 3–6, 126–131.

6. Ibid., 128.

7. Ibid., first quote 63; second quote 22; third quote 65; bibliography 159.

8. Senator Burns and Senator Aaron Quick signed; Senator Stephen Teale declined. *California Monthly,* October 1965, 25. "State Senate Probes Say Reds Ran UC Revolt," 1:4; "Kerr Is Blamed," 1:4; "Kerr's Defense," 1:6; "Why One Senator Wouldn't Sign Report," 8:1; all in *San Francisco Chronicle,* June 19, 1965. All of page 8 is on the Burns report and the responses to it. Regents meeting reported in "UC Vote of Confidence for Kerr," ibid., 1:3. The official minutes of this meeting are sparse, saying only that Pauley asked the secretary to obtain copies for each Regent. "Senate Group Report on UC Criticizes Kerr," June 19, 1965, I:1:1; "Burns, Byrne Reports Differ on Communist Role at UC: Both Score Kerr Policy as Faulty," June 20, 1965, I:B:5; all in *Los Angeles Times.* Dismissal discussion in Stadtman 1970, 484, based on a 1967 interview with Kerr; this is not confirmed by reports on that meeting in Taylor 2000, 215, or the newspapers.

9. "New Burns Report Criticizes UC Again"; "Senators Zero in on Filth"; and "'Inaccurate' Kerr Says, 'Distorted,'"; all in *San Francisco Chronicle,* May 7, 1966, 1:1. California Legislature 1966, 15–16; *California Monthly,* October 1966, 35. Kerr, October 1965. The *Supplement* cost the taxpayers $36,000; Rowland 1978, 93. Rowland (90n226) reports that Teale said he signed reluctantly after reviewing and rewriting it. Members of the Regents' committee were Jesse Tapp (an ex officio Regent as president of the State Board of Agriculture), Dorothy Chandler, DeWitt Higgs, John Mage, and Theodore Meyer. Edward Carter replaced Mage when his term expired on June 30th.

10. Burns oral history, 1981, quotes on 55, 71. Report of the Combs meeting held on October 7–9, 1958, in memo of October 16, 1958, from San Francisco FBI office to Director; Rosenfeld 2002, F:2:6.

11. *Daily Cal,* October 3, 1952, 1. Liaison plan described in California Legislature 1953, second quote on 209; Gerstel 1954; Rowland 1978, 31–35. Burns's office issued a press release on March 26, 1952, reporting on the March 24th meeting with President Sproul and the presidents of the University of Southern California, Caltech, Claremont, Scripps, Occidental, Redlands, Loyola, Pomona, and Whittier College. First quote from "Fight on the Reds: Campus Anti-Communist Groups to Screen Teachers, Organizations," *San Francisco Chronicle,* March 27, 1952, 6:3. A meeting with the presidents of northern colleges was held on June 23rd in San Francisco but was not reported in the press; "Subversive Activities," Part II, D, Records of UC Office

of the President, CU-5, series 4, Box 37:14, Bancroft Library, University of California, Berkeley.

12. Third quote from California Legislature 1966, 24. See also Rowland 1978, viii, 28, 44, Wadman's role on 41; Burns oral history, 1981, 65; and California Legislature, "Security," in 1965, 143–146, which describes Wadman but does not name him. He is named in its 1966 report on 24, 67. Regent Hearst is named as the recipient of 1958 security investigations in the Records of UC Office of the President, Bancroft Library. The FBI records indicate that other Regents received information from that agency through personal connections, not officially. Memos of August 22, 1951, and December 11, 1951, from Corley to Sproul. First quote from Corley letter of March 1, 1952, to Ray Abbaticchio, Records of UC Office of the President, CU-5, series 2, file 1957:114A, Bancroft Library, University of California at Berkeley. Second quote from FBI memo of October 4, 1954, from A. H. Belmont to L. V. Boardman. Other information in documents provided by Clark Kerr from his files; also discussed in Rowland 1978, 40–48. A statement released on July 2, 1954, after exposure by Ernest Besig of the ACLU, admits Wadman's past work but falsely claims he will now be "confined" to defense contract work; Appendix F in Kerr October 1965, 36; and Rowland 1978, 40, Appendix. This was reported in "UC Security Officer Called 'Thought Police,'" *Los Angeles Times,* 21:4; and "UC Official Accused as 'Thought Policeman,'" *San Francisco Chronicle,* July 6, 1954, 1:1. Not reported in the press was a four-hour meeting held on September 28, 1954, with the Academic Freedom Committee of the Academic Senate and Sproul, Corley, Kerr, and Wadman. Corley covered for Wadman because Corley agreed with Burns, but after Kerr became president that was no longer possible; Rowland 1978, 45–47.

13. Quotes from California Legislature 1965, 145, 146, as part of a short history of security at UC. Rowland 1978, 40–48. Quotes on CIA observation from minutes of the Regents meeting of February 16, 1962, item 12. Kerr sent Sherriffs to Washington to fetch a letter from the CIA clearing Kerr in time for this Regents meeting; Sherriffs oral history, 1980, 57–58.

54. Graduation

1. *California Monthly,* June 1965, 56. "Savio Retires from FSM," *San Francisco Chronicle,* April 27, 1965, 1:1. This was followed by a story on "Why the FSM Is Washing Away," *San Francisco Chronicle,* April 28, 1965, 1:4.

2. "UC Rebels New Name," April 29, 1965, 1:2; "Small UC Squall Over FSU's Tables," May 5, 1965, 2:2; "A Small Turnout for FSU," May 6, 1965, 3:1; all in *San Francisco Chronicle.* "'Student Union' Urged: FSM to Fade Away," April 29, 1965, 1:4; "UC Police Confiscate FSU Tables," May 5, 1965, 1:1; "Complies with Administration," May 6, 1965, 1:2; all in *Daily Cal.* For the fate of the FSU, see Felsenstein's statement in Goines 1993, 470–471.

3. The first Viet Nam War teach-in was at the University of Michigan, which also had the distinction of hosting the first big panty raid in March 1952; Kerr 1956.

4. Heirich's book says he interviewed me on May 19th, but it was the day before my mother arrived in June.

5. Degrees from "Commencement 1965 in Berkeley Tradition," *California Monthly,* July/August 1965, 44. Quotes from commencement address provided by Clark Kerr from his files.

55. The FBI Files

1. *ACLU v. Mabus,* 719 F. Supp. 1345 (S.D. Miss. 1989); *ACLU v. Fordice,* 969 F. Supp.403 (S.D. Miss. 1994); Rowe-Sims 1999. Other information from the MSC files in the Mississippi Department of Archives and History.

2. First quote from FBI memo of December 18, 1959, to Director from SAC, San Francisco, referring to Wadman's report to SA Jones of December 9, 1959. Second quote from memo of March 10, 1961, to Director from SAC, San Francisco.

3. First and second quotes from "Llewellyn Declaration" and "Lieberman Declaration," otherwise unidentified; third from FBI memo of December 14, 1964; all quoted in 761 F. Supp. 1440, 1445, 1448 (1991). Fourth from FBI memo of January 25, 1965, Baumgardner to Sullivan, as cover for report of January 19th. He added that only "14 students and five faculty members of the UCB with subversive backgrounds were observed participating in the demonstrations. Several of these are current Communist Party (CP) members, such as Bettina Aptheker and Robert Kaufman. . . . Of those arrested, 46 individuals are known to have had some type of subversive affiliations and 18 individuals are known to have parents who have been affiliated with subversive groups." Last quote from memo of January 28, 1965, from the Director to several people reporting on his meeting with McCone about the Berkeley situation. Other information in reports to Director from Wesley G. Grapp, Special Agent in Charge, Los Angeles, about his February 2, 1965, meeting with Pauley.

4. In 1996, Seth Rosenfeld was given two $5,000 awards (along with other honors) for "his 15-year fight to pry loose documents" on FBI activities at Berkeley; "Professional Journalists Honor Examiner Reporter: Award for Prying Loose FBI Files," March 3, 1996, A:2; "Examiner Reporter Honored Yet Again for Winning Release of Secret FBI Files," March 24, 1996; all in *San Francisco Examiner.*

5. All quotes from the court; *Rosenfeld v. United States Dept. of Justice,* 57 F.3d 803, 809 (9th Circuit 1995). First quote based on a Rosenfeld declaration; document of the Hoover note is not identified, but the handwritten phrase "I know Kerr is no good and doubt Kragen is" appears at the bottom of page 2 of FBI memo of March 20, 1961, from Mohr to DeLoach rejecting the vice-chancellor's invitation to the FBI to send someone to speak after Frank Wilkinson in order "that both sides will be presented." The court added that "the government has presented no other evidence" to rebut the presumption that the post-1958 documents in the Kerr file were aimed at having him fired; *Rosenfeld v. United States Dept. of Justice* at 810. Kerr gave Rosenfeld permission to obtain his file with the expectation that copies would be provided to him, but Rosenfeld only gave Kerr a few pages. The court decision did not identify which Regents received FBI information, but Kerr believes they were Pauley and Canaday, who were his biggest critics on the Board of Regents; personal communication. The FBI memos in my possession are consistent with the court's findings but identify only Pauley. Pauley also asked for negative information on three liberal Regents—Coblentz, Roth, and Heller—who opposed his efforts to get rid of Kerr. The FBI provided him with "public source" information on them, which revealed nothing "subversive." The Burns Committee also gave information to individual Regents; Burns oral history, 1981, 57. Background on Kerr's "disrespect" is in Horowitz 1962, chapter 6, though the FBI's negative reaction is in its memos.

6. Hoover's congressional testimony wasn't made public until May 17th; "Hoover Links Reds to Berkeley Strife," *New York Times,* May 18, 1965, 1:3. The

1975 Senate hearings provide information on the FBI's activities; U.S. Senate 1975. Quote from memo of January 28, 1965, in *Rosenfeld v. United States Dept. of Justice* at 810. *San Francisco Examiner* reporter Ed Montgomery ran three articles on FSM participants on November 25, 26, and 27, 1964, from information supplied by the FBI, and FBI "reporters" were at FSM press conferences.

56. Aftermath, Afterword, and Afterthoughts

1. "Reagan Lashes 'Morality Gap,'" *San Francisco Chronicle*, May 13, 1966, 16:1. The 1966 supplement to the 1965 Burns report had just been released. Reagan admitted that he hadn't read the document, only press reports about it. He also cited a report by Alameda County district attorney Frank Coakley for another incident at Berkeley when no such report existed and news stories had grossly exaggerated what had happened; Dallek 2000, 193–194.

2. Brown 1970, 143.

3. Meyer quote in insert to *California Monthly,* January/February 1967; "Regent Meyer Discusses Why Kerr Dismissed," *Daily Cal,* January 24, 1967, 14. The shift in the Regents' sentiment toward Kerr began with his March 1965 offer to resign, not with the FSM; Heller oral history, 1984, 585–595. Press coverage was extensive throughout California, but the best background story is "1964 Turmoil Caught Kerr in Ironic Web," by William Trombley, the education reporter for the *Los Angeles Times,* January 21, 1967, 12:1. Carl Schorske thought Trombley was the best reporter in the field; Schorske oral history, 2000, 91–92. Second quote from Trombley story on "UC Regents to Tackle Reorganization Puzzle," *Los Angeles Times,* June 14, 1965, 3:7, 16:1, where he says a half-dozen Regents never liked Kerr and another half-dozen "cooled" toward him during the spring. Kerr's view in Stadtman 1970, 486–493. *California Monthly,* January/February 1967, has statements from Acting President Harry R. Wellman, insert, and Kerr's press conference, 3–5, 56. Regents Pauley and Canaday had supported the loyalty oath in 1949 and were also the most adamant about disciplining "the 800," demanding that all arrested students be suspended. Canaday had been given information from the Burns Committee files and Pauley from the FBI. Pauley turned against Kerr when he persuaded the Regents to rotate their chairmanship rather than vest it in Pauley permanently. Kerr made more enemies through some of his reorganizations and his 1964 removal of Corley as university business manager (though he stayed vice president for government affairs); Rowland 1978, 102–103. Although Kerr's presidency coincided with Brown's governorship, he was chosen for the post and inaugurated when Republican Goodwin Knight was governor. Reagan made UC's presidency "political" by refusing to work with or even to speak to Kerr after his election.

4. Motion to dismiss made by Kennedy, seconded by Forbes. Voting to dismiss were Governor Ronald Reagan, Lieutenant Governor Robert Finch, H. R. Haldeman, DeWitt Higgs, Philip Boyd, William Forbes, Edward Carter, Catherine Hearst, Dorothy Chandler, John Canaday, Allan Grant, Laurence Kennedy Jr., Theodore Meyer, and Edwin Pauley. Voting to retain were William K. Coblentz, Frederick G. Dutton, Elinor R. Heller, Samuel B. Mosher, Einar O. Mohn, William M. Roth, Norton Simon, and Assembly Speaker Jesse M. Unruh. Although no one commented on the partisan character of the Regents' vote, almost all of those voting for dismissal were Republicans and those voting for retention were Democrats. An exception to this pattern was Pauley, a Democrat who did not like Kerr but supported Brown and de-

ferred to him as long as he was governor. Max Rafferty, an ex officio Regent who disliked Kerr, was the only Regent not present. Both before and after the vote, Kerr declined an offer that he resign to avoid being fired. Reagan beat Brown by 3,742,913 to 2,749,174 votes.

5. Hitch had been hired to replace Vice President Corley as head of business affairs in 1965. Feeling pushed out, Corley retired, but President Hitch brought him back as a "consultant" with the state legislature. Corley died on December 26, 1974. Hitch retired in 1975 and died in 1995; *New York Times,* September 12, 1995, D:23:1.

6. *California Monthly,* October 1965, 25. After Meyerson took over, Kerr told Vice-Chancellor Constance to fire Malloy. Later Constance had to console Meyerson when he found out he was not Kerr's candidate to be the permanent chancellor; Constance oral history, 1987, 283–284. Strong was quite bitter about Malloy's fate, more so than about his own; Strong oral history, 1992, section XV. "Obeyed Kerr Order on FSM—Strong," *San Francisco Chronicle,* February 12, 1966, I:B:1. Quote on Meyerson from the *Los Angeles Times,* July 16, 1965, 28:1. Why he was not retained was kept very quiet and this reason is inconsistent with a story Trombley had written earlier in the *Los Angeles Times* on "Regents Get Meyerson Plan for Strong Disciplinary Hand," April 23, 1965, 3:5. See story on Regents' views in "UC Regents to Tackle Reorganization Puzzle," June 14, 1965, 3:7, 16:1. John Searle (Philosophy) became special assistant for student affairs along with Officer James L. Scheneder; *California Monthly,* April 1966, 10. Strong obits in *San Francisco Chronicle,* January 17, 1990, B6; *New York Times,* January 18, 1990, D:21:3; *Los Angeles Times,* January 25, 1990, A:23:1.

7. Sherriffs oral history, 1978, 67–72.

8. Faculty oral histories assessing the effects of the FSM include those of Delmer N. Brown (2000, faculty groups 143–147; departures 150); Kenneth M. Stampp (1998, faculty who became disillusioned conservatives in the post-FSM period 254–257); Henry F. May (1999, faculty divisions, 129–131; disillusioned faculty, 133). Scalapino's and Seabury's negative assessment, along with other faculty views, are in the *California Monthly*'s "Reflections" on the 20th anniversary of the FSM; December 1984, 17, 21. Seabury died in 1990. See also Searle 1971, 34.

9. "Unrest Hits U.S. Colleges," *Daily Cal,* April 2, 1965, 11. First quote from Schorske oral history, 2000, 51; second quote from Brown oral history, 2000, 141–142. May described the new classroom as "friendly combat," May oral history, 1999, 160. All were historians; faculty in other departments may have felt differently. *Education at Berkeley* 1966. Faculty books on the topic of student protest include Feuer (1969), who sees it as generational rebellion and Searle (1971), who examines structural causes. Feuer was antagonistic to the FSM from the beginning. Searle was not, but his views on student protest shifted drastically during his two years as a special advisor to Chancellor Heyns on student affairs.

10. "SLATE Fails in UC Senate Vote," *Daily Cal,* May 8, 1965, 2:4; "Slate Defeated in Run-Off Race," *Daily Cal,* May 10, 1965, 1. The ASUC senate had eighteen elected student representatives, half of whom were elected each semester. Three ex officio non-students were appointed to represent the chancellor, the faculty, and the alumni. The spring election gave SLATE nine votes out of twenty-one; the fall reduced it to seven. "Slate Outlives Usefulness After Ten Years," *Daily Cal,* October 14, 1966; "SLATE Gives Up The Ghost," October 12, 1966; editorial, "Farewell to SLATE," October 13, 1966; both in *San Francisco Chronicle.* "SLATE Wiped Clean," *San Francisco Examiner,* October 11, 1966.

11. "New *Slate Supplement*: ASUC Takes Over Evaluations," November 23, 1966, 1; "*Slate Supplement*—A Sinking Ship," January 30, 1970, 1; "Funeral Knell Tolls," January 11, 1971, 1; "*Slate* Returns to Campus," September 27, 1973, 1; "*Slate* Missing Due to Winter Time Squeeze," January 4, 1974, 1; "The New ASUC Course Guide," April 24, 1974, 5; "*Primer* on *PRIMER*," September 9, 1974, 13; "Primer Guide Licks Its Wounds," January 20, 1975, 11; "Maligned Profs May Have Last Laugh on Primer," September 18, 1978, 10–11; all in *Daily Cal*.

12. *California Monthly*, October 1966, 35.

13. Quote from *California Monthly*, October 1966, 35. "Jack Weinberg Still Fights the Good Fight to Keep Environmentalism from Fading Away," *Chicago Tribune*, April 21, 2000.

14. Letter to the *Daily Cal*, November 9, 1965; *California Monthly*, January 1966, 34; *TIME*, December 3, 1965; rules violations in *California Monthly*, March 1966, 42; April 1966, 10.

15. Coons 1968, 71, 76, 216–221. Condren 1988. The revised Article IX § 9 of the state constitution also requires that the "regents shall be able persons broadly reflective of the economic, cultural, and social diversity of the state, including ethnic minorities and women."

16. Searle 1971, 100–101; "Sproul Steps Receive New Name to Honor Noted Student Activist," *Daily Cal*, December 3, 1997.

17. Interviewed by and quoted in "UC Berkeley—Legacy of Turmoil," by Ann C. Roark, who replaced William Trombley as the education writer for the *Los Angeles Times*, October 1, 1984, 1:1, 18:1.

18. Rowland 1978, x, 14n49, 110. Quote from "State Snoop File: 20,000 Named, Sen. Mills Says," *Los Angeles Times*, March 12, 1971, 1:6. Burns lost the senate leadership when the Republicans won a special election in March of 1969, giving them a bare majority in the senate; "Burns Long Reign Over Senate Ends," *Los Angeles Times*, May 14, 1969, 1. He did not run for reelection in 1970, when the Democrats retook control, instead running against Brown's son Jerry for secretary of state; Burns oral history, 1981, 89. As Burns had endorsed Nixon for president in 1968 and Reagan's reelection as governor in 1970 over Democrat Jesse Unruh, Reagan appointed him to the state Alcoholic Beverage Appeals Board. He died in 1988 at age 86; *San Francisco Chronicle*, November 29, 1988; *Los Angeles Times*, November 29, 1988, I:3:4. Combs was appointed a U.S. magistrate for the eastern district of California on May 1, 1970, and served until June 30, 1986; *The American Bench* (Minneapolis: Forster & Assoc., 1979), 211; *Los Angeles Times*, October 14, 1985, I:3:1. He died in 1995 at age 94.

19. The study is in Appendix 7 of Williams oral history, 1990; some figures are summarized in Goines 1990, 642–643. Although I haven't provided background on most of the Steering Committee, a disproportionate share of the militants came from New York, especially Brooklyn. Most of the moderates came from Los Angeles. Having spent the first sixteen years of my life in Los Angeles and more than twenty in Brooklyn, I believe that the political cultures of these two cities created different political styles, which clashed at Berkeley.

20. Gales 1966, quotes on 10 and 12.

21. The survey of 894 students' attitudes toward civil liberties was sponsored by the Bill of Rights Project of Stiles Hall (the campus YMCA) under a grant from the Fund for the Republic, directed by Robert H. K. Wilson. The results were analyzed by Selvin and Hagstrom (1960). It does not appear to be a random survey, but exactly who was interviewed is not described in this article.

22. Kerr later recognized that "I should have overruled the Chancellor"; "Kerr Foresees Quieter Campus," *San Francisco Chronicle,* February 7, 1966, 1:4, 6:1; see also Hall 1967, 31.

23. Although a conservative Republican senator, Knowland strongly supported the 1957 Civil Rights Act and helped persuade other Republican senators to do so. Clarence Mitchell, chief congressional lobbyist for the NAACP, said "he was a decent person" who "almost invariably . . . was for civil rights legislation"; Clarence Mitchell interview, Civil Rights Documentation Project, December 6, 1968, 58–60. In 1956, Mitchell asked Stiles Hall director Harry Kingman to lobby Knowland about the Civil Rights Act. Kingman later said Knowland "was a key man in the victory that we finally won"; Kingman oral history, 1973, VII.

References and Sources

Archives, Personal, and Institutional

Personal files of Beverly Axelrod, Pacifica, California
Personal files of Ken Cloke, Southern California Library for Social Studies and
    Research, Los Angeles, California
Personal files of Jo Freeman, Brooklyn, New York
FSM Archives and University Archives at the Bancroft Library, University of
    California at Berkeley
Meiklejohn Civil Liberties Institute, Berkeley, California (now the Ann Fagan
    Ginger Collection at Bancroft)
Personal files of Mike Miller, San Francisco, California
Mississippi Sovereignty Commission, Department of Archives and History,
    Jackson, Mississippi
Regents of the University of California. University Office of the President,
    Oakland, California. Minutes of Board and Committee meetings, open,
    closed, and executive sessions, including special committees, for Novem-
    ber 19, 1959; May 19–20, 1960; September 22–23, 1960; February 16,
    1962; June 21, 1963; December 13, 1963; January 17, 1964; May 21–
    22, 1964; June 19, 1964; October 16, 1964; November 20, 1964; Decem-
    ber 18, 1964; January 2, 1965; January 8, 1965; January 15, 1965; Janu-
    ary 21–22, 1965; January 26, 1965; February 18–19, 1965; March 3,
    1965; March 13, 1965; March 26, 1965; April 23, 1965; May 7, 1965;
    May 13, 1965; May 19–21, 1965; June 17–18, 1965; July 16, 1965; Au-
    gust 13, 1965; November 19, 1965; May 20, 1966; June 6, 1966; June 15,
    1966; June 28, 1966; August 23, 1966; October 21, 1966; January 20,
    1967.

Interviews by Jo Freeman

Axelrod, Beverly, April 20, 1997
Burnstein, Malcolm, e-mails in March and September 2000
Cleaveland, Brad, May 13, 2000, e-mails of June 18 and September 10 and 15,
    2000
Cloke, Ken, May 13, 2000
Evans, Mona Hutchin, e-mails in October 2000
Frank, Kathie Simon, letter of March 29, 2000; e-mails in September 2000

Fuchs, Sandor, May 13, 2000
Ginger, Ann Fagan, April 21, 1997
Goldberg, Arthur, May 13, 2000
Goldberg, Jackie, April 26, 1997
Goldberg, Suzanne, July 6, 2000, and August 29, 2002
Kagan, Richard, May 12, 2000
Miller, Mike, May 13, 2000, e-mails in September 2000 and June and October
    2002
Myerson, Mike, January 24 and April 11, 1997; e-mails of September 2000
Rossman, Michael, e-mails in October 2000
Savin, Nathan Eugene, e-mails in November 2000
Savio, Tom, April 5, 1997
Schmorleitz, Richard, e-mails in June 2003
Shaffer, Ralph, e-mails in September 2000
Shannon, Brian, e-mails in September 2002 and April 2003
Solomonow, Allan, May 13, 2000
Stapleton, Syd, e-mails in February 2001 and September 2002
Stein, David, e-mails in October 2000
Sternberg, Marvin, e-mail of June 15, 2000
Turner, Brian, e-mails of June 28, 2000, and September 16–18, 2002
Weissman, Steve, e-mails in June and September 2000
White, Rick, May 13, 2000
Zaretsky, Malcolm, e-mail of December 4, 2000

Interviews by Max Heirich

Conducted in 1965 for his doctoral dissertation; transcripts and notes read by Jo Freeman

Aptheker, Bettina, July 2, 1965
Freeman, Jo, June 1965 (date of May 19 is incorrect)
Goldberg, Art, May 18, 1965
Goldberg, Jackie, May 14, 1965
Goldberg, Suzanne, June 8, 1965
Kaufman, Robert [1965]
Miller, Dustin [1965]
Rossman, Michael [1965]
Savio, Mario, June 8, 1965
Towle, Katherine, June 14, 1965
Turner, Brian, June 3, 1965
Weinberg, Jack, June 11, 1965

Interviews by Mark Kitchell

Conducted for his film *Berkeley in the Sixties,* Los Angeles (largely undated but done in the mid-1980s); transcripts read by Jo Freeman

Aptheker, Bettina
Goines, David
Goldberg, Jackie
Hamilton, Steve
Iiyama, Patti
Miller, Mike
Rossman, Michael
Searle, John
Smith, Mike
Weinberg, Jack, October 10, 1985

Interviews Done for the Civil Rights Documentation Project, Moorland-Spingarn Research Center, Howard University, Washington, D.C.

Burbridge, Thomas N., interview by Robert Martin, July 18, 1969, in San Francisco
Comfort, Mark, interview by Robert Wright, November 16, 1968, in Oakland, California
François, Terry, interview by Robert Wright, November 13, 1968, in San Francisco
Hallinan, Terrence "Kayo," interview by Robert Martin, July 24, 1969, in San Francisco
Mitchell, Clarence, interview by Robert Martin, December 6, 1968, in Washington, D.C.

Oral Histories

Brown, Delmer M. *Professor of Japanese History, University of California, Berkeley, 1946–1977.* 1995 interview by Ann Lage, 1998. University History Series, Regional Oral History Office, Bancroft Library, University of California at Berkeley.
Burns, Hugh M. "Legislative and Political Concerns of the Senate Pro Tem, 1957–70." Interviews by Amelia R. Fry, Gabrielle Morris, and James H. Rowland in 1977 and 1978. In volume II of *California Legislative Leaders,* 1981. California State Government Oral Histories, California State Archives, Sacramento, California.
Byrne, Jerome C. 1993 interviews by Dale E. Treleven. UCLA Oral History Program, for the California State Archives State Government Oral History Program, 1993.
Constance, Lincoln. *Versatile Berkeley Botanist: Plant Taxonomy and University Governance.* 1986 interview by Ann Lage, 1987. University History Series, Regional Oral History Office, Bancroft Library, University of California at Berkeley.
Corley, James H. *Serving the University in Sacramento.* 1967 interviews by Verne A. Stadtman, 1969. University History Series, Regional Oral History Office, Bancroft Library, University of California at Berkeley.

Draper, Hal. Interview with Bret Eynon, April 11, 1984. Sixties Interviews, Columbia University Oral History Office.

Garson, Barbara. Interview with Bret Eynon, August 12, 1984. Sixties Interviews, Columbia University Oral History Office.

Hamilton, Steve. Interview with Ron Grele and Bret Eynon, April 9, 1984. Sixties Interviews, Columbia University Oral History Office.

Heller, Elinor Raas. *A Volunteer Career in Politics, in Higher Education, and on Governing Boards.* 1974–1980 interviews by Malca Chall for California Women Political Leaders oral history project, 1984. Regional Oral History Office, Bancroft Library, University of California, Berkeley.

Kerr, Clark. *University of California Crises: Loyalty Oath and the Free Speech Movement.* 1969 interview by Amelia Fry, 1976. University History Series, Regional Oral History Office, Bancroft Library, University of California at Berkeley.

Kerr, Clark, and Morton Meyer. *Eyewitnesses to UC Campus Turmoil in the Mid-1960s.* 1995 interviews by Nancy M. Rockafellar for the University of California at San Francisco Oral History Program, 1996.

Kingman, Harry L. *Citizenship in a Democracy.* 1971–1972 interviews by Rosemary Levenson, 1973. Regional Oral History Office, Bancroft Library, University of California, Berkeley.

Kragen, Adrian A. *A Law Professor's Career: Teaching, Private Practice, and Legislative Representation, 1934–1989.* 1989 interview by Carole Hicke, 1991. University History Series, Regional Oral History Office, Bancroft Library, University of California at Berkeley.

Leinenweber, Charles. Interview with Ron Grele, April 7, 1986. Sixties Interviews, Columbia University Oral History Office.

May, Bernice Hubbard. *A Native Daughter's Leadership in Public Affairs.* 1974 interviews by Gabrielle Morris for California Women Political Leaders oral history project, 1976. Regional Oral History Office, Bancroft Library, University of California, Berkeley.

May, Henry F. *Professor of American Intellectual History, University of California, Berkeley, 1952–1980.* 1998 interview by Ann Lage, 1999. University History Series, Regional Oral History Office, Bancroft Library, University of California at Berkeley.

Savio, Mario. Interview with Bret Eynon, March 5, 1985. Sixties Interviews, Columbia University Oral History Office.

Schorske, Carl E. *Intellectual Life, Civil Libertarian Issues, and the Student Movement at the University of California, Berkeley, 1960–1969.* 1996 and 1997 interviews by Ann Lage, 2000. University History Series, Regional Oral History Office, Bancroft Library, University of California at Berkeley.

Sherriffs, Alex. "The University of California and the Free Speech Movement: Perspectives from a Faculty Member and Administrator." 1978 interview by James H. Rowland for the Governmental History Documentation Project. In volume on *Education Issues and Planning, 1953–1966*, 1980. Regional Oral History Office, Bancroft Library, University of California, Berkeley.

Snyder, Elizabeth. *California's First Woman State Party Chairman.* 1976 interview by Malca Chall for California Women Political Leaders oral history project, 1977. Regional Oral History Office, Bancroft Library, University of California, Berkeley.

Stampp, Kenneth M. *Historian of Slavery, the Civil War, and Reconstruction, University of California, Berkeley, 1946–1983.* 1996 interview by Ann Lage, 1998. University History Series, Regional Oral History Office, Bancroft Library, University of California at Berkeley.

Strong, Edward W. *Philosopher, Professor, and Berkeley Chancellor, 1961–1965.* 1988 interview by Harriet Nathan, 1992. University History Series, Regional Oral History Office, Bancroft Library, University of California at Berkeley.

Towle, Katherine. *Administration and Leadership.* 1967 interview by Harriet Nathan, 1970. University History Series, Regional Oral History Office, Bancroft Library, University of California at Berkeley.

Treuhaft, Robert E. *Left-Wing Political Activist and Political Leader in the Berkeley Co-op.* 1998–1999 interviews by Robert G. Larsen, Consumers Co-operative of Berkeley Oral History Collection, 1990.

Wellman, Harry R. *Teaching, Research, and Administration, University of California 1925–1968.* 1972 and 1973 interviews with Malca Chall, 1976. University History Series, Regional Oral History Office, Bancroft Library, University of California at Berkeley.

Williams, Arleigh. *Dean of Students Arleigh Williams, The Free Speech Movement and the Six Years' War, 1964–1970.* 1988 and 1989 interviews with Germaine LaBerge, 1990. University History Series, Regional Oral History Office, Bancroft Library, University of California at Berkeley.

Wyman, Rosalind Wiener. *"It's a Girl": Three Terms on the Los Angeles City Council, 1953–1978, Three Decades in the Democratic Party, 1948–1978.* 1977 and 1978 interviews by Malca Chall for California Women Political Leaders oral history project, 1979. Regional Oral History Office, Bancroft Library, University of California, Berkeley.

Younger, Mildred. *Inside and Outside Government and Politics, 1929–1980.* 1976–1981 interviews by Malca Chall for California Women Political Leaders oral history project, 1983. Regional Oral History Office, Bancroft Library, University of California, Berkeley.

Legal Materials

People of the State of California vs. Mario Savio et al., 388 U.S. 460, 87 S.Ct. 2115, 18 L.Ed.2d 1320 (1967) *cert denied.*

Appellants' Opening Brief, *People of the State of California, Plaintiff and Respondent, vs. Mario Savio and 571 Others, Defendants and Appellants* Criminal No. 235, On Appeal from the Municipal Court Berkeley-Albany Judicial District, in the Appellate Department of the Superior Court, County of Alameda, State of California, September 15, 1966.

"A Suggestion for Dismissal" of No. C-7468 through C-7547, by Certain Faculty Members of the University of California, Berkeley, January 20, 1965. Excerpts in Draper, 1965, 176–178, 237–240.

Motion to Dismiss or Affirm, *Mario Savio, et al., Appellants, vs. People of the State of California, Appellee,* No. 1399, On Appeal from the Judgment of the Superior Court of the State of California, in and for the County of Alameda, Appellate Department, Thomas C. Lynch, Attorney General of the State of California, October 1966.

Transcript of Trial, in Nos. C-7468 through C-7547, Municipal Court for the Berkeley-Albany Judicial District, County of Alameda, State of California, before the Honorable Rupert P. Crittenden, Judge, April 1, to June 11, 1965. Each day paginated separately.

In re: Bacon, 240 Cal.App.2d 34, 29 Cal.Rptr. 322 (1st Dept. 1966).

Seth Rosenfeld vs. U.S. Department of Justice and the Federal Bureau of Investigation, 761 F. Supp. 1440 (N.D. Cal, 1991), 57 F.3d 803 (9th Cir. 1995).

FBI Files

Freeman, Jo, ##100-SF-53628, 100-LA-68680, 100-HQ-446176, 173-HQ-2678

Free Speech Movement, ##100-LA-66367, 100-HQ-443437, 100-LA-66367, 100-SF-54086

Savio, Mario, ##44-26027, LA File 157-984, 100-443052, 100-54060, 176-1388, 9-43500

SLATE, ##100-43823, 100-432105

University of California/Berkeley, #100-151646

Wadman, William W., Jr.

Videos and Documentaries

CBS News, *The Berkeley Rebels,* 1965

Kitchell, Mark, *Berkeley in the Sixties,* VHS video, First Run Features, New York, N.Y., 1990

Stack, Barbara, *Women of FSM Central,* 65-minute unedited videotaped interview of Marilyn Noble and Kathleen Piper, July 6, 1997. Available by special arrangement from Barbara Stack, BTStack@aol.com.

Web Sites

http://Bancroft.berkeley.edu/FSM/
http://www.fsm-a.org/
http://www.jofreeman.com
http://www.mdah.state.ms.us/arlib/contents/er/index.html
http://www.slatearchives.org

Bibliography

Barlow, William, and Peter Shapiro. *An End to Silence: The San Francisco State Student Movement in the 60s.* New York: Pegasus, 1971.

Barrett, Edward L., Jr. *The Tenney Committee: Legislative Investigation of*

Subversive Activities in California. Ithaca, N.Y.: Cornell University Press, 1951.

Belfrage, Sally. *Freedom Summer.* New York: Viking Press, 1965.

Berry, John F. "Student Demonstrations in San Francisco, May 12–14." M.A. thesis, University of California, 1961.

Brown, Edmund G. (Pat). *Reagan and Reality: The Two Californias.* New York: Praeger, 1970.

Burnstein, Malcolm. "The Un-American Committee." *New University Thought* 1, no. 2 (Fall 1960): 9–15.

Byrne, Jerome C., Special Counsel. "Report on the University of California and Recommendations to the Special Committee of the Regents of the University of California," submitted May 7, 1965. Abridged versions in *California Monthly,* July/August 1965, 49–59; Draper 1965, 230–237. Unabridged version in the *Los Angeles Times,* May 12, 1965, Part IV. This became a 20-page pamphlet published by the Free Student Union, May 15, 1965. It was also Appendix B of Appellants Opening Brief, 1966.

California Legislature. *Un-American Activities in California: Seventh Report of the Senate Fact-Finding Committee on Un-American Activities.* Sacramento: Senate of the State of California, 1953.

———. *Un-American Activities in California: Eleventh Report of the Senate Fact-Finding Subcommittee on Un-American Activities.* Sacramento: Senate of the State of California, 1961.

———. *Un-American Activities in California: Twelfth Report of the Senate Fact-Finding Subcommittee on Un-American Activities.* Sacramento: Senate of the State of California, 1963.

———. *Un-American Activities in California: Thirteenth Report of the Senate Fact-Finding Subcommittee on Un-American Activities.* Sacramento: Senate of the State of California, 1965.

———. *Supplement on Un-American Activities in California: Thirteenth Report Supplement of the Senate Fact-Finding Subcommittee on Un-American Activities.* Sacramento: Senate of the State of California, 1966.

California Monthly. Published by the California Alumni Association, devoted all of its February 1965 issue to the events of the fall of 1964. Particularly valuable is a "Chronology of Events," 35–74, based on stories published in the *Daily Californian.* Reproduced in Lipset and Wolin 1965, 99–199. Chronologies of the spring events are in the issues for June 1965, 52–56, and July–August 1965, 48–49.

Carney, Francis. *The Rise of the Democratic Clubs in California.* New York: Henry Holt and Co., 1958.

Carson, Clayborne. *In Struggle: SNCC and the Black Awakening of the 1960s.* Cambridge, Mass.: Harvard University Press, 1981.

Casstevens, Thomas W. *Politics, Housing and Race Relations: California's Rumford Act and Proposition 14.* Berkeley: University of California Institute of Governmental Studies, 1967. Reprinted in Eley and Casstevens 1968.

———. *The Defeat of Berkeley's Fair-Housing Ordinance.* Berkeley: University of California Institute of Governmental Studies, 1965. Reprinted in Eley and Casstevens 1968.

Clifford, Geraldine Joncich. *"Equality in View": The University of California, Its Women, and the Schools*. Berkeley: Center for Studies in Higher Education and Institute of Governmental Studies, University of California, Berkeley, 1995.

Cloke, Kenneth. "Democracy and Revolution in Law and Politics: The Origin of Civil Liberties Protest Movements in Berkeley, from TASC and SLATE to FSM (1957–1965)." Ph.D. diss., Department of History, UCLA, 1980.

———. *A Brief History of Civil Liberties Protest Movements in Berkeley: From TASC to SLATE to FSM (1957–1965)*. A condensed version of Cloke's dissertation published by the author as CDR Press, 2411 18th St., Santa Monica, CA 90405, 1994.

Cloud, Roy W. *Education in California: Leaders, Organizations, and Accomplishments of the First Hundred Years*. Stanford, Calif.: Stanford University Press, 1952.

Cohen, Robert. *When the Old Left Was Young: Student Radicals and America's First Mass Student Movement, 1929–1941*. New York: Oxford University Press, 1993.

———. "The Rise of a New Left Labor Union: Berkeley's Union of University Employed Graduate Students (AFT Local 1570) 1964–65." In Cohen 1994, 217–221.

———, ed. "The FSM and Beyond: Berkeley Students, Protest and Social Change in the 1960s." Unpublished anthology. Berkeley, Calif.: n.p., 1994.

Cohen, Robert, and Reginald Zelnik, eds. *The Free Speech Movement: Reflections on Berkeley in the 1960s*. Berkeley: University of California Press, 2002.

"Comment: The University and the Public—The Right of Access by Non-students to University Property." *California Law Review* 54, no. 1 (March 1966): 132–174.

Committee on Discrimination in Housing. "Segregation: Professional Ethics of the Berkeley Realty Board." 9-page mimeographed pamphlet. Berkeley, Calif.: Berkeley Law Students Democratic Club and East Bay Council of Young Democratic Clubs, n.d. [1961]. Author's files.

Condren, Clive P. *Preparing for the Twenty-First Century: A Report on Higher Education in California Requested by the Organization for Economic Cooperation and Development*. Sacramento, Calif.: California Postsecondary Education Commission, 1988.

Coons, Arthur G. *Crises in California Higher Education: Experience under the Master Plan and Problems of Coordination, 1959 to 1968*. Los Angeles: Ward Ritchie Press, 1968.

Dallek, Matthew. "You've Got to Get Those Kids Out of There." In *The Right Moment: Ronald Reagan's First Victory and the Decisive Turning Point in American Politics*, 81–102. New York: The Free Press, 2000.

The Defender: Free Speech Trial Newsletter. April 18 and 25, and May 9, 16, and 30, 1965.

Douglass, John Aubrey. *Setting the Conditions of Undergraduate Admissions: The Role of University of California Faculty in Policy and Process*. Report to the Task Force on Governance, University of California Academic Senate, Center for Studies in Higher Education, 1997.

———. "The Evolution of a Social Contract: The University of California Before and in the Aftermath of Affirmative Action." *European Journal of Education* 34, no. 4 (December 1999): 393–412.

———. *The California Idea and American Higher Education: 1850 to the 1960 Master Plan.* Palo Alto, Calif.: Stanford University Press, 2000.

Draper, Hal. "The Mind of Clark Kerr: His View of the University Factory and the 'New Slavery.'" 1964 pamphlet, reprinted without the subtitle in Draper 1965, 199–215.

———. *Berkeley: The New Student Revolt.* New York: Grove Press, 1965.

Education at Berkeley: Report of the Select Committee on Education. Berkeley, Calif.: University of California, Berkeley, Division of the Academic Senate, 1966.

Eley, Lynn W., and Thomas W. Casstevens, eds. *The Politics of Fair-Housing Legislation: State and Local Case Studies.* San Francisco: Chandler Publishing Co., 1968.

A Fact-Finding Committee of Graduate Political Scientists. *The Berkeley Free Speech Controversy (Preliminary Report).* 42-page pamphlet prepared by Eugene Bardach, Jack Citrin, Eldon Eisenbach, David Elkins, Shannon Ferguson, Robert Jervis, Eric Levine, and Paul Sniderman, December 13, 1964.

Farmer, James. *Freedom—When?* New York: Random House, 1965.

Feuer, Lewis S. *The Conflict of Generations: The Character and Significance of Student Movements.* New York: Basic Books, 1969.

Fowle, Eleanor. *Cranston: The Senator from California.* Los Angeles: Tarcher, 1980.

Freeman, Jo. "From Freedom Now! to Free Speech: How the 1963–64 Bay Area Civil Rights Demonstrations Paved the Way for Campus Protest." Paper given at the annual meeting of the Organization of American Historians, San Francisco, April 19, 1997. Posted at <http://www.jofreeman.com/sixtiesprotest/baycivil.htm>. Abridged version published as "From Freedom Now! to Free Speech: The FSM's Roots in the Bay Area Civil Rights Movement" in Cohen and Zelnik 2002, 73–82.

———. "The Berkeley Free Speech Movement and the Mississippi Sovereignty Commission." *Left History* 8, no. 2 (Spring 2003): 135–144. Also posted at <http://www.jofreeman.com/sixtiesprotest/FSMMiss.htm>.

———, ed. *Social Movements of the Sixties and Seventies.* New York: Longman, 1983.

Free Speech Movement. A collection of legal papers from *Savio v. California,* plus some other documents and articles, compiled and microfilmed by the Meiklejohn Civil Liberties Institute.

Free Speech Songbook: Songs of, by, and for the F.S.M. 18-page booklet, with introduction by Lee Felsenstein, December 1964. Reprinted in Goines 1993, 712–728.

FSM Newsletter. 5 issues, erratically dated, between October and December 1964.

Gales, Kathleen. "A Campus Revolution." *British Journal of Sociology* (March 1966): 1–19.

Gardner, David P. *The California Oath Controversy.* Berkeley: University of California Press, 1967.

Garson, Marvin. *The Regents.* 22-page pamphlet, 1965. Partially reprinted in Draper 1965, 215–221.

Gatti, Arthur. "Mario Savio's Religious Influences and Origins." Paper given at a conference on Italian-American Radicalism, New York City, May 1997. Published in *Radical History Review* 71 (Spring 1998): 122–132.

Gerstel, Walter. "G-Men on the Campus: The California Plan." *The Nation,* January 30, 1954, 93–94.

Ginger, Ann Fagan, for the San Francisco Chapter of the National Lawyers Guild. "San Francisco Sit-In Trials." *The Guild Practitioner* 24, no. 1 (Winter 1965): 10–15.

Gitlin, Todd. *The Sixties: Years of Hope, Days of Rage.* New York: Bantam Books, 1987.

Goines, David Lance. *The Free Speech Movement: Coming of Age in the 1960s.* Berkeley: Ten Speed Press, 1993.

Goodman, Paul. "Berkeley in February." *Dissent* (Spring 1965). Reprinted in Miller and Gilmore 1965, 285–301.

Grant, Joanne, ed. *Black Protest: History, Documents, and Analyses, 1619 to the Present.* Greenwich, Conn.: Fawcett Publications, 1968.

Halberstam, David. *The Fifties.* New York: Villard Books, 1993.

Hall, Mary Harrington. "Interview with Clark Kerr." *Psychology Today* 1, no. 6 (October 1967): 26–31.

Hayden, Tom. *Reunion: A Memoir.* New York: Random House, 1988.

Healey, Dorothy, and Maurice Isserman. *Dorothy Healey Remembers: A Life in the American Communist Party.* New York: Oxford University Press, 1990.

Heberle, Rudolph. *Social Movements.* New York: Appleton-Century-Crofts, 1951.

Heirich, Max. "Demonstrations at Berkeley: Collective Behavior during the Free Speech Movement of 1964–1965." Ph.D. diss., Department of Sociology, University of California at Berkeley, 1967.

——. *The Spiral of Conflict: Berkeley, 1964.* New York: Columbia University Press, 1971.

Heirich, Max, and Sam Kaplan. "Yesterday's Discord." *California Monthly,* February 1965, 20–32. Reprinted in Lipset and Wolin 1965, 10–35.

Henretta, James A., W. Elliot Brownlee, David Brody, and Susan Ware. *America's History.* Chicago: Dorsey Press, 1987.

Heyman, Ira Michael. "Some Thoughts on University Disciplinary Proceedings." *California Law Review* 54, no. 1 (March 1966): 73–87.

Horowitz, David. *Student: What Has Been Happening at a Major University— The Political Activities of the Berkeley Students.* New York: Ballantine Books, 1962.

Huie, William Bradford. *Three Lives for Mississippi.* New York: WCC Books, 1965.

Hyink, Bernard L., Seyom Brown, and Ernest W. Thacker. *Politics and Government in California.* 9th ed. New York: Crowell, 1975.

Isserman, Maurice. *If I Had a Hammer . . . : The Death of the Old Left and the Birth of the New Left.* New York: Basic Books, 1987.

Jacobs, Paul. "A Movie with a Message." *The Reporter* 23 (November 24, 1960), 41.

Jensen, Joan M., and Gloria Ricci Lothrop. *California Women: A History.* San Francisco: Boyd and Fraser, 1987.

Kerr, Clark. "The Student Riots of May 16." *California Monthly,* June/July 1956, special insert.

———. *Uses of the University.* Cambridge, Mass.: Harvard University Press, 1963.

———. "The University: Civil Rights and Civic Responsibilities." May 5, 1964, Charter Day Speech at UC Davis. *California Monthly,* July/August 1964, 7–11; excerpted in Heirich 1971, 94.

———. "President Kerr's Proposals for the Reorganization of the University of California, Presented to the Board of Regents, May 21, 1965." *California Monthly,* July/August 1965, 60–61.

———. "Analysis of the Thirteenth Report of the State Senate Factfinding Subcommittee on Un-American Activities, 1965." University of California, Office of the President, October 1965.

———. *The Gold and the Blue: A Personal Memoir of the University of California 1949–1967.* Vol. 2: *Political Turmoil.* Berkeley: University of California Press, 2003.

King, Martin Luther, Jr. *Why We Can't Wait.* New York: Harper and Row, 1963.

Larson, Rodney, Paul Halvonix, and James Crilly. "Housing Discrimination: A Time for Action." 10-page mimeographed pamphlet. Berkeley, Calif.: Berkeley Law Students Democratic Club and East Bay Council of Young Democratic Clubs, n.d. [1961]. Author's files.

Leary, Mary Ellen. "California's Lonely Secret Agent." *West* magazine, *Los Angeles Times,* April 2, 1967, 33–40.

Lee, Eugene C. *California Votes, 1928–1960.* Berkeley: University of California Institute of Governmental Studies, 1963.

Lenske, Aryay, and Sara Shumer. "The San Francisco Civil Rights Trials." 10-page pamphlet prepared by the Committee for Justice in Civil Rights Cases, July 18, 1964. Axelrod files.

Lewis, Anthony, and *The New York Times. Portrait of a Decade: The Second American Revolution.* New York: Random House, 1964.

Lipset, Seymour Martin, and Sheldon S. Wolin, eds. *The Berkeley Student Revolt: Facts and Interpretations.* Garden City, N.Y.: Anchor Books, 1965. An extensive compilation of documents and commentary.

Lunsford, Terry F. *The "Free Speech" Crises at Berkeley, 1964–1965: Some Issues for Social and Legal Research.* A Report from the Center for Research and Development in Higher Education, University of California, Berkeley, December 1965. Best bibliography to date.

Lyonns, Glen. "The Police Car Demonstration: A Survey of Participants." In Lipset and Wolin 1965, 519–530.

Mar, Pat. "Convincing the Legislature." *California Monthly,* October 1966, 7–14.

McAdam, Doug. *Freedom Summer.* New York: Oxford University Press, 1988.

McEntire, Davis. *Residence and Race.* Berkeley: University of California Press, 1960.

McWilliams, Carey. "Mr. Tenney's Horrible Awakening." *The Nation,* July 23, 1949, 80–82.

Meier, August, and Elliott Rudwick. *CORE: A Study in the Civil Rights Movement, 1942–1968.* New York: Oxford University Press, 1973.

Miles, Michael, and Martin Roysher. "The Berkeley Thermidor." *The New Republic,* March 16, 1968, 17–21.

Miller, Colin. "The Press and the Student Revolt, 1964." In Miller and Gilmore 1965, 313–349.

Miller, Loren. "Government's Responsibility for Residential Segregation." In *Race and Property,* edited by John H. Denton. Berkeley: Diablo Press, 1964.

Miller, Michael V., and Susan Gilmore, eds. *Revolution at Berkeley.* New York: Dial Press, 1965.

Miller, Mike. "Ruminations Prompted by the SLATE Reunion." Speech given at the 2nd SLATE reunion, May 2000.

Miller, Richard M. *Under the Cloud: The Decades of Nuclear Testing.* New York: Free Press, 1986.

Mills, Kay. *This Little Light of Mine: The Life of Fannie Lou Hamer.* New York: Dutton, 1993.

Morgan, Edward P. *The Sixties Experience: Hard Lessons about Modern America.* Philadelphia: Temple University Press, 1991.

Murray, Pauli. *Human Rights U.S.A.: 1948–1966.* Service Center, Board of Missions, the Methodist Church, 1967.

Myerson, Michael. *These Are the Good Old Days: Coming of Age as a Radical in America's Late, Late Years.* New York: Grossman Publishers, 1970.

O'Brien, James P. "The Development of the New Left in the United States." Ph.D. diss., Department of History, University of Wisconsin, 1971.

Otten, C. Michael. *University Authority and the Student: The Berkeley Experience.* Berkeley: University of California Press, 1970.

Peck, James. *Freedom Ride.* New York: Simon and Schuster, 1962.

Pierovich, Andrew L. "FREEDOM and Campus Unity." *California Monthly,* May 1965, 10–13.

Raskin, A. H. "The Berkeley Affair: Mr. Kerr vs. Mr. Savio & Co." *The New York Times Magazine,* February 14, 1965, 24–25, 88–91. Reprinted in Miller and Gilmore 1965, 78–91.

Room, Robin. "Peace, Student Rights Are Semester's Biggest Issues at Berkeley; Socialist Groups Seen Gaining Strength." *New University News* 1, no. 1 (January 1962): 6.

———. "SLATE and the Spirit of a Generation." Paper given at the SLATE reunion, 1984. Reprinted in Cohen 1994, 13–17.

Rorabaugh, William J. *Berkeley at War: The 1960s.* New York: Oxford University Press, 1989.

Rosenfeld, Seth. "The Berkeley Files: 17 Years of FBI Surveillance in Berkeley." *Daily Californian,* May 28, 1982, 1, 13–15.

———. "How the Feds Kept Track of the FSM." *Daily Californian,* June 1, 1982, 1, 8–11.

———. "FBI Supplied Governor with Info about FSM." *Daily Californian,* June 2, 1982, 2, 7, 10–11.

———. "The Campus Files." A *Chronicle* Special Report on the FBI files on UC Berkeley and Clark Kerr, *San Francisco Chronicle,* June 9, 2002, A1:6, A20:6, F:1–8. Posted at <http://www.sfgate.com/campus/>.

Rossman, Michael. "Civil Rights and the FSM: Some Background Notes." *Occident* (Fall 1964–1965): 1–14.

———. *The Wedding within the War.* Garden City, N.Y.: Doubleday and Co., 1971.

Rossman, Michael, and Lynne Hollander, eds. *Administrative Pressures and Student Political Activity at the University of California: A Preliminary Report.* 8-page pamphlet, followed by over 100 pages of documents and appendices written by others. Berkeley: Michael Rossman and Lynne Hollander, 1964.

Rothschild, Mary Aickin. *A Case of Black and White: Northern Volunteers and the Southern Freedom Summers, 1964–1965.* Westport, Conn.: Greenwood Press, 1982.

Rowe-Sims, Sarah. "The Mississippi State Sovereignty Commission: An Agency History." *Journal of Mississippi History* 61, no. 1 (Spring 1999): 29–58.

Rowland, James H. "Un-American Activities at the University of California: The Burns Committee and Clark Kerr, 1952–1967." M.A. thesis, Department of History, San Francisco State University, 1978.

Roysher, Martin. "Recollections of the FSM." In Cohen and Zelnik 2002, 140–156.

Sale, Kirkpatrick. *SDS.* New York: Random House, 1973.

Savio, Mario. "An End to History." Speech made in Sproul Hall, December 2, 1964. Transcribed and reprinted in *Humanity,* December 1964, 1, 4; Draper 1965, 179–183; and Lipset and Wolin 1965, 216–219.

———. Commencement speech delivered at his son's graduation from Sidwell Friends School, Washington, D.C., on June 10, 1988.

Schlesinger, Arthur, Jr. *Robert Kennedy and His Times.* Boston: Houghton Mifflin Co., 1978.

Seaborg, Glenn, with Ray Colvig. *Chancellor at Berkeley.* Berkeley: Institute of Governmental Studies Press, University of California, Berkeley, 1994.

Searle, John. "The Faculty Resolution." In Miller and Gilmore 1965, 92–104.

———. *The Campus War: A Sympathetic Look at the University in Agony.* New York: World Publishing Company, 1971.

Selvin, Hanan C., and Warren O. Hagstrom. "Determinants of Support for Civil Liberties." *British Journal of Sociology* 9, no. 1 (March 1960): 51–73.

Sevilla, Teresa. "Student Authority: Its Development and Role in Governance of the University of California." Ph.D. diss., University of California, Berkeley, 1967.

Shapiro, Fred C., and James W. Sullivan. *Race Riots: New York 1964.* New York: Crowell Company, 1964.

Silver, James W. *Mississippi: The Closed Society.* New York: Harcourt, Brace and World, 1966.

Sitkoff, Harvard. *The Struggle for Black Equality, 1954–1980.* New York: Hill and Wang, 1981.

Somers, Robert H. "The Mainsprings of the Rebellion: A Survey of Berkeley Students in November, 1964." In Lipset and Wolin 1965, 530–557.

Stadtman, Verne A. *The University of California, 1868–1968.* New York: McGraw-Hill, 1970.

———. "Is There a Student Movement at Berkeley?" *California Monthly,* April 1961, 8–10, 54–55.

———, ed. *The Centennial Record of the University of California.* Berkeley, Calif.: University of California, Office of the President, 1967.

Starobin, Robert. "Graduate Students and the Free Speech Movement." *Graduate Student Journal,* Spring 1965, 17–26.

Stewart, George R. *The Year of the Oath: The Fight for Academic Freedom at the University of California.* Garden City, N.Y.: Doubleday, 1950.

Stoper, Emily. "The Student Non-Violent Coordinating Committee: Rise and Fall of a Redemptive Organization." *Journal of Black Studies* 8 (1977): 13–28. Reprinted in Freeman 1983, 320–334.

"Symposium: Student Rights and Campus Rules." *California Law Review* 54, no. 1 (March 1966).

Taylor, Angus E. *The Academic Senate of the University of California: Its Role in the Shared Governance and Operation of the University of California.* Berkeley: Institute of Governmental Studies Press, 1998.

———. *Speaking Freely: A Scholar's Memoir of Experience in the University of California, 1938–1967.* Berkeley: Institute of Governmental Studies Press, 2000.

Towle, Katherine A. "Comments on the Berkeley Situation." *Journal of the National Association of Women Deans and Counselors* 29, no. 3 (Spring 1965): 101–103.

Trillin, Calvin. "Letter From Berkeley." *The New Yorker,* March 3, 1965. Reprinted in Miller and Gilmore 1965, 253–284.

Tussman, Joseph. *Obligation and the Body Politic.* New York: Oxford University Press, 1960.

Unger, Irwin. *The Movement: A History of the American New Left, 1959–1972.* New York: Dodd, Mead and Co., 1975.

U.S. Civil Rights Commission. *Hearings before the U.S. Commission on Civil Rights.* San Francisco, January 27–28, 1960.

U.S. House, Committee on Un-American Activities. *Communist Target—Youth: Communist Infiltration and Agitation Tactics.* A Report by J. Edgar Hoover, Director of the Federal Bureau of Investigation, Illustrating Communist Strategy and Tactics in the Rioting Which Occurred during House

Committee on Un-American Activities Hearings, San Francisco, May 12–14, 1960. Washington, D.C.: Government Printing Office, 1960.

———. *The Communist-Led Riots against the House Committee on Un-American Activities in San Francisco, California, May 12–14, 1960.* House Report No. 2228, 86th Cong., 2nd Sess., October 7, 1960. 23 pages. Washington, D.C.: Government Printing Office, 1960.

———. *The Truth about the Film "Operation Abolition."* Supplemental Report to House Report No. 2228, 87th Cong. 1st Sess., October 5, 1961. 58 pages. Washington, D.C.: Government Printing Office, 1961.

U.S. Senate. *Intelligence Activities Hearings Before the Select Committee to Study Governmental Operations With Respect to Intelligence Activities,* vol. 6, 94th Cong., 1st Sess., November 18 and December 2, 3, 9, 10–11, 1975. Washington, D.C.: Government Printing Office, 1976.

U.S. Senate, Committee on the Judiciary. *Pacifica Foundation: Hearings before the Subcommittee to Investigate the Administration of the Internal Security Act and Other Internal Security Laws.* 88th Cong. 1st Sess., January 10–25, Senate Library vol. 1581. Washington, D.C.: Government Printing Office, 1963.

The University of California Centennial. 48-page booklet, available from the Office of University Relations, 1968.

University of California Policies Relating to Students and Student Organizations. September 1963. 22-page booklet. Berkeley: University of California.

Watters, Pat, and Reese Cleghorn. *Climbing Jacob's Ladder: The Arrival of Negroes in Southern Politics.* New York: Harcourt, Brace and World, 1967.

Weinberg, Jack. "Recent Trends in the Local Civil Rights Movement." *The Campus CORE-lator,* September 1964, 23–24. Reprinted in Cohen 1994, 37–38.

———. "The Free Speech Movement and Civil Rights." *The Campus CORE-lator,* January 1965. Reprinted in Lipset and Wolin 1965, 220–225; and Draper 1965, 183–188.

Werthman, Carl. "The Organization of Student Protest." *New University Thought* 1, no. 2 (Fall 1960): 15–18.

Wilson, James Q. *The Amateur Democrat: Club Politics in Three Cities.* Chicago: University of Chicago Press, 1966.

Wolfson, Robert. "Legal Lynching: The San Francisco Civil Rights Trials." *The Campus CORE-lator,* September 1964, 18–22. Reprinted in Cohen 1994, 39–40.

Wolin, Sheldon S., and John H. Schaar. *The Berkeley Rebellion and Beyond: Essays on Politics and Education in the Technological Society.* New York: New York Review, 1970.

Zelnik, Reginald. "On the Side of the Angels: The Berkeley Faculty and the FSM." In Cohen and Zelnik 2002, 264–338.

Zinn, Howard. *Postwar America, 1945–1971.* Indianapolis: Bobbs-Merrill, 1973.

Index

Page numbers in italics refer to illustrations.

JO FREEMAN has published extensively about feminism, women and politics, social movements, and political parties in scholarly journals, popular magazines, and anthologies. She received her B.A. from Berkeley in 1965, her Ph.D. from the University of Chicago in 1973, and her J.D. from New York University School of Law in 1982. She has lectured at more than a hundred colleges and universities in the United States and Europe. Some of her articles and photographs are posted at <www.JoFreeman.com>.

Other books by the author:

A Room at a Time: How Women Entered Party Politics, 2000, winner of the 2003 Leon Epstein award for a recent book making an outstanding contribution to research and scholarship on political organizations and parties.

Waves of Protest: Social Movements since the Sixties (edited with Victoria Johnson), 1999.

Social Movements of the Sixties and Seventies (editor), 1983.

Women: A Feminist Perspective (editor), 1975–1995.

The Politics of Women's Liberation: A Case Study of an Emerging Social Movement and Its Relation to the Policy Process (1975), winner of a 1975 prize given by the American Political Science Association for the best scholarly work on women and politics.